N

¼/97

CASPIAN SEA

Rasht

TURKMENISTAN

D0949806

Mashhad

✪ Tehran

Hamadan

◇ Qom

I R A N

AFGHANISTAN

◇
Isfahan

◇ Yazd

◇ Kerman

◇
Shiraz

PERSIAN GULF

BAHRAIN

QATAR

PAKISTAN

GULF OF OMAN

UNITED ARAB
EMIRATES

OMAN

THE
IRANIANS

Persia, Islam
and the
Soul of a Nation

SANDRA MACKEY

W. Scott Harrop, research assistant

A DUTTON BOOK

DUTTON

Published by the Penguin Group
Penguin Books USA Inc., 375 Hudson Street, New York, New York 10014, U.S.A.
Penguin Books Ltd, 27 Wrights Lane, London W8 5TZ, England
Penguin Books Australia Ltd, Ringwood, Victoria, Australia
Penguin Books Canada Ltd, 10 Alcorn Avenue, Toronto, Ontario, Canada M4V 3B2
Penguin Books (N.Z.) Ltd, 182–190 Wairau Road, Auckland 10, New Zealand

Penguin Books Ltd, Registered Offices:
Harmondsworth, Middlesex, England

First published by Dutton, an imprint of Dutton Signet,
a division of Penguin Books USA Inc.
Distributed in Canada by McClelland & Stewart Inc.

First Printing, May, 1996
10 9 8 7 6 5 4 3 2

 REGISTERED TRADEMARK—MARCA REGISTRADA

LIBRARY OF CONGRESS CATALOGING-IN-PUBLICATION DATA:
Mackey, Sandra
    The Iranians : Persia, Islam and the soul of a nation / Sandra Mackey.
        p. cm.
    ISBN 0-525-94005-7 (alk. paper)
    1. Iran—Politics and government—20th century. I. Title.
DS318.8.M3   1996
955.05—dc20   95-44135
                                                                          CIP

Printed in the United States of America
Set in Garamond 3
Designed by Jesse Cohen

This book is printed on acid-free paper.

Neither our thoughts nor our doctrines nor our minds' forces,
Neither our choices nor our words nor our deeds,
Neither our consciences nor our souls agree.

Zoroaster

To R. K. Ramazani
Teacher, Mentor, Friend

Acknowledgments

Over the course of two and a half years, I made three extensive trips to the Islamic Republic of Iran in preparation of this book. Much of this time, I traveled alone without the protection of either my own government or that of the Islamic Republic. Instead of government, my shield was provided by the people of Iran. With their help, I escaped the confines of Tehran to explore the tribal lands of the Bakhtiar in the Zagros Mountains, the old Silk Road that crosses Baluchistan, the Caspian coast, the Iraq border, the shrines of Qom and Mashhad, and the cities of Isfahan, Kerman, Shiraz, and Ahwaz, as well as dozens of villages and towns in between. At every stop, I met ordinary Iranians from all walks of life. Some took me in hand to make sure that I boarded the correct airplane, found my way through narrow twisting streets, or had a cool drink of water on a blistering hot day. Others offered me their homes, their time, and their insights into Iranian culture and the Iranian nation. Because of a number of factors, including the present political atmosphere in the Islamic Republic, I cannot list their names. They know who they are and they know how much I appreciate their kindness and all that they did for an American in what Westerners assume is the universally hostile environment of the Islamic Republic.

All books are to some degree a collaborative effort. I owe a special note of gratitude to W. Scott Harrop for his unflagging enthusiasm and his vast knowledge of the facts of contemporary Iran. It was through his contacts and efforts that the door of Iran opened to me. Separately and together we made five trips to Iran during the preparation of the manuscript. Thus a number of the observations and vignettes in the text are directly attributable to Scott. While contributing to the broad outline of the book and assembling a portion of the research for the early chapters, his real service to this book was through his careful checking of the finished manuscript to ensure that it met his high standards of scholarship and accuracy. It is for all of these reasons that I extend to Scott a heartfelt "thank you."

It is impossible to list everyone who so graciously gave me the benefit of their time and expertise. At various points along the way, I gleaned from the far-ranging experience and unique perspectives of Gary Sick and Eric Hooglund much that proved invaluable to my work. Special mention goes to Moshen Milani, Bauman Baktiari, and Abdul Aziz Sachedina, as well as to a number of people in the Iranian community in the United States. Although all did much to deepen my understanding of Iran, the focus, direction, observations, and conclusions in this book are the sole responsibility of the author. I also want to give a word of thanks to Sally Wildman for sharing not only her experiences as an American living in Iran in the last years of the Pahlavi dynasty but her sensitivity to the strains that this huge American presence inflicted on Iranian culture.

A special word of appreciation goes to Bahram and Sarvnoz Massoudi, who did so much for me on the last trip I made to Iran. I not only enjoyed their hospitality but gained from them some of my most memorable experiences, particularly on the road as "Roxanne Khanoum." I am also grateful to the ever-wonderful Nesta Ramazani who beyond her significant intellectual input often also fed, housed, and encouraged me through the long and difficult process of writing. And there is my family—my mother, Verna Sherman, who with a combination of anxiety and steadfastness sent her only child off to the far reaches of Iran; my son, Colin, whose good humor never allowed me to take myself too seriously; and my husband, Dan, who does so much to make every book I write possible.

I appreciate the encouragement and fine suggestions provided by my editor, Matthew Carnicelli; the photograph of me on the cover taken by Barbara Bowen Moore; and the patience exercised by so many of my friends, who listened to all the trials and travails associated with the completion of this manuscript.

Finally, I must thank R. K. Ramazani, the inspiration and guiding light of this book. When I arrived at the University of Virginia in

1963 as a green graduate student, the young Professor Ramazani was already a highly regarded expert on Iran. During my time at the university, he opened my mind to the tangled, turbulent, and often tragic Middle East. He never taught me what to think but how to think. As important, he gave me an appreciation for human values and the universal call to justice. Never hesitating to be critical of nations and people when criticism was warranted, he nurtured in all his students the quality of empathy for people of different cultures, historical experience, and viewpoint. When I began writing my first book, *The Saudis*, I found reason to make contact with my former professor. Through that book and two more, Ruhi never hesitated to take the time to answer questions or to explore with me ideas, observations, or conclusions. When I began this book, he helped me conceptualize the general theme, directed me to the most credible sources, sorted out my questions, redirected me when necessary, and, as during my days in graduate school, taught me how to think about Iran. It is for all of these reasons that this book is dedicated to my teacher, mentor, and friend—R. K. Ramazani.

Contents

PART IV

Author's Note

Any book that deals with a whole people claiming a very old and highly complex culture needs some explanation as to its scope and focus. This truth was brought home to me on my first trip to Iran when I was discussing with a university professor what I sought to do. With the hint of a shrug, he said, "Your task is very difficult. Not even Iranians understand Iran." He was right. The task was very difficult. And I found that an Iranian in perceiving Iran from his or her own viewpoint often fails to grasp the whole. The same thing is true for Westerners who see Iran only from the perspective of Pahlavi Iran or the Iran of Ayatollah Khomeini. Contravening both Iranians and Westerners, this book is about the Iran of Persia and Islam, of past and present, of glorious success and ignoble failure. By pulling the long and thick threads of Iranian history and culture together, I have sought to create a pattern of understanding of a country that is critical in terms of geography and resources to the industrialized world and precious in terms of identity and emotion to all Iranians—those inside the Islamic Republic and those now living in exile. While the demands of space required that I leave out much that is relevant, I hope that I have at least caused both the West and the Iranians abroad to think about Iran in a way that is new and unique, one that elicits perhaps a bit of empathy with the largely unheard people of the Islamic Republic.

I also need to provide an explanation on language. Transliteration from Farsi to English is always problematic as no standard system exists. I have chosen to use the Farsi vernacular with diacritical marks omitted. Some terms and names associated with Islam which are commonly known to the general reader have been left with their Arabic transliteration. A few exceptions have been made in cases where the term has a special relevance to Shiism in Iran as opposed to Sunni Islam in the Arab world. An example is Ramadan, which in Farsi is spelled Ramazan. In quotes from other authors, spellings stay as they are in the original. Finally, Shia, the followers of the Shia sect of Islam, is both the singular and plural form of the term.

In cases where the essence of a vignette is not affected, I have changed the names of towns as well as the names of nonpublic persons in order to protect the individuals involved.

Preface

Abadan is a hell in which the fire has finally gone out. An Iranian town separated from Iraq by the creeping marshes of the Shatt al-Arab, it wears the awful scars of the eight-year-long Iran-Iraq War. Over seven years after that war ended in 1988, the grayish brown water of the Karun River crawls more than flows through half-sunken hulls of rusting landing craft and broken debris of shell casings and missile parts. Miles back from the river's bank, steel skeletons of what were once buildings bare their nakedness in the grim devastation around them. In this atmosphere of appalling tragedy, they silently wait for the labor of people from whom the last ounce of energy has been drained.

Walking among the ghosts that haunt the ruins of Abadan are the United States, Western Europe, and the Arab states that line the western edge of the Persian Gulf. For they all played a part in its destruction. In September 1980, when the Iranian Revolution was spewing its condemnation of the West and those branded as its lackeys, Saddam Hussein ordered the forces of Iraq across the Shatt al-Arab and into Iran. With the invasion, a grim satisfaction suffused the West, Saudi Arabia, the United Arab Emirates, and tiny Kuwait. The Iraqi dictator had seemingly plugged the flowing river of passion that had surged out of Iran since 1979. Over the next eight years, Arab money and Western technology, weapons, and military intelligence fed Saddam Hussein's war machine in the name of containing Iran and the ideology of politicized Islam. Less than two years after the terrible war finally ended in a thinly disguised surrender by the Islamic Republic, the West and its Arab allies paid the price of employing Iraq against Iran.

On August 2, 1990, just a month short of a decade after he invaded Iran, Saddam Hussein gathered the weapons supplied by those who feared the Islamic Republic and marched into Kuwait. Standing on the threshold of Saudi Arabia's rich oil fields, he pressed his booted foot against the pipelines supplying the lifeblood of the industrialized world. The Persian Gulf convulsed as a coalition led by the United States poured men and matériel onto its shores and into its waters. The pounding air war started the following January, the hundred hours of combat came in February, the imperfect peace in March. Through it all, the war against Iraq carried its Iranian component. As the allied army rolled across the plains of southern Iraq, the coalition's political and military strategists continually looked eastward toward Iran. And when they ordered the sweeping advance stopped short of Baghdad, a compelling reason was that the unraveling of Iraq might benefit Iran. As a result, Iraq stayed together. In 1994 thirty thousand American troops were forced to go back to the Persian Gulf to contain the man Western and Arab fear of Iran helped create.

Thus in the afternoon when a jet fighter roars down the floating runway of an aircraft carrier to fly north over Iraq in yet another exercise in the unfinished Gulf War, the shadow of its wing reaches toward Abadan. It is a profound symbol of the link between the Islamic Republic of Iran and the seemingly permanent Western presence in the Persian Gulf.

The West's fear of Iran crystalized that February day in 1979 when hundreds of thousands of Iranians formed a churning black sea that swirled around the exiled Ayatollah Ruhollah Khomeini as he returned in triumph to Iran to complete the revolution that would create the Islamic Republic. Only a month earlier, the weeping Muhammad Reza Shah, the West's bulwark in the Persian Gulf, had fled his throne and his kingdom. At the helm of Iran now stood a pious, unyielding man of religion in command of a potent movement that the West neither anticipated nor understood.

By the following November, the fury against the West unleashed by the Iranian Revolution held fifty-two blindfolded Americans hostage behind the gray stucco walls of the enormous American embassy compound in Tehran. Outside, a milling mob stabbed the crisp air with slogans aimed at the United States, the Great Satan of revolutionary rhetoric. Yet it was not just Washington but London and Paris, Bonn and Tokyo who privately agreed with one of President Carter's senior aides. "We are dealing with a religious fanatic."

This dark vision of holy war waged against the West took form as the Ayatollah Khomeini vowed to "drive from the world of Islam the evil forces of the West." As the Islamic Republic in perception and reality pushed the revolution beyond the borders of Iran, the West moved to contain it. To the detriment of both, the forces of revolution and the forces of containment met in Lebanon. In April 1983, the American embassy on Bliss Street crumbled in the fire and force of a bomb delivered in a van by the Iranian-inspired Islamic Jihad. Militants from Lebanon's Shia Muslim population dispatched two more bombs on a quiet Sunday morning the following October. One massacred 241 United States Marines, the other 47 soldiers of the French contingent of the Multinational Force sent to Lebanon in a misguided attempt to restore order to a country ravaged by its own civil war and the 1982 Israeli invasion. Three months later, in February 1984, groups gathered under the umbrella of a shadowy organization called Hezbollah began to snatch Americans and Europeans off the streets of Lebanon. By January 1987, Hezbollah, possessing undefined but discernible ties to Iran, held hostage the nationals of the United States, Britain, France, Ireland, and the Federal Republic of Germany. As in 1979, the West again faced a waiting game measured by the days of the innocent.

Although the hostage takers were Lebanese, most in the West believed—rightly or wrongly—that it was the cursed and feared Iran which was responsible. In Western eyes, Iran hovered like a black raven over the Persian Gulf and beyond. With rasping squawks, it sounded its indignation against the pro-Western monarchies on the Arab side of the Gulf and celebrated the struggles of politicized Islam. The only force seeming to hold the power of the Islamic Republic in check was the endless war with Iraq. Thus as blood washed the Iran-Iraq border, the West feigned blindness in public and pumped support to Saddam Hussein in private.

The Iraqi president's treachery in 1990 did nothing to lift from the West its abiding fear of Iran. Fueled by those in the Islamic Republic who still rage against the enemies of Islam, Western anxiety about Iran continues to smolder in the face of the rhetoric and actions of the Muslim Brotherhood, Hamas, and other political movements pushing Islamic revolution. It burst into flame in the late spring of 1993 when terrorism apparently employed by Islamic militants crashed

through the walls of the United States. In the explosion at the World
Trade Center in New York, the agencies of government and the suspicions of the public searched for the hidden hand of Iran. But in the
minds of Western intelligence experts and military planners an even
greater danger looms in the laboratories of Tehran's obscure Sharif
University, the suspected cradle of Iran's nuclear program. With evidence mounting that the Islamic Republic seeks to join the exclusive
nuclear club, the West's anxieties about Iran have moved to a new plateau. Military power thus takes its place alongside state-sponsored terrorism and the message of Islamic resurgence in the triad of dreads the
West perceives from Iran. The result is that Iran has become for the
West, particularly the United States, the new evil empire, the towering threat against Western values and Western interests.

But Iran is something else. Contrary to post–cold war mythology,
which denies the reality of national rivalries and the mechanism of
peace known as the balance of power, Iran constitutes the great strategic prize, or the great strategic peril, of the industrialized West.

For two hundred years that spanned the Ottoman Empire to the
cold war, Iran's geographic location and natural resources made it a
pawn of great political rivalries. Through much of the nineteenth century and into the twentieth, imperial Britain and czarist Russia maneuvered Iran in the strategic contest for empire, warm-water ports,
and the black gold of petroleum. At the midpoint of the twentieth
century, the United States employed Iran in its titanic struggle with
the Soviet Union. When the Soviet Union collapsed in 1988, the muscular word "strategic" lost its sinew in a world seemingly freed from
superpower rivalry. Like other former pressure points in the cold war,
Iran lost its designation as a strategic territory. That is a false and dangerous assumption.

Iran's resources alone elevate it to a position of vital necessity to
the West. For no amount of political change can alter the basic truth
of the twentieth century—the great industrialized countries that dominate the international community run on oil. Sixty-four percent of the
world's known oil reserves lie below and around that shallow saltwater
lake known as the Persian Gulf. Iran, the most populous nation of the
Persian Gulf, occupies its entire eastern shore and straddles that strategic global choke point known as the Strait of Hormuz.

The world's industrialized giants also live by natural gas. Again
Iran not only claims the second largest reserves of natural gas in the
world but also lies adjacent to central Asia, where perhaps as much as
212.8 trillion cubic feet of gas await development by Western compa-

nies for the hungry European market. That gas will move through
pipelines, the strategic and economic equivalent of nineteenth-century
railroads. The routes must cross Turkey, Russia, Ukraine, and—Iran.
Thus resources and territory join as they have always joined in the
twentieth century in Iran, a country lying between Russia and the
Persian Gulf, bridging the Middle East and Asia. Today the Islamic
Republic cannot be ignored any more than the Iran of Muhammad
Reza Shah could be ignored in the deep-freeze of the cold war.

In a classical scenario that transcends the false euphoria that
marked the end of the cold war, national rivalries between the West
and Russia are once more asserting themselves. To its dismay, the
West is learning that Russia harbors ambitions and interests that may
clash with those of the West. They are territorial. They are economic.
And they are psychological, driven by the need of the Russians to remain a great power in the world. The grand alliance of peace in which
the West and Russia joined in 1988 is fraying into what Boris Yeltsin
describes as "cold peace." There is no guarantee that it will not shatter
totally, returning Russia and the West to the depths of hostility with
the accompanying threat of nuclear war. The issues of confrontation
are present—the expansion of the North Atlantic Treaty Organization
into Eastern Europe, United Nations sanctions against Iraq, Serbian
aggression in Bosnia, and competition for central Asia. Russia has
proved in Chechnya its willingness to go to war in the Muslim under-
belly of the old Soviet Union to achieve hegemony over central Asia.
While Iran seeks to establish its own influence over the same region,
the West is becoming painfully aware that two rivals—Russia and the
Islamic Republic of Iran—share enough compatibility of interests to
stitch together an alliance of convenience extending from the Caucasus
to the Persian Gulf. Its possible goals: to deny the West the opportunity to develop central Asia's gas and oil and to control access to the
energy resources needed to fuel Western economies.

Iran can also play handmaiden to the power of Asia—the People's
Republic of China. China supplies Iran high-tech weapons and a market for its oil. Iran provides China a land bridge to the West. In a period when U.S. relations with China are difficult and those with Iran
frozen, the giant of Asia and the giant of the Persian Gulf find compatibility of interest. In a growing alliance of convenience, only the
United States is the loser.

Thus Iran sits at the very core of the West's strategic interests as
defined by geography and resources. But Iran also poses an ideological
challenge in an atmosphere in which the cold war against the Soviet

Union is being replaced in the Western psyche by the war with Islam. Across the Middle East, Islam as a culture is asserting itself against the Western domination it has felt since the end of the eighteenth century when the West marched into the Islamic world on the feet of Napoleon's army. And from Turkey to Algeria, resurgent Islam is clashing against the secular regimes that have controlled the economies and politics of the Middle East since the colonial era ended. Of the Muslim countries, only Iran has staged its Islamic Revolution.

A basic element in the Islamic Republic's ethos is the ideal of Iran leading the oppressed Muslim masses against arrogant Western powers. Victory comes in exposing Western impotence, thereby lifting from the Islamic world the relationship of dominance and subservience that has existed for two centuries. This is the Islamic Republic's great battle-cry against the West.

Almost two decades after revolution turned Iran from admired ally to feared adversary, Americans still ask why. The answer can come only through understanding the complex, seemingly inexplicable Iranians. This understanding cannot start with 1979 and the hostage crisis. It must begin with Cyrus the Great in the ancient Persian Empire and span all the centuries since as the Iranians have sought to define their own unique identity and have struggled with all their own demons. That is the task of this book.

Introduction

A slender shaft of light filters through an octagonally shaped hole in the old, vaulted ceiling of the carpet market in Tehran's sprawling Bazaar-e-Bozorg (grand bazaar). It pierces the dust and the dimness to fall on the central aisle of uneven, hard-packed dirt shaped by the years of traffic it has borne. On each side, the endless varieties of Iran's carpet-making craft lie in piles and hang from wires stretched the length of the small shops that line the passageway. The *gelims* and carpets are large and small, woven of threads fine and coarse. Together they create a collage composed of the distinct colors and patterns of their weavers. The Lurs of western Iran lay giant elongated snowflakes of soft reds, apricots, and grays against backgrounds of dark blue; the Kurds juxtapose brilliant reds in precise geometric patterns against black and the deepest blue; the Bakhtiari weave large stylized flowers interconnected by bold curving vines; and the Baluchis recreate the sands and browns of the harsh eastern desert where they roam. Down a narrow stairway leading to an ancient subterranean room dug beneath the old bazaar, jewels woven from silk and wool hide from the dust raised by shoppers. Illuminated by a string of naked lightbulbs dangling from frayed black cords, the delicate flowers of a Bijar, the soft blues and beiges of a Nain, the deep colors of a Tabriz, and the intricate designs of an Isfahani parade the timeless art of Iranian carpet weaving.

But Tehran's bustling carpet market displays more than rugs. It portrays Iran itself. Like a Persian carpet, Iran is a complex pattern of ethnic groups, languages, religions, and regions. This diversity is fundamental to Iran's character. For territorially and politically, the country is as much an empire as a nation. In conflicts that are as contemporary as historical, Iran is afflicted by enmities between the nation's geographical heartland located on the vast Iranian plateau and the regions on its periphery; between Shia Islam and minority faiths; between the speakers of Persian and those who speak the language of their own ethnicity.*

Iran's diversity was bred by location. Resting between the steppes of Asia and the Fertile Crescent, Iran is an island in the land ocean of Asia, a stepping-stone between East and West. Beginning perhaps five thousand years ago, the Iranian plateau, the heartland of contemporary Iran, attracted waves of nomadic tribes roaming its periphery. In the centuries that followed, the plateau that straddled the main trade routes between central Asia and Mesopotamia became a road trod by traders, travelers, and men of learning. But the open corridor that was the Iranian plateau also beckoned invaders. For centuries, they marched from the west, the north, and the east. Carrying names like Arab, Turk, and Mongol, they came as conquerors. Yet many stayed to be digested by the culture they had challenged. But some of the invaders were never completely absorbed. Settled in natural refuges provided by Iran's mountains and deserts, they and their descendants preserved their own languages, religions, and ways of life.

The original Iranians were the Persians who settled about one millennium B.C. on Iran's high central plateau. Descendants of an Indo-European group that originally migrated out of central Asia, they were known as Aryans. It is for them that Iran, "the land of the Aryans," is named. Today the Persians are the largest and most important group in Iran, claiming approximately 50 percent of the Iranian population. Although often ethnically mixed, those who identify themselves as Persian all speak Farsi and almost all adhere to the Shia sect of Islam. Possessing a distinct sense of superiority over other Iranians, the Persians regard themselves as the true heirs of Iran's history and traditions and the guardians and perpetrators of its legacies.

Yet while Iran is cast in the mold of Persian language and culture, it contains within its borders other groups who speak their own languages and possess variations of Persian culture. They came in differ-

*Persian is more accurately known as Farsi.

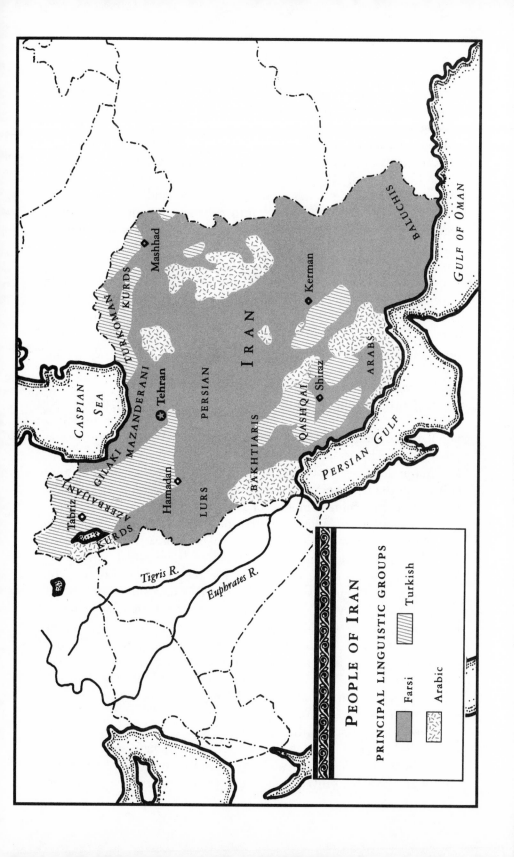

PEOPLE OF IRAN

PRINCIPAL LINGUISTIC GROUPS

Farsi · Turkish · Arabic

IRAN

CASPIAN SEA

GULF OF OMAN

PERSIAN GULF

BALUCHIS
TURKOMAN
KURDS
Mashhad
Kerman
MAZANDERANI
GILAKI
Tehran
PERSIAN
Shiraz
QASHQAI
ARABS
Hamadan
LURS
BAKHTIARIS
AZERBAIJANI
Tabriz
KURDS
Tigris R.
Euphrates R.

ent periods of history as the Persians had come—by migration. They include 12 million Azerbaijanis who speak Turkish rather than Farsi, and the 6 million Kurds whose fierce sense of Kurdish nationalism has challenged Iranian governments for most of the twentieth century.[1]

Large, historically nomadic tribes also strain against the authority of the Iranian state. They were born of ethnic identification and brutal economics dictated by Iran's mountains, deserts, and its scarcity of water.[2] These tribes, often divided into subtribes, number as many as four hundred. Those large enough to wield some power over any Iranian government include the approximately 1 million Baluchis of southeastern Iran, seven hundred thousand Lurs from the central Zagros Mountains, and roughly 1 million Bakhtiari rooted in the southern Zagros, all of whom share language and religion with the Persians; 1.2 million Turkomans spreading out from the eastern shore of the Caspian Sea who speak a dialect of Turkish and follow the Sunni branch of Islam; and seven hundred thousand to 1 million Qashqais of central Iran who speak a dialect of Turkish and essentially ignore religion. All are both part of Iran and separate from it.

Still other groups, less numerous than the Azerbaijanis, Kurds, and the tribes, compose other segments of the heterogeneous Iranian population. The half million Arabs, concentrated in the southwestern province of Khuzistan, are the only Arabic speakers in Iran. Gilakis and Mazanderanis, numbering 2.5 million, live within their own folk culture on the Caspian Sea's coastal plain. Yet they too form an important part of the human mosaic of Iran.

Inlaid within this mosaic crafted from ethnicity and linguistics are the fragments of religion. Like tiny flakes, Zoroastrians, Christians, Jews, and Bahais dot the heavy varnish of Islam which covers Iran. The Zoroastrians are the remnant of the religion of pre-Islamic Iran who, in a sense, tend its memory. The Christians subdivide into the Eastern Orthodox Assyrians, Protestants, and Armenians, who are also an ethnic minority claiming their own distinct history, language, literature, and music. Of the religious minorities, the Jews are the most closely integrated into an Iranian culture structured on Islam.[3] They suffer little of the ostracism historically visited on the Bahais, a mid-nineteenth century offshoot of Islam, who have always lived as a suspected, even hated, minority in Iran.

The great paradox is that out of this varied mix of language, ethnicity, and religion rises an intense sense of Iranian identity that is shared by all people of Iran with the possible exception of the Kurds. Although those who invaded and then settled in Iran over the centuries brought with them their own identity, they fell under the powerful influence of the cultural tradition originally planted on the Iranian plateau by the Persians in the fifth century B.C. and fertilized since the sixteenth century A.D. by the Shia sect of Islam. Because they perceive themselves as the protectors of an ancient culture and as the custodians of the Shia sect of Islam, the Iranians as a whole feel their cultural roots with a sensitivity shared by few other people on earth. Consequently, Persians, Bakhtiaris, and Azerbaijanis; Muslims, Zoroastrians, and Christians share an intense pride in the distinction of the Iranian past; in the structure of society; in the character of artistic expression; in the importance placed on questions concerning the meaning and purpose of life; and in a unique outlook and attitude toward the surrounding world. All have combined to give the Iranians an intense nationalism that ignores the standard measures of a common language and religion and the existence, or at least the perception, of racial homogeneity. Yet the final element in the great paradox of division and unity among the Iranians is the dual nature of that very identity to which almost every Iranian so emotionally adheres.

The Iranians are a people claiming two complex and interlocking traditions. One comes out of ancient Persia, the other out of Islam. Like a tormented Janus, Iran has survived since the seventh century with its Persian and Islamic faces sometimes relaxed in harmony but as often creased with tension. In the twentieth century, the traditions of Persia and Islam became swords with which the Iranians have fenced in an often deadly struggle over control of Iranian culture and government. In important ways, the Iranian Revolution of 1979 as well as the ideology and behavior of the Islamic Republic represents an intense, sometimes brutal, contest between two powerful traditions competing for possession of a nation.

Iran began as Persia. First Cyrus and then Darius led their armies out of the Iranian plateau to conquer and to rule a vast empire that stretched from the Indus River in the east to Egypt in the west. Out of its loins came the religion of Zoroaster, the philosophy of the just ruler, the art and architecture, mores and traditions which so tightly wove Persian culture. But in the seventh century A.D., Persia, in the sense of a defined political-territorial unit, faded when the Arab armies swept out of the Arabian Peninsula to conquer the world for Islam. High Persian culture fell to men shaped by the constant fight for survival on the harsh desert of the Arabian Peninsula and who, beyond a rich oral tradition, were unlettered and unlearned. To the Persians whom they had vanquished, the Arabs brought nothing except the religion of Muhammad. But in the end, Persia conquered the Arabs. The Golden Age of Islam that set the standard of civilization between the eighth and eleventh centuries A.D. came largely out of Persian art and knowledge. Even so, Persia from within the Islamic Empire continued to strain to express its own distinct identity. Ultimately it broke from Islam's main body to embrace and refine the Shia sect of Islam. Although its roots lay in Islam's great schism in 680, Shiism did not lay hold of Iran until 1501, when an adolescent zealot galvanized the Turkoman tribes of northern Iran in an assault on the existing order in Persia. By the sword and the word, Ismail and the great king Abbas mobilized Shiism to bind Persia's ethnically and linguistically diverse population. In declaring Shiism the state religion, the Safavid dynasty began the process by which Iran would be defined by Shia theology as well as Persian culture. This merging of religion and the state was celebrated in the art and architecture of magnificent Isfahan. But it was at Mashhad and Qom that Shiism's followers sought their soul and confirmed their Islamic identity.

In the nineteenth century, Shia Persia met the Christian West. Until 1979, it was an uneven encounter in which Western nations sought individually and collectively to use Iran as a pawn of their own interests. Concurrently, the Iranians confronted the deeply disquieting challenge of creating a modern civilization. In this weaving of Iran and the West, tradition and modernization, the threads of Iranian identity knotted. On its most basic level, twentieth-century Iran, its revolution, and its future can be understood as the great cultural contest between the Iranians' Persian and Islamic identities. Each of those identities has possessed its own icon—Muhammad Reza Shah and Ayatollah Ruhollah Khomeini.

In terms deeper and more relevant than the free license given to Western technology and Western popular culture, the last shah of Iran sought to achieve his personal vision of Iran by exorcising that part of Iranian identity that dwells in the Shia branch of Islam. Through neglect and repression, Muhammad Reza Shah abandoned Iran's Islamic traditions and institutions in favor of a shallow resurrection of the glories of ancient Persia. With Western television crews and magazine writers acting as fawning courtiers, the shah's reclamation of the Iranians' Persian past reached its metaphorical peak on October 12, 1971.

On that day, the tall, slender columns that mark the ruins of the ancient Persian capital of Persepolis cast their narrow shadows toward an enormous round tent striped in broad strokes of blue and gold. Together stone and canvas poised in wait for Muhammad Reza Shah to launch the internationally heralded celebration of the 2,500th anniversary of the Iranian nation founded by Cyrus the Great. At Pasargadae, fifty miles from the great Persian capital at Persepolis, the shah, wearing a midnight blue military uniform encrusted with heavy gold embroidery, stepped to the foot of the simple, timeworn tomb of the legendary Cyrus. Saluting his self-proclaimed predecessor, he intoned, "O Cyrus, the great king, king of kings, Achaemenian king, king of the land of Iran, I, the shahanshah of Iran, offer thee salutations from myself and from my nation."

The shah then moved back to Persepolis, founded in the fifth century B.C. on the swell of Persian power. While trumpets blared, bearded men who had not shaved for a year on the orders of their shah marched up the wide entrance staircase garbed in the tunics and carrying the spears of Achaemenian warriors. Behind them, drum-beating foot soldiers costumed in orange and purple robes that recalled Persia's centuries-long wars with the Romans preceded stately chocolate-colored camels bearing men in silver mail and high pointed helmets that remembered Persia's conflicts with Byzantium. As the procession of 6,200 characters wound on and on, men clad in costumes that evoked the era of Cyrus stood as sentries high atop the ruins of Persepolis. Over it all, Muhammad Reza Shah, the self-decreed heir of Cyrus, the shahanshah of Iran, led his people in celebration of his own perception of the Iranians' history and their identity. Conspicuously absent was any acknowledgment of that accompanying part of Iran's history and culture shaped by Islam.

A mere decade later, passion and power had recaptured the Iranians' Islamic tradition. On June 21, 1981, just four months short of the tenth anniversary of the lavish celebration of Cyrus at Persepolis, Abolhassan Bani-Sadr, the secular president of revolutionary Iran, surrendered Iran's government to the Shia theologians. Iran had completed its move from the Persian past defined by Muhammad Reza Shah to the Islamic present presided over by Ayatollah Ruhollah Khomeini. The signs appeared everywhere.

In the international arrivals section of Tehran's Mehrabad Airport, gilded frames that once held photographs of the proud monuments of ancient Persia now hung empty and dusty. Beneath them, a sign scrawled with a felt-tip pen and propped on the foreign-exchange counter of the Melli Bank trumpeted Iran's new greeting. "Dear Guest. God is the Greatest. Welcome to the Islamic Republic of Iran."

Iran had turned within itself. In the process, government led by clerics attempted to purge from Iranian society the remaining symbols of alien influences. Tehran, a capital that had set Westernization on a Persian base, stood stripped of its illusory past. The Hilton and Intercontinental hotels that ran Western-style operations splashed with Persian decors had lost their ambience as well as their names. The Hilton was now the Esteqlal, or "independence," and the T-shaped Intercontinental had become the Laleh, or "tulip," in reference to the mythical red flower that grows from the blood of a Shia martyr. Stately Pahlavi Avenue was now Vali-ye-Asr, "the expected one."

The convivial cafés of north Tehran that once spread out on the sidewalks under shady branches of sycamore trees had pulled back inside their walls or locked their doors. The theaters and most of the movie houses idled as dark, silent relics of a bygone era. Across group and class, Iranians declared their return to their Islamic tradition. Hands wielding aerosol cans had renamed Kentucky Fried Chicken "Our Fried Chicken" and turned the colonel into something that vaguely resembled a mullah. Kiosks along the streets that had once sold *Newsweek*, the *Economist*, and *Paris Match* now dispensed the magazines of the revolution carrying articles on such topics as where to place toilet fixtures within bathrooms to make it impossible for the user to face Mecca while disposing of his or her bodily wastes.

In its piety, the revolution literally shut down the shah's fast track of modernization. Across Tehran, the proud shah's capital, tall steel cranes stilled by a revolution stood in mournful attendance at abandoned construction projects where unfinished buildings provided backgrounds for scribbled slogans and stenciled portraits of the Ayatollah Khomeini.

It was a time in which those intent on establishing Islam at the pinnacle of Iran's political system secured the revolution. In the name of their own vision of Islam, Khomeini's Revolutionary Guards imposed their order while revolutionary tribunals executed the enemies of the Islamic state and drew the lines of proper Islamic behavior. As a result, life moved to the cadence of the spiritual. At the University of Tehran, one time the monument to Western technical knowledge, women students draped themselves in the chador, the bell-shaped garment Islamic tradition assigns to the protection of female chastity. State-run television poured out prayers, readings from the Koran, and instruction in the faith delivered on videos of swirling lights and transmuting calligraphy narrated in the deep monotones of the clergy. Under the imperative to be Islamic in all things, one cleaner of Persian carpets changed the name of his establishment to "Islamic carpet-washer."

But the Ayatollah Khomeini's concept of Islamic Iran was no more valid than the shah's concept of Persian Iran. Like the shah's glorification of Persia, the Islamic Republic's exaltation of Islam denies the two traditions existing within the Iranian national psyche. Rather than bringing synthesis to Iranian cultural identity, the revolution has only written the latest complex chapter in Iran's long, painful quest for definition of itself and its place within the world around it. These dual challenges of internal harmony and national security have engaged the Iranians in all their ethnic, societal, and religious complexity across the fourteen centuries since Islam invaded the realm of Persia. Today the conflicting strands of Iranian identity are no more evident than on Iran Air, the Iranian national airline.

It had taken me months to negotiate a visa to enter an Iran closed to Americans claiming exclusive U.S. citizenship. But now I was, at last, departing for Tehran. In the Frankfurt airport, I stood before a large electronic board flipping over notices of departures—Amman, Johannesburg, New York, Singapore. Finally "Tehran—Iran Air #609—G22—16:10" whirled into place. Lugging a camera with three lens, two tape recorders, and a laptop computer across what seemed like miles, I finally reached gate G22. It looked like most other gate areas of the massive international airport. No stern security personnel with piercing eyes searched through luggage as they often do on flights into the Persian Gulf. The airline employees wore Western-style uniforms like the employees of other airlines. Among the passengers, no women hid beneath the folds of black sacks or tucked their hair under tightly drawn scarves. I thought that maybe the revolution had exhausted itself. But when the call to board came, I discovered that the Islamic Republic controlled the plane if not the gate.

The female flight attendants who welcomed me on board were wrapped in head scarves that covered every hair and were draped in big black overcoats called *manteaus* that concealed every curve of their anatomy. At my seat, the pocket contained the usual emergency instructions but no menu listing alcoholic drinks available on board. As the plane pulled back from the gate, a mournful chant of prayer vibrated in the heavy atmosphere of Islamic piety which pervaded the cabin. But for the next six hours, I heard nothing else of Islam.

As the 747 droned on its path eastward, stewards delivered dinner—steaming *chelo kabab*, Iran's national dish since the time of the Persians. When the movie began, it was a classic morality play set in pre-Islamic Persia. In frame after frame, it celebrated Persian virtues of understanding and compassion while ignoring Islamic themes of sin and punishment, discipline and vengeance. But as the plane touched down in Tehran and taxied to a stop in the dusty darkness of the night, Islam once more took charge.

I joined every woman on board in pulling a head scarf low on my forehead to cover every last hair of my wispy bangs. I donned the long black raincoat two sizes too large that would satisfy the Islamic Republic's law that women be properly covered. Finally I removed all my makeup. When the doors of the plane opened, I moved down the aisle encased in the Islamic Republic's mandated Islamic dress. Immediately inside Mehrabad Airport, behind the forbidding cubicles of immigration, a large, stern portrait of the Ayatollah Khomeini glared down from the wall. The deceased ayatollah seemed to say once more, "Neither East nor West—Only Islam." With a moment's hesitation, I laid my American passport before the uniformed immigration officer, who applied his stamp. The door to Iran opened. Inside lay the answer to the question that has perplexed the West for over a decade and a half—who are the Iranians?

PART I

1

The Glory of Persia

THE ANCIENT TOWN OF YAZD SAT IN THAT PERFECT MOMENT when darkness breaks to dawn. Across the landscape, early grasses were thrusting their green shoots through the hard brown soil and the fruit trees held swollen buds waiting to burst into bloom. As the sun rose on March 21, the vernal equinox, Yazd and the rest of Iran welcomed the Iranian New Year—No Ruz.

In a modest, flat-roofed, middle-class house belonging to the Rajavi family, the festivities had actually begun the preceding Wednesday, Joyous Wednesday. Relatives had arrived in drips and waves from as near as Tehran and as far as France. They came bearing fat bouquets of yellow daffodils mixed with red tulips and oversize containers holding enough food to feed everyone in the family for the next week. Before darkness fell, a match touched the sticks and straws stacked in the little garden at the front of the house, producing a miniature bonfire. Everyone old enough or young enough to walk jumped the fire, chanting a couplet directed toward the sun: "May your red radiance come to me, May my yellow tiredness go to you."

Inside, the No Ruz table held seven vessels, the number of the holy immortals of Zoroastrianism, filled with food, seeds, coins, or anything beginning with the letter *s*. Why the letter *s* is lost in the mysteries of time. But each of the other objects held a precise meaning. Two candles represented light and dark; a mirror reflected evil; a bowl of goldfish symbolized life; and painted eggs depicted fertility.

The Rajavis as Muslims placed a Koran on the front left corner of the little table. In Christian, Zoroastrian, and Jewish homes the holy book was the Bible, the Avesta, or the Torah.

The Iranians have been celebrating No Ruz since before the reign of Cyrus the Great in the fifth century B.C. Originally the planting festival of prehistoric, agrarian Iranians, it was later given ethical meaning by the teachings of the prophet Zoroaster. The twelve-day holiday garbed in all its Persian trappings has survived at least twenty-five centuries of invasion and foreign rule, as well as the Islamic Revolution. Ignoring its history as a holiday dedicated to the three holy elements of Zoroastrianism—fire, earth, and water—every Iranian celebrates No Ruz as the commemoration of his nation's Persian past.

In the twelve hundred years between the founding of the Persian Empire and the arrival of Islam in the seventh century A.D., Persian culture and Persian identity took form on the Iranian plateau. It developed under the four dynasties of pre-Islamic Iran—the Achaemenian, Seleucid, Parthian, and Sassanian. Each dynasty made its own history of successes and failures. But central to each were the themes of governance and culture that are as relevant today as they were in the ancient past. Although there are others, the three predominant themes that pre-Islamic Iran handed down to succeeding generations are the concepts of a powerful king ruling in the name of justice, the continuity of a distinct culture, and a sense of nationhood rooted more in cultural identity than in either government or territory. For 2,500 years, the inheritance that ancient Persia bequeathed to Iran has exerted its powerful influence over Iranians culturally, socially, and politically. And its ethos binds those within the Islamic Republic to those Iranians now in exile. In certain core values, basic attitudes, and self-perception, Iranians have lived in a continuum that stretches from Cyrus the Great through Ayatollah Khomeini.

In the history of the Iranian plateau, the sun has risen and set on nearly a million days. That history began toward the end of the third millennium B.C. when the hunter-gatherers of Neolithic times gradually gave way to organized society. Among the most advanced of these societies was Elam, spreading over the lowlands east of the Tigris and Euphrates and climbing into the western Zagros Mountains. Drawing from the Sumerian culture of the Fertile Crescent and adding to it elements that were uniquely its own, Elam by the middle of the eleventh century B.C. had reached an extraordinarily high level of artistic achievement. But by 646 B.C., its days of power and independence were over and its knowledge and skills passed on to Persia.

Before Elam fell, successive groups of Aryans migrated out of the steppelands of central Asia, moved down the eastern side of the Caspian Sea, and into western Iran.* The Medes came first, around the ninth century B.C. To avoid confrontation with the mighty Assyria to the west, the Medes settled in the Zagros Mountains. Perhaps a century later, the leather-helmeted Persians riding horses hung with bronze ornaments followed. Eluding both the Assyrians and the Medes, they wandered south along a narrow route drawn by mountains to the west and deserts to the east. When they reached Fars, near the center of the Iranian plateau, they stopped. There in the dry plains and barren mountains of Fars, they planted the seeds of Persian culture.

During the sixth century B.C., the Persians, along with other societies on the Iranian plateau, assumed more complex forms as they made the transition from nomadism to settlement. Hostage to climate and topography, people could survive only by harnessing the great force that sustains life—water. Water meant hydration and food. It meant trees capable of providing shelter from the blaze of the sun and the desert. But rainfall in Iran averages only twelve inches a year. Cities and settlements stay alive with the melting snow running off the major mountain ranges that flows through *jubes*, or concrete conduits, that border streets like narrow canals. Yet it is the *qanats* that testify in stark, visual terms to the Iranians' constant quest for water. Seen from the air, these miles of gently sloping underground tunnels intersected by well shafts that resemble giant mole holes lie on the landscape like ribbons. As old as Iran itself, the *qanats* bequeath or deny fertility to the land. The ancient Persians, recognizing the crucial link between water and life, summoned their first system of government to equitably distribute the precious, sparse resource. But equitable distribution also required an ethic. They found it in Zoroastrianism.

The prophet Zoroaster was born sometime between the tenth and seventh centuries B.C. in the Azerbaijan area of what is now Iran. Claiming to have received divine revelation, Zoroaster set out across the Iranian plateau on a pilgrimage to teach mankind the nature of the world and the individual's responsibility within it.† In the process

---

*The term Aryan refers to an Indo-European family of languages.
†Also known as Zarathushtra, Zoroaster is believed by some to have been a group of priests rather than one man.

of defining one of the world's first systems of theology, he laid the cornerstone of Persian civilization.

Zoroaster preached to people who worshiped animals, ancestors, the earth and sun, or the whole galaxy of deities common to the Hindus of the Vedic Age. Yet societies on the plateau even before the time of Zoroaster also recognized the god Ahura Mazda, the cosmic force of good, as well as a vaguely defined sense of evil. They sometimes worshiped at fire temples in which the eternal flame both represented the supreme godhead and fostered community by providing a place to draw fire for cooking and warmth. Embracing both the existing ideas of a deity and man living in community, Zoroaster carried these concepts on to a higher, more complex level. Although he framed the central point of his doctrine in simple words, the theology was profound. There are two forces at work in the world—one the Creator and the other the Destroyer. According to Zoroaster, the Creator is Ahura Mazda, who is all goodness and light. The Destroyer is Ahriman, who is all wickedness and full of death. Thus Zoroaster defined the great cosmic dualism: darkness and light; good and evil; Ahura Mazda, the Sire of Truth, and Ahriman, the agent of falsehood. Unlike the shared concept of Judaism, Christianity, and Islam, where Satan, the personification of evil, is a fallen and, therefore, lesser creation, Zoroastrianism holds that the realm of evil equals in power the realm of good. As creatures of Ahura Mazda's realm of good, man and woman are called to engage morally in the eternal conflict between two equal forces. Exercising his or her own free will, each decides whether or not to stand with Ahura Mazda against Ahriman. This dualistic struggle between the host of light and the commander of darkness is present in every aspect of human life from the conduct of the individual to the functions of organized society. It is, in fact, the challenge of life. "[For] life is at its highest intensity when the struggle is fiercest, because then, all vital activities are greatest; waste is incessant, and restoration is constant. When the struggle ceases, life is done."[1]

Under the commands of Zoroastrianism—good works, good thoughts, good deeds—man and woman have been set at the center of a flawed world to serve as perfecter and redeemer. The ultimate fate of the individual depends on how well he or she acts in the cosmic battles between the powers of light and the powers of darkness. For at death, the good person enters into paradise, the doer of evil into eternal hell.

In essence, Zoroastrianism teaches one God instead of many, a God of justice and beneficence rather than a God of vengeance, a moral code for all to live by, final judgment, and immortality.* The faith holds high the concept of social justice, propagating the belief that the whole purpose of man's engagement with good against evil is the betterment of society. Consequently, Zoroastrianism carries a powerful social content. Religion is not only spiritual, it is political. In terms of contemporary Iran, the profound and lasting legacy of Zoroaster is that he imposed God's moral will on society and implanted in Iran from its earliest beginnings a strong religious character that has shaped the Iranian and his culture ever since.

Zoroastrianism was taking root in Iran about the time Cyrus the Great, the founder of the Persian Empire, was born. In one of those momentous twists of fate on which history sometimes hangs, one of the most significant religious figures of all time and one of the greatest political-military geniuses ever to stride across the human landscape both occupied the cradle of the Iranian nation in the same era. Their creations—one religious, the other political—blended. Zoroaster gave Cyrus's earthly realm a soul and Cyrus gave Zoroastrianism a body.

The great Persian Empire of the fifth to the third century B.C. was almost the by-product of the search for security by the Persians of Fars. As they moved from nomadism to settled agriculture, the Persians, along with the Medes and other groups on the Iranian plateau, sought to control as much land as possible on the perimeters of their settlements. In this quest for land, water, protection, and order, the quality of leadership within each group played a decisive role in that group's success. For protection lay in numbers, and numbers were possible only through loose confederations between groups who were natural rivals. By their very nature, these confederations could retain their cohesiveness only through a strong leader exhibiting a charismatic personality. It was this environment that produced the most remarkable leader in Iranian history. In essence, the history of ancient Iran began when Cyrus of Fars deposed the king of Media to unite the Persians and the Medes.

Ironically, Cyrus hovers offstage in the Iranians' conceptualization of their history. When asked who are the major figures of their past,

---

*In the doctrine of the final judgment of each soul at death, Zoroastrianism profoundly influenced the monotheistic religions of Judaism, Christianity, and Islam. On circumstantial evidence, Zoroastrianism also gave each a savior or messiah, angels, heaven, hell, a millennium, and even the halo.

most Iranians will name the Persian Empire's Darius, the sixteenth-century Shah Abbas I, or, depending on the individual's perspective, the Ayatollah Khomeini. Yet whether the man on the street readily recognizes it or not, Cyrus is central to the history of Iran. He was among those leaders of ancient times who Machiavelli once said "owed nothing to fortune but the opportunity which gave them matter to be shaped into what form they thought fit." With his mind and his sword, Cyrus created and nurtured the basic elements in Iranian culture—the nature and philosophy of leadership, a unique collection of art and mores, and the sense of Iran and its people as particular and special. All reappear in varying degrees and in various forms in the rulers and dynasties that followed him and on into the centuries in which Iran is described in terms of Islam. But it took until the twentieth century before Cyrus was raised as a symbol of Iranian nationalism and political tradition. The Pahlavi shahs—Reza and Muhammad Reza—creatively invoked Cyrus's name and defined his legacy to remind Iranians of their pre-Islamic past. While justifying their own rule, the Pahlavi shahs also caused Iranians to not only remember Cyrus but to appreciate him as a touchstone of Iranian culture.

The origins and even the likeness of Cyrus have fallen down the well of time. Leaving aside Herodotus's heroic account of his birth, Cyrus was probably the son of Cambyses, the king of the Persians of Fars, and possibly Mandane, daughter of Astyages, king of the Medes.*
On ascending the throne around 559 B.C., Cyrus began to build his empire. In 550 B.C., he wooed as much as conquered the Medes under his principles of conquest.† First, persuasion and accommodation would take precedence over brute force. And second, the vanquished would never be humiliated. With a deft political touch, Cyrus granted the captured king Astyages all reverence due his position and preserved intact Media's existing military and administrative organizations along with the people who managed them. Avoiding needless reprisals against the subjugated, Cyrus created partners rather than adversaries in the expanding Persian Empire.

In the consolidation of the Persians and the Medes under Achaemenian rule, Cyrus placed Persia alongside Lydia and Babylon in the ancient world's triangle of power. But the triangle did not last long.

---

*Cambyses carried the dynastic name Achaemenian adopted from the first Persian king, Achaemenis.
†In joining the Medes and the Persians, Cyrus also won the Elamites, who had been incorporated by the Medes.

In the Lydian capital of Sardis, Croesus—the king whose name is synonymous with vast wealth—felt the threatening wind blowing from the Iranian plateau. Although he solicited advice from the oracles of Ionia, Greece, and Lydia, the cautious Croesus hesitated year by year to engage the Achaemenian king. These were years that Cyrus critically needed to harmonize his existing territories, expand his army, and establish a highly efficient intelligence network within the enemy's camp. From his spies, Cyrus learned that Croesus was ready to use his famous cavalry to defeat Persia in the opening act of Lydian expansion eastward.

In a deadly game of empire, Cyrus moved his pawn first. Crossing the Tigris River in the spring of 547 B.C., he marched westward, gathering mercenaries to augment his well-drilled, superbly disciplined army. Croesus answered by crossing the Halys into eastern Asia Minor. There, in late summer, the Lydians met the Persians. Caught by surprise by the size of Cyrus's army, Croesus pulled back into his citadel at Sardis. Cyrus was left to make the fateful decision to follow or to retreat back to Persia. If he stayed in place, he faced the problems of communication lines perilously extended; an alien population capable of turning on him; and weather awaiting the inevitable coming of winter. Yet if he turned back to Persia to wait for the spring, he handed Croesus the opportunity to call on his treaties with Egypt, Babylon, and Lacedaemonia for the men needed to overpower him. Cyrus gambled that Croesus was a conventional general who avoided battle in winter. He was right. Croesus sent word to his allies to hold their reinforcements while his standing army waited out the coming winter in the seemingly impregnable Sardis.

According to legend, a plague of snakes, an ominous sign of impending doom for the superstitious Croesus, suddenly descended on the meadows around Sardis. The creatures slithering through the grass sent grazing animals into panic. As they charged toward the city, Cyrus followed. That part of the Lydian cavalry within the citadel rode out to meet the Persians on the broad treeless plain. Their long spears caught the sun as Persian infantry, preceded by bowmen in flowing saffron robes, marched toward what appeared certain slaughter. Then at the critical moment, the lines of infantry parted. Out poured looping, long-legged camels transported from the northwest of Fars and secreted in the baggage train. At the sight and smell of beasts they had never seen, the terrified Lydian horses reared, throwing their riders, still clutching their deadly spears, to the ground. The remnants of the Lydian army fled back into Sardis and positioned themselves on the acropolis. Cyrus laid a siege. With the threat of winter creeping ever closer, Persians, Medes, Elamites, and Cyrus's mercenaries scaled the ramparts, breached the defenses, and claimed the capital of Lydia. From its high walls, the emerging Persian Empire cast its shadow across the Hellespont toward Greece.* It would not move for two hundred years.

The beauty and grandeur of Lydia's impeccably executed architecture and opulent, colonnaded palaces opened Cyrus's eyes and imagination to the trappings of power. With the riches of Lydia providing the funding, Cyrus drafted the skilled stonemasons and artisans he found in the western part of his expanding empire and sent them to an isolated spot in Fars to build him a capital.

In the southern reaches of the Persian heartland, sixty miles northeast of Shiraz, it is possible to stand quietly and actually feel the juxtaposition of geography and history. Coming across the barren, bleached landscape, a narrow road winds to the foot of a steep hill formed of hard-packed dirt and scaling rock. An uneven path climbs from a gentle incline, zigzags up the near vertical face, and ends on the flat plateau of the summit. From there, it is clear why Cyrus the Great chose Pasargadae for his first capital.

Located on the Dasht-e-Morghab, the Plain of the Waterbird, Pasargadae nestles in a natural bowl carpeted with green vegetation denied to the barrenness beyond. On three sides, hills rise like protective walls. The fourth opens like a gate into a broad valley that seems to stretch forever. What the exact function of Pasargadae was at the time of Cyrus remains a mystery. It was not a capital in the usual sense, as Cyrus spent most of his life in the saddle moving from place to place within his empire. Plutarch described Pasargadae as "the sacred place" where each new king in the Achaemenian line was to be crowned. Perhaps the linguistic analysis of the word *Pasargadae* describes this place in Fars the best—"the dwelling of the Persians."

After the construction of Pasargadae, Cyrus once more took up wars of defense and conquest conducted according to the Zoroastrian mandate of justice. In 540 B.C., the Achaemenian king began his assault on Babylon, the last threat to Persia to the west. Deploying part of his army as a decoy, Cyrus drew the corrupt king, Nabonidus, and his army from the city. Then he and the remainder of his forces stood before the walls of Babylon. Slowly the gates opened and the people beckoned Cyrus to enter. Once inside, the king of Persia walked down

*The Hellespont is now known as the Dardanelles.

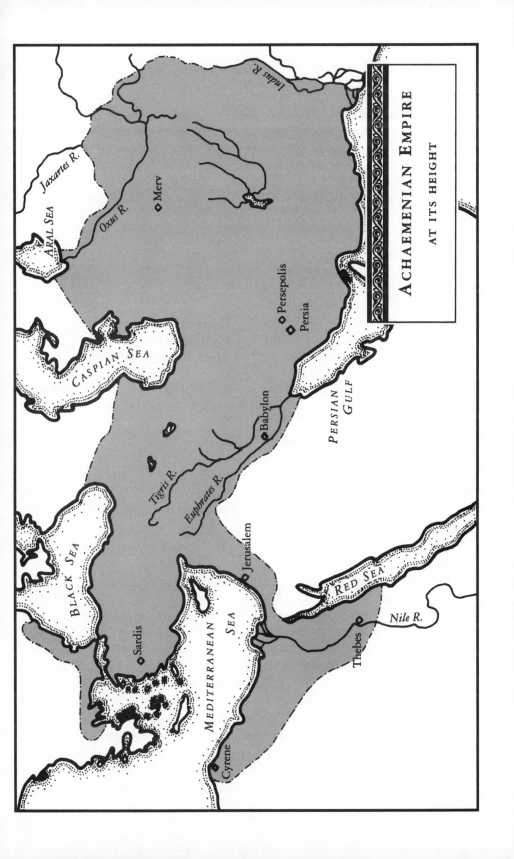

ACHAEMENIAN EMPIRE

AT ITS HEIGHT

Indus R.

Jaxartes R.

Merv ◇

Oxus R.

ARAL SEA

Persepolis ◇
Persia ◇

CASPIAN SEA

PERSIAN GULF

Babylon ●

Tigris R.

Euphrates R.

Jerusalem ◇

RED SEA

Nile R.

BLACK SEA

Sardis ◇

MEDITERRANEAN SEA

Thebes ◇

Cyrene ◇

a carpet of fragrant leaves strewn on the great processional mall of once mighty Babylon liberated from the unjust rule of Nabonidus. Rejecting the image of conqueror, Cyrus assumed the traditional titles of Babylonian kingship and reached out to embrace the Babylonian gods. According to an account of Babylon's surrender written on a cylinder by a Persian, "All the inhabitants bowed to him and kissed his feet. . . . Happily they greeted him as a master through whose help they had come again to life from death and had been spared damage and disaster and they worshiped his very name."[2] This acknowledgment of Cyrus as a liberator was also confirmed by non-Persians. It was Cyrus, the liberator, who freed the Jews from their Babylonian captivity, restored to them what remained of their gold and silver confiscated by Nebuchadnezzar, and sent them home to rebuild their temple in Jerusalem.

From Babylon, Cyrus went on to the west and to the east. His exalted reputation of tolerance preceded his armies, adding to Persian military power the cooperation of dissident elements within the territories he sought to annex. In one generation, he built an empire that exceeded in size those of the Egyptians, the Assyrians, and the Babylonians. Its boundaries spanned the Nile, the Aegean, and the Indus, and stretched north to south from Africa to China.

As a tribute to his politics of idealism and pragmatism, Cyrus's empire was not only large, it was stable because ". . . the Persians realized what had never occurred to the Assyrians and the other imperialist powers of that age: that national interest does not have to express itself solely in vindictiveness, that it is not necessarily impaired by respect for lesser national interests, and that tolerance pays off."[3]

Underlying this tolerance was the ability to understand and appreciate different cultures, which sprang from the Persians' own ideological orientation. It was an ideology shared by Cyrus. Beyond his personal motives of conquest and glory, Cyrus believed that the Supreme God defined by Zoroastrianism had entrusted him with the task of uniting the people of the earth in one kingdom of justice and peace. As the king of that empire, Cyrus exercised the Zoroastrian concept of the just ruler.

Even before the prophet Zoroaster put his stamp on Iran, people of the Iranian plateau believed that only the good ruler who destroyed the evil done by the wicked deserved the allegiance of his subjects. This contract between the ruler and the ruled was not one of passive submission by subjects to king. Rather, popular conception held that hardship would fall to those who helped the wicked to gain kingship and blessings would accrue to those who hurled the wicked from power. To establish in the eyes of his subjects that he stood on the side of right, the king of various early groups on the Iranian plateau visited the great fire-temples to offer his supplications to Ahura Mazda for help in the war upon which he was embarking or to offer thanksgiving for a victory already won.

In embracing and strengthening existing religious beliefs, Zoroastrianism increased the expectations of leadership by speaking forcefully to the moral conduct of government and politics. Since Zoroastrians regarded their place on earth as part of the continuing renewal of the whole Creation, the faith conferred on the king, as representative of the state, the obligation to rule in the interest and defense of good. Consequently for the Persians, the title "King of Kings" expressed less the relationship of the Persian king to the minor kings within the empire than to the nature of kingship in Persia. By the time of Cyrus, the king was regarded as the instrument of God on earth. His right to rule came from righteous conduct, the outward sign that the "divine force" shone upon him. But ensuring that his rule was indeed "right" proved an awesome task. The great king was to be the perfect man, the column of light connecting the upper world of ideals with the lower world of concrete facts. His task was not just to improve the human condition but to rise to a supernatural level on which he renewed the world according to the celestial pattern. This re-creation could not merely serve the abstract. Proof of regeneration lay in the realm of material certitude. Upon the king's virtue depended not only the release of his people from poverty, anguish, need, illness, and disorder but cosmic matters such as the expected course of spring and fall, rain and sun on which the fertility of the land depended. Catering to this expectation, Cyrus attended the fire-temples housing the sacred flame "given to the land of Persia to protect us from disastrous and terrible events, to keep us safe from evil."[4]

But in Zoroastrian epistemology a king, like any other man, might abandon divine guidance. Acting through his own free will, he could turn to malignant spirits and demons. Yet this ability for the king to turn from the light to the darkness also carried with it the denial of his legitimacy to rule. Only by presiding over the order of a just society could the king maintain the *farr*, the sign of divine favor, which confirmed his inherent right to rule. It was this sacred principle of kingship which linked monarchy and religion as the dual forces of power, the symbolic manifestations of God's will.

From this theory of sacred kingship, the Zoroastrian concept of a leader's engagement in the mystical liberation of humankind was firmly planted in the Iranian political consciousness. Until the latter years of the reign of Muhammad Reza Shah, the Iranians, through all the tormented vicissitudes of their history, always held to the mystical ideal of kingship. Within this mythology, they never discarded the hope that someday myth and history would converge to create happiness for all mankind.

As a result, justice is the single most important concept in Persian political culture. The force of the idea is not diminished by the fuzziness of exactly what constitutes justice. Rather than a structured guarantee of individual freedom, the Iranian concept of justice is the preservation of balance and order in a society aligned on the side of good. Because the concept of justice is as much a mystical as a concrete bond between ruler and the ruled, Iranians feel justice more than define it. The great tragedy of the Iranians is that in the 2,500 years from the Achaemenians to the Islamic Republic rarely have they experienced good government, much less ideal government based on justice and equity. Yet the expectation of the ideal is still a powerful force haunting all governments, including the Islamic Republic, that will not, or cannot, meet the expectations of a just society.

Cyrus, who set the standard of just rule, was still robust and in the saddle when he reached his sixties. His efficiently administered empire generally lived in peace. The exception was a corner in the northeast where the Massagetaes, a nomadic branch of the Scythians who ranged the steppes around the Jaxartes River, continued to defy Persian control. In 530 B.C., Cyrus led his army across the Jaxartes, where it engaged the Massagetaes. In the battle, the son of the Massagetaes' strong-willed queen, Tomyris, died. The furious Tomyris rallied the Massagetaes, who in their rage overwhelmed the hitherto invincible Persian army. But the savage queen demanded more than mere military victory. She wanted the life of Cyrus. Succeeding in capturing the Persian king in a fall from his horse, Tomyris raised her sword, severed his head, and threw it into a bag of human blood. It was left to the men who had followed the great king through the battles for empire to bear the dismembered body back to Pasargadae.

Today there is little left of Pasargadae except a palpable sense of time. One lone column stands intact on the broken floor of Cyrus's palace. The others still locked to their pedestals are broken, stubby remnants of their former grace. The rest of the pillars that once supported the roof lie on the ground in roughly ordered rows surrounded by fibrous weeds. There is also little left that celebrates Cyrus. Two sandaled feet and a length of robe are all that remain of the relief carved on the stone of a doorjamb. It once depicted the Persian king as a towering winged figure wearing a tall crown on which rested a covey of mythological figures. Only a timeworn, gabled edifice poised on top of six descending tiers is intact. It stands alone in an open field, facing toward the ruins of the palace. There is something very grand and very dignified about the simple tomb of Cyrus. Perfectly proportioned in a scale that is human, the worn stone bears only the faded epitaph the Achaemenian wrote for himself: "I am Cyrus, son of Cambyses, who founded the Empire of Persia, and was King of Asia. Grudge me not therefore this monument."

Cyrus was succeeded by his son Cambyses, who pushed the Persian empire into Egypt. The campaign consumed three years, too long for the internal politics of a Persia grown weary of war. Pacifism, encouraged by an alliance between a usurper named Bardiya and the priesthood, spread across Fars, threatening to consume those who lived by the martial traditions of the Persian Empire.* Cambyses rushed home. Before he reached Persia to secure the Achaemenian throne, he died.

In 521 B.C., Darius, the dead king's twenty-eight-year-old royal spear bearer and the youngest of three possible heirs from an auxiliary branch of the Achaemenians, picked up the royal shield. With a precocious grasp of politics, he mobilized the nobility and the military to claim the Achaemenian throne and then married both the widow of Cambyses and a daughter of Cyrus to cement that claim. Nonetheless the empire which had seemed so secure at the death of Cyrus weakened as the aura of the righteous king which bound subject to ruler dimmed in the bloody struggle for the throne. Over the next two years, every one of the ancient provinces of the kingdom, including Fars and Media, revolted against Darius. Although each of these provincial revolts represented an uncoordinated challenge against Achaemenian authority, together they threatened to rip the empire apart. In response, Darius launched a two-pronged attack on the insurrection. The first was moral. Charging that a false king planned to appropriate herds, fields, and riches belonging to the citizens of the empire, Darius convinced a sufficient number of people that only he, through his sacred bond with Ahura Mazda, could restore justice. With the moral high ground staked out, Darius gathered his resources and sent them

*History has never accurately determined who Bardiya was or if that was actually his name.

into battle. In the ensuing bloodbath, thousands died in the field and thousands more at the hand of the executioner. When it was over, Darius cut the story of the rebellions into a sheer rock face staring out of a three-thousand-foot mountain northeast of Hamadan. Three hundred feet above the plain below, a rectangular frame the size of a giant billboard carries a carving of twelve figures standing on a densely packed inscription in three languages—Persian, Elamite, and Akkadian. The historical document that Darius commissioned is actually a folk epic with Darius himself cast as the mythic hero fighting hand in hand with the forces of light and goodness. Repeatedly invoking the name of the Zoroastrian deity, Darius asserts that each victory came "by the favor of Ahura Mazda; Ahura Mazda bore me aid; by the favor of Ahura Mazda my army smote that rebellious army exceedingly." Responding to the expectations of his subjects, Darius placed himself into the cosmic realm, assumed divine blessing for his kingship, and proclaimed himself the supreme mortal agent of the deity.

Recovering from his rocky start, Darius reshaped the Persian Empire in his own image. He organized a highly efficient army and developed an administrative system so efficient that it served as a model for the Romans. He governed the conquered territories through satrapies, or provinces, held to Persia through a communications system unmatched in speed until the telegraph doomed the horse to obsolescence. Post stations precisely spaced at intervals equaling one day's ride dotted the royal road stretching two thousand miles from Pasargadae to Sardis. They were linked together by way of fast, muscular horses ridden by strong, skilled men carrying royal messages as far as sixteen hundred miles in one week. Herodotus marveled, "Nothing mortal travels so fast as these messengers. . . . [They] will not be hindered from accomplishing at their best speed the distance which they have to go, either by snow, or rain, or heat, or by the darkness of night."

A grander, more authoritarian figure than Cyrus, Darius nonetheless respected and defended the standards of rule laid by the great Cyrus. Justice reigned over a system of laws that reflected the Zoroastrian theology of kingly power exercised hand in hand with Ahura Mazda. But Darius also tended the flame of empire.

In 517 B.C., the Achaemenian king led his army eastward into the Punjab of present-day India and plunged south into Sind, where he expropriated troves of gold. Having perfected the chariot, the guided missile of the time, he took the flag of Persia west along the North African coast as far as Libya. Operating as much from habit as from need, Darius drove the Persian army as far as the lower Danube in 512 B.C. In the withdrawal back to Persia, he won more than forced the submission to Persian rule by both the Greeks of Thrace on the Aeagean coast and the king of Macedonia. The empire that Cyrus built and Darius first defended and then expanded had reached its apex. It would be celebrated at Persepolis.

The isolated splendor of Persepolis suddenly materializes around a curve on the flat, vacant road leading south across the Marv Dasht plain fifty miles from Pasargadae. Hovering on a massive platform jutting out of a limestone hill, thrusting its classic columns upward like naked spears, fabled Persepolis stands shrouded in a misty purplish blue created by the seemingly mystical light characteristic of Iran. Seldom are the skies anything but cloudless. Yet the entrance to the legendary Achaemenian city always appears enveloped in a dry fog. It disappears at the foot of the grand staircase which leads upward. Fifty-two feet above the surrounding plain, Persepolis becomes an elevated stage on which the Achaemenians displayed the assembled glories of Persia and its king.

Despite the effects of centuries of weather and wreckage, Persepolis is where one best senses the once-upon-a-time power of the Persian Empire that Iranians still regard as a watermark of their national identity. There the restraint so evident at Pasargadae dissolves. The two huge winged bulls that formed the entrance gate and the Apadana, a hall large enough to hold ten thousand people, were only the beginning of the 181,500 square yards of grandeur which existed at the time of the Achaemenians. From buildings covered in brilliantly painted plaster embedded with jewels to the gold-plated doors that swung on mammoth stone hinges to gold lace curtains and rich tapestries, Persepolis was meant to awe its visitors with the power of the empire ruled by the king in alliance with Ahura Mazda.

Persepolis was a ceremonial city more than a capital. Every year when the harshness of winter gave way to the softness of spring the people of the empire came to Persepolis to celebrate No Ruz. An exquisite carving on the huge foundation stones of the Apadana portrays the lion of winter and the gazelle of spring locked in mortal conflict between the forces of the old year and the new, between good and evil. No Ruz, perhaps more than any other event in Achaemenian Persia, demonstrated the growing body of customs and traditions which stamped Persian culture as unique. For at Persepolis on No Ruz, the Persians knew who and what they were—a special people sitting at the center of the universe.

On the day of the vernal equinox, the Immortals, ten thousand men from the leading families of Media and Persia who formed the king's bodyguard, stood in attendance as the subjects of Persia's empire paraded past the Achaemenian throne. The spectacle is preserved in stone on the eastern staircase of the Apadana where delegates of twenty-three different peoples bear their gifts of camels, bulls, horses, rams, gilded weapons, bracelets, bowls, and textiles to the Persian king. Powerful in their effect, these reliefs depict a decorative quality exceeding mere representation. There is high art in the grouping of figures, their stance, and their gestures. But these act as only hand-maidens to detail—tight little clusters of whorled stone create the curls of beards and hair; slanting lines and flattened curves press folds into robes of limestone; etchings of incredible delicacy turn a sheep into a creature of stately dignity; and a loop, elongated just enough, gives an animal leash the grace of an arabesque.

The offerings that these magnificent figures bear are as eclectic as the empire in which Indians, Asians, Syrians, Ethiopians, Libyans, Sogdians, Egyptians, and Babylonians acknowledged a common bond under the Achaemenian king enthroned at Persepolis.* The platform on which Persepolis was built was itself a symbolic throne, a metaphor for the seat of empowerment from which the Persian king reigned over an ecumenical world order. That same metaphor appears in reliefs that picture the king sitting on a throne mounted on a gigantic stool lifted a few inches off the ground by rows of men, each dressed in the peculiar costume of the foreign tributary land he represents. The throne itself rests on lion's feet, the stool on bull's feet, symbolizing the king on the throne of Persia resting his feet on the stool of the empire. It was an empire of interdependent provinces willing to submit to Persian authority in exchange for stability, prosperity, and an expectation of equity under the law. They did so because the source of Darius's authority, like the source of Cyrus's authority, lay in the Zoroastrian concept of the king as the symbol of divine sovereignty on earth. Although Darius, the architect of Persepolis, was significantly more authoritarian than Cyrus, he still carved into the stone of his tomb at Naqsh-e-Rustam his commitment to the side of good. "Saith Darius the king: by the favor of Ahura Mazda I am of such a sort that I am a friend to right, I am not a friend to wrong. It is not my desire that the weak man should have wrong done to him by the mighty; nor

---

*By the end of his reign, a total of twenty-nine separate peoples were giving Darius their allegiance.

is it my desire that the mighty man should have wrong done to him by the weak. What is right, that is my desire."

Zoroastrianism as a faith had steadily gained influence in Persia since the reign of Cyrus. By the time Darius had systematized the empire's administration, it was a well-developed and generally accepted faith in Persia and the empire. Yet in spite of fire-temples positioned at public sites and Darius's instruction that the Avesta, the scriptures of the Zoroastrian faith, be recorded in gold and silver on twelve thousand ox hides, Zoroastrianism was by no definition a state religion. But as the most widely accepted faith of Persia and the theology that affirmed the authority of the king, it served an essential role in the political life of both Persia and the territories. During the reign of Darius, the magi, the official priests of the Achaemenian kings, became akin to a caste. Obligated to preserve religious tradition and proselytize the faith, these "guardians of the flame" ripened into the authenticators of truth and justice. Thus the king and the priests, the secular and religious, formed another dualism in Persian culture.

By the time Darius died in 486 B.C., a distinctive Persian culture had established itself. Fluid rather than fixed, it engulfed the new ideas that constantly fed it. Xerxes, Darius's successor and the last of the great Achaemenian kings, continued to oversee the cross-fertilization of Persian culture encouraged by his predecessors. Recognizing the talents of foreign architects and artisans, Xerxes put their skills to work at Persepolis. At the epicenter of the Persian Empire, the best of Assyria, Egypt, and Greece successfully melded with the best of Persia. Xerxes, like his father Darius, attached Greek physicians to his court and employed distinguished Greek intellectuals exiled by their compatriots. Along with the game of chess, intellectuals from India also brought Eastern ideas to a Persia anxious to incorporate any notion it considered beneficial or simply interesting. But the admired ideas of others were never slavishly copied by the Persians. Instead they were restudied, reworked, and reexpressed in a uniquely Persian fashion that was in harmony with the Zoroastrian creed of uniting good forces in the name of the Supreme God. This ability of the Iranians to adopt, remold, and assimilate the art and ideas of others became another of the hallmarks of Persian culture. It was an ability that would not be seriously tested until the nineteenth century A.D., when Iran encountered the West.

Persia's artistic life cohabited with its military life. Like Cyrus and Darius, Xerxes took Persia to war in the quest for territory and security. In the spring of 481 B.C., he marched out of Susa in command of the biggest war machine ever assembled in Asia. Heading west, the Persian king aimed to engage the Greeks in another contest for domination of the ancient world.

Crossing the Hellespont and passing quickly through Macedonia, the Persian army met and defeated the Spartans at Thermopylae and swept on through Attica, burning towns and villages as it went. Taking Athens, the Persians stormed the Acropolis and set fire to the partially finished Parthenon, the pride of Athenian architecture. Xerxes sent word of victory back to Persia. But stripped of much of its naval support by the Battle of Salamis, the Persian infantry, still uniformed in the capes and flowing gowns handed down by the Elamites, lost Persia's war to the armor-clad Greeks at Plataea.

Returning to Persepolis in defeat, Xerxes spent much of his time seeking pleasure in the *haram*. Despite the stone doorjambs of the new portals at Persepolis that portrayed him in combat with the mythological beasts of evil, Xerxes increasingly exercised his absolute power as king without tending its underpinnings—justice and tolerance. The decline of Achaemenian Persia had begun.

In 465 B.C., Xerxes was murdered by a palace conspirator. By 401 B.C., brother fought brother for the right to be sanctified by the robes of Cyrus the Great. As the rivals for fading Persia circled one another, the empire's Greek-speaking western provinces girded for revolt and Greek imperialism from west of the Hellespont waited on the two factors which would allow it to rip the Persian Empire to pieces—a resolution of Greece's own political schisms and a leader.

As the Achaemenians allowed the best of Persian tradition to drain away, the young Alexander of Macedonia looked on. In 332 B.C., a hundred and thirty-three years after the death of Xerxes, he crossed to the eastern side of the Hellespont. Reluctant to fight, Persia watched. Twice the Achaemenian king Darius III offered to buy peace by ceding all Persian territory from the "Euphrates to the Greek sea." Alexander refused, preferring to humble Persia at Cunoxa on the battlefield of Mesopotamia. From there, the Macedonians plunged through the Zagros Mountains toward the heart of Fars. What lay ahead was the Marv Dasht plain and the spiritual center of Persia—Persepolis.

Halting his army, Alexander climbed the ceremonial staircase not as a suppliant of Persian power but as its conqueror. Before him spread the wealth of the Achaemenians: the gold-plated rim of the Apadana's roof; hundreds of reliefs studded with gems; a golden vine dripping with jewels; and 120,000 talents of silver and 8,000 talents of gold. Like Cyrus at Lydia, Alexander was suddenly relieved of the problem of financing his conquests. Employing ten thousand horses and five thousand camels, he emptied the city. Then Alexander, the student of Aristotle, the avowed servant of truth and beauty, ordered Persepolis burned. Committing one of the most senseless acts of destruction in human history, Alexander intended to take from the Persians their sense of self. He was only the first in a long line of conquerors who would consume the Persians' territory but not their identity.

In less than a hundred years—from Cyrus's rise to the death of Xerxes—the Persians had produced a religion that replaced idols and blood rites with a God and a moral system; a government reigning over a diversity of nations living in peace; a philosophy concerned with ethics, tolerance, and justice; and finally an art that celebrated an extraordinarily high level of civilization. Thus in the empire that began with the Achaemenians, Iranians—with a perception born of truth—see their greatness. And it is the culture which took root in Achaemenian Persia that constitutes the potent Persian component of Iranian identity.

Persian culture's first test of resilience came under the Greek Seleucids. For forty-two years after Alexander the Great died, his generals squabbled over possession of his legacy. In the end, the empire was divided. Egypt went to the general Ptolemy. The remainder, including Persia, was seized by Seleucis, Alexander's Macedonian cavalry commander. His Seleucid line ruled Persia between the third and first centuries B.C.

The Seleucids pursued Alexander's Hellenistic vision, which saw subject peoples incorporated into a superstate directed by Greek ideals, governed by Greek laws, imbued with the Greek language, and swayed by Greek art. In the Seleucid territories of Syria and Asia Minor, Hellenism flowered and bore the fruit of new cultural patterns. But in Iran, it remained only an influence. While the elite mimicked the Greek way of life, the majority of Persians held to their traditional culture and nursed their differences with their Greek masters. Consequently, one generation after another of Persians sustained their basic identity and sense of belonging to the Iranian plateau. That the Persians, the most imitative of people, should have remained indifferent to Greek culture, one of the most potent in history, is extraordinary. The reason may be that the Greeks and the Persians were simply too different to meld. They were, in many ways, cultural opposites. Politically the Greeks had the city-state and the Persians the absolute monarch. Artistically, the Greeks loved representation, the Persians decoration. Geographically, the Greeks were of the West, the Persians of the East. Thus in 160 years of Seleucid rule, the Greeks succeeded only in laying a veneer over the Persian body. They never seduced the Persian heart that dwelled in the blackened ruins of Persepolis.

Seleucid rule was lifted from Persia by a tribe of nomadic Aryans, the Parthians. Advancing down the eastern side of the Caspian Sea about the time Alexander died, the Parthians settled in Iran, where they began to absorb the culture of Persia. Gradually creeping out of the nucleus of their first settlement, the Parthians nibbled at the nerve ends of a weakening Seleucid Persia. In 163 B.C., the Parthians severed the main artery connecting Persia to the rest of the Seleucid Empire, reuniting the northern and southern ends of the Iranian plateau. Persia was reborn.

Wedged between the resplendent dynasties of the Achaemenians and the third-century A.D. Sassanians, the Parthians were the bridge between alien Hellenism and resurgent Persia. Although breathing new life into Persian culture, the Parthians' single most important achievement was to fight and check the Romans for three hundred years, ensuring that Persia escaped the orbit of the West.

The military strength with which the Parthians protected Persia and its culture came from both beasts and men. When they surrendered their nomadic life, the Parthians took their horses out of the open fields, put them in stalls, and fed them on grain. The result was a new breed. Larger, possessing more stamina, these horses were outfitted with armor and mounted by archers armed with powerful bows capable of sending arrows through Roman breastplates. Together man and beast became a devastating weapon of war. In 53 B.C., the Parthian army killed twenty thousand Romans in one battle. In 36 B.C. in Azerbaijan, the mounted bowmen faced the famous Roman general Mark Antony. In one confrontation, Rome lost thirty-five thousand men out of a force of approximately one hundred thousand. As a result, Mark Antony fled to the arms of Cleopatra and Rome retreated west of the Tigris, surrendering its chance to further expand its empire eastward.

The Parthians lasted a little less than four hundred years, from 163 B.C. to A.D. 224. From the beginning of the dynasty, the Parthians appropriated Achaemenian culture and philosophy as well as its royal lineage. Rejecting Greek political thought, which postulated that a king ruled through the goodwill of his subjects, the Parthian kings, like the Achaemenians, claimed legitimacy from the supreme deity. In the arts, they fostered the small, delicate paintings which constitute the most recognizable form of Persian art other than carpets—the miniature. Controlling a valuable segment of the Silk Road between China and Rome, the Parthians placed Persia once more at the crossroads of cultures, restoring the Persians to their historic position as receivers and transmitters of ideas. But all their wealth, power, and achievements could not overcome their fatal weakness— the inability of any king to establish and maintain control over his kingdom.

While the Parthian Empire plunged into tribal war, Fars, the original seat of Achaemenian power, watched. As early as 280 B.C., Fars had established its independence in an uprising against the Seleucids. With no unified government to rule it, Fars reverted to a series of tribal monarchies similar to those from which Cyrus sprang. One of these lay between the ruins of Persepolis and Pasargadae, at a place called Istakhr. It was ruled by a man named Papak, the keeper of the shrine of Anahita, the Zoroastrian provider of water.

In A.D. 208, Papak's son, Ardeshir, succeeded to a throne surrounded by the chaos of Parthian rule. Across Fars, villagers and noblemen alike were drawing into fortified enclaves to protect themselves from the anarchy. Treading the fine line between conquest and conciliation, Ardeshir, in the tradition of Cyrus, began to reassemble the Persian state. By 224, his opponents had narrowed to one— Ardavan, the last of the Parthian kings. When Ardavan accused Ardeshir of usurping his power, Ardeshir replied in tones that echoed the Achaemenians. "This throne and this crown were given me by God."[5]

Leaving their armies aside, Ardeshir and Ardavan met in hand-to-hand combat. With a kingdom hanging in the balance, two mailed figures on a vast treeless plain cautiously circled each other awaiting divine blessings to fall on one or the other. Ardeshir was chosen. Standing over the corpse of his rival, he claimed the title of "King of Kings." From 208 to 637, the Sassanian dynasty he established consciously raised the torch and honed the edges of the culture which began with Cyrus.*

The Sassanian epoch constitutes one of the notable ages of Iranian history. It took form in a renaissance of Persian culture, the charisma of kingship, and the religion of Zoroastrianism. Even today the artistic

*The dynastic name, Sassanian, came from Ardeshir's grandfather.

footprints of the Sassanians track Islamic Iran. The dome and the vault so identified with Iranian Islamic architecture are, in fact, Sassanian. The first known Persian carpet, "Spring of Khosrow," came out of a Sassanian royal palace. The technique of miniature painting developed by the Parthians reached a new plateau during the Sassanian era. And contemporary poetry, in some of its themes and motifs, recalls Sassanian Iran.

The Persian cultural revival begun by the Sassanians went hand in hand with their need to secure political stability. Ardeshir realized from the moment that he claimed kingship that the Parthian curse of unresolved leadership could only be lifted if the king acquired the aura of divinity prescribed by Zoroastrianism. Between the fall of the Achaemenians and the rise of the Sassanians, the magi of Persia had kept the "Good Religion" of Zoroaster alive. They had done so independent of kings. But religion met politics when Ardeshir recognized that religious conformity served his need to centralize authority within his kingdom. Zoroastrianism could also provide a rallying point for empire as the Persians pushed west against the eastward advance of the Roman Empire. To Ardeshir's advantage, the interests of the King of Kings and the interests of the priests represented two dimensions of the same desire—power. Hand in hand, king and priest organized Zoroastrianism into a coherent force in control of Persia's spiritual and temporal life. The sacred texts in the care of the priests grew into a powerful instrument of dogmatic definition and ritualistic institutions. Through them, the priests granted legitimacy and authority to the king, and the king ensured the survival of the priests.

In a grand manipulation of symbols, the sacred flame of the temple at Istakhr became the flame of the king as well as Ahura Mazda. Having asserted himself as God's agent on earth, Ardeshir surrounded himself with the trappings of divine authority. His first palace, the Qaleh-e-Dokhtar, poised at the top of a sheer-faced gorge connecting the northern and southern spheres of the Sassanian Empire, became a towering symbol of royal power. Everyone who passed it felt the king's omnipotence. Those invited into the presence of the king climbed the steep cliff terrace by terrace, traversed a large courtyard, filtered through rigid protocol, and, finally, passed out of blinding daylight into the dimmed opulence of the palace to fall prostrate before the King of Kings.

Around the king, the social order stratified into rigid classes. First came the clergy, incorporating priests, judges, temple guardians, teachers, and ascetics; second, the military; third, the scribes, including the writers of official communications and chronicles as well as physicians, astronomers, poets, and accountants; and fourth, the artisans, embracing farmers, herdsmen, merchants, and skilled craftsmen. A writer of the period likened the social system to man. The priests were the head; the warriors the hands; the agriculturists the stomach; and the artisans the feet. And each class represented an aspect of man's character. The first, virtue; the second, manliness; the third, steadfastness; and the fourth, diligence. Between these classes, privileges on the one side and interdictions on the other built almost insurmountable barriers. The position of the priests and the aristocratic landholders was hereditary. Neither class was allowed to intermarry with the lower classes, who in turn were forbidden to acquire property. Basically, society cleaved between the few highly privileged and the rest. It was the beginning of the social-political oppression that would mold Iranian culture and political behavior for centuries. Still existing in a modified form populated by different families at the time of Muhammad Reza Shah, the call to level this heirarchical system was one of the most forceful elements in the Iranian Revolution of 1979.

These carefully constructed and regulated stations in Sassanian society represented the Sassanian obsession with control. For the Sassanians faced the same basic problem of stability as the Parthians before them and almost all governments of Iran that have followed. The Sassanian Empire was composed of parts—the Persian heartland and the restless, polyglot periphery. In the existing tension, the evenhanded, predictable justice maintained by Cyrus and Darius wavered as Ardeshir discovered early on the value of terror produced by calculated caprice in which only the godlike figure of the king could choose between mercy and severity. Yet Ardeshir's overpowering authority was held in check by the Zoroastrian tradition that required a king to rule with a general sense of social justice.

But tolerance, that seed of understanding between the master of the Persian Empire and its subjects so carefully tended by the Achaemenians and defended by the Parthians, withered under the Sassanians. The Sassanian Empire in its later stages too often supported a religion far more concerned with rites and practices than beliefs, a king far more concerned with power than justice. Establishing a pattern that would stretch through Iranian history to Muhammad Reza Shah, the call for radical social change appeared in religious garb.

During the reign of Ardeshir's son, Shapour, a religious visionary by the name of Mani appeared out of a village near Ctesiphon in Mesopotamia. Born in A.D. 216, Mani became the second great prophet of pre-Islamic Iran. Claiming to be the last apostle in a line from Zoroaster to Buddha to Jesus, he borrowed teachings from all three and combined them into Manichaeism. Like Zoroastrianism, Manichaeism dealt in the great dualism between good and evil. In Mani's theology, good and evil manifested themselves in the individual in the separation of body and soul, heart and mind, the sensual and the spiritual. In society, this duality reflected itself in the conflict between "divine" spiritualism and "satanic" materialism.

All Manichaeans believed that spiritual piety could free the light deep within the human soul imprisoned in the darkness that was the world. Only when this light was released would the world vanish and God emerge victorious. In pursuit of this spiritual purity, some of Mani's followers refused to marry and others castrated themselves in order to devote their lives completely to spiritual enrichment. For a while, Mani himself was accepted at the Sassanian court of Shapour I. But when the established priests judged that Mani posed a threat to their power, he was put to a slow and diabolic death.

The second heresy to strike the theocratic Sassanian state was Mazdakism, a theology propagated by a religious visionary named Mazdak. It was born at the end of the fifth century A.D. when Persia was ravaged by famine, drought, and military defeat, all signs that the king no longer possessed the divine aura. A kind of positive radicalism, Mazdakism took Manichaeism a step further in defining perfect good. In a direct challenge to the Sassanian system, Mazdakism taught that in order to put an end to such evils as hatred, discord, and war, their natural causes must be neutralized. These were defined as the desires for women and wealth. Hence women and property were to be held in common in a classless society of equal individuals. This call for a society in which all were peers proved too much for an establishment granted power through a rigid social hierarchy. In 524, a corrupted Zoroastrian priesthood ordered Mazdak assassinated and his followers purged.

But neither Mazdakism nor Manichaeism totally died in Iran. Their influence survived in part because they touched the deep concerns of Persian culture with the aim and purpose of life. In its most basic terms, Manichaeism retained the Zoroastrian principle of opposing forces of good and evil, of light and dark, by teaching that man must redeem his soul by the rigorous denial of fleshly appetites; and Mazdakism summoned each individual within society to fight for truth against darkness and lies. Both sought to level the class hierarchy in order to establish a just society. This theme of social justice, of the king standing with Ahura Mazda on the side of right, came directly out of Zoroastrianism at the time of Cyrus.

Despite the minor tremors produced by deviant religious thinkers, the Sassanians presided over a noble age. With the Silk Road between China and the West producing ever higher revenues, a new Sassanian city rose at Firuzabad, roughly a hundred miles south of the present city of Shiraz. Its circular shape symbolized a growing attitude among the people of Sassanian Persia that they occupied the center of the world. The gates out of the city literally put spirit in stone. Placed at each of the four points of the compass, they led out to China, India, Arabia, and Rome. Connected to the world, exhibiting confidence born of stability and prosperity, Sassanian Persians felt they could go anywhere and do anything.

This new spirit found form in another push for empire. Ardeshir's successor, Shapour I, once more took Persia into war against Rome. In two successive campaigns, he defeated the Roman army. In the third, he crushed it, capturing the emperor Valerian in the process. In the afterglow of the victory of Persian power, Shapour ordered his image carved below the tomb of Darius at Naqsh-e-Rustam. Adorned with a tall crown, a heavy sword strapped at his side, Shapour sits astride a horse dwarfed by its royal rider. Before him, the emperor Valerian, stripped of his ornaments of office, cowers before the mighty Sassanian king, the ruler of resurrected Persia.

In 560, a new king, Khosrow I, sat on the Sassanian throne. Although he is rightfully celebrated as "the just," Khosrow's power was anchored in the bedrock of absolute monarchy. Like so many of his predecessors, he built his charisma on heroic legend and fed the mystique of the throne by embellishing his court. During his forty-eight-year-long reign, Khosrow exercised justice both as philosophy and political pragmatism. But despite his political acumen, Khosrow pulled the kingship from its roots in Fars. Moving his capital to Ctesiphon in Mesopotamia, the Sassanian king left behind once and for all the simplicity Cyrus established at Pasargadae.* Ctesiphon became an exercise in the glorification of the monarchy. The king's vaulted audience hall reached 121 feet high and spanned 84 feet. In winter, the floor was laid with the legendary "Spring of Khosrow." A Persian carpet ninety feet square, woven of silk and embellished with gold and silver threads, it represented the traditional Persian garden in

*Ctesiphon was located just south of the present city of Baghdad. It was one of the sites spared in the bombing of Iraq during the 1991 Gulf War.

spring. Thousands of jewels studded its weave—diamonds for water, emeralds for greenery, rubies and pearls and a dozen other precious gems for blossoms. At the end of the vast hall in which it lay, a transparent curtain divided the king from his subjects. Behind it, Khosrow sat beneath a crown so heavy with gold and jewels that it had to be suspended on chains from the ceiling. In his presence, the royal banquets, sometimes requiring up to twelve days to prepare, served as gargantuan displays in which the King of Kings "showed the riches of his glorious kingdom and the honor of his excellent Majesty."[6] At his side, exercising the rites of orthodoxy, stood the Zoroastrian priests.

This alliance of religion and king no longer served the cosmic battle between good and evil. Instead it allowed the state to exercise its will and religion to protect its position. For three centuries of Sassanian rule, the Zoroastrian priesthood had formed the heart of Sassanian power. In their white robes and conical caps, the magi had zealously gone to Persia's wars to cleanse the conquered lands of demons. In peace, they had certified the kings' authority. The kings, in turn, purged any whiff of heresy and stood guard over a monolithic orthodoxy that ensured the priests privileged position in the political and social hierarchy. Having lost touch with its mission of divining light over darkness, goodness over evil, Zoroastrianism was no longer accessible or relevant. When Sassanian kingship brought disaster to Persia, Zoroastrianism would be fatally implicated.

Before he died in 579, Khosrow had succeeded in reestablishing Persia as a military power, enabling his successors to push again into the West in pursuit of security and territory. In 602, the Persians drove into Byzantium, the eastern part of the former Roman Empire. Antioch fell to Persian might in 613, Jerusalem in 614, Sardis and Ephesus in 616, Alexandria and then Egypt in 619. By 620, Persia had pushed Byzantium all the way back to Constantinople.

But in 626, Byzantium struck back. Restructured into a fast-moving offensive force, the army of Byzantium swung north, sailed across the Black Sea, and positioned itself in the Caucasus. Plunging south, the Byzantine juggernaut tore through Armenia and Azerbaijan and into Mesopotamia, to the glittering seat of the King of Kings—Ctesiphon. The city fell into panic. The king fled, decapitating the empire of the Sassanians. In less than a decade, the Sassanian dynasty itself fell.

Yet the Persian culture that came to life under the Achaemenians survived. The themes of ethics and behavior bred by religion, kingship and justice, art and customs, tolerance for diversity and an eagerness for assimilation lived on as they had lived on after the Achaemenians. In that earlier time, the Seleucids might well have succeeded in tying Persia to Greece and its Western culture. Under the Parthians, the culture of Rome shaped in the West might have prevailed over the Iranian plateau. And when the old Roman Empire split between West and East, an alliance between Byzantium and Persia could well have developed. After all, Christianity that rose out of Judaism was as much a religion of the East as Zoroastrianism. That the uniquely Persian culture and identity survived and prospered must be credited to the Sassanians, for it was they who took the traditions they inherited and cast them into a distinct kind of identity. However, in the end, it was the Iranians themselves who defended a unique form of nationalism which came from an emotional commitment to culture. When Iran fell to the Arabs in the seventh century, Persian culture stayed intact to fertilize Islam and define it for Iran.

2

The Invasion of Islam

THE ALBORZ MOUNTAINS LAY BLANKETED IN SNOW AND THE cold winter air that blew down on the city below hurried people along Shahid Drive. On this day in Iran, as on all days, the sights, sounds, and smells of Tehran competed with one another for attention. I was standing under the canopy of the Esteqlal Hotel, the prerevolutionary Hilton, waiting to be picked up for a tour of the city. On schedule, a boxy, brown Iranian-made Paykan jerked to a stop in front of the hotel. The door on the driver's side flew open and a short, mustached man bounced out. Smiling broadly, raising his arms in greeting, he proclaimed, "I am Jamshid. Welcome, welcome!"

What Jamshid lacked as a driver, he made up for in exuberance. Weaving the car through the city's mad, suicidal traffic with the four fingers of his right hand on the wheel and his thumb on the horn, he threw his left hand out the window to point out the Majlis building, the bazaar, and the Central Bank. All the while his commentary cascaded like a waterfall. Then came the humor. Still pushing the car at breakneck speed through the pell-mell traffic, he turned his head toward the backseat and abruptly asked, "You have heard the scientific explanation of the difference between the Iranians and the Arabs?" I answered, "No." It was the answer he wanted. As he swerved to avoid an oncoming car, he explained. "The Arabs are interested in only two things—sex and making money. The Iranians are interested in the first two plus culture." Laughing uproariously, Jamshid had voiced one of the basic attitudes of Iranians—contempt for the Arabs, their brothers in Islam.

Islam originally belonged to the Arabs. Yet when the faith of Muhammad swept across the border of Iran, it fell under the influence of Persian culture. And it was Persian culture which led the Islamic Empire into its golden age that encompassed the eighth through the tenth centuries. Yet the Arabs continued to hold Islam through its great emotive force: the Arabic language, the tongue of the Prophet and the sacred language of the Koran. Through the Islamic Empire's centuries of glory, the Iranians adhered to Islam and incorporated much of the Arabic language into Farsi. But at the same time, they rejected Arab culture, choosing instead to hold to the values, mores, and aesthetics of pre-Islamic Persia. Before Islam's golden age ended, Persian identity within the world of Islam found its voice in the poetry of Ferdowsi, who revived the images of pre-Islamic Persia within the religion of Muhammad. By the eleventh century, the Iranians and the Arabs had begun to move into separate rooms in the house of Islam, each painted in the differing colors of sect and culture.

Today Islam is split into two main branches—the Sunni tradition and the Shia variation. In the most simplistic terms, Sunni orthodoxy portrays Arab culture, Shia nonconformity mirrors Persian culture. As such, each sect reflects the great and enduring ethnic and cultural schism between Arabs and Persians. Since the seventh century A.D., these ethnic, cultural, and religious variations have bred contempt and animosity between Arabs and Iranians. This cultural-religious cleavage of Islam is as immediate as it is historic. For within the issues of sect and culture lie clues to the direction and leadership of contemporary revolutionary movements in the Middle East that call themselves Islamic.

Islam was born in the desolate landscape of the Arabian Peninsula. For a millennium, the Arabs of the peninsula had lived in isolation from the repetitive contest for control of the Fertile Crescent that lies between the Mediterranean and the Iranian plateau.* During the centuries in which the Fertile Crescent experienced Persian power applied

---

*The Arabs of the Arabian Peninsula were the original Arabs. Organized by tribes, they were ethnically and linguistically distinct from the people of the Fertile Crescent. The contemporary definition of the term Arab incorporates all people who claim Arabic as their first language.

by the Achaemenians, Alexander's Hellenism, Rome's eastward drive for empire, and Byzantium's reach for political hegemony through Christian faith and Greek culture, the Arabs lived in isolation, protected by walls erected of sand, heat, and distance. Condemned to deserts deprived of fertility and water, most Arabs survived either by farming the widely scattered oases or by herding goats and sheep over the ocean of barren land in a constant search for water and scrubby vegetation. A few backwater towns lay along the spice and frankincense route that ran from Yemen to the Mediterranean. In the early seventh century, a main stop on that north-south track was Mecca, fifty miles inland from the Red Sea and roughly halfway between the tip of the Arabian Peninsula and the southeastern corner of the Mediterranean. Mecca had claimed a certain prosperity as a trade center during the years that the wealth of the competing Byzantine and Persian empires consumed the expensive products of Yemen. In the sixth century A.D., the Meccan merchants, dominated by the Quraysh, a clan of mercantile families, hustled in the marketplace to maximize the commercial advantage created by geography and timing. In the process, the Arabs' traditional loyalties rooted in family and tribe and their values of honor and morality grounded in nomadic society suffocated in the stampede for wealth and status. As a result, a great chasm opened between the ethical system of the tribesmen and the materialism of the ruling class.

In A.D. 570, Abu al-Qasim Muhammad ibn Abdullah ibn Abd al-Muttalib ibn Hashim was born into this social turmoil. Orphaned at the age of six, he lived in his grandfather's house for two years before being passed on to an uncle, Abu Talib. Abu Talib, like Muhammad and his father before him, claimed membership in the Banu Hashim, a poor clan within the Quraysh. As a young adult, Muhammad, the progeny of respectable bloodlines with little power and even less money, went to work as a driver in the camel caravans. Soon the handsome man with wavy hair, a full beard, thick-lashed dark eyes, and a radiant smile married the widow who owned the camels.

Freed from daily toil, Muhammad began to withdraw into the desert for long periods of time to meditate on the sins of Meccan society. In 610, just before his fortieth year, a troubled and distracted Muhammad slept alone on Mount Hira. According to the classic biographies of the Prophet, the angel Gabriel descended from heaven to bring Muhammad a message. It contained only one word: "Recite!" Muhammad hesitated. And three times the angel commanded, "Recite!" The shaken Muhammad asked, "What shall I recite?" And the angel said, "Recite in the name of the Lord who created all things, who created man from the clots of blood." The next morning Muhammad came down off the mountain bringing his revelation to the people of Mecca. He called them to abandon the idolatrous practices propagated for profit by the Quraysh and accept the one, universal God—Allah, the all-powerful, the creator of the universe, the everlasting.

Muhammad's message validated the worth of traditional Arab life followed by the nomadic Bedouins. Harvesting the tribal values of generosity, courage, loyalty, and veracity, Muhammad put them in a religious context structured with clear rules. There is paradise and there is hell. Splendid rewards come to those who obey Allah's commands and terrible vengeance awaits those who disobey. Giving voice and form to the restiveness of his time, Muhammad began to attract converts. The poor responded to his denunciations of the quest for wealth. The young who were shut out of the councils of power grasped his vision of equality for all men. The Bedouins responded to his repudiation of the dreaded *jinn*, the evil spirits, and his restoration of the ethics of the tribe. But in attracting the lowest classes—the meanest of society—Muhammad threatened the aristocracy. Sounding a theme similar to that which Mazdak had sounded in Sassanian Persia, Muhammad tore at the entire social system by preaching that the destitute have the right to share in the wealth of the rich. Like the Zoroastrian priesthood, the Quraysh, lords of the caravan trade and masters of the city, struck back by employing every weapon from economic retaliation to poetic barbs. In 622, Muhammad and his community escaped Mecca for Medina, two hundred miles to the north. Known as the *hijra*, or "flight," the move to Medina transformed Muhammad from a private person preaching a new faith to a leader wielding political and military authority. With that authority, Muhammad, at the head of a thousand followers, returned triumphantly to Mecca in January 630 to claim the city for Islam.

At the beginning of his ministry, the Prophet had harbored no ambition to found either a religion or a government. He saw himself as nothing more than an ordinary man chosen by God to convey to the people of Mecca the truths that would save them from divine wrath on the Day of Judgment. But by the time the Prophet died on June 8, 632, near the age of sixty, he had gone beyond simply preaching Allah's message. Presenting himself as the culmination of all the Old Testament prophets and the New Testament prophet Jesus, Muhammad had delivered a monotheistic religion containing precise ethical doctrines to most of western Arabia. In addition he had established a new community that was in essence an organized and armed state governing in the name of religion.

The victory of Islam was religious and it was social. Muhammad had not only given God definition, but like Zoroaster, had redefined relations between one human being and another. Replacing tribal fragmentation with the unity of religious belief, Muhammad instilled the idea of the *Ummah*, the community of believers, with the words, "Hearken, O ye men, unto my words and take ye them to heart. Know ye that every Muslim is a brother unto every other Muslim, and that ye are one brotherhood."[1]

Religiously, Islam was a completion. Muhammad had delivered the comprehensive word of Allah. There would be no more prophets and no more revelations. But Islam was also a new beginning—the foundation of a new empire and a new civilization. When he died, Muhammad bequeathed to his followers the mission of delivering Islam's message to the rest of mankind. Rallying to the Koranic injunction "Fight those who believe not in God and the Last Day," a ragtag Muslim army drawn from the deserts and towns of the western coastal plain of what is now Saudi Arabia took to the field. In a lightning campaign consuming a few months, it converted the tribes of southern, central, and eastern Arabia to Islam.

The Prophet had been dead only a year when Islam's soldiers raced north out of the Arabian Peninsula in pursuit of converts and booty. They first drove west toward Syria and the empire of Byzantium. In 634, Damascus, Christian Byzantium's "pearl of the East," surrendered. Two years later, on a boiling hot August day on the Yarmuk River, fifty thousand Byzantine Christians commanding all the military technology of the age fell to a Muslim army half its size, armed with nothing but bows and curved-blade axes. On the western flank of the Arab army that had come out of Arabia, the way opened for the Muslim conquest of all of Syria. Before the eastern flank lay Mesopotamia and Sassanian Persia.

Victories came swiftly to the Muslims because they rode into a political and spiritual vacuum. The centuries of warfare in which Byzantium and Persia had hammered away against each other had debilitated both, leaving the wide swath of territory for which they fought largely defenseless against the Arab invaders. Yet as impressive as these quick military successes were, the ease with which the conquered people from Egypt to the western edge of the Iranian plateau underwent Arabization is even more astounding.

Before the Arab invasion, the Fertile Crescent was a patchwork of languages, religions, and ethnic identifications. Running west to east from the Nile to the Tigris and north to south from the southern Taurus Mountains of Asia Minor to the northern deserts of the Arabian Peninsula, the Fertile Crescent lay on the historic invasion routes between Europe and Asia, with an occasional intrusion from Africa. For almost three thousand years—from the days of the pharaohs to the arrival of the Muslim armies—the Fertile Crescent had been subjected to one invasion after another. Armies moved from the west and then they moved from the east, conquering, occupying, and finally withdrawing in response to a greater force. They all came—the Egyptians, Hyksos, and Hittites; the Macedonians and the Persians; the Romans and the Assyrians; the Byzantines and once more the Persians. And when each of them retreated, they left a little of themselves behind. Yet despite the bombardment of different empires with all their accompanying languages and philosophies, the people of the Fertile Crescent possessed a certain fragile cultural unity imprinted by some of its earliest immigrants, Semitic tribes migrating north from the Arabian Peninsula. When the Arabs entered Syria in the first wave of the Islamic conquests, the Semitic people of Syria and western Iraq fell to Islam in part because they identified more with their Semitic cousins from Arabia than with either the Greeks of Byzantium or the Sassanians of Persia. As for the non-Semites in the region, they saw the Arab armies not so much as conquerors as emancipators from the tyranny of the region's dominant power, Byzantium. As a result, groups, cities, and regions more often than not surrendered to the army, language, and religion of the Arabs. By the eleventh century, less than four hundred years after the first Islamic conquests, Arabic and Islam constituted the essence of the Arab ethos and drew the geographical boundaries of what is now the Arab world. Persia would be different.

Through a thousand years of history, Persia had never feared invasion from the primitive, sparsely populated Arabian Peninsula. But in 636, the Persian Empire of the Sassanians that only a few years earlier had stood before the best Byzantium could throw against it prepared to face an enemy of fewer numbers from a civilization as rudimentary as Persia's was elaborate. Alarmed by Arab successes against Byzantium, the Sassanians gathered their army to defend their empire's western frontier. They drew the line at Qadisiya, a small town on the west side of the Euphrates where an estimated eighty thousand well-armed Iranians looked with contempt at perhaps ten thousand

Arabs—sun-scorched, dusty men in sandals and torn, dirty clothes, carrying ox-hide shields and swords sheathed in rags. For four months, the two sides negotiated. Finally on a day in June 637, the Sassanian commander, Rustam, reluctantly opened the battle. But the Sassanian army, like Sassanian society, had grown ponderous. With its spirit drained off in the futile campaigns against Byzantium, the famous Persian cataphracts became clumps of fat, immobile men battling a swarm of wasps. The heavily armed cavalry with its supporting elephants which had punished Romans and Byzantines proved powerless against the Arabs on swift camels who attacked and then withdrew into the desert. Over three days, the two sides engaged. On the fourth, the Persians' reluctant commander, Rustam, died. His army went into pell-mell retreat, leaving the Sassanian Empire open to invasion.

In 638, the vaulted palace at Ctesiphon, the physical embodiment of late Sassanian art and knowledge, fell to the Arabs. Its fabulous prizes dazzled the poor, unlearned tribesmen of the Arabian Peninsula. A life-size camel crafted of silver and a golden horse with emerald teeth and a garland of rubies draped around its neck were only two among the hundreds of objects of art that passed from the cultured hands of the Sassanians into the rough, callused hands of Arab warriors. The incredible carpet, "Spring of Khosrow," went to Mecca, where Islam's religious leaders, disdainful of material possessions, cut it into pieces. The destruction wreaked by the ignorant Arabs went on. The massive libraries so carefully collected by the Sassanian kings scattered in the capricious wind of the Arab edict:

> If the books herein are in accord with Islam,
> then we don't need them.
> If the books herein are not in accord with Islam,
> then they are kafir (of the infidel).[2]

The capture of Ctesiphon changed Arab objectives on Islam's eastern front. Initially the Arab leadership in Mecca had been reluctant to press ahead into Persia. But the vision of booty that came out of Ctesiphon drew the armies of Islam on. Justification for crossing into the territories of the Sassanians came from the Prophet himself, who had spoken of the riches of Persia that were destined to belong to the Arabs.

With the Sassanian king, Yazdagird III, in retreat, the Sassanian presence in Mesopotamia crumbled. Two battles in 642, the first at Jalula and the second at Nihavand, opened the passes through the

Zagros and into Fars—the heart of the Iranian plateau. There the Arab armies met Persian defenders refusing to surrender historic Persia, as opposed to Sassanian territory, to a foreign conqueror. These Persians, living within the cradle of Persian culture, proved to be the Arabs' most difficult adversary in all of the Islamic conquests. In their last stand at Istakhr in Fars in 648–49, the Persians endured a terrible siege that ended in the slaughter of forty thousand people. In the aftermath, the Arabs rode toward Persepolis, the emotional center of Persian history and culture. There men, carrying out Islam's prohibition against representation, broke the crowns and beards from the colossal winged bulls. On a pillar of the Apadana, a plaque written in Arabic joined those in cuneiform. And the cyprus tree, the symbol of Persia, began to bend its top to become the paisley. By 651, the Persian heartland, the territories to its west, and the regions of central Asia under the influence of Persian culture were united under one state—an Arab state. The reasons were political, economic, social, and ultimately religious.

When the Arab armies challenged Sassanian Persia, no great feudal lords in command of their own armies came forth to defend the empire against the Arabs as they had once defended it against Rome and Byzantium. The explanation was that they no longer claimed a stake in the political system. In the latter years of the Sassanian era, an increasingly imperial court presiding over a bureaucracy commanded by minor aristocrats undercut the position, authority, and income of the regional kings who had pledged allegiance to the King of Kings in return for just rule. By the time the Arabs arrived, the traditional deference between king and subject people that had once held the periphery of the empire to the center was gone, leaving Sassanian Persia vulnerable.

Economic grievances followed political grievances. During the last decades of the Sassanian dynasty, economic conditions everywhere in the empire moved steadily downward. Yet the court continued to flaunt its riches and tax its subjects at a level necessary to support its excessive life-style. With the peripheral areas already alienated from Sassanian rule, the Persians of the heartland also saw just rule, that sacred link between the ruler and the ruled, violated. Just like the people of the periphery, few were willing to stand against the Arab invader in defense of the Sassanian system.

Socially, the rigid ordering of classes which had taken place under the union of the king and the Zoroastrian priesthood had drained from society any concept of the common good. Zoroastrianism, the religion of Iran for a thousand years, rotted among its stultified rituals and arcane liturgies. In its stead, numerous heterodoxies, including Manichaeism and Christianity, attracted Iranians culturally steeped in religion. When the Arabs arrived carrying Muhammad's message of the equality of all believers, the remaining Zoroastrians declined to defend the fire temples and the faith against an invading army promising justice.

In the end, Sassanian Persia fell to the Arabs because the king had lost the *farr*, the sign of divine favor. In the perception of most Iranians, the King of Kings, the commander of authority and power within a just and tolerant order, had moved from the side of light into the shadow of darkness. Still respectful of the central theology of Zoroastrianism which called men and women to stand on the side of good, his subjects refused to follow him into material and spiritual bankruptcy.

With the Arab occupation of historic Persia, Iranian history broke in half—Islamic and pre-Islamic. For the coming of Islam produced profound alterations in Iran's political, economic, and social structures. And once Islam was established, it would mark Persia more profoundly and more lastingly than any other alien invasion in the long, turbulent history of the Iranian plateau.

Previous conquests of Iran had followed a general pattern whereby a corrupt, decadent dynasty suffered humiliation at the hands of a small, disciplined force under the command of a dynamic conqueror. Except for the Seleucid torchbearers of Greek culture, the conqueror inevitably fell under the influence of Persian culture, adopting much of the essence of Persia. Consequently, little fundamental change occurred in the lives of the majority of the Iranians. But the Islamic conquest proved radically different. Accepting Islam required adoption of a new way of life constructed on the cultural traditions of the Arabs. This religious conversion came easily to the Iranians in part because Islam carried within it elements of their own pre-Islamic beliefs: monotheism; the fear of evil; the existence of angels; and the acceptance of Judgment Day, the time in which every individual passes over a narrow bridge between heaven and hell, falling into one or the other. Finally there was Islam's promise of justice, the wellspring of authority in Persia since the reign of Cyrus. Thus through the Iranians' gradual transition from Zoroastrianism to Islam much of the essence and religious character of Iranian identity remained intact. Religion stayed central to existence; Allah replaced Ahura Mazda; Muhammad substituted for Zoroaster as the spiritual force sent into a world full of evil and injustice to lead the cosmic battle for goodness and compassion.

But Islam could never be a carbon copy of Persian religious thought and tradition, for it negated as well as confirmed the ancient beliefs of Persia. Muhammad's religion demanded that a believer's total allegiance should be to Allah, not shared with any cultural system or geographic entity. By dictating the equality of every human being before his maker, Muhammad left no room for a king. Consequently, Islam broke the centuries-old Zoroastrian bond between subject and ruler, faith and state. In its place, Iranian Muslims were called to commit to something greater than the state—the *Ummah*, the community of believers whose only boundaries are faith. As a result, the cherished notion Iranians had harbored since the time of Cyrus that Persia was a defined entity supporting Persian culture faced subordination to the empire of Islam created and dominated by Arabs. But the Iranians refused to yield. Although language, literature, art, and architecture all acquired Arabic influences under the mandate of religion, the soul of the Persian ethos remained untouched by the Arabs. Its essence continued to determine the basic nature of Persian culture in all of its manifestations. The Iranians' pride in the Persia of the Achaemenians and the Sassanians rejected the Arabs' contention that the past before Islam was a time of "ignorance." To the Iranians, "Islam became Islam only when it reached the [Sassanian] settlements between the Tigris and Euphrates. . . . Before that it was nothing but the *jahiliyat* [ignorance] and the *badviyat* [Bedouinism] of the Arabs."[3] Thus between the sixteenth and eighteenth centuries, the Iranians would take their adopted religion of Islam, reshape it along the lines of Shiism, and consecrate it with Persian culture and identity. (See chapter 3.) The irony is that the great symbol of the Iranians' Shia faith, the caliph Ali, was himself an Arab.

The Prophet Muhammad died without designating a successor. As a result, it fell to his closest associates to choose the next leader of the Muslim community. The men of Mecca and Medina, the products of the Arabian Desert's tribal culture, knew only two models to follow. The first was bloodlines, the second tribal consensus. Since the Prophet left no direct male heir, bloodlines proved murky. Fatima, Muhammad's only living child, was the wife of the Prophet's cousin and first convert, Ali. With both religious credentials and family ties, Ali seemed the logical choice to assume the mantle of the Prophet. Instead Abu Bakr, Muhammad's closest confidant, was named caliph, or successor to Muhammad's temporal authority. To prevent a similar dispute on his own death, Abu Bakr designated as his successor Umar, a member of the Quraysh, the old aristocratic clan of Mecca. Once again Ali found himself passed over. Refusing to fill any office in the Islamic state, the short, bald, white-bearded Ali devoted himself to teaching a growing number of disciples. During the ten-year reign of Umar (634–44), Ali remained noticeably absent from the great wars of conquest that the caliph waged in the name of Islam, including the invasion of Persia. Nonetheless, Ali's following continued to grow for reasons beyond political power and military exploits. Ali's image as a champion of egalitarianism within the pristine Islam of the Prophet amplified the deep emotional appeal of his personal attributes— modesty, self-sacrifice, knowledge of the sacred texts of Islam, and a passion for justice. Yet when a Persian slave murdered Umar, Uthman, another of Muhammad's early converts and a member of the Umayyad clan within the Quraysh, became caliph.

The choice of Uthman over Ali stirred waves of discontent within the community of Muslims. Some took umbrage at the lack of religious conviction and deep moral purpose they perceived among the leadership in Mecca. Others reacted to increasing personal corruption and political injustice. Consequently, as Uthman took his place at the helm of Islam, scattered knots of Muslims in Arabia and in some of the territories of the Islamic Empire designated themselves as Shia Ali, supporters of Ali. Rejecting the reigning system of choosing leadership by consensus, they believed that the caliph must come out of the Prophet's house, for it was only Muhammad's descendants who possessed the knowledge and wisdom of the Prophet. In contradiction, those who became known as Sunnis believed that any man within the Meccan aristocracy could assume the leadership of Islam through the process of consensus among Muhammad's early converts.* A third group, the Kharijites, ranked as the most egalitarian of all the Muslims. They held that any male believer, regardless of blood, tribe, or class, possessed the right to assume the leadership of the Muslim community. Thus a little more than a decade after the Prophet's death, the pieces which would determine the future direction of Islam fell into place.

From 644 to 656, the third caliph, Uthman, presided over a corrupt and repressive regime funded by the Islamic conquests. While the old Meccan aristocracy as the new aristocracy of Islam amassed tre-

*The Sunnis were known as the "people of the custom and the community." They constitute roughly 90 percent of Muslims today.

mendous wealth, Ali continued to live in the simple manner in which the Prophet had lived. Outside the boundaries of political power, he taught his followers that all believers are created equal, that only through virtue is one Muslim more dear to God than another. Thus visibly and theologically, Ali counterpoised Muhammad's teachings of piety and equality against the growing wealth and elitism of Islam's establishment. This strengthening perception of Ali as the upholder of personal and moral virtues against the corrupt and unjust Muslim state began to open cleavages within the Islamic community that followed lines of class, tribe, and theology. In Kufa, a garrison town on the southern end of the Euphrates, in present-day Iraq, Islam's divisions often corresponded to the dictates of ethnicity and culture.

Kufa was in many ways a non-Arab town on the edge of the Arabized Fertile Crescent. Location alone made it a cultural crossroads of the eastern and western parts of the Islamic Empire. The great number of prisoners of war funneled in from Iran and elsewhere readily mixed with one another because Kufa was a new town claiming no traditions of its own and certainly feeling no loyalty to the Meccan establishment. Most of these prisoners of war deposited in Kufa soon embraced Islam and won their freedom. But faith and freedom did not mean equality with the Arabs in control of the town and the Islamic Empire. In a time when Arabs were still defined as inhabitants of the Arabian Peninsula, the Arab soldiers of Islam carried their long tribal genealogies with pride and arrogance. Believing that these tribal credentials set them above other Muslims, the Arabs looked on all non-Arabs as racially inferior. It was this second-class status imposed by the Arabs that drew Iranians, Yemenis, certain Iraqis, and other non-Arab groups toward Ali. Impoverished Arabs, those who had benefited the least from the Islamic conquests, joined them in gravitating toward Ali's teachings. They came together with others of Islam's dispossessed to form the core of the Shia revolt.

Protesting against brutal rule, the dissidents in a number of areas within the Islamic Empire appealed to Uthman to right the injustices of his governors. But Uthman chose instead to punish the protestors by sending them to Syria to be persecuted by the Umayyad governor, Muawiya. In 656, rebel contingents from Kufa, nearby Basra, and Egypt marched on Medina calling Ali's name. Responding to what amounted to a rebellion, Ali broke his silence to become the spokesman and leader of a reform movement within the still-young religion of Islam.

Ali favored deposing the caliph Uthman by withdrawing his mandate. But events charged beyond his control. In an orgy of hate, Uthman's opponents literally hacked the caliph to death. As a consequence, Islam was left without a leader for the third time since the Prophet's own death. Out of the anarchy that followed, Ali, at last, emerged as caliph.

But doom seemed to hang over Ali's caliphate from the beginning. To Islam's elite, the Quraysh aristocracy in Mecca and their Umayyad cousins in Damascus, Ali's base of support in the lower ranks of society was anathema. For the more traditional elements of Arab society who continued to hold onto tribal loyalties and the privileged status of ethnic Arab, his widespread following among non-Arabs undermined his authority. Finally, Ali, by his very nature, proved incapable of playing the game of power politics. Capitalizing on opposition to Ali and the caliph's own personality, Muawiya launched his campaign for the leadership of Islam. Vowing vengeance against Ali for the death of Uthman, he sounded the call for allies. Aishah, the Prophet's favorite wife, answered.* Mobilizing an army against Ali, she took to the field to restore the caliphate to the Umayyads. With most of his support concentrated in Kufa, Ali was forced to go to the banks of the Euphrates to raise his defensive corps. Aishah followed. With Muhammad's widow directing her troops from a litter on the back of a camel, the two sides engaged on the flatlands of Iraq in what became known as the Battle of the Camel. Ali won. But he never went back to Medina, and he never firmly established himself at the head of the Islamic state.

Ali's reign as caliph lasted less than five years, 656 to 661. It spanned a time in which the Muslim community, still clinging to the ideal of its sacred unity, saw itself being torn asunder by its own internal divisions. Within the turmoil, Ali preached to the Islamic establishment in Mecca that Islam's unity could be preserved only through strict adherence to justice and equality among all believers. In this challenge to elitism, Ali reigned as a towering figure of righteousness engaged in moral battle with the corrupting temptations of wealth and power. He represented to his followers not only descent from the Prophet but the piety demanded of the leader of Islam. To Iranians among the Shia, Ali fulfilled within Islam the Persian tradition of charismatic kingship. He became the manifestation of divine

---

*Grudge may have been the motive. Years before, when Aishah dropped behind the Prophet's entourage, supposedly to look for a lost necklace, Ali voiced suspicions of her infidelity with the young Bedouin with whom she arrived in Mecca.

authority who in partnership with a supreme being exercises the rule of virtue and justice. Thus the Iranian Shia again heard the words of the just king when Ali spoke to the governor of Egypt about the relationship between the ruler and the ruled:

> You must be just, and the serving of the common man must be one of your prime objectives; the gratification of the aristocracy is insignificant and can be ignored in the face of the happiness of the masses. . . . Look after the deprived (*mahrum*) and dispossessed (*mostazaf*) who need food and shelter. They deserve your help. Give to them generously from *bait al-mal* (public fund). It is your duty to protect them and their families. Be kind to those you rule. The people will obey their ruler if they are immune from his abuse. . . .[4]

The seventh-century controversy within Islam that centered around Ali reflected profound questions about the nature of Islamic government, the method by which the leader was chosen, and the status of Arabs vis-à-vis non-Arabs within the *Ummah*. The failure to answer these questions to the satisfaction of all within the community of believers resulted in Islam's great schism that severed the deviating Shias from the orthodox Sunnis.

As Ali tried to establish his authority as caliph, Muawiya, the governor of Syria, and his Umayyad relatives continued to press to unseat him. Having lost most of his Arab supporters in the Battle of the Camel, Ali's defense against the Umayyad usurpers fell to the army in place in Kufa. But elements within it disliked Ali as much as they disliked the Umayyads. The Kharijites, the most egalitarian of all the early Muslim groups, were largely Bedouin. As such, they felt shut out by both the elite of Mecca and the blood descendants of the Prophet. Seeking their own power, they called forth their poets to weave together vindictive words that hurled the same charges at Ali as they had at Uthman—nepotism. In 661, Ali left his house in Kufa to go to the mosque for prayers. At their conclusion, he emerged from the mosque to meet a Kharijite, who struck the caliph across the head with a sword. According to religious tradition, the dying Ali whispered that he was to be placed on a camel and laid to rest wherever it knelt. Najaf, now in Iraq, became his burial place. Over it, Ali's followers built a shrine to the theological force of Shia Islam.

Because the Iranians are overwhelmingly Shia, Ali, in death as well as life, would profoundly mold Iranian morality, values, and character. "The entire spiritual edifice of the Shia was built on the *walaya* (love and devotion) to Ali, . . . the sole criterion for judging true faith. Faith was conceived in terms of personal devotion to Ali . . . [for] he alone could bring a true Islamic rule of justice and equity in the world. . . ."[5] In Ali, Iranians see the most perfect model of the noble virtue of justice which they believe has always been a central part of their cultural tradition. This is why the portraits of Ali so often found on the walls of mosques and in Iranian religious literature portray a handsome man with unmistakably Aryan features. It is as if the Iranian propensity to ignore reality in favor of the ideal has conspired to deny that Ali was what he was—an Arab.

After Ali's death, his oldest son, Hassan, surrendered all claim to the title of caliph and retreated into his palace in Medina. The capital of Islam moved to Damascus in the conquered province of Syria to reside in the house of the Umayyads. Yet the success of the Umayyads in wooing Ali's oldest son into retirement failed to settle the issue of how the caliph should be chosen. Defending tribal tradition, the Kharijites continued to hold that any believer, of whatever origin, was worthy of the office of caliph if the believers chose him. Followers of Ali persisted in their claim that the caliphate belonged in the House of the Prophet. Rejecting the Umayyad caliph Muawiya as possessing no authority because he was neither a direct descendant of the Prophet nor chosen by the community of the faithful, Ali's followers and the Kharijites buried their differences to make alliance against the Umayyads. They brought with them subject peoples, including the Iranians, who had embraced Islam but remained relegated to a social class lower than that of the Arabs descended from the tribes of the Arabian Peninsula and lower still than that of the aristocratic Umayyads. If the assassination of the caliph Uthman sparked Islam's first civil war, the rebellion against the Umayyads marked its second.

Hussein, the second son of Ali, the grandson of the Prophet, placed himself at the head of the insurrection against Umayyad power. Condemning Umayyad rule as unjust, Hussein called the faithful to stand in the light of good against the darkness of evil. When warned of the extreme odds against winning a fight with the Umayyads' well-manned and well-armed forces, Hussein echoed Ali's passion for social justice: "O people, the Apostle of God said during his life, 'He who sees an oppressive ruler violating the sanctions of God, reviling the covenant of God, opposing the Sunna of the Apostle of God, dealing with the servant of God sinfully and cruelly; [If a man sees such a ruler] and does not show zeal against him in word or deed, God would surely cause him to enter his abode in the fire.' "[6]

The Umayyads, now led by Yazid, responded. In 680, they met Hussein, his family, and his followers at Karbala on the flat, salty plains south of what is now Baghdad. Hussein's force numbered seventy-two, including women and children. The Umayyad army, employing the famed training and tactics of both the Byzantines and the Sassanians, counted thousands. Despite the odds, Hussein took the high ground of principle by declaring that death is preferable to compromise between right and wrong. In the ensuing battle on what is now known as the "Plain of Sorrow and Misfortune," the Umayyads butchered Hussein along with the rest of his companions. Heads severed from throats parched by thirst went to Yazid in Damascus. As the news spread, waves of anguish and anger flowed with the blood of the Prophet's grandson. Islam ruptured into its two great branches—the orthodox Sunnis, who accepted the Umayyad caliphate; and the breakaway Shia, the followers of Ali and Hussein. Thus the Battle of Karbala changed Shiism from a loosely knit group of Ali's devotees into a separate sect inspired by the potent themes of sacrifice, guilt, and death. To this day, Karbala for Shia reigns as the tragic moment when piety sacrificed itself for justice.

There is an air of immediacy about Karbala which dispels the thirteen hundred years since Hussein died the martyr's death. Before the 1991 Gulf War and its aftermath turned southern Iraq into a battleground where Saddam Hussein wrings life from his Iraqi Shia opposition, Karbala moved to its own special tempo. Cars filled with passengers and trucks loaded with produce competed for space on the crowded streets leading toward the commercial center. Within Karbala's core, people came and went in the shops lining the narrow streets. Much of that is gone now. But Karbala's reason for being is still found in a large mosque flanked by slender minarets. It is here where tradition says Hussein gave his life for the ideal of justice. Waves of pilgrims from Shia communities in Iran, Iraq, Lebanon, India, Pakistan, and elsewhere who once washed over Karbala have been reduced to a trickle. Nonetheless, they represent the millions of Shia who emotionally continue to come to Karbala, not to pay homage to a long-dead man, but to celebrate the living spirit of both Ali and Hussein. That spirit takes form in the flags of mourning and the images of Hussein and his father, Ali, that hang as banners from buildings or cling to small wooden sticks stuck in piles of oranges and melons laid out on the stands of the fruit vendors. But it is in the courtyard of the mosque itself that the grief for Hussein and the passion of what he represented express themselves. Before mosaics of blue, turquoise, and white pockmarked by bullets, men tremble as tears flow from their eyes and women wail their laments for the martyred Hussein and for the imperfect world in which they live.

Defeated in life, Ali and Hussein were victorious in death. Their legend and the mythology surrounding them has inspired and mobilized millions of their followers for centuries. In the devotion, religious zeal, self-sacrifice, and strict adherence to Islamic principles originally set by Ali, the Shia see the ideals of the faith. And every Shia Muslim accepts the notion that after the Prophet Muhammad, Ali stands as the most virtuous, courageous, and just human being who ever lived. Consequently to Islam's most profound saying, "There is no God but Allah and Muhammad is his prophet," Shia add, "and Ali is his vice-regent." This call to the oppressed sounded again in the tragic life of Hussein. Its message to the Shia transcended blind belief in Ali as an idol. Instead the message Hussein's death still delivers to the Shia is to become like Ali, to live like Ali, and to die like Ali.

Despite the themes of pre-Islamic Persia that echoed in the Shia branch of Islam, Iranians would not become predominantly Shia until the sixteenth century. (See chapter 3.) Until the mid-eighth century, Muslim Persia along with all Islam's territories gave obedience to the authority of the Umayyad caliphs. But the Umayyad dynasty carried within it the seeds of its own destruction. With roots dug deep into the soil of Mecca, the Umayyads saw Islam as an Arab religion delivered within the parameters of Arab culture. Refusing to recognize the expanding Islamic empire as a meld of many peoples and cultures, the Umayyads continued to keep non-Arabs in the category of lower-class aliens. Beginning in 715, a succession of dissolute caliphs added decay to the arrogance of the Umayyads. Gathering into their sumptuous bathhouses and pleasure palaces, the Umayyad caliphs mocked the example set by the Prophet, who never gave up mending his own clothes in the courtyard of his stark mud house. The excesses of court life poured like flammable oil over the existing political and social grievances that most Muslims, both Sunni and Shia, held against the Umayyads. Discontent exploded into revolt in Khorasan in what is now northeastern Iran. Across the empire, the white banner of the Umayyads turned in retreat before the black banner of the challenging Abbasids, yet another branch of the Prophet's family. In January 750, on a tributary of the Tigris, the supporters of the Abbasids utterly destroyed twelve thousand troops of the Umayyads. The fourteenth Umayyad caliph, Marwan, fled to Egypt. Caught hiding in a Christian church, he was decapitated. While frenzied mobs in Damascus scattered the bones from Umayyad tombs, the dynasty died.

The shift from the Umayyad to the Abbasid regime represented more than a dynastic change. With the victory of the Abbasids, the caliphate and the empire altered geographically and politically. The capital moved once more, from Damascus to Baghdad. As a result, the distance between Mecca and Islam's capital lengthened again not only in miles but in culture as the new caliphate oriented itself more to Persia than to Arabia. The Arab aristocracy of Medina and Mecca that had exercised control over the empire since its first days gradually diminished. And Arabs as a separate identifiable group faded into the geography of the Islamic Empire. What remained of the Arabs' exalted status in Islam was their language.

There is an old cliché which says that the Umayyad dynasty was Arab, the Abbasid Persian. As with most clichés, it contains a measure of truth. The Abbasid capital built at Baghdad carried the hallmark of the Persians more than that of the Arabs. The city's walls formed a circle just like the walls of the classic Sassanian city of Firuzabad. The caliph's palace, incorporating the architectural style of imperial Persia, was crowned by a dome and punctuated by four *ivans*, or courtyards. Within the court itself, everything from the clothes the caliph wore to the executioner he employed carried the stamp of Sassanian Persia. And it was from pre-Islamic Persia that the imagery of the caliph's title came: "the Shadow of God on Earth." Almost by default, nearly fifteen hundred years of Persian art, learning, and culture provided the catalyst for Islam's golden age, which extended from the eighth to the eleventh century. It was a function the Persians could be expected to fulfill. Since Cyrus's conquest of Lydia in 547 B.C., the Iranians had behaved like a great cultural sponge. Tolerant of diversity, quick to absorb from others that which was of value, the Iranians undertook the Persian conquest of Islam. With Iranian intellectuals as the conduit, the Islamic Empire drew together the learning of Greece and India as well as the areas in between. From 813 to 833, the Persians within the House of Wisdom established by the Caliph Mamun translated Aristotle, Plato, Euclid, Ptolemy, Archimedes, and Hippocrates into Arabic and added to them the scientific works of Persia and India. While Europe remained mired in the Dark Ages, emissaries from Islam's caliph went out over the empire in search of literature, philosophy, theology, and science to be translated into Arabic under formal Arabic grammar largely devised by an Iranian scholar named Sibveyh. It was almost as if the Iranians meant to confirm the truth of the

Prophet's words: "If scholarship hung suspended in the highest parts of Heaven, the people of Fars would reach to take it."[7]

In the energy of their intellectual activities, the Iranians were not seeking to supplant the structure of the Islamic Empire with Persian ideas and institutions. Nor was the question the Iranians raised during the Abbasid caliphate Islam or Iran. Rather they asked how Islam would be defined—in terms of Persianized Islam that encompassed the great diversity of the empire or Arab Islam that confined the faith and the empire within the narrow limits of its origin. At its core, the Iranian-Arab dichotomy over the definition of the new Islamic state boiled down to whether Islam would become a reembodiment of Persian culture into which Arabic and Islamic elements would be absorbed or a culture in which Persian contributions would be subordinated to Arab tradition and strictly delineated Islamic values. In the case of the Iranians, there was no question that Islam would be absorbed into Persian culture. For the Arabs, Persian contributions could only feed into Islam dominated by Arab culture.

Before the universalization of Islam and its culture was completed according to either the Persian or the Arab model, the Iranians revived their specifically Persian identity. While Islam in the ninth century A.D. saw the apogee of Arab Baghdad, the tenth century marked the Persian renaissance. Unfurling once more its determination to survive, Persian culture broke the Arab bonds of Islam. As they had under the Greek Seleucids, the Iranians would again prove under Arab rule that unlike the mighty oak broken by hurricane winds or the tumbleweed that rolls across the plain, Iran is the supple, deep-rooted cypress that bends but never breaks.

Language led the Persian awakening. Paradoxically, it was a language revitalized by Arabic. In the aftermath of the Arab invasion, Middle Persian, or Pahlavi, which was spoken in the Sassanian Empire, quickly gave way to Arabic.* The change occurred rapidly partly because Pahlavi was the language of discredited Zoroastrianism. Perhaps more important, Pahlavi, neither rich in vocabulary and grammar nor easily adapted to new demands, surrendered to an Arabic script and nomenclature easier to use and far more expressive. In short, Arabic appealed to Iranians always ready to adopt new ideas. Consequently, those who learned to read and write in Islamic Iran learned

*The Iranian dynasty overthrown in 1979 by the Iranian Revolution took its name from the language of the Sassanians.

in Arabic, leaving Pahlavi almost exclusively to the uneducated Persians and the dying Zoroastrian priesthood. For three centuries, Arabic reigned as the language of administration and culture. But in the ninth century, Persian, sewed with Arabic script and embroidered with Arabic words, began to reappear as a written language. On one level, this synthesis of Arabic script and vocabulary with existing Persian recreated the Persian language, producing modern Farsi. On another, more profound level, the emergence of a revitalized language seemed to say that if Persian culture were to survive in an Arab empire it would do so through the Persian tongue. Flourishing the elaborate figures of speech common to Arabic poetry, the Iranians began to produce their own poems. While not un-Islamic, great quantities of this poetry were not strictly Islamic, either. Many of the verses which flowed from the pens of Iranian poets echoed themes of ancient Persia, Zoroastrianism, and Manichaenism laced with elements of mysticism.

In the rise of new Persian and the corresponding decline in the use of classical Arabic, the cultural incompatibility of the Iranians and the Arabs manifested itself in the *shuubiyah* movement among Iranian intellectuals. Although primarily centered on literature, the *shuubiyah* controversy contained within it the ongoing dispute over the relative virtues of Persian versus Arabic cultural traditions as well as the issue of what role Iran deserved to play within the Islamic Empire. Rather than engaging in political issues which would involve changes in government, the *shuubis* discussed the relative merits of Arab customs and the customs of the people they had conquered. Invectives flew from both Iranians and Arabs. The Iranians sneered,

> *Retreat to the Hijaz and resume eating lizards and herd your cattle*
> *While I seat myself on the throne of kings supported*
> *by the sharpness of my blade and the point of my pen.*[8]

And the Arabs answered that the ancient Persians relished brother-sister and mother-son marriages which they charged Zoroastrianism sanctioned. In the end, the *shuubiyah* controversies solved neither the question of cultural superiority nor that of Iranian status within the Islamic Empire. What it did accomplish was to lead the Iranians to discover that they were united by a language and its literature, which rendered them distinct from the community of the Arabs. In a paradox of the time, those who would first reject the Arabs, if not their religion, came not from the Persian heartland but from the periphery of the old Sassanian Empire.

The Arab invasion had destroyed the Sassanian Empire but had left intact many of the small states within it. Some scattered through the western part of Iran, others in the east. Some were Shia, most were Sunni. In retrospect, they found commonality in the tenth, eleventh, and twelfth centuries in the preservation, in varying degrees, of Persian culture, which, in turn, kept alive Iranian identity within the Islamic Empire.

In the West, it was the Dailamites, an elusive and indomitable people in the Alborz Mountains during the ninth century, who protected surviving pockets of Zoroastrianism and hosted Islam in its deviant form—Shiism. Although formidable soldiers, the Dailamites were usurped by a mercenary in their employ by the name of Abu Shuja Buye. Together with his three sons, he created the Buyid dynasty.

In the first years of the tenth century, the Shia Buyids extended their empire from the mountains of western Persia into Iraq. Taking advantage of the debilitated Abbasid caliphate, the Buyids, in 945, marched their army into Baghdad. But they stopped short of deposing the Sunni caliph. Instead they devised the title of sultan, or military chief, for one brother and made the other the shahanshah, the king of kings. Displaying unmistakable Sassanian proclivities, the Buyids wrote their own inscriptions alongside those of the Achaemenians at Persepolis and stamped their coins with the profile of the shahanshah wearing a bungled copy of a Sassanian crown.

The Buyids prevailed for a century before they were undermined by the Turkish faction in their own army. Although obscured in the fog of history, the Buyids left an important legacy. During the time they controlled Baghdad, the seat of the caliph, the Buyids as Shia strengthened Shiism's status within Islam by formalizing the sect's beliefs and establishing Shia theological colleges in Islam's capital alongside those of the Sunnis. The Buyids also established Qom, the religious city in which Ayatollah Khomeini first gained fame, as an important center of Shiism. This propagation of Shiism by an Iranian dynasty marked a crucial point in the history of Islam. In a sense, the Buyids did for Shiism what Martin Luther did for Protestantism—gave form to a dissenting sect within the faith.

But prior to the early sixteenth century, Shiism stayed largely confined to the western part of Iran. In the East, a series of small city-states on the edge of central Asia stayed with orthodox Islam. In their courts, princeling rulers presided over feudal societies built on pre-Islamic Persian models and provided a refuge for the old traditions of

Persian culture. In the ninth century, as the Abbasid dynasty of Baghdad continued to decline, the allure of independence beckoned these distant provinces of the Islamic Empire. In east-central Iran, a buccaneer dynasty called the Saffarids moved north and east out of Khorasan into central Asia and what is now Afghanistan and Pakistan, creating the first great breach in the territorial integrity of the Abbasid caliphate. In another blow to Abbasid power, the cultural life in the Saffarids' sparkling cities along the Oxus River—Tashkent, Bukhara, and Samarkand—created a counterbalance to the Arabian cities of Mesopotamia.

By the first years of the tenth century, the Saffarids had given way to the Samanids, a dynasty claiming descent from the Sassanians. Into their palaces, the Samanid kings gathered an array of men of art and learning who were Muslim by religion and Persian by culture. Under Samanid tutelage, Bukhara and Samarkand, Islamic cities mirroring the heritage of Persia, soon challenged Baghdad for supremacy as cultural centers.*

Yet the most powerful testament to the revival of Persian culture came from the court of Mahmud of Ghazan, who ruled the farthest reaches of historic Persia, an area south of what is now Kabul, Afghanistan. Even more than the Saffarids and Samanids, the Turkic-speaking Ghaznavids identified with historic Persia and applied to their Islamic state the model of the Sassanians. In the titles of king and the "Right Hand of the Dynasty, Fiduciary of the Islamic Community, Representative of the Prince of Believers," Mahmud in the years 994 to 1030 brought together the legacies of Persia and Islam. Creating a huge standing army complete with a camel-borne infantry and a cavalry supported by armored elephants, the Ghazan kings, in the tradition of the Achaemenians, built an empire as far east as Kashmir and as far west as the Zagros. And like the Sassanians, Mahmud, the military commander, was also Mahmud, the patron of poets and scholars. Probably less motivated by the love of learning than by the desire for status, he called the giants of learning and literature to his capital. It was here that modern Persian literature came of age in the poetry of Rudaki and Daqiqi and Iranian identity resurrected in Ferdowsi's *Shahnameh*.

Ferdowsi was the nom de plume of Abdul Qasim Mansur, who was born in 935 near Mashhad in northeastern Iran. Believed to have been a landowner who needed money for his only daughter's dowry,

---

*The Samanids so deeply imprinted parts of central Asia with Persian culture that it survived even under the iron hand of the Soviet Union.

Ferdowsi undertook a commission from Mahmud for an epic poem. Over the next thirty-five years, he composed the sixty-thousand-line *Shahnameh*, the Book of Kings.* Four times longer than the *Iliad*, the *Shahnameh* winds through a thousand years of history from the Achaemenians to the Sassanians—from the Iranian genesis to the intrusion of the Arabs. Through a series of heroic acts in defense of the homeland, Iranians are led—and sometimes betrayed—by their kings. Reaffirming the principle of charismatic kingship, the entire work pulsates with a drumming meter suggestive of men engaged in a cosmic struggle. At the center of this cosmic struggle is the complexity of the cultural conflict between pre-Islamic Iranian identity and Arab Muslim religious beliefs. By the time Ferdowsi was writing, Islam had become an undeniable part of Iranian culture and identity. Consequently, Ferdowsi in the *Shahnameh* "had to weigh Islamic values of foreign origin against pre-Islamic Iranian culture, arriving at a compromise of nostalgic pride in the pre-Islamic Iranian grandeur and past, balanced by an acceptance of the wisdom of the Arab Allah."[9] Thus written in the context of faith in Allah, the *Shahnameh* nonetheless resurrects Iranian identity within the world of Islam by celebrating the history and mythology of Persian kingship.

In his long narrative poem, Ferdowsi, a Shia Muslim, recounts the Arab conquest of Iran without hatred or a desire for vengeance. Nor does he question Islam's main social and philosophical values, some of which echo ideals that flourished in Iran before Islam. Ferdowsi, in essence, separates Islam from the Arabs, whom he holds responsible for the diminution of what he judges a superior Persian culture. Before the Battle of Qadisiya, the luckless general Rustam curses the Arab invader for what he sees as the coming suppression of Persian culture.

> *O, Iran! Where have all those kings, who adorned you*
> *with justice, equity, and munificence, who decorated*
> *you with pomp and splendor gone?*
> *From that date when the barbarian, savage, coarse*
> *Bedouin Arabs sold your king's daughter in the street*
> *and cattle market, you have not seen a bright day, and*
> *have lain hid in darkness.*

*Tradition holds that Mahmud reneged on his financial arrangement with Ferdowsi. Instead of gold, he paid the poet in silver. Later repenting, he sent bales of indigo worth sixty thousand dinars to Ferdowsi in his home city of Tus. It arrived on the backs of the royal camels at one gate of the city as Ferdowsi's funeral bier was passing out another gate.

Writing in new Persian pruned of Arabic excesses, Ferdowsi awakened the soul of the Iranians. Making no distinction between myth, lore, and fact, the poet poured the folk history of Iran into the *Shahnameh*. The result is a long hymn to honor, valor, wisdom, and patriotism—virtues conceived in the springtime of the Iranian nation and embodied in the mystical *farr*, the charisma of kingship. The kings—both those he idealizes and those he condemns for their failure to rule justly—are all charged with the preservation of Iranian sovereignty and defense of Iranian territorial integrity against all enemies, mythical and real. In that challenge, the *Shahnameh* evokes a whole range of images—heroism, justice, national glory, and tragic defeat—that Iranians as a people hold essential to their culture and their identity.

In size and scope, the *Shahnameh* stands with Persepolis as a symbol of Iranian identity. Persepolis communicated in stone a self-awareness of Persian prosperity and the hope for its continuity. The *Shahnameh* depicts in words the immortality of Iran's unique culture resting within the quintessential figure of its kings. But as Persepolis and the *Shahnameh* both celebrate Iranian greatness, so do they also testify to its defeat at the hands of others—Alexander of Macedonia and the Arabs of the Arabian Peninsula. Ferdowsi could forgive Alexander but not the Arabs.

> *From feeding on desert lizards and camel's milk,*
> *So have the affairs of the Arabs prospered.*
> *That they long for the empire of Khosrau,*
> *Shame on thee, O circling Heaven, shame.*

Neither can most Iranians forgive the Arabs. Almost any educated Iranian can passionately quote Ferdowsi's lament uttered by a Persian general facing the Arab army.

> *Damn on this World, Damn on this Time, Damn on Fate,*
> *That uncivilized Arabs have come to force me to be Muslim.*

Ferdowsi is buried in the cool rolling hills just south of Iran's border with Turkmenistan, near the former town of Tus. The tomb itself stands majestically at the end of a reflecting pool surrounded by scarlet roses. On each side of the square white marble structure, stone slabs repeat in chiseled script Ferdowsi's words. One reads, "Let not this body live if there is no Iran." This is the essence of Ferdowsi's composition, explaining why it has worked its extraordinary emotional power on the Iranians for almost a thousand years. I saw this power standing on the top tier of the tomb's high base, just below this inscription, looking down to ground level. There a robed and turbaned Muslim cleric and his teenage son looked up at the words. Over a long moment, they stood perfectly still, as if mesmerized by the message. I also saw it at the agricultural school at Shahr-e-Kord located in the Zagros Mountains, where the Islamic Republic's Organization of Nomadic Peoples played host to a conference.

As the audience filed in, four tribesmen sat cross-legged on the stage of the school's auditorium. On one side hung a portrait of Ali Khamenei, the spiritual heir of the Ayatollah Khomeini, and on the other, the white-turbaned likeness of Ali Akbar Hashemi Rafsanjani, the president of the Islamic Republic of Iran. In front, a line of bearded mullahs, political commissars in the Islamic Republic, occupied the first row of seats. But for an Iranian neither position in the Islamic government of Iran nor membership in a tribe dulled the effect of Ferdowsi's poetic hymn to Iran.

A hushed moment of anticipation fell on the audience as one of the men on stage, a Lur, extended his bony arms from the long pointed sleeves of his orchid-colored tribal coat, reached into a silk sack lying in front of him, and pulled out a large leather-covered book. Opening its pages, he began the slow measured cadence of the Sharveh, a section of Ferdowsi's *Shahnameh*. When he finished, a Qashqai wearing a traditional flop-eared felt hat picked up his own large, leather-bound volume. The words, quivering with emotion, poured forth. Closing his text, he turned to the next reader, a Bakhtiari dressed in the black and white of his tribe. Rejecting the microphone, he rolled out one line after another in a deep baritone voice as the audience clapped and cheered through verse after verse. When he finished, he surrendered the stage to an old, weather-beaten Kurd wrapped in a worn, faded turban. His voice was coarse gravel, but his cadence mesmerized and then pulled his audience with it. On the first word of a recognizable verse, voices within the crowd joined in unison. Together, reader and audience spoke of their commitment to the Iranian nation and to their assurance of their uniqueness among the peoples of the world.

The *Shahnameh* is the great hymn of Iranian nationalism. When it was written, nationalism by its contemporary definition had yet to take form. Yet the ethos of the *Shahnameh* gives voice to the sense of separate identity within Islam that the Iranians had felt from the time the Arab invaders dusted the long history of Persia into the trash bin of pre-Islamic ignorance. In the early sixteenth century, Iran would find the answer to its cultural-religious dilemma by joining Persian culture to Shia Islam. Out of this union, Iran established its emotional and aesthetic nationalism. Today this wedding of culture and religion defines Iran as a nation.

3

God and State

IRANIANS SAY TEHRAN IS IRAN'S BRAIN, QOM ITS SOUL, AND cherished Isfahan its heart. Isfahan, located two hundred miles south of Tehran, lies on Zayandeh-rud, the "Giver of Life." The broad river that quietly flows in summer and swiftly rushes in winter gives reason to the perfectly positioned Allahverdi Bridge. The sixteenth-century bridge of two stories precisely balances an arched, open gallery high above the river on a line of small, dark coffeehouses, brushed by the water running below. But it is the *maidan*, a long rectangle twice the area of Red Square, seven times larger than St. Mark's, that forever burns Isfahan into the memory of those who see it. There are no walls or gates to herald its presence, for none are needed. The *maidan*'s drama is delivered by ordinary streets that simply end in the square's faultless proportions that present as visual poetry that which is best in Persian architecture. Like points on a compass, the tall, slender minarets of the Royal Mosque mark the south, and the low, broad entrance to the vaulted passageways of the bazaar, the north. On the east and west, the Ali Qapu, or "Lofty Gateway," faces the jewel of Persian-Islamic architecture—the Sheikh Lutfullah Mosque. The mosque's ceramic-covered dome, patterned in the graceful curves and conjunctions of classical Persian design, grabs the sun and throws back its radiance while the peaked arches and the intricately cut mosaics of the massive Royal Mosque pull those rays back again into its massive size. The magnificence of Isfahan peaked in the sixteenth century as a glorious statement of Iran's nationhood and its will to survive.

Beginning in the eleventh century, a series of invaders overwhelmed Iran. The Seljuk Turks came first. More migrants than conquerors, they absorbed more than destroyed what they found. Beginning in the early thirteenth century, the Mongol hordes out of central Asia plunged into Iran in an infamous orgy of killing and destruction. In the late four-teenth century, Tamerlane followed, driving Iran further toward physi-cal extinction. But Iran did not die. Out of the desolation wreaked by barbaric invaders, Persian culture rose, as it had after the invasions of the Greeks and the Arabs, to kindle another renaissance. And as in the Iran of the Achaemenians and Sassanians, Persian culture blossomed in the sun of religion. Shia Islam in the hands of a powerful new dynasty collected the fragments of Sassanian Persia to give Iran nationhood and the Iranians a separate identity within Islam. With nation and identity came the Iranians' passionate sense of nationalism, which has never waned. In essence, Iran of the sixteenth century is the Iran of today—a nation defined by Persian culture and Shia Islam.

As if part of the grand plan designed by nature, the junction of the great salt desert of Dasht-e Kavir and the eastern end of the Alborz Mountains provides an unobstructed pathway from central Asia to the Iranian plateau. In the 1960s, Iranian writer Jalal Al-e Ahmad lamented,

> Every few decades [a tribe] would pack up their tents and drive west-ward in search of new pastures in order to make up for the untimely but chronic droughts of the Qipchak plains. . . . In short, no century in our legendary or historical past has gone by without being marred once or twice by the hoof prints of nomadic invaders from the northeast. . . . Each time we tried to build a house, as soon as we got to the ramparts, some hungry invading tribe would come from the northeast and pull the ladder out from under our feet, destroying everything from the foundation up.[1]

In 1045, twenty years after the completion of the *Shahnameh*, the Seljuk Turks came out of central Asia and pushed westward into Iran.*

---

*This was the beginning of a succession of migrations of Turkic-speaking people from the central Asian steppes that would continue until the beginning of the sixteenth cen-tury. Establishing themselves as a military class, they would supply most of the rulers of the Middle East generally, and Iran particularly, into the twentieth century.

The Seljuks came as converts to Sunni Islam and with an appreciation of Islamic civilization, including the Persian contribution. Once in control of Iran, the Seljuks employed Iranian *vazirs*, or ministers, to govern their domain while they rode on west to destroy the remnants of the Buyid Empire, the Shia dynasty ruling northwest Iran and much of Mesopotamia.

Perhaps more by accident than design, the Seljuks put the Islamic Empire in new clothes. Culturally, the Seljuks acted as patrons of Persian culture within the house of Islam. Theologically, they debilitated Shiism. And politically, they transferred authority to the sultan, the Seljuk military-political leader. The caliph, the successor to Muhammad, the symbol of the Islamic state personified in Abu Bakr, Ali, the Umayyads, and the Abbasids, would never again exercise political power. As a result, the caliph became nothing more than an impotent spiritual leader tending the ghost of the Islamic Empire. Yet the Seljuks, in control of a vast area from the Bosporus to Chinese Turkestan, lasted just over a hundred years. They were gone by the beginning of the thirteenth century, the century of the Mongols.

The nomadic Mongols roamed the unrelenting steppes of central Asia following life free of physical or political confinement. Tough, durable, and mobile, they possessed the raw power to rule central Asia. But divided into separate, competing tribes, the Mongols remained what they had always been—herders of animals. In 1206, the Mongols found unity and destiny under Genghis Khan. Possessing both charisma and a genius for organization, he drew the disparate Mongol tribes under his white banner edged with nine yak tails. Firing them with a divine mission—"One sole sun in the sky; one sole sovereign on earth"—Genghis Khan laid claim to a vast force capable of running over anything that stood in its way.

Mongol power lay in numbers, speed, and way of life. By the nature of their nomadic life, the Mongols, unlike sedentary states, maintained a highly skilled and mobile army manned by almost every male. A Mongol learned to ride before he could walk, and to fell a fast-moving animal with a deadly accurate bow before he reached adolescence. As a man, he learned the intricacies of the *nerge*, the annual hunt that employed a large-scale encircling operation to trap stocks of meat for the winter. To these skills of traditional life, Genghis Khan added the classic military formation of wings and a center which he combined with precision of movement and unbroken discipline. It was on these elements that the Mongol chief constructed his plans for empire.

Originally Genghis Khan posited two objectives: to secure his eastern flank with China and to reduce the threat the Turkish tribes to the west posed to Mongol pasturelands. In 1215, a massive Mongol force helmeted in fur hats with earflaps and mounted on swift, hardy horses rode eastward against China. Two years later, it swung west, dispersing the Turks. At the border of the kingdom of Khwarazm, in a region where the Oxus River flows into the Aral Sea, the Mongols paused. But when Khwarazm's governor detained a Mongolian merchant and his caravan and then executed the emissary sent by Genghis Khan to secure their release, the Mongols invaded.

Beginning in 1219, the army of Genghis Khan swarmed toward the frontiers of Iran like a horde of locusts. Over the next three years, the Mongol followers of shamanism, a faith incorporating superstitions and sacrifice to the sky god Tengri, ravaged territories built on Persian culture and the faith of Muhammad. The savage assault was cultural as well as physical. At Bukhara, the eastern jewel of Islam, Genghis Khan contemptuously rode his horse into the city's main mosque, dismounted, and ascended the pulpit reserved for those delivering the message of the Prophet. Demanding food for his army's mounts, the Mongol leader ordered the massive wooden chests containing the mosque's Korans emptied and carried to the courtyard to become mangers from which to feed Mongol horses. A watching servant, trying to calm a cleric outraged by infidels trampling over scattered Korans, whispered, "Be silent: it is the wind of God's omnipotence that bloweth, and we have no power to speak."[2]

With no military force capable of defending themselves against an attack force that numbered anywhere between seventy thousand and eight hundred thousand, cities were left to their fate.* When the tide of booty-hunting Mongols poured through the gates of these cities, streets turned into rivers of blood as whole populations were put to the sword. In Nishapur, the great university city of Khwarazm, the Mongols beheaded every person in the city. Then the warriors, their swords dripping with blood, separated and stacked the severed heads of men, women, and children into carefully constructed pyramids around which they placed the carcasses of the city's dogs and cats. Turning from this macabre monument to death, they systematically disemboweled the headless bodies of Nishapur's residents according to

*Actual numbers of Mongol warriors were always suspect due to the Mongol tactic of placing dummies on surplus horses to make the attack force look larger than it actually was.

a custom begun when a captive was once caught swallowing a pearl. The populations of other cities found themselves herded into a field outside the city wall. Practicing the *nerge* on their human captives, the Mongols separated out those they wanted as slaves and pressed the rest toward the center to be slaughtered in a torrent of arrows.

The brutal suppression of Khwarazm opened the way to northern Iran. In its march south and west, the massive Mongol army surrounded, captured, raped, and plundered the cities lying in its path. Those spared lived in terror fed by the reality that the death and destruction inflicted by the Mongols was not random, nor was it senseless butchery committed by an army out of control. Mongol devastation was systematic and organized, executed on command. Even those who escaped the Mongol sword knew they could suffer death and deprivation from the men of the steppes who wrecked the *qanats,* the irrigation works critical to coaxing crops out of arid terrain, and salted the land around them. Consequently, starvation as deadly as Mongol butchery descended on the countryside and the cities dependent on its produce.

The horrors of the Mongol invasion of Iran came not once but twice. Genghis Khan brought the first, his grandson Hulagu the second. After ravaging Iran between 1256 and 1258, Hulagu moved into Mesopotamia and toward Baghdad, the seat of the caliphate, the remaining symbol of the unity of the Islamic Empire. As he bore down on the city, Hulagu received a warning delivered by Abassid messengers: "If the caliph is killed, the whole world will be disorganized, the Sun will hide his face, the rain will cease to fall and the plants will no longer grow."[3] Ignoring the admonition, the Mongols kicked the caliph to death, sacked Baghdad's rich treasure, and massacred as many as eight hundred thousand people.*

From Mesopotamia, Hulagu and his army rode on west to take Aleppo, Damascus, and most of Syria. But Iran and Mesopotamia had drained the raw power of the Mongol hordes. In Palestine, an army out of Egypt ended the Mongols' westward expansion. Accepting the reality of overextension, Hulagu withdrew to northwest Iran, where he took the title of il-khan, khan of the tribe. Iran became an Ilkhanate, an essentially independent Mongol territory maintaining a nominal allegiance to the Great Khan of China. Thus once again, the proud core

---

*In a letter to King Louis IX of France in which he was exploring a possible alliance between the Mongols and the European Crusaders, Hulagu took responsibility for only two hundred thousand deaths.

of Achaemenian and Sassanian territory became part of someone else's empire.

The Mongol invasions that ravaged Iran between the arrival of Genghis Khan in 1217 and the death of his grandson Hulagu in 1265 slaughtered or starved uncounted millions of Iranians. At the beginning of Mongol rule, a contemporary Persian historian wrote, "Every town and every village has been several times subjected to pillage and massacre and has suffered this confusion for years, so that even though there be generations and increase until the Resurrection the population will not attain to a tenth part of what it was before."[4] At its end, another historian concluded, "There is no doubt that the destruction which happened on the emergence of the Mongol state and the general massacre that occurred at that time will not be repaired in a thousand years, even if no other calamity happens."[5] It did not take quite a thousand years, but it was not until the mid-twentieth century that the population of modern Iran reached the level that existed before the arrival of the Mongols.

The damage that the Mongols wreaked on Iran can be roughly measured in numbers of people and agricultural production lost. But it also must be judged by the more subtle measurements that exist in the mind. It requires very little experience with Iranians to realize that the Mongol invasion is burned deeply into their collective psyche. One story Iranians often tell about the Mongols is probably more folklore than fact, but the frequency and passion with which they tell it demonstrates just how acutely they still feel the thirteenth-century national trauma. Salaheddin, a quiet little man who has worked for a family in Mashhad for years, told the story as well as anyone. The sun was setting on his prize red roses when he informed me that the intensity of color came from Iranian blood in the soil. Taken aback, I thought in terms of Muhammad Reza Shah's SAVAK or the mass executions during the 1979 revolution. I asked him if he was talking about one or both of these. He clipped a flower and handed it to me. Speaking in a voice of resignation, he said, "No, no madam. I am talking about the Mongols. That is why my roses are so red."

That memory is perhaps worse than reality is beside the point. What matters is the Iranian perception that they, as a people, must always live with the terrible threat of outsiders who have so often plundered and debilitated the Iranian nation.

In 1384, the Iranian will to survive was summoned again when Tamerlane, Mongol by descent, Muslim by religion, and Turkish by language, rode into Iran along the same route taken by Genghis

Khan.* This time the men of the steppes bore the name Tatar. And this time they went south as well as north, engulfing all of Iran in plunder and massacre. At Isfahan, they piled seventy thousand skulls into a grisly tower before they moved on to other targets. By 1405, they were gone, leaving behind a ravished Iran with its culture in full flower.

In the intrusion of the Seljuks, the Iranians saw almost two thousand years of Persian culture endangered. In the invasions of the Mongols and Tatars, it could have been extinguished. Yet as it had survived the Greeks and Arabs, Iranian culture gathered itself from the dust beneath the hooves of Seljuk, Mongol, and Tatar horses to begin its renaissance.

The Seljuks, like other invaders who had gone before, had added their part to that renaissance. In control of much of the Islamic Empire, the Seljuks, through the Persian *vazirs* in their employ, essentially granted Iran regional independence. No longer subsumed within an empire employing the Arabic language and largely reflecting Arab culture, Iran became a separate political unit. More important, it stood as a cultural entity in its own right. Freed of lingering Arab dominance, Persian intellectual life soared. Persian architects in the service of the Seljuks fused proportion and shape to produce walls, pillars, and domes that restated the laws of geometry and beauty. The style, artistry, and genius of these Iranian craftsmen eventually found their way into such later architectural marvels as India's Taj Mahal and Spain's Alhambra.

It seemed that in the barbarity of the Mongol tenure in Iran, the rich resources of the Iranian mind and culture unfolded to make life bearable. Within thirty years of Hulagu's death, the Mongols themselves had done what other invaders of Iran had done—settled within the folds of Persian tradition. The Mongol court at Tabriz, the capital city, took on a Persian as well as a Muslim character as the khan Ghazan inspired and funded a cultural revival. But it was Tamerlane and those who followed him in the Timurid dynasty who presided over one of the peaks of Iranian civilization. Tamerlane had proved to be a connoisseur as well as a vandal. Into his military organization that caused such destruction, he tucked a company of scholars and painters. And along the road of conquest, he collected artists of special talent

---

*Tamerlane was also known as Timer the Lame, a name that came from a short leg and hunched back.

like prizes of war to ship back to his capital, the beloved Samarkand. Some of his successors showed the same divergent personality traits. The prince Hussein Bayqara, for example, exhibited an inordinate love for fighting cocks and mystical poetry.

During the Timurid period, faience mosaic—an art form that covers the entire surface of a building with brilliant color by setting segments of different-colored tiles on a plaster bed—joined mass and form to produce the most perfect examples of the Persian mosque. And miniature painting reached toward its pinnacle of achievement. Evading the religious taboo on representation of the human figure which Persians never considered applicable to them, miniaturists reduced the animate to a scale that could be secreted between the covers of a book. Painting with brushes made from the throat hairs of two-month-old kittens, they created swirling pictures of battles, hunts, and polo games rendered in red, blue, turquoise, and gold as well as portraits of downy-faced youths embracing a thick-thighed girl with one hand and a hock of wine with the other. Joining the miniature in the renewal of Persian art forms were ceramics, metalwork, and carpet weaving. Science also flourished. Omar Khayyam, one of the most gifted men of his day, is credited with the first solution to the quadratic equation and the reform of the Iranian calendar that corrected its accuracy to only one day in every five thousand years. Although celebrated as a mathematician, Omar Khayyam was also a poet. And it was poetry more than any other art form to which Persian culture owes its debt of gratitude to the Timurids. For the Timurid period produced an avalanche of brilliant epic and lyric poets—Rumi, Saadi, Mowlana, Jami, and Hafez. Together they wrote of ruin and confusion, love and hope, death and survival.

To most Iranians, Hafez reigns as the giant of Persian poetry. Almost nothing is known of him except that he wrote in the fourteenth century and that he lived in Shiraz, an object of devotion in his poems. As a poet, Hafez brought perfection to the *ghazal*, a lyric poem of six to fifteen couplets linked by unity of thought and symbolism rather than by a logical sequence of ideas. Traditionally the *ghazal* deals with love and wine, motifs that, in association with ecstasy and freedom from restraint, relieved classical poetry of its tedious formalism. But the real appeal of Hafez's *ghazals* are themes in which the poet writes of his love of humanity and his sympathy for the problems of ordinary people. In his many poems, Hafez exhibited the ability to universalize everyday experience and relate it to an unending search for the reality of God. The *Divan*, the best known of his works, is a collection of poems that Iranians of the Islamic Republic read just as their ancestors who lived under kingship read for guidance at critical junctures in their lives.

Hafez, like Rumi and Mowlana, was guided in life and art by Sufism, a mystical movement whose adherents reject the restraints of conventional religion in order to pursue union with God, the Ultimate Reality.*

Sufism took root among devout ascetics within Islam during the Umayyad caliphate (660–750). Originally a reaction by pious believers to the growing worldliness of the ruling Umayyads, Sufism gravitated toward forms of mysticism that enabled believers to escape the sober, legalistic traditions of the Sunnis in order to seek through hidden meanings in the faith personal bonds with God. Bit by bit, the Sufis, or "wearers of wool," won converts in every part of the Muslim world and among nearly every category of Muslim.†

Sufis, like other Muslims, believe that the Koran enshrines Muhammad's ultimate message: Love the one God. They deviate from orthodox Islam in how they see that love expressed. In addition to its mystical content, Sufism also contains a social-political component. Sufism, in fact, began as a social protest against the *ulama*, the learned clerics of Islam, who, in Sufi perception, exhibited more interest in political power than religion. While the Sunni *ulama* saw God primarily in terms of omnipotence, the Sufis perceived God in terms of love. By participating with God in the creation of a just moral order, the Sufi engages in the first stage of his or her pilgrimage to the believer's ultimate goal—union with God. The second stage of that pilgrimage is mysticism. By searching the inner meaning of the words of the Koran, the Sufi endeavors to recreate for himself the spiritual state in which Muhammad received the word of God. With the guidance of his all-important master and his application of religious knowledge, the Sufi discards all concern for the material world around him. Through retirement and meditation, he seeks to become part of the universal order by standing in the light of God. Repeatedly renewing his

---

*Sufism is familiar to most in the West through the fabled longhaired "whirling dervishes" who rapidly spin around and around until they achieve a near hypnotic state. Employing their own unique method for coming into the presence of God, the dervishes are only one sect within Sufism.

†The term "wearers of wool" came from the hair shirt asceticism of some of the founders of the movement.

meditations, the Sufi moves, step by step, toward another level of consciousness. Finally, responding only to the mystical rhythms deep within him, he finds union with God. In the words of the Sufi poet Hallaj:

> *I am He Whom I love and He whom I love is I,*
> *We are two spirits indwelling in one body.*
> *When thou seest me, thou seest Him,*
> *And when thou seest Him, then thou doest see us both.*

Mysticism within Islam did not arrive full-grown. Rather, masters of mystical theology, largely ignored by Sunni scholars and caliphs, coaxed their students in the unorthodox approach to the divine. In this way, mysticism slowly moved out from a narrow intellectual realm into Islam's main body. It started with the Seljuk Turks.

Toward the end of the tenth century, the Sufis won converts among some of the Turkish tribes of central Asia. Thus when the Seljuks rode into Iran in 1045, they were Sufis as well as Sunnis. And it was during the Seljuk Empire that Sufism, after years of denial, distrust, and persecution by the Sunni establishment, found its way, in a modified form, into Sunni orthodoxy across the Middle East, including Iran. But in Iran and other affected areas, it was the invasions of the Mongols and Tamerlane which gave new impetus to Sufism. Sufism grew during the thirteenth and fourteenth centuries because the basic values of humanity were no longer honored in the chamber of horrors created by the hordes coming out of central Asia. The death and destruction that surrounded them encouraged Iranian poets and writers to escape into religion. In the first linguistic voyage of the Sufis outside Arabic, Iranian poets like Rumi wrote of the need to yield to destiny.

> *Placing your pack on board a ship,*
> *in trust alone you do so,*
> *Not knowing which you'll be,*
> *drowned on the voyage or safely come to home.*
> *If you say "Until I know which way for certain,*
> *I will not rush on board or put to sea . . .*
> *You'll do no business,*
> *for the two fates' secret lies ever with the Unknown.*[6]

Hafez wrote of the satisfaction of personal escape from harsh public reality into a private realm of dreams:

Lie down beside the flowing stream
and see Life passing by and know
That the world's transient nature
this one sign is enough for us.[7]

The Sufis, through the poets, taught that mysticism provided the vehicle by which one sheds all sense of identity with the material world in order to achieve union with God. In the *Divan of Shams-e Tabrizi*, Rumi wrote:

I am neither Christian nor Jew, Zoroastrian nor Moslem.
I am not of the East, the West, the land, or the sea;
I'm not of Nature's mint, nor of the circling heavens.
I'm not of earth, water, air, fire;
I'm not of the empyrean, nor of the dust,
  nor of existence, nor of entity.
I'm not from India, China, Bulgaria, or Turkestan;
I am neither from Mesopotamia nor from Iran.
I'm not of this world or the next,
  nor of Paradise or Hell;
I am not of Adam or Eve, nor of Eden and Paradise.
My place is the Placeless, my trace is the Traceless;
It is neither body nor soul: I belong to the soul of the Beloved,
I have put duality away
  and have seen the two worlds as one;
I seek only one, I know, see, and call only one.
He is the first and the last,
  the outward and the inward;
I know none other than "O lord" and "O lord, lord."[8]

Sufism represented only one variation among many that had occurred in Islam after the death of Muhammad. In 680, Islam's great schism between the Sunnis and the Shia had occurred at Karbala over the issue of who was entitled to wear the mantle of the Prophet. In the centuries immediately following, most of Shiism's adherents as well as its centers of learning resided in the Arab world. Persecuted by both Umayyads and Abbasids, Shia theologians secreted themselves away to develop their particular view of Islamic law and learning and to cultivate the sect's own forms of piety. In this unfolding Shia theology, the Sunni doctrine that the community of believers as a whole is charged with upholding the collection of teachings and interruptions that make up Islamic law was not enough. Rather, the faith, as in the time of Muhammad, required the presence of an authoritative figure possessing the wisdom and knowledge to interpret divine will to the faithful. To the Shia, Ali was the first imam, the divinely inspired leader of the Muslim community. As the Prophet's cousin and son-in-law, Ali possessed the necessary knowledge of Islam to determine that which is lawful and just. As such, only he commanded the authority to direct the consciences and lives of true Muslims. This privileged knowledge included the notion of a secret, hidden wisdom which was inaccessible to the masses. And only through Ali's descendants could this knowledge and wisdom be passed from generation to generation. This raised the inevitable question of who within each generation ranked as the most knowledgeable and the most just among Ali's descendants and, therefore, the most authoritative to guide the Shia Muslim community. (See chapter 4 for a further discussion of Shia authority figures.)

In the eighth century, the Shia split over the question of the rightful successor to Jafar al-Sadiq, the great-great-great grandson of Ali and the sixth Shia imam. In a period in which differing views of the imamate, or system in which the imam exercises authority, were still vague, Jafar had been acknowledged as his father's successor almost without dissent. The choice of Jafar's own successor proved more difficult. Originally Jafar named his oldest son, Ismail, as successor, but Ismail died first. Simply moving to the next son turned out to be fraught with complications. In a theology in which the imam is considered infallible, the question arose about Imam Jafar's fallibility in choosing a successor who would not survive to assume the position. A second question concerned whether or not Jafar's eldest surviving son, Abd-Allah, possessed sufficient knowledge in Islamic law and learning to become the imam. That turned out to be a moot point when Abd-Allah died without heirs within weeks of his father Jafar. A majority of the Shia accepted as imam, by default rather than from conviction, Musa al-Kazim, another of Jafar's sons. However, many Shia clung to Jafar's original designation of Ismail and proclaimed his son as imam. These became the Ismailis, or Seveners, of Shia Islam. Still others believed that Jafar himself, dead or alive, was the only true imam.

In this turbulent sea of faith, theologically sound answers continued to become more difficult for the supporters of Musa al-Kazim as the heir of Jafar. Musa and then his son died. That son left his own son and a grandson, both too young to have received adequate instruction in the hidden knowledge of the religion to qualify as imam. It was only with Jafar's great-great-great grandson, Hasan al-Askari, that someone in the line emerged as undisputed imam. But in 873, Hasan died without an heir or a successor. Rather than grappling with the question of who among the descendants of Jafar now held the *ilm*, the knowledge to be an imam, the faithful reasoned that Hasan must have had a son and that he disappeared in order to escape persecution at the hands of the Sunni caliph, an Abbasid. A whole range of stories sprang up to fill in the details. Yet what mattered was not how that son disappeared but rather the extraordinary precautions taken to protect him. This alone persuaded believers that he must be a very special imam. From this supposition grew the conviction that the son of Hasan al-Askari was the Mahdi, the savior that Shia eschatology said would return at the end of time to deliver the suffering faithful from injustice. In the meantime, this twelfth imam in the line of Ali would live in occultation. This belief in the Islamic messiah in the form of the Twelfth or Hidden Imam undergirds what is known as Twelver Shiism. "The twelve imams [from Ali to the Hidden Imam] came to be invested with cosmic worth, and their lives reflected the sad vicissitudes of the divine cause among ungrateful mankind. As Ali had been abandoned by the Muslims and finally murdered, so the Twelvers came to feel that each of the imams that had followed him had been persecuted and finally executed or at least secretly poisoned by the wicked and worldly Muslims in power, both Umayyads and Abbasids."[9] As a result, the Twelvers set themselves apart as a minority against a world ruled by the strong. They wept at the tombs of their heroes on the anniversaries of the wrongs done to them and raised the Shia prayer to the Mahdi, "May God hasten release from suffering through his rise."

It was Twelver Shiism, delivered by the Turkish-speaking followers of an adolescent zealot, that would forever imprint Iran. Between the sixteenth and eighteenth centuries, Twelver Shiism shifted from its strictly Islamic base to link with the historic traditions of Persia to resurrect Iranian identity and create Iranian nationalism.

The path Twelver Shiism took toward becoming the dominant religion of Iran began with Sufism. Over several centuries, the theology of the mystical Sufis spread from the west of the Islamic Empire to the east. There it found eager followers among those alienated by orthodox Islam. They included the tribes of central Asia, a people who had worshiped the elements of nature or a panoply of gods endowed with mystical powers, who found in the mystical elements of Sufism emotional satisfaction. For others on the edge of Asia, Sufi doctrine that consciously escaped the strictures of the Koran made it possible for Islam to live beside Hinduism and Buddhism, the other faiths of the region. Inside historic Iran, men and women culturally steeped in ideas rather than legalisms had tired of the endless debate among the *ulama* on minor points of Islamic law. Looking to Islam for the answers to the problems of everyday life rather than the controversies surrounding esoteric points of dogma, they sometimes found possibilities, if not solutions, in Sufism. These possibilities came from the local Sufi "holy man" living in almost every town or village. Through meetings, singing, repetitive prayers, and even mass hysteria, these pious men touched hearts and minds with the promise of supreme ecstasy reached in communion with God. Especially in the pain of the calamitous thirteenth and fourteenth centuries, a small but respectable percentage of people from all strata of society came to the Sufis.

One of the Sufi orders that sprang to life during the Mongol period was the Safavids. They date to the late thirteenth century when Sheikh Safi al-Din Abdul Fath Ishaq Ardabili established the order at a place called Ardabil, roughly halfway between Tabriz and the western shore of the Caspian. Safi al-Din, a man of mixed ethnicity, was a Sufi out of the Sunni tradition. Exhibiting great wisdom and a saintly way of life, he drew followers from both the ruling classes and the common people. Gradually his followers assigned to him heroic qualities that passed on to his descendants. They became a line of charismatic leaders radiating special spirituality. That image intensified in a popular history composed of the disappearance of one of Safi al-Din's descendants at the age of seven who reappeared seven years later; the survival of another left on a pile of corpses with a sword wound in his neck four fingers wide; and the indestructibility of another forced to drink a cup of poison. Combining piety and perception, the Safavids came into the second decade of the fifteenth century in command of a thriving center of Sufism and the ability to disseminate Sufi doctrines throughout Azerbaijan; Anatolia, the eastern part of Turkey; and into the Iranian plateau. Believers thronged to the Safavid seat at Ardabil to pray in the presence of the great sheikh Ibrahim, the fourth head of the order. Renowned for the scale of his charity to the poor and needy, Ibrahim's order continued to grow. Although acquiring more and more disciples and property, the Safavids remained a strictly religious organization harboring no political or territorial ambitions.

But with the accession to leadership of Ibrahim's son, Junayd, the

two-centuries-old Safavid order entered a new phase. No longer satisfied with a solely religious role, the Safavids reached for political
power. The reasons remain murky. The Sunni writer Ruzbihan Hungi
provides as good an answer as any. "When the boon of succession
reached Junayd, he altered the way of life of his ancestors [when] the
bird of anxiety laid an egg of longing for power in the nest of his
imagination."[10]

Forced into exile by estrangement from his uncle and guardian,
Junayd spent long years living among the Turkoman tribes of what is
now southern Turkey and northern Syria. The unschooled Turkomans,
through what might be termed folk Islam, placed with Ali, the first
imam, all their expectations of justice and all their devotion. Responding to the magnetic charisma he emitted, the Turkomans gave this
same devotion, based on the same premise, to Junayd. He became the
heir of Ali.

Mobilizing his personal following among the Turkomans, Junayd
transformed his Sufi order from an ascetic religious brotherhood to a
militant military organization. Inciting his disciples to holy war
against the infidels, Junayd in 1460 rode out of Anatolia and into the
territory of the Shirbavan tribe en route to battle with the Christian
Circassians of the Caucasus. Before he reached his target, he died on
the bank of the Kur River at the hands of the Shirbavans.

Junayd's son Haydar inherited his father's personal aura and the
Safavid movement. Through that movement, Haydar wielded both
spiritual and temporal authority. He was both a leader in the Safavid
tradition, walking the path of spiritual guidance and defending the
faith, and a prince on a throne. Accelerating the religious order's drive
toward temporal power, Haydar made alliances and increased the size
of his army. Reflecting the concern of those around him, the wary
ruler of an adjacent region observed, "At the moment Haydar owns no
territory but he has mobilized a warlike army, and his ambitions will
not be contained within the confines of the district of Ardabil."[11]

Haydar downgraded mystical Sufism as the Safavids' central doctrine to a respected tradition. Shiism became the theology of the order
perhaps because of the following it commanded among the Turkomans
and perhaps because of the emotional appeal provided by Ali. Yet the
change was neither abrupt nor complete. In essence, Sufism served as
a bridge between orthodox Sunni beliefs and the Shia interpretation of
Islam that the Safavids, as well as many others, easily crossed. Thus
Haydar could, without inordinate contradiction, lower the flag of Sufism and raise the flag of Shiism over the Safavids. Claiming to follow

instructions from the imam Ali delivered in a dream, Haydar put the Turkoman tribesmen in a distinctive scarlet turban constructed from twelve gores, each commemorating one of the twelve imams of Shiism. Derisively called the *qizilbash*, the "redheads," by their opponents, Haydar's disciples marched once more into battle against the Shirbavan. And once more their leader was killed. On July 9, 1488, the Safavid order passed to Haydar's son, Ali. But he, like his father and grandfather, fell on the battlefield. With his death, the order, debilitated by the crisis of leadership, passed to Ali's seven-year-old brother Ismail. Snatched away from the enemies of the Safavids by the sect's loyalists, Ismail passed from hand to hand until he reached Gilan on the Caspian coast. There he entered the court of a local ruler named Kar Kiya Mirza Ali, where he was educated by a Shia tutor.

The true grandson of the charismatic Junayd, the precocious Ismail soon proclaimed his divinity. To some devotees of the Safavid order, he was the "Living One," the incarnation of God. Accepting the designation, the young Ismail wrote poems acknowledging his divine nature.

> *I am Very God, Very God, Very God!*
> *Come now, O blind man who has lost the path,*
> *behold the Truth!*
> *I am that* agens absolutus *of whom they speak."*[12]

While still a child, Ismail, the most charismatic of all the Safavid sheikhs, wrapped the Turkoman tribes in his aura. Sending his agents to live among the tribesmen, he won their unquestioning loyalty by convincing them that he was the true descendant of Ali and the Shia imams. In Ismail, leader and moment met. Insecurity caused by war, anarchy, bandits, catastrophes, plagues, and famine fueled religious expectations that concentrated in the hope that the Mahdi would return to cleanse the world. In the young Ismail, the Turkomans saw the Mahdi, or at least his harbinger. Man by man, tribe by tribe, the Turkomans separated from their tribal leaders and the Sunni Ottoman Empire controlling them to follow the charismatic Ismail.*

*The Ottoman Empire was built by the Ottoman Turks beginning in the early fourteenth century. In 1453, the Ottomans, in one of the major landmarks of history, took Constantinople from the Christian Byzantines. Eventually incorporating the former Western territories of the Seljuks plus northern Africa and the Balkan Peninsula north of Budapest, the empire played a major role in the events of the Middle East and Europe until it died in World War I.

In August 1499, Ismail, at age twelve, moved to claim his secular-religious kingdom.* He sent the scarlet-turbaned *qizilbash* into battle against princes, kings, and empires, carrying these words:

> *We are Hosain's men, and this is our epoch.*
> *In devotion we are the slaves of the Imam;*
> *Our name is "zealot" and our title "martyr."*[13]

Shia came out of Syria and Asia Minor to join the Turkoman tribes of northern Iran to fight for the figure they venerated. Over the next two years, Ismail would fulfill the words spoken by his brother Ali when he designated him his successor: "The die of Heaven's choice has been cast in your name. . . . You will come out of Gilan like a burning sun and with your sword sweep unbelief from the face of the earth."[14]

With Ismail leading the way, the Turkomans and the Shia zealots drove north toward Christian areas and then turned south toward a Muslim region that was ripe for a new order. Shouting the *qizilbash* battle cry—"My spiritual leader and master, for whom I sacrifice myself!"—they took Tabriz for Ismail in 1501. Assuming the title of shah, Ismail told his subjects, "I am God's mystery." In his first act as shah, he declared Shiism the official faith of his new kingdom. A royal edict went forth ordering the public cursing of Islam's first three caliphs. "Men should loosen their tongues in street and square for the profanation and cursing of Abu Bakr, Umar, and Uthman, and that they should chop off the heads of any that stood in the way of this."[15] Warned that Tabriz's overwhelmingly Sunni population might resist a Shia ruler, Ismail answered: "I fear no one; by God's help, if the people utter one word of protest I will draw the sword and leave not one of them alive."[16]

With Azerbaijan in hand, the Safavid forces marched south, delivering Shiism to a people already familiar with Islam in its mystical form. During the eight years it took to subdue historic Persia, Ismail and the *qizilbash* won converts and imposed their creed through example, zeal, massacre, pillage, and torture. In Khorasan, Ismail freed the city from Sunni control by personally killing the Uzbek king, the ruler of what is now Uzbekistan. Taking the skull, he ordered it set in gold to create a drinking cup for the sultan of the Ottoman Empire, a gruesome statement of rising Safavid power. When the *qizilbash*

---

*In all likelihood, Ismail's decision was made by the *ahl-i iktisas*, the seven close advisers around him.

finally completed their sweep of Iran, Ismail stood at the helm of a political kingdom won under the banner of Twelver Shiism. For the first time since the Arab conquest of the seventh century, reconstituted Iran stood within the rough borders of Sassanian Persia.

Having established his kingdom, Ismail had to defend it. His greatest threat came from the Ottomans, the Turkish Sunni who were building an empire across the Middle East. At the root of the Ottoman-Safavid conflict was not only control of territory and population but nascent nationalism developing among the Iranians and the Turks as well as sectarian strife between Shia and Sunni. Both issues were reflected most clearly among the *qizilbash*. Iran and the Ottomans claimed the common frontier in northwest Iran that included the Turkoman tribesmen who made up Ismail's army. As Turkish speakers, it seemed that *qizilbash* loyalty could be won by the Ottomans. But common language with the Ottomans simply was not enough to break the link between the *qizilbash* and the Safavids. Many of the "redheads" who had created the Safavid kingdom saw themselves as Iranian through their loyalty to the Safavid royal house and, more particularly, to Shia Islam. In this context, the Turkomans consciously and willingly took their position as the guardians of what Ferdowsi in the *Shahnameh* called the soil of Iran.

When the Ottomans invaded the Safavid Empire in 1514, the *qizilbash* fought furiously for Ismail and his kingdom against an Ottoman army of greater numbers in command of artillery. The Ottomans won, taking with their victory a swatch of the border area. Although Shah Ismail still controlled most of what was once Sassanian Iran, Tabriz now lay hazardously close to the enemy. The capital shifted southward to Qazvin, south of the Caspian Sea, and then to Isfahan.

As Iran changed, so did Ismail. The defeat the Ottomans inflicted on Ismail, particularly in the Battle of Chalderan, profoundly affected the shah's character and behavior. Egotism and arrogance gave way to self-doubt and despair. Essentially going into mourning, Ismail put on a black turban, donned black robes, and ordered his military standards dyed the symbolic color of death. Falling from self-proclaimed divinity to drunken debauchery, he spent his later years, in the words of a Safavid chronicler, "hunting, or in the company of rosy-cheeked youth, quaffing goblets of purple wine, and listening to strains of music and song."[17] The invincible, divine figure possessing the all-important charisma was gone. In his absence, the mystical vine holding the spiritual leader to his disciples withered. Ismail died May 23, 1524, in the

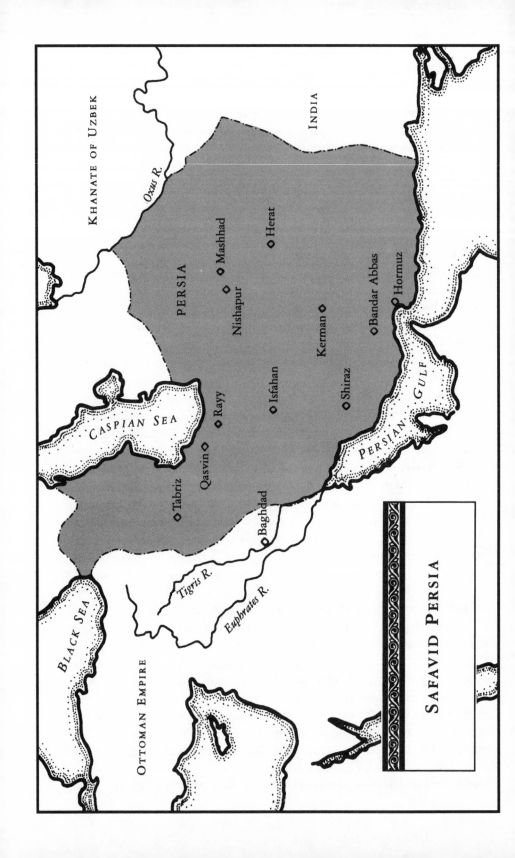

SAFAVID PERSIA

twenty-third year of his rule and two months short of his thirty-seventh birthday.

Ismail's kingdom withstood his death. Within it, Iranians continued to convert to the imposed, official religion—Shiism.* The reasons were multiple, encompassing both a sense of territorial identity and familiarity with an Islamic sect containing within its theology elements found in the religion of pre-Islamic Persia.

When Ismail pronounced Twelver Shiism the official religion of his new Safavid state, he clearly differentiated Iran from the Sunni Ottoman Empire, the major power in the Islamic world in the sixteenth century. Shiism, in effect, gave Iran the specific territorial and political identity that Iranians had been searching for since the Arab conquest. Through the Shia sect, the inhabitants of historic Iran could be Muslims within a specific Iranian identity. Shiism also gave a religious basis to the Iranians' instinct of self-preservation and self-assertion. In the sixteenth century, the Iranians watched the nearly simultaneous rise of two mighty Sunni empires, the Ottomans of Turkey in the west and the Moghuls of India in the east, as well as the continuing threat from the Sunni of central Asia. Particularly determined to resist conquest by the Sunni Ottoman Turks, Iranians allowed the Safavid rulers in 1514 to defend Shia Iran by scorching the earth under their feet in order to slow the Ottoman advance.†

Iranians also eventually converted to Shiism and accepted Shiism as an integral part of Iranian identity because it spoke to Persian culture and the Iranian experience. From the first century of Islam, the martyrdom of Ali and Hussein held particular meaning for Iranians. Within the recesses of their minds and souls, Iranians saw in the Shia martyrs shadows of themselves. For they too were a defeated and humiliated people whose rights and deepest convictions had been trampled. But even more, Ali provided the Iranians with their archetypal model for political order—the just ruler. In a parallel with Persian kingship, the Iranians accepted the cause of Ali and the house of the Prophet because it coincided with their pre-Islamic traditions of legitimacy. And in Shiism, the Iranians found the stoicism of Manichaeism and the Zoroastrian hope for the return of the savior who would restore justice on earth. In Zoroastrian eschatology, the Last Judgment is to be announced by a messiah named Saoshyant, who overthrows the forces of evil led by Ahriman. In the Shia version of the Day of Judg-

---

*It took until the eighteenth century for Shiism to claim 95 percent of all Iranians.
†Milton described the contest between the Safavids and the Ottomans in *Paradise Lost*.

ment, the Mahdi returns to preside over a final battle between Ali and Satan. All told, there were enough points of similarity between Shiism and pre-Islamic religious tradition to allow Iranians to comfortably convert Zoroastrian shrines into Shia pilgrimage sites.

Shiism also touched the Iranians intellectually. The mystical elements within Shiism and its reluctance to accept the Koran as final revelation presented to the Iranians the world of ideas with which they had always been fascinated. The Iranian Shia, freed from Sunni legalisms, released Islam into an ever-expanding arena of creative theology. (See chapter 4.) Responding to a special identity, aspects of pre-Islamic religious thought, and a universe of ideas, the Iranians over the next two centuries embraced Shiism as the potent preservative of their historic and cultural traditions within the faith of Islam.

But sixty years after Ismail died, Iran's outward unity masked the internal turmoil boiling primarily between the *qizilbash*—the Turkish-speaking military who had forged the Safavid kingdom—and the Persians—the Farsi-speaking bureaucrats who regarded themselves as the rightful heirs of historic Persia. In the equation, it was the *qizilbash* rather than the Persians who held the military power that bestowed the ability to challenge the king. In 1587, the *qizilbash* governor of Mashhad moved Muhammad, the reigning shah, off the tottering Safavid throne and replaced him with his sixteen-year-old son, Abbas, Muhammad's heir apparent.* To their regret, those who created the boy king failed to calculate what a brilliant leader Abbas would turn out to be. Through his long reign of forty-one years (1588–1629), Abbas held together Ismail's territorial legacy and sealed its internal fissures.† In the process, he created another of Iran's golden ages, comparable in the minds of Iranians with those of the Achaemenian Darius and the Sassanian Khosrow.

While Ismail had mobilized Shiism to reconstitute territorial Iran, Abbas called religion to build national unity. Identifying with Shiism as the Achaemenians and Sassanians had once identified with Zoroastrianism, Abbas raised above a people long drawn to charismatic leaders the emblem of the shah as the perfect spiritual guide. According to the English adventurer Sir Anthony Sherley, "The king knows how potent a uniter of men's minds the religion is for the tranquility of an estate. . . ."[18] The reality was that Abbas had little other choice. The

---

Shah is the Farsi word for king.
†The reign of Abbas roughly coincides with that of Elizabeth I of England (1558–1603) and Philip II of Spain (1556–1598).

ethnic, tribal, and class divisions of sixteenth-century Iran left Abbas's subjects with almost nothing in common except religion.

In the first year of his rule, the adolescent Abbas sat on his shaky throne facing near anarchy fed largely by the *qizilbash*. On his frontiers, almost all the provinces lying along the western and northwestern borders had been occupied by the Ottomans, and in the east the Uzbeks had overrun half the province of Khorasan. Complicating all of his other problems, Abbas's treasury was empty.

Meeting the challenge head on, the Safavid king prioritized his goals: restoration of internal order; expulsion of the Uzbeks; and recovery of territory from the Ottomans. Seeming to go backward instead of forward, Abbas signed a treaty with the Ottomans in 1590 that ceded to them some of Iran's richest provinces, including Azerbaijan. Only the town of Ardabil, the original seat of the Safavid order and the site of the throne of Sheikh Safi al-Din, remained in Abbas's hands. It was the price the shah was required to pay to neutralize external threats while he dealt with the *qizilbash* renegades.

The *qizilbash* could be put down only if the shah possessed an army whose first loyalty lay with the state. The manpower to build such an army resided in the large number of Circassians, Georgians, and Armenians who had been brought to Iran as slaves during the wars fought by Tahmasp, the second Safavid shah. It was from the ranks of these subjects claiming neither Turkish nor Persian identity that Abbas levied the several regiments that created the nucleus of a standing army owing allegiance only to the shah. Numbering about forty thousand, this new army enabled Abbas to deal ruthlessly with the *qizilbash* or anyone else who might choose to challenge the power of the throne.

By 1602, Abbas's army had eliminated the Uzbek threat on the northeastern frontier, enabling Abbas to turn west to take on the Ottomans. As the shah's troops marched toward Tabriz, the *qizilbash* whom Abbas had quelled pulled on their red, twelve-gored Safavid headgear and joined the king's forces against a Sunni enemy occupying Shia Iran. Siege, devastation of parts of eastern Anatolia, transfers of populations, and finally a decisive battle at Sufiyan near Tabriz expelled the last Ottoman soldier from Iranian territory defined by a 1555 agreement between the Ottomans and the Safavids. Although the war dragged on, the Iranians had essentially reestablished the borders of Iran constructed by Ismail, borders that, in turn, generally reflected the territory of Sassanian Persia. Over that territory stood Shah Abbas.

Drawing on the Persian model, Abbas reasserted royal power,

magnifying the style and aura of Safavid kingship. To the Shia concept of the ruler as the regent of the imams, Abbas joined the Persian concept of the divine right of kings derived from possession of the *farr*. Thus, through his titles, Abbas reigned as both the "Shadow of God on Earth" and the "Splendor of Darius." He was the sun king of Iran, bringing together the authoritarian traditions of Persia and Islam. In 1618, Pietro Della Valle, an Italian businessman visiting Isfahan, described the great Abbas:

> In stature he was as small as me and perhaps smaller; his face is not thin, but well-formed; his limbs and body are slender, but lusty and robust. . . . He is rather handsome than ugly in appearance, though venerable. In complexion countenance is dark. . . . His hands he carries very darkly painted with henna. . . . He has an aquiline nose, moustache and eyebrows also completely black (if they are not dyed). . . . His moustaches are drooping, this being curiously for reasons of religion, as they say that moustaches which point upwards . . . show pride, and thus in a certain way they desire to fight with heaven. . . . He finds it hard to stay still; nonetheless his natural fancifulness and restlessness are accompanied by an indefinable gravity, revealing true regal majesty.[19]

Yet amid the ostentation of his court, Abbas dressed simply. In the hunt, he skinned and gutted the kill and tended the fire while it cooked. Walking the streets and bazaars incognito or sitting in the teahouses telling jokes to ordinary men, Abbas portrayed the Persian ideal of the just ruler. Thus, in his court "there was not a Gentleman but the king: the rest were shadows which moved with his body."[20]

Using Shiism as the Sassanians used Zoroastrianism, Abbas undergirded his temporal power with theology. He traveled, once entirely on foot, the six hundred miles between Isfahan to Mashhad as a pilgrim to the tomb of the eighth imam. Although pragmatic in his dealings with non-Muslims, he took care throughout his reign to keep his own piety above attack in order to play off the keepers of the faith against any political faction that might choose to threaten him. But he also saw danger in the fanatical Shia who have always been present in the faith. Planting his own religious establishment, Abbas founded Shia *madresehs*, or schools, in numbers which had never existed before. Benefiting from royal patronage, these religious schools dedicated to Twelver Shiism drew a stream of Shia learned men from across the Islamic world. As a result, Shia Iran came to exercise enormous influence among adherents of the sect from India to Iraq to Syria and eastern Turkey.

But Iran's new status did not solely come from religious dogmatism. With a military base and a shrewd diplomatic mind, Abbas played realpolitik between Europe and Asia. Economically, he exploited Iran's crucial position on the continental trading routes. More interested in Iran's position in the world than Islamic piety, Abbas ignored some of Islam's strictures. To convince European merchants that the climate in Iran favored trade, he encouraged Carmelites, Augustinians, and Capuchin friars to found Roman Catholic convents within his kingdom. In a system pleasing to most, the non-Muslim Jews and Armenians produced fine wine from Iranian grapes, and the court, including members of the religious class, consumed it. Perhaps this tolerance of alcohol in a Muslim country escaped scandal because the Iranians, reflecting both their Persian and Islamic sides, felt a sense of peace with themselves. Yet it was more. Iran and the Iranians had slipped the bonds of Arab Islam. They had survived the Mongols and the Timurids. They had fended off the Ottomans and the Uzbeks. Now for the first time since the seventh century, no group or nation seriously threatened Iran's heartland, and Iranians owed allegiance to no one but their king. As if to acknowledge their place in the sun, the Iranians joyously celebrated their future through another revival of art and architecture. Their testament to Iran's ascendancy was Isfahan.

There is a magic about Isfahan that is impossible to describe. In terms of size and beauty, Isfahan outside the historical center is not a particularly impressive city. But from the moment I caught a glimpse of the Zayandeh-rud and followed it to the Allahverdi Bridge, I felt no doubt that Isfahan is special. Like so many places in Iran, it emits its own specific light. Unlike the purple mist that encompasses Persepolis or the crisp radiation of the Alborz, Isfahan's light is clear yet soft, gently laying itself equally over beds of roses and asphalt streets, ancient glazed tiles and new storefronts, a quiet walled courtyard and the huge square before the Royal Mosque. As I wandered the streets, I was reminded of what Vita Sackville-West wrote about Isfahan in 1925. "In sixteenth century Isfahan Persians were building out of light itself, taking the turquoise from their sky, the green of the spring trees, the yellow of the sun, the brown of the earth, the black of their sheep and turning these into solid light."[21]

Another kind of light besides the sun illuminates Isfahan. It is artificial light produced by electricity. Strings of small colored bulbs hang over the doorways of mosques that are centuries old. And big multicolored bulbs wind around tall, willowy pine trees planted in traffic circles, creating what Isfahanis quip are Iranian Christmas trees. But it is the bright, bare bulbs that light the old bazaar that most brilliantly shine on Isfahan's age and uniqueness. Architecturally, the bazaar is a work of art. The vaulted ceilings spray out intricately laid brick and little alleys that end in courtyards where the precise angles of stone and mortar draw perfect scale and proportion. These are the passageways Abbas walked when Isfahan was the center of Iran.

Abbas's grand design encompassed four and a half miles and integrated the secular, religious, commercial, and royal strands of Persian society. The Chahar Bagh—a magnificent wide boulevard with four rows of plane trees and a central water channel—connected gardens, pavilions, and small palaces. Along it Safavid high society preened and promenaded. Like the other major thoroughfares, it ended in the *maidan*, the great square that served as both a polo ground and a stage for Persian life—respectable and seamy, dignified and riotous, virtuous and venal. There, in the soft earth required by the sport of kings, jugglers, wrestlers, storytellers, puppeteers, acrobats, hucksters, and whores all vied for the passing trade. Above them, sonorous music blown from copper trumpets eight feet long sounded from a deep porch pillared like an Achaemenian hall. Islam was there also. At one end of the vast *maidan*, the blue gateway and turquoise dome of the Royal Mosque rose majestically above everything human. Yet it faced toward the dark, gaping entrance to the bazaar. It was as if the religious and the secular were deliberately counterpoised one against the other.

The Safavids had given Iran itself—a proud state with a clear sense of identity built on the legacy of Persia and bound together by Shia Islam. But the Safavid dynasty also bequeathed to Iran a bedeviling dichotomy. In Sassanian Persia, the king and the Zoroastrian priests joined state and faith. In Safavid Iran, absolute monarchy in its secular form ruled as the dominant feature of the state built on Islam. Consequently, the king and the Shia clerics became dual poles in which political power based on the traditions of Persian kingship weighed against the legitimacy of the clerics derived from the theology of Shia Islam. At the same time, the king and the clerics reflected more than the question of authority. They stood as symbols of a whole culture in which Persia and Islam continually meet and mesh, repel and divide.

PART II

4

The Faces of Authority: Father, King, and Cleric

ROM THE TIME THEIR ANCESTORS GATHERED INTO SOCIAL units at the dawn of history, the Iranians as individuals and as a people have lived and died within the overlapping orbits of powerful authority figures. And for centuries, Iranian culture has held within itself a deep-rooted authoritarian tradition in which society demands submission to the will of those who hold a position, higher than oneself. The family, the cornerstone of the social structure, is ruled by the patriarch. The nation, for most of its two-and-a-half-millennia history, gloried and suffered under the ancient Persian concept of authoritarian kingship attended by a rigid social hierarchy. In religion, authority figures to whom the faithful owe obedience are central to the theology of Shia Islam. Thus the authoritarian tradition of father, king, and cleric has shaped a whole culture into a pattern of dominance and subservience.

This same authoritarian tradition has imprinted Iranian political behavior. With frequency, Iranians have behaved like a nation of sheep. Ignoring philosophy and issues, they follow a charismatic authority figure who, like a surrogate father, commands obedience. Yet the aura around this authority figure is the promise of internal order, national autonomy, and, most of all, a just society. Between the sixteenth century and 1979, the Iranians sought security and national independence through the authority figure created by the institution of Persian kingship and justice through the authority figures consecrated by Shia

Islam. Together king and cleric held Iran to the tradition of monarchy and the promise of Islam.

The omnipresent authoritarianism that engulfs Iranians begins in the family. In the Iranian patriarchal society, the senior male rules over the family, the alpha and omega of every Iranian's universe. With his position and power rooted in common experience as ancient as Iran itself, he is the all-powerful king within a domain structured on the bonds of kinship. Acutely aware that historically the family often provided the only available physical defense against marauding tribes and invading aliens, Iranians hold to an abiding fear that an individual can trust no one but his kin. And only within the family do Iranians escape the rivalry, conflict, manipulation, and oppression inherent in a political system that has never escaped absolutism in one form or another. Thus, in pursuit of group survival in an environment characterized by insecurity, the patriarch has always directed the family's defense, provided its material needs, defined its interests, managed its affairs, and demanded its obedience.

In crowning the father the head of the family, patriarchy also decreed males superior to females. This ordering of Iranian society into dominant men and subordinate women paralleled patriarchy itself. Long before Cyrus mounted the Achaemenian throne, nature had already defined the specific roles of male and female. Women bore and nursed the next generation. Men, unburdened by pregnancy and child care, physically larger and stronger, hunted the food and protected the family. Later, as settled agriculturalists, men not only plowed the land but allocated the crops. By the time Cyrus assembled his kingdom, man ruled woman.

In the endless debate on the origin and practice of veiling in the Islamic world, which many see as symbolic of woman's inferior status to man, some historians argue that it was Cyrus the Great who, ten centuries before Islam, established the custom of covering women to protect their chastity. According to this theory, the veil passed from the Achaemenians to the Seleucids. They, in turn, handed it to the Byzantines, from whom the Arab conquerors inherited it, transmitting it over the vast reaches of the Arab world. Whether or not Persian tradition is responsible for the custom of veiling, the indisputable fact is that at Persepolis, where stone preserves the ideas and ideals of ancient Persia, women are absent. All the splendid reliefs and noble statues carved at the peak of empire represent bulls, maned lions, winged stallions, and warring men. Even the servants who walk behind kings swinging fans or swatting flies are men. But it is not ancient ruins that attest to the power of Iranian patriarchy. It is society itself.

Family is the cornerstone of the social order. In the interest of preserving the basic building blocks of society, hallowed tradition requires that the family be led by an all-powerful leader commanding unquestioning obedience from every member of the kinship group. In effect, the patriarch, the senior male of the family, creates in miniature the Iranian hierarchical structure of ruler and subject. His silent power can be observed in the hovering wife serving her husband's dinner and in the sudden quiet that descends on children when their father enters the room. Enthroned by age and dethroned only by death, the patriarch collects the blind obedience of the family that accepts both his right to rule and their duty to obey as part of the inviolable order sanctified by tradition. Iran has paid a high political price for the system of patriarchy. For the age-old order in which the father sat at the head of the family as a mysterious superhuman force created the model and environment for absolute monarchy.

The exalted grandeur of Persian kingship, faded by almost two decades of Islamic government, still dwells in Iran. It can be seen in a relief on the tomb of Darius at Naqsh-e-Rustam in which the king stands on a two-layered throne supported by his Persian and foreign subjects; in illustrations of the timeworn arch of the palace of Taq-e Kasra at Ctesiphon, the great memorial to the Sassanians; in the jewel-encrusted Peacock throne on which all Iran's kings since the eighteenth century have sat; and in Gulistan Palace in the heart of Tehran, the legacy of the Qajars. But it is in the archives of Iran's last king, Muhammad Reza Shah, where the nature of Persian kingship most powerfully expresses itself. Here photographs rather than jewels and architecture portray the glorified position of the Pahlavi king as a powerful authority figure commanding the suppliance of his subjects. In 1963, a peasant receiving a deed to a bit of land lies prostrate before the shah. In late 1977, an army general wrapped in gold braid with a sword strapped to his side walks toward his king crouched in a half kneel, his hands held together in a gesture of prayer. On No Ruz of 1978, high-ranking government officials line up to bow and kiss the hand of their sovereign just as their predecessors once paid obeisance to the absolute authority of the kings of Persia.

The institution of Persian kingship spans the history of Iran from the Achaemenians of the fourth century B.C. through the Pahlavis of the twentieth century A.D. During that great arc of time, a core element within Iranian identity linked Iran's heroic past and its exalted civilization to monarchical rule. Perhaps more than any other people, Iranians perceive their history as a history of their monarchs. Under their rule, the nation swept to every victory and rallied after every defeat. In culture, as in politics, kings fostered poetry and painting, carpets and tiles, intricate works of gold and massive structures of architectural art. Whether beneficent or tyrannical, Persian kings sat on the throne enveloped in the Iranian expectation of imperial rule.

The Iranian ideal of monarchy comes out of the ancient Zoroastrian concept of a king governing hand in hand with Ahura Mazda. Thus he derives his authority from possession of the *farr*, a sign of favor bestowed on those who stand on the side of good against evil. Conversely, a king who leaves the light to enter the darkness sacrifices the *farr* and with it his authority. Evidence of who possesses the *farr* and, therefore, the right to leadership takes the form of personal charisma.

In the Iranian concept of leadership, a leader possesses charisma because he is endowed with supernatural powers, or at least exceptional qualities, that set him apart from ordinary humans. He commands a special grace, an otherworldly quality that engenders trust, commitment, and an irresistible desire to follow. The reality that charismatic figures bearing a new dynasty often appeared during pivotal points of history to sustain the Iranian nation reenforced the concept of the hero king. Thus monarchy became a function of personality where authority flowed to the charismatic leader rather than being imposed by the institution of the throne. Furthermore, this ideal and expectation of charismatic leadership constitutes one of Iranian culture's defining characteristics. Although historically applicable to kings, charismatic leadership never has been limited to monarchs. From time to time in Iranian history, a king has sat on the throne while power surged to someone else. Within the twentieth century alone, the Iranians saw the prime minister Muhammad Mossadeq in the early 1950s as the charismatic leader. In the late 1970s, it was the Ayatollah Ruhollah Khomeini. But it was kings who usually filled the role of charismatic leader.

Cyrus the Great created the model of charismatic Persian kingship at the birth of the Iranian nation. In possession of a magnetic personality, Cyrus seemed to stand in the light of Ahura Mazda to rule over a just society and to build a mighty empire. Those of the Achaemenian dynasty who followed Cyrus, particularly Darius and Xerxes, glorified the position of king, raising it to exalted heights which reenforced the institution. By the end of the dynasty, kings bereft of natural charisma created their own through imagery that cast them as the chosen of Ahura Mazda. In these acts orchestrated to elevate him above the mortals who surrounded him, the king might appear outside his palace only mounted on a fine horse or carried on an elaborate litter borne by commoners. Within the palace, the king advanced to his throne in measured, majestic steps beneath a shallow parasol attached to a long ornamented handle held by a servant following at a respectful distance. On the great ceremonial occasions when a large number of guests dined at the palace, the king sat on a raised dais, separated from his guests by a gossamer curtain. Yet behind all the pomp in the service of charisma the culture nurtured the ideal that a king sat on the throne only as long as he presided over a just society. Sadly for the Iranian nation, the history of Achaemenian kingship reveals that in the near constant struggle between justice and power, power most often won.

With the notable exception of Khosrow, the Sassanian kings concerned themselves less with the idea of justice than with enforcing the political allegiance of their subjects through the state-imposed religion of Zoroastrianism. In cooperation with the Sassanian monarchy, the Zoroastrian priesthood presided over minute forms of etiquette designed to create the charisma that undergirded monarchical authority. According to its rules, only the top strata of the realm's elite entered the king's presence. On approaching his august sovereign, the landowner, scholar, or military man threw himself at the feet of the throne and kissed the earth until the king commanded him to rise. Standing reverently in his place, the suppliant pulled a clean white handkerchief out of his sleeve and held it before his mouth to prevent his breath from profaning the royal surroundings while he spoke. For the masses of the people, the king appeared on New Year's Day as a distant, venerable figure seated on a lofty perch to receive the homage of his subjects. Wrapping themselves in the trappings of divine personage, almost all Sassanian kings failed to uphold the ideal of just rule which theoretically bestowed their authority. Rather, they reigned as absolute monarchs enforcing authority through coercion underwritten by religion. When the Arabs came, the *farr* was gone and with it the Sassanian dynasty.

During the centuries Iran lay within the Islamic Empire, the ideal of the just and charismatic king never totally died. Theologically, the Persian concept of the divine king in partnership with Ahura Mazda found a parallel position in the Islamic concept of religious rule over the faithful by the legitimate successor of Muhammad. Whether the legitimacy of that successor was determined by Sunni standards or Shia standards, Iranian Muslims accepted the idea of a powerful authority figure at the head of the Islamic state. Yet as the Islamic Empire crumbled, kings once more laid claim to authority. Persepolis and Pasargadae, those magnificent stage sets that Cyrus and his successors built for royal display, once more became revered ceremonial sites for a panoply of local Muslim monarchs. Nurtured in the courts of these minor kings of eastern Iran, the ideal of Persian kingship flowered again in Ferdowsi's *Shahnameh.*

Ferdowsi chronicled many myths of Persian kingship. At the center of one stands Jamshid, a king who ruled for seven hundred years. In possession of the divinely ordained *farr,* he organized society into social classes and patronized the arts and learning that nourished Persian culture. Two hundred years into his reign, Jamshid boarded a ship to travel from land to land before returning to Persia to celebrate the grandeur of his kingdom. In the words of Ferdowsi, "With the aid of the royal *farr,* he fashioned a marvelous throne, which at his bidding was lifted by demons into the air. He sat upon that throne like the sun in the firmament. That day was called a new day—the festival of No Ruz—the first day of the new year."[1] For another three hundred years, Jamshid guided the peace and welfare of his people. But gradually pride consumed the just king. As his virtue declined, the *farr* dimmed and then died when an evil usurper sawed the fallen king in two. For the next thousand years, Iran lay in darkness before a righteous, charismatic youth carrying the royal *farr* once more claimed the throne in the name of justice.

The Persian ideal of kingship survived the chaos of the Seljuks, Mongols, and Tatars to follow the Safavid dynasty into power. Ismail, the dynasty's creator, laid claim to the charismatic legacy. Like the founders of the Achaemenian, Parthian, and Sassanian dynasties, he had lived in exile and privation before being rescued by the forces of destiny. He would rule as an absolute monarch in the Persian tradition, using religion and its message of justice to enforce his legitimacy. But like other dynasties, the Safavids too sacrificed justice to the god of power. Abbas, immortalized as the great shah who gave unity and stature to the Iranian nation, also began the Iranian strand of despotism. Tormented by his own inner demons, challenged by internal and external threats to his nation, Abbas ruled as a tyrant.

The intrigue and betrayal of a childhood in which he served as the tool of the political ambitions of others convinced Abbas that he could trust no one, including his family. When the *qizilbash* chief who acted as guardian of Abbas's second son revolted against the king, Abbas locked all his direct male heirs in the *haram.* Cut off from the outside world and deprived of companions, the princes grew up among eunuchs and women with nothing to do but feed the sexual appetites of their royal charges. When they were allowed out of their erotic prison to accompany their father on his military campaigns, they went not as soldiers but as hostages to Abbas's fear that any legitimate claimant left in the capital posed a threat to his throne.

Still Abbas felt haunted. Believing a February 1615 conspiracy to displace the king included his oldest son, Abbas ordered him murdered. Six years later, in 1621, he ordered another son suspected of conspiring for the throne blinded. In a repeating pattern, Abbas blinded and imprisoned his fifth son, his father, and his two brothers.

Over the forty-one years of his reign, Abbas, the king famed for walking the streets in simple clothes among ordinary people, tortured and killed his subjects as a matter of justice and as a warning to anyone who might reach for his crown. Motivating everything he did, beneficent and cruel, was his one overwhelming ambition—power. He was the shah, the omnipotent ruler of Iran. His wishes, his policies, and his priorities drove the country. Breaking the ancient bonds with religion, the legitimizing force of both Zoroastrian and Islamic kings, Abbas made the state secular, despotic, and absolute. Yet in achieving absolute authority over everyone and everything, Abbas paid a price.

Just west of the *maidan* in Isfahan, a large garden hides behind big, shaggy cedar trees. A graveled path, almost as wide as a narrow street, leads toward a pavilion of weathered wood. The height of two stories, it stands majestically at the head of a slender reflecting pool. The forty-columned Chehel-Sotoon which served Abbas as a throne room is another of those places in Iran where centuries seem to drop away, allowing a moment of the past to crystalize. Here is where he received his subjects by day and wrestled with his demons by night. Pietro Della Valle, the Italian businessman who wrote of court life in Isfahan in 1618, captured the internal torment of Abbas in these words: "He . . . went to stand leaning against one of the pillars holding up the roof . . . of the *divan-chane.* And the musicians came near to him, all the while he stood listening attentively with an air of deep melancholy. . . . The King, from what I heard, stays thus silent and alone to listen to the singing; and when he wishes to, he retires to the *haram* of women, much troubled by his natural melancholy. . . ."[2]

Abbas died in 1629 without an heir adequately prepared to succeed him. Incarcerated in the *haram* and addicted to its pleasures, those who followed the celebrated shah knew nothing about how to rule. The Safavid kings of subsequent generations proved, for the most part, weak. The next major dynasty to follow the Safavid, the Qajar (1795–1925), would contain strong men and weak men, acceptable rulers and appalling rulers. Yet all were the shah, the ruler, the master of secular authority. Unrestricted by law, strengthened by tradition, accepted as the force of an ordered society, and undergirded by legitimacy derived through the defense of territorial Iran and Shia Islam, the absolute power of the monarch extended as far as the ambitions, whims, or personal competence of the reigning shah permitted. As a result, autocratic rule encompassed every group and stratum of society.

This monarchical system of government, with variations applied by whoever sat on the throne, would dominate Iran until 1979. Thus from the Achaemenians through the Pahlavis, the concept of Iranian monarchy never really evolved. Except for two popular movements that exploded in 1906 and 1951, the monarchy remained absolute and, in its own view, infallible. By its very nature, it was government by elites. The shah sat at the apex of power. Below him, in both a descending or lateral order stood the *vazirs,* or ministers of the king; the *ulama,* constituted from among the religious elite of Shiism; the tribal chiefs known as khans; and the aristocracy, the lords of land and water.* The next level in the hierarchy included craftsmen and the bazaar merchants; still lower were the village elders. At the bottom grouped the great mass of peasants. Decisions based on the interests of those at the top passed down level to level to people who possessed descending abilities to resist the traditional patterns of power and authority. With no ideology beyond elitism itself, the shah governed through force and coercion, subjecting individuals and groups to acts of repression and savagery regarded as vital to the preservation of the throne.

*Although large landowners held an important position in the social structure, Iran never developed a hereditary nobility nor even a well-articulated theory of aristocracy of the type that characterizes most feudal systems. The reason lay in the nature of the monarchy, particularly as defined by Abbas. The king, whose unlimited power gave him the right to bequeath or confiscate land, determined membership in the aristocracy. As a result, the nobility, dependent on the ownership of land, changed as dynasties rose and fell. Bits, pieces, and segments of the privileged survived from dynasty to dynasty. They joined with the new aristocrats created with each new king to reconfigure the "Thousand Families," the major landowners of agricultural Iran. Along with smaller landlords and religious foundations, they owned about 95 percent of the land in the long period from the Safavids to 1963, when Muhammad Reza Shah instituted land reform. See chapter 8.

The political system ruled by the all-powerful king reflected the highly structured society that dated to Iran's origins. The Achaemenians ruled over a population divided by the tasks necessary to the overall strength of the community and the empire. The Sassanians even more precisely ranked and graded society in the interests of the king and state. Cracking during the Arab conquest, the hierarchical order underwent repair and codification under the Safavids. Reenforcing the traditional social pyramid, the administration of Safavid Iran assigned a title to every occupation and precisely ranked every position in the state from the shoemaker up through the entourage of the shah. At the top, the Safavid elite comprised the same groups that had constituted the ruling class of Iran for centuries. Thus the king, his extended family, the landed aristocracy, the khans of the important tribes, members of the *ulama* who supported the shah, the upper echelons of the military, the upper and lower levels of the bazaar, and the masses of peasants stayed locked in the ancient hierarchy. In this system of absolute monarchy and rigid social division, every level of society harbored its own insecurities. Yet insecurity is exactly why absolutism survived. It was the range of catastrophes threatening to life, property, and psyche that led peasants clustered in their villages to welcome rulers strong and tyrannical enough to scare everyone else into submission. This same desperate need for security from enemies within and without carried over to the people of the towns and cities. As a result, fear kept in motion the dynamics of feudal politics: Make alliance with whoever is strong; promote powerful kings; surrender nebulous personal freedom in return for some promise of stability. On these premises, the strong and the weak entered into a relationship in which one was the master and one the servant, each recognizing and dutifully fulfilling his obligation to the other. In this real world, the ideal of the just king holding within him the divine light gave way in the scramble for survival. Consequently, what the British minister to Iran acidly described in 1838 would be just as true in 1978. "The Monarchs of Persia, as far back as memory reaches, or is preserved in history, have always been despotic over Persian subjects, in like manner over their lives, and property, and families, and reputations, and lands, and goods; so that even if they should order a thousand innocent persons to be put to death, it would be in no one's power to call them to account."[3]

Yet the great paradox of Iranian monarchy is that the ideal of just rule by a charismatic leader stubbornly survived for 2,500 years despite the harsh realities of a political and social hierarchy in which one level inflicted injustice on the level below. Through all the tyranny and despotism, Iranians never accepted man's inhumanity to man as either natural or inevitable. Instead, Iranians found in Islam a counterweight against the all-encompassing power of the secular hierarchy that grew out of Persian kingship. Although Islamic kings proved to be as despotic as the kings who went before them, religion provided, in theory, some sanctuary for those who lived under their power. There was the palliative promise of paradise for the faithful. But there was more. Islam in its Shia form provided a theology which spoke to the oppressed and bestowed on certain religious leaders the authority to define the just society.

For the four plus centuries between the time the Safavids established Shiism as Iran's state religion and the 1979 Iranian Revolution, the king wielded the power of the state and the Shia clergy exercised the moral authority of the faith. In many respects, secular and religious authority have always intertwined in Iran. At the birth of the Iranian nation, monarchy arrived wrapped in swaddling clothes woven of religion. In the seventh century A.D., Islam combined secular and religious authority. The caliph, the heir of Muhammad, was the king ruling over the *Ummah*, the Islamic state. When Iran came out of the ruins of the Islamic Empire and the Mongol invasion as a Shia state, the king of the nation also acted as the servant of the faith. In expectation, if not in reality, the concept of secular leadership blessed by religion survived almost as long as the Iranian monarchy. For the fabric of Iranian life was, and is, woven on the loom of Islam. Its endlessly repeated motif is God rather than king. And religion instead of the state embroiders it with the expectation of equality and justice for the masses so often victimized by kingship and hierarchy. But Shia Islam contains its own patterns of authority.

Theologically, Shiism is the great equalizer of society and the mighty shield protecting the masses against the elite. In practice, Shiism is authoritarian and elitist, supporting an imprecise but powerful hierarchy commanding obedience from the faithful. In a configuration only occasionally interrupted over a period of five hundred years, kingship born of Persia and the clergy born of Shia Islam constituted parallel tracks of authority. The constantly changing drama in which the king ruled and the clerics acted as nonparticipants, collaborators, or adversaries in the political process would end only when Ayatollah Ruhollah Khomeini gathered the theological and hierarchical elements of Shiism into the powerful political movement that overthrew the Iranian monarchy.

The original source of Shia Islam's leadership tradition with its defense of social justice came from the Prophet Muhammad. He was perhaps the ultimate charismatic leader, the powerful personality who exhibited deep spirituality in his personal, social, and political life. While Iranians lived within the rigid hierarchical institution of Persian kingship structured by the Sassanians, Muhammad taught his followers in Arabia that all believers who faithfully follow the tenets of the faith are equal one to the other. Each man or woman who surrenders to Allah forms an integral part of the Islamic community and each contributes to the strength of the whole. Branding riches as disruptive to communal harmony, the Prophet prohibited usury and drew lines of behavior aimed at preventing the excessive accumulation of wealth, particularly at the expense of others. According to the Koran, "Nothing shall be reckoned to a man but that for which he has made efforts."[4] In his condemnation of unearned wealth, Muhammad pronounced the oppression of the poor immoral, warning that a society that fails to care for its needy can achieve neither piety nor virtue. In the words of the Prophet, "Proclaims a woeful punishment to those who hoard up gold and silver and do not spend it in Allah's cause. The day will surely come when their treasures shall be heated in the fire of Hell, and their foreheads, sides, and backs branded with them."[5]

In the model of government Muhammad created for the early Muslim community, the Prophet ruled as the spiritual and temporal leader of society. He represented "perfect passivity before God and perfect activity before man. He was the mirror who reflected the world of God and he saw nothing except God and through God."[6] Muhammad, the prototype of the charismatic leader, reigned over a theology that stresses submission to the will of God. When he died, he left his followers without a leader to guide the community toward the divine promise of an ethically just order that comes from obedience to God. As with the same concept in pre-Islamic Iran, the ideal of justice in Islam was, and is, ingrained in the yearnings of the soul rather than the logic of the mind. In its simplest terms, Islamic justice means restraining evil to provide the greatest good for the greatest number. That requires leadership by righteous individuals committed to the corporate welfare. In the seventh century, the question of who among the faithful constituted the righteous leader led to Islam's great schism.

The original cracks in the *Ummah* appeared when Muhammad's

disciples passed over Ali, Muhammad's closest relative by blood and marriage, to choose another as the first caliph. By the time Ali became the fourth caliph, the Muslim community divided into two factions— the Islamic establishment of Mecca, who believed the leadership of Islam belonged to them; and the antiestablishment forces within the Islamic Empire, who held that only those out of the house of the Prophet possessed the qualifications to lead the faith. The Shia, the antiestablishment supporters of Ali, saw in the virtues of the fourth caliph the ideal leader, the defender of the rights of the oppressed.

But Ali's reign as caliph only lasted from 656 to 661. Yet to the Shia, he remained the shining leader of what was, in essence, a political protest movement demanding equality, compassion, and justice in a world his followers saw dominated by inequality, oppression, and injustice. Iranian Shia still regard Ali as the hero of the downtrodden. He is both the symbol of the ideal of justice that had its origins with Cyrus and the emblem of the pure goodness found in the life and teachings of the Prophet. So it is that through many centuries and every kind of venal and unjust government, the Iranians have harbored within themselves the example of the glorious, charismatic Ali standing for the ordinary men and women of Islam. The same emotions flow to his son Hussein, who died at Karbala. In choosing martyrdom at the hands of the overwhelmingly superior force of a tyrant, Hussein became for the Iranian Shia steeped in the tradition of monarchy the symbol of both the Prophet and the ideal king. In the words of a nineteenth-century poet,

What rains down?
Blood!
How?
Day and Night!
Why?
From grief!
What grief?
The grief of the Monarch of Karbala![7]

Like Ali, Hussein's revered position within Iranian culture is the result of the interaction of history, experience, and perception. In the collective mind of Iranians, Hussein's agony is the symbol of oppression from which they have suffered individually and collectively at the hands of tyranny wielded by powerful aliens and their own social-political systems. As Hussein died the martyr's death at the hands of evil forces which he was too weak to defeat, the masses of Iran have also suffered for centuries at the hands of unjust and venal rulers they also have had no power to resist. Perhaps this is why Iranian culture bears a palpable if not quite definable burden of grief. It is as if the precarious social-political milieu in which Iranians have so often lived has preconditioned them to always perceive the negative, the sad, and the tragic. This weariness of misfortune is clearly voiced as a common theme in Persian poetry, which often speaks of the futility of all human desires in the face of inevitable death.

In contrast to mainstream Sunnism, which accepts the vicissitudes of life as God's will, Shiism is characterized by suffering and passion in the name of righteousness. There are within the sect legends and rituals that keep alive that part of Iranian identity rooted in a sense of communal pain. All are directed toward the day when God will deliver the community from tyranny in its multiple forms. But it is Ashura, the tenth of Muharram, the annual day of mourning for Hussein, who died the martyr's death at Karbala, when the Shia physically and emotionally also become martyrs.

In an isolated village near Mashhad, men crowded around the little hardware stall in the tiny bazaar to buy *zanjeers*, wooden handles from which hang links of chain tipped with barbs. Outside on the rutted, unpaved street, women draped in the blackest of chadors strung out carpets, woven mats, and worn blankets in preparation for the Ashura procession.

In midafternoon, at the hour tradition says Hussein died, a jagged procession began to move slowly from the direction of the now-empty bazaar. Within it, men, wrapped in white symbolizing their readiness to die, swung the barbed chains over their shoulders in the measured, repetitive motion of self-flagellation. Others repeatedly hit themselves on top of their shaved heads with the flat sides of crude swords. With each blow, the point of impact swelled as dark, red blood pooled under the skin. Then in one dramatic moment, the marchers turned their swords to the sharp edge and struck their crowns once more, sending blood cascading down their faces. The distinct salty smell of blood mixed with the scent of rosewater sprinkled from a crowd visibly trembling with emotions that seemed released from the very depths of the soul. Once more the bizarre and the profound blended in the macabre ritual of Ashura, the consummate celebration of martyrdom.

The theme of martyrdom replays itself over and over between Ashura of one year and Ashura of the next year. *Rowzeh-khans*, professionals who specialize in giving recitals that recount the sufferings of the sacred figures of Shiism, stand outside the religious shrines offering their services to pilgrims, pious women hosting a group of friends in their homes, and *hayats*, neighborhood men's associations committed to religious work. The *tazieh*, the Shia passion play which recreates the death and martyrdom of Hussein, is performed regularly across Iran by polished professional troupes and village amateurs possessing the same level of professionalism found among the principals of local Christmas pageants in the Christian West. Together Ashura, the *rowzeh-khans*, and the *tazieh* draw forth emotions never far below the surface. These feelings of pain and suffering Iranians hold within themselves are collective as well as personal. For as the individual has suffered, so has the nation.

Within a culture engraved with martyrdom and laced with distrust of secular authority, the Iranians have historically looked to their religious leaders for spiritual guidance and the promise of justice. Who Shia Islam's leaders are and how they claim authority is a defining characteristic of the sect. In contemporary political terms, the authoritarian tradition within Shia Islam explains, in part, the Iranian Revolution and poses profound questions for the future of the Islamic Republic. (See chapter 13.)

After the deaths of Ali and Hussein, the Shia continued to hold fast to the belief that only members of the Prophet's family possessed a special knowledge of religious matters that set them above all others. From this hereditary premise, a form of elitism developed in which each of a select group of men came to be regarded as the source of truth. He was the imam, the ultimate spiritual authority. Together the imams formed a chain of infallible leaders who ruled over Twelver Shiism in the name of God between 680 and 873. In life, they were, in the eyes of believers, the repositories of all truth and knowledge. This knowledge bestowed on them the authority to interpret God's revelation. In death, they are considered by the faithful to hold the power to intercede with God on behalf of the needs of the believer. They number twelve—beginning with Ali and ending with Muhammad al-Muntazar, the Hidden Imam, who will return one day as the Mahdi to preside over an age of justice that precedes the final Judgment. With these perfect persons, the Iranian Shia deposited the elements of hereditary leadership, absolutism, elitism, and obedience that underlay the idea of authority in Iran. In this sense, the Iranians found in the concept of the imam the deeply rooted traditions of sacral kingship and social justice so basic to pre-Islamic Iran. But the imams are of Islam, not Persia. Representing the authoritarian aspect of Shia Islam, they are the link between Allah and his people on earth. In Shia theology, they possess the essence of God and understand His plan for the world. As the vice-regents of God, the imams interpret His will and guide the faithful toward the completion of that will. With them there is salvation; without them there is only damnation. Consequently for the believer who feels trapped in the evil of a suffering world, their ministry and their intercession are essential to the relief of pain. As a student at the female theology school in Qom told me with the conviction of the divine promise, "All the imams are infallible. They can hear us, see us, and answer us. Whatever we ask for they give it to us with God's permission."

The eighth imam, Reza, is the only Shia imam buried in Iran. He died in 817, just one year after he had been nominated as caliph for all Muslims, both Sunnis and Shia. Suspecting that he was poisoned by a son of Harun al-Rashid, the Abbasid ruler, the collective mind of the Iranian Shia see him as the victim of the range of machinations the Iranians perceive the Arabs inflicted on them during the Islamic Empire. Every year, thousands of Shia visit the tomb of Imam Reza at Mashhad, bringing with them their piety, sorrows, and petitions.

Mashhad rests in a broad, narrow valley on the high plateau of northeast Iran. Enveloped in cool, dry air and blanketed in green, its physical setting alone differentiates it from the rest of Iran. But the uniqueness of Mashhad is not physical, it is spiritual. The city's reason for being is the Imam Reza Shrine, a magnificent complex of golden domes, blue mosaics, mirrored walls, and bubbling fountains.

It was the day before Eid-e Fitr, the feast day at the end of Ramazan. Pilgrims had arrived from all over Iran as well as from central Asia, Pakistan, and other areas claiming Shia populations. Some came as individuals, others in groups riding on big, cross-country buses with Ya Muhammad painted in red across their back windows. The city literally hummed as the hours ticked away, bringing ever closer the prayers at the shrine.

Long past nightfall, I walked down the broad main street of Mashhad toward the enormous mosque. Hundreds of colored lights draped from every dome, and dozens of flood lamps bathed every tower. Pulled toward the splendor created by illumination, I was swept along in the current of people flowing through the front gate. Inside, I stood in an enormous courtyard where fountains played and glimmers of gold inlaid in mosaics and flashes of silver from intricate mirror work created an atmosphere of magic. Reluctant to leave, I gathered my chador tightly around me and snaked my way through the crowd camped before the heavy, brass-grilled window that provides a view of the imam's tomb from the outside. Among the quiet and weeping people huddled before it was a little boy of about eight, his emaciated body curled on a pallet and covered by a thin blanket. Moving away a few feet, I watched his father plead for the life of his child with thin cords of yellow and pink. Winding through the crowd, the colorful strings physically connected the child to the metal covering the window to Imam Reza's tomb. As people became entangled in one or the other, breaking the link to the imam, the father left the side of his son, frantically located the severed ends, tied them together, and returned to the fretful child. With an acute sense of grief, I wondered what terrible burden lay on each of the people weeping before that window or if they, as the Shia had done for centuries, wept for the world in which they live.

This grief for the human condition has always been within Shiism. Theologically, it was during the lives of the imams that good was enjoined against evil and the oppressed defended against the oppressors. Although the weak failed to prevail against the strong, the imams, with their gift of religious knowledge, guided the faithful along the path of righteousness that promised ultimate salvation. When the Twelfth Imam went into occultation in 873 without leaving behind an heir, the chain of infallible imams broke. The Shia were left to face the critical question of who among them was qualified to give guidance to the community of believers. For only the imams possessed the ability to interpret, with infallibility, divine revelation. Only the descendants of Ali could act as the vice-regent of God, directing and guiding the believers toward the ideal society.

Although there were no more imams, the promise of the Mahdi's return remained, and with it, the promise of justice, the highest of all values in Twelver Shiism. Viewing existing social conditions as temporary, the Twelvers, the Shia who follow the twelve imams, continued to believe that the Mahdi could appear at any time to test the faithful. At that moment, in a final act of history, they would be summoned to launch a great social transformation under his command.

But in the absence of the Mahdi, the Shia, during the centuries before the 1979 Iranian Revolution delivered the Islamic Republic, judged all governments profane, impure, and corrupt. For all power, temporal as well as spiritual, remained vested in the Hidden Imam. Consequently, institutions of secular authority stood as nothing more than makeshift structures necessitated by the ever-present threat of anarchy. Rather than corrupting themselves through involvement with secular government, the Shia, in effect, surrendered political power to whatever ruler or system, usually the monarchy, supported and defended Shia Islam. The pious believer who did take part in secular government did so only as part of the moral challenge to create a divinely ordained public order on earth or if the refusal to serve secular authority clearly endangered the believer's property or his life. Or the devout Shia could become part of secular government under the principal of *taqiyeh*, concealment in defense of the faith.*

Traditionally, the believer who did participate in secular government assumed no real moral duty. In the eleventh century, the theologian al-Hasan al-Tusi illustrated the almost Alice in Wonderland atmosphere created by a believer's de facto presence in a secular government for which he took no responsibility. "It is incumbent to enjoin the good and to forbid the evil in the heart, by the spoken word and by act whenever the *mukallaf* (those upon whom there is an obligation) is able to do this and know, or considers, that it will not lead to harm to him or to a believer at that time or in the future. If he knows that it will lead to harm to him or to a third party at that time or in the future, or thinks this probably it is not incumbent upon him in any way—it is only incumbent if he is safe from harm in all cases."[8] This combination of Shia acceptance of governments that supported the faith along with Shia participation with secular rulers in certain circumstances strengthened religion's own authority, creating an intricate system in which submission to religion often also meant submission to Iranian political authority and, at the same time, the submission of Iranian political authority to religion.

Spiritually, the real question for a Shia was not who sat on the throne but who commanded authority within the faith. The disappearance of the Twelfth Imam in the ninth century came at a time when

---

Taqiyeh developed out of the Shia's minority position within Islam, particularly during the Abbasid caliphate. It later served those Iranians of Safavid Iran who lived under the threat of the Ottoman Turks, followers of Islam's Sunni branch. It is a theological concept that calls for "dissimulation of the truth" in order to protect the faith against its religious and secular enemies. This can mean proclaiming allegiance to the Sunni sect and publicly following its rituals. It can mean denying the Shia faith by joining profane, secular government. Historically and operationally, it has meant concealment of the truth in any situation in which that seems propitious. In contemporary politics, the Islamic Republic suffers the abiding suspicion among many foreign governments experienced in the Iranian philosophy and practice of *taqiyeh* that pronouncements of policy on everything from economics to terrorism may be concealment instead of truth.

all of Islam, not just Shiism, again faced the recurring question of leadership that had plagued the Muslim community since the death of Muhammad. The Abbasid dynasty, holder and defender of the imperfect caliphate established after the fall of the Umayyads, was disintegrating. When the Mongols stomped the breath out of the last caliph in 1258, the Sunnis, like the Twelver Shia already left by their imam, found themselves without leadership. Into the vacuum flowed the most learned men in Islamic law. Although vested with no political power and living under government exercised by others, these scholars of Islam began to gather significant influence among Sunni Muslims through their ability to interpret the body of traditional religious writings. Eventually they became the custodians of the sharia, the body of Islamic law composed of the Koran; the hadith, Muhammad's sayings and actions recorded by his followers; opinions of highly regarded scholars; and public consensus.* In Shiism, where the whole question of religious leadership was always significantly more important than in Sunnism, the scholar, the master of Islamic law, became the functional imam. To him fell the charge to interpret all moral questions—social, political, and religious—until the return of the Mahdi. Together the men of great learning developed "a profile of a just Shiite figure of authority, however temporary and fallible, who could . . . follow the Quranic mandate of creating a public order that would 'enjoin the good and forbid the evil'."[9] By the seventeenth century in Shia Iran, those individuals most knowledgeable in the law of God were recognized as the legitimate leaders, not of government, but of society. The reasons lay as much in Iranian culture and society as in religion.

Although disputed theologically, the deference shown to the most learned of the Shia scholars is part of the authoritarian tradition in Iran. Members of the family obey the father. Subjects of the kingdom followed the powerful charismatic king. In this cultural setting, Iranians of the Shia faith look to a divinely inspired guide believed capable through his knowledge of the faith to lead them toward the ideal community devised by God and the Prophet. The choice of this leader is complicated by the multiple facets of Shiism. They include mysticism, folk practices of believers with no intellectual grounding in the faith, and the kaleidoscope of practices and attitudes in what might be called mainstream Shiism.

*Sharia literally means "the path." Beyond the Koran and the hadith, the value assigned to the opinions of particular legal scholars varies from place to place, group to group.

Mysticism has always dwelled in Iranian culture. Some claim it began in the Zoroastrian concept of light and dark. Early Muslims found mystical thought in the Koranic verse, "To God belong the East and the West; wherever you turn, there is the face of God—for God is All-pervading, All-knowing."[10] Whether Zoroastrian, Muslim, or agnostic, most Iranians seem to be mystics at heart. And Iranian culture itself reflects a long tradition of contemplating the spiritual realm and the meaning of existence. In this atmosphere, "mysticism, the ambiguity of poetry, belief in the many-faced subtlety of evil, and the never fully resolved choice between the roles of hedonistic cynic and selfless devotee have created the great interior spaces in which the Iranian soul has breathed and survived. . . ."[11] Whether or not they classify themselves as mystics, Shiism's great intellectuals have led the way in this search for truth and meaning.

At the other end of the spectrum stands folk religion. Here the uneducated masses include in their religious practices magic, charms, and the worship of saints which occurs at simple shrines with some claim to the miraculous. One such shrine in rural Fars is revered because it contains what is purported to be a hoofprint of Ali's horse. In other locations, a special tree flutters with bits of colored cloth and absorbs the glow of votive candles because some unknown person in an unknown time was supposed to have experienced a miracle in its shadow. This wide gap between the folk practices of the villager and the complex intellectualism of the highly educated cleric is one of the paradoxes of the Shia faith. Yet it is between these extremes that most of the great theological debates over what constitutes real truth as opposed to false truth take place. Out of these debates emerge the authority figures of Twelver Shiism.

Shia clerics are a large and visible presence in Iran. They are identified by the turban, black for those descended from the Prophet, white for the rest. Wherever he is seen, the cleric with his turban and a cloak draped over an ankle-length robe emits an air of authority. Those he meets know exactly where he belongs in the scheme of society and what duty is owed to him by others.

At the Tehran airport, all of the flights were running late. The people milling about in the stark expanses of the domestic terminal divided into two groups—those waiting to board an overdue plane and those waiting to meet a passenger delayed by Iran's overburdened air transport system. As a ticketed passenger burdened with luggage, I sat like a caged bird near the center of the building. Before me, impatient people, often carrying big bouquets of flowers, flowed back and forth between the big electronic board listing arrival times and the wide glass doors through which all arriving passengers flowed. In the crowd, four perturbed, animated men drew my attention. Their khaki clothes, scruffy sandals, thick, rough hands, and close-cropped hair identified them as working class. As I watched, they tried with growing frustration to decipher the posted combinations of flights and times before moving en masse to one of the counters of Iran Air. Calmed by the information they obtained, they sat down in a row of molded plastic chairs near the sliding glass doors where incoming passengers enter the terminal from the tarmac. The minutes ticked by. None of the four seemed able to sit still. They exchanged tense words, ran plastic worry beads through their callused hands, and craned their necks every time they saw another wave in the intermittent stream of arriving passengers. Suddenly, they sprang to their feet and rushed toward a shriveled old man with thick glasses wearing a black clerical turban, a worn cloak of faded brown, and bright yellow patent-leather slippers. Each kissed the cleric's hand and his cheeks in gestures of adoration. With one of the quartet leading the way, another following with the small black suitcase that constituted the cleric's baggage, and the other two guarding the flanks, they led the aged clergyman through the crowd. Hovering around him with exaggerated respect, these humble men turned the simple act of exiting an airport into a rite of supplication. The cleric, clutching his cane with an air of authority, moved with the dignity of one who accepted as a matter of right the lavish attention being showered on him. Thus together master and followers disappeared into the night.

The clerics are the aristocracy of Shiism, the elite to whom commoners pay obedience. This is the great paradox of Shiism. A theology rooted in the equality of all believers follows authoritarian lines that divide those who interpret religious law from those who are qualified only to obey that law. Within the clergy, imprecise judgments concerning knowledge of Islamic law arrange religious authority figures in a fluid hierarchy.

The lower level in this clerical hierarchy is composed of the mullahs, the broad collection of men who claim some level of religious learning.* Until the 1940s, any man could grow a beard, put on a turban, sling a cloak over his shoulders, and declare himself a mullah.

---

*The word *mullah* is the Persian pronunciation of the Arabic word *maula*, meaning "master." In everyday Persian, it borders on being a slang term for cleric. In English, it translates simply as "cleric."

Earning a living through a variety of occupations that ranged from craftsman to merchant to the owner of a single plot of land, he taught a few small boys recitations from the Koran and, perhaps, from time to time acted as the judge in disputes involving the least educated of the community. Although often ridiculed by the religious establishment, no individual or institution commanded the authority to defrock him.

Some of the mullahs living in villages or neighborhoods within large population centers did possess some formal religious training enabling the most educated among them to preside over matters involving marriage, divorce, and inheritance. Today all mullahs are better educated, but they still function within imprecise definitions of who is and who is not the fully trained equivalent of the local parish priest in Christian Catholicism. Yet regardless of how he is defined by the rules of religion, the local mullah is an integral part of Iranian life. While secular government traditionally remained distant from those it governed, the cleric lived and worked among the ordinary people for hundreds of years. Consequently, society's most humble have always turned to him for advice and guidance. They seek him out to perform religious ceremonies. And they look to him as the only buffer they have against the powerful forces which always rage against Iran's poor. There is no prototype of a mullah. Their commonality has always been the direct and intimate contact they maintain with the people they serve.

Historically Iranians have known good mullahs who upheld the ideal of religious service. And they have endured notoriously venal mullahs who have fed like leeches off the people they lived among. They have seen mullahs who have used their limited education as a beacon of light to those who look to them for guidance. And they have suffered mullahs who interpret in the most narrow terms both religion and the world to their largely illiterate followers. In contrast to the ethical and educational diversity of the mullahs, the top of Shiism's clerical hierarchy has almost always represented great integrity and the Iranian intellectual tradition.

For a number of centuries, the clergy massed in an amalgam of ignorance and intellectualism. As late as the nineteenth century, Shia clerics functioned in an environment of blurred distinctions and ill-defined jurisdictions. They carried titles granted by their peers, titles bestowed by the king, and titles assumed by themselves. It was in the twentieth century that the religious hierarchy organized itself into a more definitive structure with accompanying designations that carried real theological meaning. In a tradition stretching back to Ali, knowledge of the sacred texts of Islam separates the low from the high in Shiism's clerical order. And intellectual command of Islamic law and tradition determines who in the faith leads and who follows. For what might be called the "church" in Shia Islam is actually a brotherhood of the learned. Its headquarters is in the town of Qom.

If Persepolis is the monument to Iranian kingship, Qom is the seat of Shia religious authority. The town sits between bare, scruffy hills near the great salt lake of Daryache-ye-Namak, seventy-eight miles south and east of Tehran. This dry, dusty, desolate environment sets the tone of a city given to scholarship and mourning. Qom itself is a collection of low, dun-colored buildings anchored by a great shrine from which fragments of color—gold, green, and blue—glint in the desert sun. Below its massive dome is the tomb of Fatimah, the sister of Reza, the eighth imam. Around it cluster the *madresehs*, the colleges that train the intellectual elite of Shiism. They are the ultimate reason for Qom's importance. Originally established by Arabs who fled Iraq following the Battle of Karbala, the schools of Qom draw Shia religious students from all over Iran as well as the greater Islamic world. Rather than being housed in majestic buildings expected of great old universities, Qom's schools are for the most part ordinary square boxes of three or four stories that look more compatible with business than either education or religion. Yet within their walls, the great teachers of the faith instill the basic precepts of Islam, teach the intricacies of Islamic law, drill students in the principles of Aristotelian logic, contemplate Islamic society, and define just government.

A young man wishing to formally establish himself within the clergy tries to secure a place as a *talabeh*, or student, at one of the respected *madresehs* in Qom or elsewhere. If he is admitted, he begins the rigorous study of law and logic "chest to chest" with one or more teachers who through their own studies have earned their reputations and positions as Islamic scholars. The curriculum and length of study varies depending on a student's ambitions and abilities. The average student is most often sent out within a year, two, or three to go to a village or a neighborhood as a mullah respected because he studied at Qom or Mashhad or another in a descending order of theological schools. The gifted can stay for years working their way through the tortuous curriculum that gives a cleric the right to claim the title of *mujtahid*.

The *mujtahid* ("jurist") is a combination of theologian and judge who through his learning possesses the ability to interpret until the return of the Mahdi all religious, social, and political issues facing the Islamic community. The authority of the jurist to interpret Islamic law began even before the disappearance of the Twelfth Imam, when it was prophesied that "the earth shall not remain without there always being a learned authority from among us, who will distinguish the truth from falsehood."[12] In the theology undergirding the imamate, rule by the descendants of Muhammad, the imams provided that guidance. But when the line of visible imams ended with the twelfth, it was necessary to the survival of the Shia community to find other divine guides enabling the faithful to live in accordance with the laws of God until the Hidden Imam reappears in the triumph of justice at the end of time. It was the religiously learned, the *mujtahids*, who gradually assumed the social and religious leadership of the Shia community as functional imams.

The role of the jurist within Shiism is to engage in the interpretive reasoning of Islamic law that is forbidden to ordinary believers. He does so after training for years and passing through rigorous examinations by his peers that bestow the authority to apply his own interpretations to a broad range of religious questions. This emphasis on theological inquiry is one of the great differences between the Shia and Sunni branches of Islam. In the simplest terms, the great minds of Sunni Islam are lawyers; those of Shiism are theologians. The difference comes because Sunnis believe the Koran, the hadith, and the basic laws of early Islam represent complete revelation. Within them are all the truths which God has conveyed to man. Thus, since the tenth century, Sunni clerics have neither added to nor amended the legal opinions contained in each. They only comment on the existing texts. The Shia, on the other hand, hold that the ability of humans to reason is not essentially different from that of God. Consequently, humans are capable of deciphering, rearranging, and reinterpreting the tenets of Islam which form the moral order of Islamic society. This lofty regard for reason explains why a major emphasis is put on Aristotelian deductive logic in the colleges that train Shia clerics. In these schools, every student learns to take a major article of the faith, such as the prohibition on alcohol, establish its premises, and derive subsidiary rules which can be applied to it. In this highly charged intellectual atmosphere in which man perpetually tests existing boundaries, Shia scholars constantly engage in debate with one another not only on issues of holy writ but regarding philosophy, reason, and the whole range of disciplines which influence the life of the faithful. Different clerics reach different decisions. But the opinion of one *mujtahid* is as valid as another's as long as it conforms to Shia traditions. These conflicting opinions between jurists are a vital part of Shia theology, which holds that only through the process of discussion and debate can the faith differentiate between good and evil, reasonable and unreasonable. It is in this milieu that the Ayatollah Ruhollah Khomeini devised his doctrine of "Islamic Revolution" and that Shia clerics now debate the theological validity of his Islamic state.

Although all *mujtahids* have the right to engage in theological reasoning, the weight given to an individual's opinion varies according to where he stands within the clerical hierarchy. How individual position in that hierarchy is established is as complex as Shiism itself. Rungs on the ladder of authority are gained in part by the number of years of study, how many students seek a particular *mujtahid* as a teacher, and the number and quality of that *mujtahid's* publications. Yet despite all of the examinations taken to determine learning and knowledge, all of the students taught, and all of the published writings, any *mujtahid* must still operate in a world of face-to-face relations. A man's ambition to advance through the levels of titles within the clerical hierarchy of Shiism requires above all else the agreement of his peers. Ultimately, the coveted titles of Shiism are granted through the complex and unstructured system of deference and consensus of the religion's learned.

The elite of Shia Islam climb out of the broad category of *mujtahid* to *hojjat ol-eslam*, the "proof of Islam," and then to ayatollah, the "miraculous sign of God," a title reserved for a small cadre of clerics who are the most admired and respected for their learning and personal integrity. Finally, the rare cleric becomes a *marja-e taqlid*, "source of emulation," the most authoritative religious title in Shiism. By virtue of his sound faith, knowledge, and character, the *marja-e taqlid* is recognized as a deputy of the Twelfth Imam, authorized to assume the duty of guiding the community during the occultation. Yet while his title is conferred by the clerics, his authority comes from the masses. There the ayatollah and the rare *marja-e taqlid* fill the ancient Iranian expectation of leadership—charisma. But it is charisma composed less of personality than of knowledge and personal virtue that emulate the imams themselves.

In a religion where every *mujtahid* is a theoretical equal, there is no religious body vested with the authority to grant the great jurist the title of "ayatollah." Rather, when a clerical leader achieves a certain eminence, his followers simply begin to call him "ayatollah," and if enough of the respected theologians accept the title, it becomes fact.

British scholar Sir John Malcolm wrote in the nineteenth century about the status of ayatollahs, "It is not easy to describe persons who fill no office, receive no appointment, who have no specific duties, but who are called—from their superior learning, piety and virtue—by the silent but unanimous suffrage of the inhabitants . . . to be their guides in religion and their protectors against the violence and oppression of their rulers, and who receive from those by whose feeling they are elevated a respect and duty."[13]

Because ayatollahs hold their position only with the acclamation of their followers, the hierarchical structure of Shiism possesses the tensile strength of Jell-O more than steel. Position and authority depend on a constituency, a group of followers who look to a particular cleric as a model of emulation. Rather than commanding this following, a cleric attracts disciples to him. The greater the number of lower-level clerics and ordinary people who pray behind any given *mujtahid*, the greater his standing and power. But just as every *mujtahid* can issue his own opinion on questions of faith, every believer can select which *mujtahid* he or she accepts as a spiritual guide. In this sense, Shiism is a populist religion that chooses its leadership. The ability to command a following and to hold the obedience of those followers creates the great ayatollahs.

For uncounted generations, Iranians from all walks of life have made their way to the main mosque of their city to pray the Friday prayers with the famous ayatollah who occupies the pulpit. The rich, but mostly the poor, move with the merchants of the bazaar through the *haram* and on into the mosque. Separating into male and female, they kneel on large carpets laid end to end and side by side across the wide stone floors. They come to pray but they also come to hear the sermon delivered by the man they look to as their spiritual guide. It is with this sermon that the Friday prayers begin. "In the name of Allah, the Beneficent, the Merciful" vibrates off the thick walls as the ayatollah prays for the community of Muslims before launching into his theme for the day. The sermon can be purely theological or it can be potently political. It can draw from the worshipers' deep emotion watered by weeping, or it can, in periods of political turmoil, send the people into the streets in protest against governmental authority. The person able to decide how he wants the crowd to react is the cleric who controls the pulpit.

Beyond religious knowledge and charisma radiated from the pulpit, money constitutes another important source of clerical authority and power wielded by the ayatollahs. A cleric receives a range of contributions from his personal followers. Contributions come in the form of *zakat*, donations to charity required by one of the five pillars of Islam; *khoms*, one-fifth of a believer's annual income given to Shia religious authorities; and *sahm imam*, an additional and optional amount given for the general support of Shia religious causes. The cleric receiving these contributions is free to dispense them as he sees fit as long as the money goes to the broadly defined causes of Shiism. Consequently some flows into the shrines, schools, publications, and other areas which promote the faith. But most goes to charity. Traditionally, clerics have functioned as glorified social welfare agents who gather money from those who have a pittance or a fortune and disperse it among those with little or nothing. But regardless of how it is dispersed among Shiism's causes, this money bestows on a high-ranking cleric independent power. For in a system where a *mujtahid* answers to no one but his followers, no government can demand any portion of religious revenues and no cleric can require from another what are privately administered funds.

No matter how famous or powerful, a *mujtahid* who allows any of the money he collects in the name of religion to settle in his own hands suffers damage to his reputation that is beyond repair. And if he fails to maintain his scholarship or ceases to attract followers, including the least educated, he loses the right to lead. Thus regardless of the hierarchical nature of Twelver Shiism, it is always difficult to determine the point at which the leader leads and the follower follows. Laymen look to their leader for guidance and pattern their behavior accordingly. At the same time, the cleric from his position of authority seeks to understand the will of his followers and then to shape his policies to reflect that will. As a result, religious leadership, unlike kingship, is circular rather than vertical. The leader both leads and follows and the followers both follow and lead.

Before the Iranian Revolution, this same imprecise application of power applied to religious and secular authority of the Iranian state. Over almost a thousand years after the Arab invasion, administration of justice in Islamic Iran consisted of a loosely sewn and frequently resewn patchwork of conflicting authorities in which the different and sometimes competing sources of Islamic law vied for the right to dispense order and justice. Gradually a loosely organized structure of religious authority took a position parallel to the authority of the king. Asserting the imperfection of secular government, Shiism held out the ultimate promise of just rule. In the absence of the Twelfth Imam, it claimed the authority to stand guard against the corrupt power of secular kings. That authority rested with the *mujtahids*, who poised as the counterbalance to Iranian secular authority. Consequently kings and clerics, secular power and religious power—each commanding its own sources of revenue and authority—lived in perpetual tension. The religious leaders with their close relationship with their followers and their reputations for veracity built on personal integrity held the potential to act as conduits of public protest against the repression and venality of the ruling regime. Particularly the ayatollah with an exalted reputation exercised such a level of obedience from his followers that he possessed the power to instruct them to endure any situation or instill in them the willingness to die for a cause. Yet the *ulama* declined to keep secular authority engaged in a constant battle for primacy. Rather, conflicts between the religious and secular came and went from the time of the Safavids until the last years of the Pahlavis. Issues excited the religious guardians of the masses. But in the end, the *ulama* usually drew to the side of the individual or group that affirmed the traditional position of Shia Islam as the state religion of Iran, recognized the independence of the Shia clergy within the monarchical system, and defended the national independence of Shia Iran.

For their part, Iranian monarchs prior to the Pahlavis legitimized their authority by linking themselves with the *ulama* and religion in general. They did so under the assumption that the *ulama* would uphold secular authority in order to protect the interests of religion. To close the circle from the religious to the temporal back to the religious, the *ulama* justified this obedience to theologically profane secular government as necessary for the protection of the Shia state and Shia society. The clerics of Shia Islam even added a patina of morality by claiming the futility of political action in the absence of the Twelfth Imam.

The manner in which Twelver Shiism and Persian monarchy dealt with the question of leadership and authority created a strong duality in which the king controlled the power of the state and the *ulama* possessed the allegiance of the masses. Consequently, there existed in Iran prior to 1979 a state within a state. The government of the king, the shahanshah, ruled Iran under the shadow of the clergy ruling from Qom. In the village and the urban neighborhood, the local police represented Tehran but the mullah represented God. Nonetheless, both stood as powerful authority figures confirmed by tradition.

So it was that every Iranian lived as he or she had always lived under powerful forces of authority—familial, political, religious. The father dominated the family, the king ruled his subjects, the jurist guided his followers. But at the break of the twentieth century, the authoritarian tradition of kingship stumbled, gained different footing, and finally fell as Iranians searched for the elusive promise of justice for themselves and their nation. They did so in the face of the one alien invader the Iranians never tamed—the cultural intrusion of the West.

PART III

5

King and Nation:
Iran's First Revolution

Tehran is a monotonous city, relieved only by the dramatic natural beauty provided by a spine of the Alborz Mountains that stretches across its northern suburbs. From the foot of those mountains to the southern edge of the city, one flat-roofed, boxlike building after another lines the streets. Some are large, some small, some new and pristine, some old and dilapidated, but each repeats the same dull line. This sameness gives way only to the pocket parks that dot the neighborhoods and the squares that segment the major thoroughfares. They too share a certain repetition of low shrubs, shaggy grass, and a fountain that is often dry. Yet in the very center of the city, little glimpses of Tehran as it was at the turn of the twentieth century remain. Just south of the bazaar, a tight semicircle of decaying buildings curves around a nondescript intersection. Buff brick, arched windows, and tall, narrow finials that break the roofline mimic late-nineteenth-century Paris. Laid within this Western facade are chipped and stained mosaics of turquoise and yellow, the aged remnants of classical Iranian tiles. Together brick and ceramic, one imposed on the other, symbolize Iran's early engagement with the West. Within a compact area of maybe two square miles, Tehran offers up other aging symbols of the early twentieth century, when Western intrusion and despotic government drove Iranians to revolution. There is the solemn Gulistan Palace, with its grand audience hall where the Qajar rulers sat on the Peacock throne like oriental potentates. And there is the bazaar, where merchants in small, dark shops pulled the strings of Iran's economy. From the bazaar, a short, narrow passageway where a blind man recites the Koran for a few coins, leads to an expansive courtyard. Above it, the towering central mosque, blackened by the exhaust of countless cars, stands as a massive statement of the power of religion when turbaned men choose to wield it. Finally, there is a templelike gray stone building fronted by a garden that sits like an island at the confluence of several streets just beyond the palace, bazaar, and mosque. Once the building where the Majlis, the parliament, met, it is now a simple monument to the 1905–1911 Constitutional Movement, in which the forces of modernization, traditionalism, nationalism, and authority collided in Iran's first revolution of the twentieth century.

In less than a hundred years, three powerful political upheavals have convulsed Iran: the Constitutional Revolution of 1905–1911, the nationalist revolt of 1951–1953, and the Islamic Revolution of 1979. All stand as parallel movements driven by the same core issues: opposition to a corrupt, unjust king and resentment against the intrusion of foreign powers into Iran. Ignited by nationalism, each carried within it aspects of political philosophy, Shia theology, national identity, and Iran's response to the West. In their reaction to the West, the Iranians confronted the ultimate issue of culture. Each of these popular revolts wound to its own conclusion. But it was the Constitutional Revolution, through the establishment of a parliament, which defined a new source of authority in Iran—that of the people. Although originally conceived in terms of Western liberalism, Iran's "house of justice" took root in soil containing the Persian concept of the righteous king and the Islamic tradition of justice. Deprived of most of its goals by domestic dispute and foreign intervention, the Constitutional Revolution had grappled with ideas introduced by the West, took a stand for national independence, philosophically limited the power of the king, and debated the relationship between the law of man and the law of God. All laid the foundation of contemporary Iran.

Iran's transition out of its medieval past began in the eighteenth century, when the Safavid dynasty conceived by Ismail through Shiism lay gasping its last breaths. Externally harassed by the Ottoman Empire and Russia, internally decayed and corrupted, it could not rise from its bed in its own defense. So when eighteen thousand Afghan tribesmen from the east rode into Iran in 1722, Sultan Hussein, the alcoholic descendant of Abbas, surrendered the Safavids' disintegrating amalgam of territories. While the Afghans took Fars and eastern Iran, the Ottomans moved east out of Turkey to occupy large tracts of Iran's western provinces, including the cities of Tabriz and Hamadan. At the same time, Russia reached south, seizing the western Caspian coast.

The Afghanis, who tried to reimpose Sunni Islam on the Iranian Shia, proved unable to rule. In 1736, they retreated before a warlord named Nadir Qil Beg. Restoring the monarchy, Nadir Shah pushed into Mesopotamia and north into central Asia in quest of another Persian empire. In 1737, he thrust into India. After destroying the Moghuls, the patrons of the Taj Mahal and other architectural monuments of northern India, he turned homeward, carting with him sacks of rubies, sapphires, and emeralds and the seven-foot-high, jewel-encrusted Peacock throne.* Despite his military successes, Nadir Shah could build neither nation nor empire. Increasingly brutal in recurring bouts of madness, Nadir Shah died in 1747 at the hands of his own commanders. With his death, Iran plunged into civil war that did not end until 1750, when the Zands, a tribal group, established themselves at Shiraz. Their hold on Iran lasted only through the rule of one man, Karim Khan, before a civil war fought along ethnic lines ripped Iran apart. Fifteen years later, in 1794, the Qajars, a Turkish tribe from Mażandaran, defeated the last Zand pretender to claim the right to rebuild Safavid Iran. The Qajar dynasty would rule Iran until 1925, when it, in turn, gave way to the Pahlavis, the last Iranian royal family.

Originally the Qajars comprised one of the seven Turkish tribes which helped Ismail pull Safavid Iran together. As part of the *qizilbash*, the Qajar chiefs came into Ismail's court as noblemen. But in a later strategy to rein in the disrupting power of the *qizilbash*, the Safavid king dispersed the Qajars. One section found itself protecting an area around the present border of Georgia. Another went east to Khorasan to fight the Tatars. The third returned to Mazandaran to defend Safavid Iran against the Turkomans. It was this third group, under the leadership of Agha Muhammad Khan, which reappeared on the political scene in the eighteenth century to contest for the throne of Iran.

Agha Muhammad Khan looms as another of those extraordinary characters to found an Iranian dynasty. As the child of a rival tribal chieftain, he became a hostage of the Zands. Castrated and caged while he grew to manhood, Agha Muhammad Khan turned into a

*The Peacock throne is believed by many to have disintegrated en route, making the present Peacock throne with its 26,733 inlaid jewels a copy.

monster. At last escaping imprisonment in Shiraz, he fled north to his tribe. Motivated by unbridled rage, he gathered the Qajars to fight the Zands in a sadistic war of revenge and spoils. Region by region, Agha Muhammad Khan and his tribesmen captured Zand territory by sword, siege, and terror. When the last Zand surrendered in 1795, Agha Muhammad Khan strapped on a sword consecrated at the tomb of the founder of the Safavid order and declared himself shah.* But neither nation nor kingship could quell the hatred and ferocity which characterized Agha Muhammad Shah. In 1797, a year after he seized the throne, several of the shah's own fearful servants assassinated him.

Under Agha Muhammad Shah, Tehran, the seat of tribal power since 1786, converted to the seat of the Qajar dynasty. The move of Iran's capital from its historic location in Fars to Tehran in the north represented a quantum shift in the nation's history. How abrupt and complete it was struck me one night in Tehran during a rainstorm. I had been staying for several weeks in a room with a big window that looked out on the Alborz Mountains. Every morning when I woke up, the first thing that I saw was rugged, gray-blue rock that plunged down toward the city. At dusk on a spring evening, a storm sent the cool air rushing down that mountain and through my window. Sitting on my bed, breathing in air and moisture, I realized how completely Tehran of the Qajars divided from Persepolis of the Achaemenians and Isfahan of the Safavids. I could almost see Tehran at the turn of the nineteenth century. The town, not much larger than a settlement, lay in a valley whose greenery and flowing streams contrasted with the brown of the desert to the south. Its people spoke Turkish instead of Persian and its ruler came out of a tribe instead of a court. But the Turkish Qajars would take the model of Persian kingship and twist it in their own image.

Fath Ali, a nephew of Agha Muhammad, led Qajar Iran into the nineteenth century. Inordinately handsome, possessing the languorous Qajar eyes and a wasplike waist, he set the new royal style. Agha Muhammad had been a tribal khan. Fath Ali was the shahanshah. Turning his back on the rough Turkish-speaking tribesmen who had won Iran for his uncle, Fath Ali brought back the Persian court. Embracing the traditional etiquette and endless ritual that characterized the courts of his predecessors, the shah ruled his empire from a specially commissioned throne that harked back to the Achaemenians and

---

*Agha Muhammad Khan buried the bones of the last Zand ruler under his doorstep so he could walk on them every time he entered or left his house.

Sassanians. Seated on it, the shah perched three feet off the ground with his head hidden in shadow and his feet resting on a platform adorned with the lion of Persia. Consumed with illusions of grandeur, he ordered his portrait painted on the wall of the Sassanian grotto at Taq-e-Bustan, adjacent to that of Khosrow II. Like other dynasties before them, the Turkish Qajars had become Persians.

Outwardly, Fath Ali and his successors commanded enormous power. The shah owned all secular lands except those granted to military commanders and court favorites. At his sole discretion, he called his subjects to arms. He possessed exclusive right to grant economic concessions, privileges, and monopolies. He intervened directly in the commercial markets by fixing prices, buying, selling, and stockpiling food. He made and unmade the officials of the realm. And he held the power of life and death over his subjects. But one more element orbited the sun of authority.

In the tradition of the Safavids, Fath Ali Shah ruled under the ancient Persian precept of the just ruler and the Shia injunction to protect the faith. Within this matrix of power and expectation lay the old dichotomy of secular and religious authority. Upset in the period between the fall of the Safavids and the rise of the Qajars, the *ulama* began to reassert their role as jurists possessing the right to decide issues of right and wrong in the absence of the Twelfth Imam. Developing a more defined religious hierarchy than had ever existed before, Shia clerics administered vast religious endowments, collected religious taxes, ran schools and charitable organizations, and presided over sharia courts. In the process of enforcing their legal rulings, the mullahs maintained private armies composed of religious students and fugitives from secular authority living under the protection of Islam. Each with its own sources of authority and empowerment, state and religion coexisted in a delicate balancing act in which the clerics presided over religious matters while yielding to the king sovereignty over secular issues. And the king carefully paid deference to the *ulama* whose sanction of his rule undergirded his claim to the throne.

In the prolonged and generally deplorable Qajar dynasty, the shah ruled by manipulation more than force. He functioned like the *ilkhan*, protecting each community and tribe against its rivals and the state against foreign aggression. As long as he protected Iran internally and externally, the shah could expect the head of each community to commit himself and his people to his service. In essence, the sovereign filled the role of supreme arbitrator who sat in judgment over disputes involving Iran's many divergent communities. In the absence of written law, the shah was expected to rule according to the abstract, but real, notion of moral justice.

In this system where he acted as mediator more than despot, the shah commanded neither a large standing army nor an extensive state bureaucracy. Rather, the aristocrats from the landed families functioned as provincial administrators and military governors who, in the interest of quelling anarchy, personally paid for the upkeep of their provinces. The king could also call on the tribes for the armed men he needed to defend the country. But the tribal elite who made the decision to commit to the shah ruled their own tribes as virtual kings, governing in isolation from outside authority, administering their own laws, collecting their own taxes.

The tax system produced by this collection of autonomous regions and tribes serves as an example of the controlled chaos of Qajar Iran. Generally, the government in Tehran only knew what revenues to expect from the governor of the province. And the governor only knew what to expect from the district officers. And so it wound down to the peasant. The actual amount of money collected and the sources which paid it remained the exclusive knowledge of the official in charge at a particular level. No one cared what happened above or below him as long as it did not have impact on him personally. This included the shah. He asked no questions about how taxes were assessed or collected, only when the anticipated revenues would flow into his treasury. With no one accepting responsibility for the whole, corruption ran rampant. As James Morier, the author of *Haji Baba*, observed about nineteenth-century Qajar Iran, "The business of each individual is to amass money by every possible expedient and particularly by the obvious one of plundering all those unfortunately subjected to his power. . . ."[1]

The confusion of law and administration manifest itself in the curious Qajar concept of *bast*, "sanctuary." Through some mysterious consensus, certain sites such as the royal stables, telegraph stations, a particular point on a road, and a certain gate to a city provided protection from arrest. At religious shrines, the entire structure might give sanctuary to serious criminals, who usually huddled near the tomb, while petty thieves could claim safety only in the outer courtyard. For a while, the shadow of a monstrous cannon positioned in front of Tehran's Drum Tower gained recognition as a sanctuary for minor offenders, who slowly moved around the gun with the sun.

The Qajars stayed in power by building an enormous network of kinship and alliances reenforced with grandiose titles. Fath Ali married his twenty daughters into the leading houses of the provinces. His two hundred sons, all carrying the title of prince, married into Iran's most influential families.* Each of the male descendants of these unions became princes who, in turn, entered other marital unions that bestowed more titles and established more ties to the throne. This plethora of royal titles led to the saying, "Everywhere in Iran there are camels, lice, and princes." But it was not just titles of royalty that proliferated. Military men, bureaucrats, and members of the clergy acquired the honorifics that gave them their own stake in the Qajar system. As for those without an honorific, they constantly strove to ingratiate themselves with the shah so they too could join the ranks of the elite. Together the shah and his willing subjects created the Qajar system. At its apex perched the shahanshah. Below him, in descending order, sat members of his family; aristocratic families who held their position through loyalty to the reigning king; the tribal khans who provided military strength to the regime in return for royal favor; bureaucrats beholden to the shah; and religious leaders willing to profit themselves by taking part in secular government. Lord Curzon, the architect of British policy in the East, caustically remarked about Qajar Iran, "The law of the Medes and Persians altereth not. . . . The government of Persia is little else than the arbitrary exercise of authority by a series of units in a descending scale from the sovereign to the headman of a petty village."[2] Left out of this system of mutual benefits were members of the new merchant class created by economic developments of the eighteenth and nineteenth centuries, the intellectual class that was assuming an increased role in the affairs of the state, and the mass of peasants and menial laborers at the bottom of the social structure.

As the late twentieth century has so patently demonstrated, protest in Iran has often come packaged in religion. In the age of the Sassanians, Manichaeism and Mazdakism both constituted protest movements against the ethos and practice of the existing regime. Islam triumphed in Iran because the political system underwritten by Zoroastrianism had ossified. Shiism, in turn, arose as a protest movement within Islam. In the mid-nineteenth century, opposition to the Qajar system found a voice in the Bahais.

The Bahai religion began as a messianic movement within the Shia sect of Islam. In 1844, during the reign of the third Qajar shah,

*Fath Ali's multitude of children was produced by his many wives plus the women resident in his large *haram*.

Muhammad, a young man just past adolescence named Mirza Ali Muhammad declared himself the long awaited Mahdi. Repeating the pattern of Islamic movements of heresy and revolt provoked by a sense of injustice from those who ruled, mullahs formed a segment of the early converts to a movement within Shiism called Bahaism. However, the Bahais soon began to pull away from Shiism to develop their own religious themes. Stressing equality of the sexes, universal education, pacifism in establishing world peace, and the need to improve society through the pursuit of purity, the Bahais eventually severed the ties with their Shia origins. It was this rejection of Islam from within the faith that has inflicted on the Bahais a level of Shia resentment never applied to other religious minorities in Iran. It seems the Shia can tolerate Jews, Christians, and Zoroastrians because their faiths preceded the faith of Muhammad. But the Bahais are a Shia heresy which cannot be suffered.

From its inception, Bahaism enraged the Shia clergy. Its blasphemy denied Muhammad as the last prophet and the Koran as final revelation. A powerful corresponding issue for the clerics as well as the shah was that Bahaism, like Manichaeism in its time, posed a threat to the existing order. Trumpeting the sound of reform against mullah and king, the Bahais called for "heads to be cut off, books burnt, places demolished and laid waste, and a general slaughter made."[3]

Although the most visible and distinctive opponents of the Qajar system, the Bahais were a symptom of widespread dissatisfaction spreading through Iran. It fed on a series of disastrous wars the Qajars fought against Russia and Britain in the first half of the nineteenth century. These wars flared from a combination of geography and imperialism. Like a rug on a doorstep, Iran lay between an ambitious Russia driving toward warm-water ports on the Persian Gulf and an anxious Britain determined to protect the gateways to India. (See chapter 7.) Ignoring the realities of Iran's woeful military capabilities, Fath Ali Shah chose to fight the encroaching powers in the name of national glory. In 1813, Iran lost its first war to Russia and with it possession of Armenia, Georgia, and northern Azerbaijan. In 1828, it lost its second. This time the Caspian Sea turned into a Russian lake when the Qajars surrendered the southern shore to the czar. Ten years later, in an ill-conceived attempt to counter Iran's image of weakness magnified by the losses to Russia, the Qajar king laid claim to the city of Herat in Afghanistan. This time Britain administered the defeat. In its wake, Iran cowered on its knees, territorially dismembered, psychologically devastated.

It was in this environment of national humiliation that seventeen-year-old Nasir ed-Din became the fourth Qajar shah in 1848. For the next forty-eight years, Iran traveled in an uneven orbit around his throne. In his first crisis, he confronted rebellion in six parts of the country ignited by the military defeats of the previous decades that left restless tribes and regions with a perception of a weak central government. His second challenge came from within the court in the person of Mirza Taqi Khan Farahani Amir-i Nazam, the young shah's guardian and tutor.

Popularly known as Amir Kabir, the tutor became his pupil's first prime minister. He brought to office the intellectual heritage of Abbas Mirza, a son of Fath Ali Shah. In the early nineteenth century, Abbas Mirza had stood among the ruins of the Iranian army on the Russian front. Suffering the disgrace of his country, he saw in retreating soldiers and captured armaments Qajar Iran's backwardness and impotence. When he returned from war, he began to agitate within the court for reform of the monarchy and the nation. Tragically dying before his father, Abbas Mirza left his vision to the few enlightened minds within the palace. One of those who grasped that vision was Amir Kabir.

Utilizing his intimate association with the shah, Amir Kabir extended his control over government finances and the bureaucracy to give form to Iran's flimsy central government. In foreign policy, he introduced the principle of equilibrium that would characterize Iranian relations with its powerful neighbors into the reign of Muhammad Reza Shah. In essence, Iran protected its fragile sovereignty by balancing the interests of Russia against those of Britain. Addressing the debilitating problem presented by internal and external threats to the security of the nation, Amir Kabir raised and equipped an army capable of defending territorial Iran.

In his overriding concern to buttress the state, Amir Kabir sought to end the dualism of power between the king and the clergy, or at least to reduce it to a point where religion could no longer challenge the authority of secular government. But the breach between crown and turban repaired when Amir Kabir judged the Bahais a looming threat to Iran's internal stability. Beginning in 1848, serious disturbances between the Bahais and the clergy rumbled like thunder in the ears of the prime minister. The lightning speed with which Bahaism was spreading its message threatened more. In 1850, charges of heresy by the *ulama* paved the way for the state to execute the Bahais' central figure, twenty-five-year-old Mirza Ali Muhammad, the Bab, the Bahais' proclaimed successor of Muhammad. His followers, indicted for renouncing Islam for another religion, faced the choice of repentance or death. The wave of persecution aroused by the clergy and led by the state culminated in 1851 at Zenjan, between Tabriz and Tehran. There Qajar troops, in the name of Shia Islam, laid a siege to the town. When they saw Qajar troops storm the gates, the Bahais, with a sense of ecstasy that comes with religious certitude, fought from house to house until not a man, woman, or child was left alive. In the aftermath of this assault on the Bahais, Amir Kabir allowed the dualism of power between king and clergy to return to its former state.

Yet in centralizing administration, protecting the nation, and suppressing the Bahais in the name of Shia Islam, Amir Kabir wrapped Nasir ed-Din Shah in the aura of a strong, responsible monarch. Iran seemed ready to undergo another of the renaissances which so often followed national defeat. But hovering in the background was the shah's mother, Mahd Ulya.

From the *haram*, the queen mother supervised the private life of her son and participated in decisions of his government. In the tradition of the Qajar tribe, she expected to marry the shah's chief minister. Instead, Amir Kabir, a man in his early fifties, chose to marry Mahd Ulya's fourteen-year-old daughter. Furious at her rejection, the shah's power-hungry mother went to war with her son's influential minister. Amir Kabir won the first battle. On a charge of promiscuity, Amir Kabir deposited Mahd Ulya in the pious environs of Qom. In the second round, the enraged mother struck back through her son. On November 11, 1851, Nasir ed-Din Shah stripped Amir Kabir of office, snarling, "You are a plebeian of humble origin who took pride in the high positions I provided for you."[4] With both Britain and Russia maneuvering the situation to the respective advantage of each, Amir Kabir and his bride left Tehran in a closed black carriage on their way to exile in Kashan, 150 miles south of Tehran. Six weeks later, the guards who had escorted Amir Kabir from the capital led the fallen prime minister into a bathhouse at the back of the royal garden of Fin. There they executed him in a shroud of secrecy.

At the time, an episode involving a minister and the king he served was nothing more than another demonstration of how difficult it was to emancipate the government from the vested interests of the ruling elite and the arbitrary power of the shah. But since then, the period in which Amir Kabir boldly moved in the interests of Iran has taken its place in the Iranian collective psyche. He is the heroic nationalist destroyed by domestic conspiracy and foreign intervention. In the early 1950s, the martyred Amir Kabir came to life again in the collective Iranian psyche when Muhammad Mossadeq rose to challenge the forces of national impotence. In the years leading up to the Islamic Revolution, Ali Akbar Hashemi Rafsanjani, the future president of the Islamic Republic, wrote a biography celebrating the martyred prime minister.

At a time when Nasir ed-Din Shah refused to adopt the reforms that would build his country internally and Russia and Britain continued to play on Iranian weakness, Iran came face to face with the West. Despite the splendor of the court at Isfahan and the tenuous contacts that Abbas the Great made with the world beyond the borders of his kingdom, Safavid Iran had lived largely in isolation, particularly from the West. Much of the reason resided with the Ottoman Empire, with whom the Iranians had been repeatedly fighting since 1501. Controlling all the territory west of Iran, the empire of the Turks stood like a physical, cultural, and intellectual barrier between Iran and emerging Europe. Although the Persian-Shia tradition of learning provided a natural affinity for new ideas, Iran remained excluded from the reasoning of the Enlightenment, which, in turn, laid the foundations for the age of science. So as Europe embarked on the industrial revolution, Iran stayed mired in the learning and traditions of medieval Persia. Even Shiism had ceased to be a visionary force. Shia thinking, which thrives on testing new ideas, had petrified within institutions of learning conducted by men who knew little or nothing of the ongoing advancements in human knowledge. Traditional thought, bent on consecrating the imams and their time, held Iran while the West moved on politically and economically.

Iran's engagement with the West came in the aftermath of that series of military defeats the country suffered in the early nineteenth century. In the mid-nineteenth century, the West walked through Iran's door looking for spheres of influence that would bolster the strategic interests of individual countries and for markets to absorb the goods spewed out by the industrial revolution. Within their baggage of territorial and economic interests, Westerners also carried the ideas that were sweeping Western Europe. Education, science and technology, systems of law, economics, and politics fed the growth of rich, strong nation-states capable of extending their influence where they chose to go. It all stood in stark contrast to Qajar Iran, where despotism, traditionalism, illiteracy, and poverty made of Iran a backward, helpless, dismembered nation.

But there was another Iranian reaction to the Western intrusion. The sudden confrontation of a medieval culture composed of religion, philosophy, and literature with one emphasizing science and technology sparked the intellectual curiosity and skill of adaptation that so characterizes the Iranians' Persian heritage. There were among the intellectuals in the upper ranks of society those who possessed a profound appreciation of this aspect of their Persian identity. They embraced Dar-ul-Fonun Polytechnic Institute. Founded in Tehran in 1852 as a reaction to Iran's military defeats, it patterned itself after the great French military school St. Cyr. Although charged with training future military officers, Dar-ul-Fonun also taught engineering, math, foreign languages, and medicine. Within its walls, a new generation began to slip the bonds of traditional education comprised of poetry and religion.

By the end of the nineteenth century, the sons of the royal family and the landed aristocracy went to the West to school. To avoid hostile Ottoman territory and the plundering tribes of eastern Turkey, the young scholar loaded his trunks and headed north from Tehran. By carriage and horse, he scaled the Alborz Mountains to reach the Caspian port of Enzeli. A steamer carried him to Baku in Russian Azerbaijan. From there he went west to Tblisi in what is now Georgia. Boarding the railways, he traveled north to Moscow and then west again through Warsaw and Berlin before finally arriving in Paris. He stayed there four years, six years, or however long it took to complete his course of study. Then he began the arduous trip back to Iran. He arrived possessing a French education learned in the French language. Already balancing dual identities coming out of Persia and Islam, he now split between two cultures—Iranian and Western. But those around him failed to see the internal contradictions. Instead they saw a man molded by a modern Western education. To the intellectual in weak and backward Qajar Iran his presence served to emphasize the degree of the country's decline since the glorious peaks of Sassanian Persia and Safavid Iran. In response, these same intellectuals expressed uncritical admiration for European civilization and, even more, Western education. Holding pious dogmatism and the contamination of indigenous Persian culture responsible for Iran's deterioration, the educated cast aside what they deemed moribund religion to grasp secularization, Westernization, and cultural purification. As a result, interest in the country's pre-Islamic past surged among the elite. Through long evenings of discourse, they labored to rid the Persian language of its Arabic words and stoked the memory of the old Persian Empire that had always stayed alive in the Iranians' great literary tradition. In the myth of Kaveh the Ironsmith, canonized by Ferdowsi, the justification of political revolt against tyrannical rule flowed into the hands of a generation of Iranian reformers drawn to Western ideals of liberal democracy, individual freedom, and social justice.

Yet Shia Islam as much as the Persian tradition carried parallels to the political philosophy of Western liberalism. Shia theology rings with the theme of justice. Ali and Hussein both died the martyr's death in the struggle against tyranny. The imams guided the way toward a righteous society. In the absence of the Twelfth Imam, the *mujtahids* defined good and evil, right and wrong, justice and injustice. Thus, some authorities of Shia Islam found no difficulty in sharing the intellectual fascination with the West as an answer to national impotence. Liberal thinkers among the clergy weighed Western ideas, deciding to what degree they were compatible with Islam, which should be adopted, and how those might be blended with traditional Shiism.

Yet while secularists and clerics embraced much from the West, the Iranians as a people felt a new foreign invasion descending on a country repeatedly subjected to the alien. In its presence, they sensed that the Western invasion would be different from those of the Arabs, the Turks, and the Mongols. After all, the Arabs brought Islam and the Persians altered it. The Turks embraced Ferdowsi. And the Mongols built a shrine to Imam Ali. But Westerners seemed impervious to Iranian culture. They were simply too powerful and too sure in their own culture to give way as previous invaders had to the civilization of the Iranians. As important, the West presented the Iranians with a block of ideas so alien to their culture that it could not be absorbed without destroying the Iranians' own identity. Consequently, Iran's people, steeped in their own traditions, found themselves confronted by a form of modernization for which they were psychologically unprepared and faced with demands they could neither meet nor escape.

The traditionalists within the *ulama*, the great majority of the clerics, quaked before the ideas of the West descending on Qajar Iran. Regardless of what it might promise in the way of a national revival, Westernization to the guardians of Shiism meant secularization with its attendant rejection of Islam's central role in defining Iran's cultural and political identity. The traditionalists took an interest in the West only from the standpoint of defending the faith against the infidel. In their eyes, Iran's decline traced to one source—the disregard of Islamic principles and teachings. Conversely, resurrection of Iran could come only from a return to the norms of Islamic life where the revelations of the Prophet and the example of the imams provided all the knowledge a Muslim required.

This contraposition of two different cultures, one possessing technology and wielding great power and the other extolling spirituality and suffering from impotence, created the atmosphere in which Iran's uneven relationship with the West unfolded. In the Iranian response to the Western invasion, two diverse intellectual trends aimed at the reform of Qajar Iran pitted the Persian trait of openness and assimilation against the Islamic trait of insularity and traditionalism. They expressed themselves in the Constitutional Revolution of 1905 to 1911, where nationalism and the absolutism of the Qajar kings united the secularists and the clerics before the implementation of constitutional government divided the proponents of secular law from the defenders of sharia, Islamic law.

As the twentieth century approached, the brittle kingdom of the Qajars glittered with the artificial light of its ornaments. As the Sassanians had done, Nasir ed-Din Shah symbolically placed the Qajar capital at the center of the world. The roads that led out of Tehran to Shemeran, Hamadan, Isfahan, and Mashhad passed through stately gateways that broke the monotony of the long level line of earthworks that created the city's walls. Within Tehran, the doors of the rudest shops dressed themselves in glazed tiles or honeycombed plaster. And elaborate teahouses gave light to the night. But Tehran paraded more than architecture. Nasir ed-Din Shah had demolished wide areas of congested Tehran to make way for the large squares and broad boulevards which are still a distinguishing characteristic of the city. In Gulistan Palace, both the administrative core of the kingdom and the residence of the shah, the audience chamber celebrated the Qajar king's image of wealth and power. The ceiling dripped with stucco crafted to perfect proportions and the floor glistened with intricate mosaics worked in tile. A globe, twenty inches in diameter, eighty pounds in weight, recreated the world in 18,200 karats of precious stones—the Persian Gulf in emeralds, Iran itself a compact mosaic of diamonds. Beside it sat the Peacock throne, valued at thirteen million dollars in terms of the money of the day.

The titles of Nasir ed-Din matched his audience hall. He was the Shahanshah; Asylum of the Universe; Point of Adoration of the Universe; Subduer of Climate; Arbitrator of His People; Guardian of the Flock; Conqueror of Lands; and Shadow of God on Earth. He moved through his domain like the proverbial oriental potentate, surrounded by pomp and circumstance not seen in Iran since the Sassanians. It all played to the power and glory of the Qajar monarch.

To his credit, Nasir ed-Din Shah began to nudge Iran out of its isolation. In 1873, 1878, and 1889, the shah toured Europe with a large entourage including his wives and concubines.* With each royal tour, European influences on Nasir ed-Din Shah grew. By the end of his third trip, his oriental accoutrements and black mustache shaped like a scimitar had disappeared. The royal costume had transformed from baggy pants, loose tunic, wide-sleeved jacket, and pointed cap to European trousers, a long, fitted jacket with gold epaulets, a crimson sash, and a flat-topped Prussian-style hat. Only the feathery Qajar aigrette anchored by a spray of jewels stayed the same. In Gulistan Palace, Nasir ed-Din Shah placed beside a piece of gold and enamel work from Isfahan a clock from Europe in the form of a mechanical monkey playing a guitar in the garden of a Swiss chalet. On the walls, the shah's hunting trophies stared out between bad copies of French paintings.

Although Nasir ed-Din Shah expresses in his diaries an avid curiosity about all that he saw and heard in the strange world of constitutional monarchs and unveiled women, his interests as Iran's ruler concentrated on military hardware. Russian pressure on Iran's territory and British meddling to protect the gateways to India led the shah to seek Western technology found in munitions factories, cannon foundries, and powder plants. The more he saw, the more Nasir ed-Din Shah became convinced that to be strong, Iran must adopt the things of the West. Thus Iran tentatively engaged with Europe. Gathering Western weapons and bric-a-brac, Nasir ed-Din Shah left behind the cornerstone of Western civilization—the rule of law. Within the rot of Qajar Iran, the burden of oppression that fell on all but the elite accelerated. And the abuse of power flayed, mutilated, and impaled anyone who defied the established order. Although any man accused of a crime could be blown from a cannon, buried alive, or converted into a human torch, the standard penalty was the bastinado. Here the accused hung by his wrists while his jailers lashed the soles of his feet tens, hundreds, or thousands of times. Nasir ed-Din, the Shahanshah, the Guardian of the Flock, the Shadow of God on Earth, ignored it all.

Despite all the injustices, the shah stayed in power because he ruled a population fragmented into small units—families, tribes, villages, and sectors within the cities. One group remained separate from another on the basis of geography, language, religion, ties of blood, and the ceaseless competition for scarce economic resources and vital

*During the 1873 trip, Nasir ed-Din Shah shocked Victorian England by offering the comely Lady Margaret Beaufort five hundred thousand dollars to join his *haram*.

public offices that bestowed a measure of power on those who held them. There existed no political institutions or codified systems of law to check the shah's abuse of authority. Only the *ulama* could, in theory, provide the institutional backing for opposition to Qajar rule. But the clerics constituted part of the system. For generations, the sitting shah had defended Shiism as the state religion and the *ulama* had, through the prescription of religious duty to the faithful, enforced obedience to the monarch. Yet in the reign of Nasir ed-Din Shah, the gulf between the monarchy and the clergy that had begun earlier in the century widened in an atmosphere of growing absolutism.

Dissent was already whispering across the land in 1890 when Nasir ed-Din Shah decided that existing taxes and frequent raids on the fortunes of his subjects no longer filled the cavernous coffers that supported the Qajar style. He turned to growing European economic interests in Iran to provide the shah a new and more lucrative source of quick money—the sale of concessions to European companies. Exercising the prerogative of absolute monarchy, Nasir ed-Din Shah sold rights to minerals, railways, banking, and even a lottery to individuals, companies, and nations of Europe. In the exchange of concessions for cash, Qajar excesses moved beyond the individual to threaten the nation itself.

Opposition to Qajar rule found form in nationalism. The powerful feeling of distinctiveness which dwells in the deep recesses of the Iranian psyche stems from language and religion. Together the Persian tongue and Shia Islam have created a sense of nation among people inhabiting a unique piece of the planet from which they draw their identity. That territory had been dismembered by the wars of the early nineteenth century. Now Nasir ed-Din Shah seemed intent on selling the rest to the West piece by piece. Consequently it was preservation of the Iranian nation that became the focus of the turbulent political era that began in 1890 and faded in 1911. And it was the great emotional outpouring of Iranian nationalism, not Western ideas of democracy, that brought secularists and clerics, merchants and peasants, men and women together against the Qajars' feudalistic landholding system, their sloth and corruption, and their wholesale distribution of Iranian resources to foreigners.

In a society where the vast majority of the population consisted of illiterate peasants, tribesmen, and urban laborers, the movement to reform and strengthen Iran was composed primarily of intellectuals, merchants, and clerics. Each of these groups demanded that the influence of foreigners in Iran be reduced, social reforms inaugurated, and an institutional check placed on the tyranny of the court. But each also possessed its own unique character and interests.

The intellectuals, more specifically secular, educated Iranians, were the products of privileged families and the tribal elite. Many had gone West to school, where they learned Western technical knowledge and either toyed with or absorbed Western liberalism.* For them as well as for those they influenced, modernization represented a seductive new faith that promised to end Iran's impotence. In the view of these disciples of modernization, the institution of kingship as defined by the Qajars begged revision and the traditionally vaunted knowledge of the clerics, so important in Iranian culture, belonged within the anti-quated boundaries of religion. Yet in rejecting the crucial Shia compo-nent of Iranian society, the secular reformers could only talk to one another and to the merchants.

The interest of the merchants, or *bazaaris*, in reforming the Qajar system was anchored in economics. The traditional activities of the ba-zaar, which included domestic and international trade as well as exten-sive banking functions, suffered from the conditions and policies of Qajar Iran. In moving goods, the merchants contended with bad roads, poor communications, and marauding bandits. In their com-mercial activities, they operated in an archaic monetary system un-suited to world markets and unable to create sufficient capital to expand trade. Above all, the men of the bazaar found themselves in-creasingly unable to stem the tide of foreign manufactured goods flooding the market or to compete with foreign merchants and banks who enjoyed extraterritorial rights and privileges granted by Nasir ed-Din Shah. But to solve the existing problems by modernizing Qajar Iran, the merchants needed to mobilize the pious, tradition-bound masses who possessed the numbers to effect change. These masses lis-tened only to the clerics.

True to the nature of Shia Islam, the clerics split into two broadly defined camps. A small percentage shared the intellectuals' enthusiasm for Western education. They saw in the West's science and technology the keys to national power and wealth. For only power and wealth could protect Shia Iran and its Islamic culture from the unbelievers of the West who already possessed riches and strength. Malek al-Motakallemin, heralded as the "king of orators," cried to those who

*Part of the group advocating Western political thought was a collection of social dem-ocrats concentrated in Tabriz who drew their ideology from Marxism.

came to hear him preach, "Your destiny, and that of your nation and of your children, lies under the banner of science and nothing else."[5]

But it was the great liberal religious leader, Jamal ed-Din Afghani, who exemplified the reformist clergy. No man was more appalled by the political, economic, and cultural inroads the West was making into Iran than he. And no one articulated better than he the contention that conservative tradition rather than theological doctrine bore the blame for the backwardness of Qajar Iran. In the cleric's opinion, nothing in the Koran precluded the acceptance of some of the liberal and humanitarian values of the West. To the contrary, the acceptance and translation of Western ideas of social and political reform into an Islamic context would destroy much of the attractiveness the West held for Iranians. In essence, Jamal ed-Din wanted to snatch liberalism away from the secularists and turn it into a shield against Western influence in Iran.

Members of the *ulama* whose views Jamal ed-Din Afghani represented believed themselves the true Shia clerics. Upholding the great Shia tradition of inquiry and postulation, they called for broad changes in government and society. But even the most radical among the reform clerics never intended to undermine Shiism's theological underpinnings, impose his own religious authority, or establish a new creed as the Bahais had done. All of these guides to the future continued to wear the turban, study with established *mujtahids* whom they outwardly continued to serve, and upheld their Shia identity as well as Shiism's central place in the definition of the Iranian nation.

The other component within the clergy, the great majority of the *ulama*, theologically rejected Shiism's engagement with the affairs of secular government. They held to the duality of authority in Iran, where kingship and religion represented two centers of power, separate yet mutually dependent. But this part of the *ulama* also questioned whether the duality of authority still functioned as it had historically. In the timid efforts at modernization over the last several decades, the Qajar kings and their secular advisers had been slowly eroding the tacit compromise between Iran's spiritual and temporal leaders by extending the powers of the state even at the cost of implicitly abandoning religious sanction. Although Nasir ed-Din made intermittent attempts to restore some kind of viable relationship with the *ulama*, the state continued to adopt or entertain European models of administration and education. As a result, religious learning found itself increasingly relegated to the fringe of the state. This posed the great threat to the *ulama*. If the clergy became irrelevant to the corporate life of Iran, it lost its whole raison d'être. Already tottering, the carefully structured balance of power between secular and religious authority collapsed when Nasir ed-Din Shah sold another concession to foreigners.

This time, for a fee of fifteen thousand pounds a year, the shah granted the British Imperial Tobacco Company the right to buy the entire tobacco crop of Iran. While all concessions that Nasir ed-Din had sold raised popular ire, tobacco struck the raw nerve of public opinion. As word of the concession spread, the sense of outrage grew among all social classes. The tens of thousands of peasants who grew the highly prized tobacco, the thousands of small merchants who sold it, and the hundreds of thousands who smoked it realized that control of a product that came out of the sacred soil of Iran had been handed to the British. At that moment, the fragmented population of Iran coalesced. The intellectuals drawn to Western ideas of governmental accountability seized the issue to support their contention that the power of the shah must be limited. And the mullahs who controlled large amounts of agricultural land through religious endowments and maintained close links to the merchants of the bazaar spoke out on behalf of the economic interests of themselves and their followers. But the *ulama* also cried out as guardians of Islamic values. They charged that concessions to Western interests threatened to subjugate Iran's Shia Muslims to the economic and cultural dictates of Europe's infidels. And then they warned that Iran itself, "the citadel of Shia Islam," the sacred responsibility of the king who sat on the throne, was slipping into the hands of Westerners willing to satisfy the personal greed of Nasir ed-Din Shah. In December 1891, Sheikh Shirazi, the chief *mujtahid* of the day, broke the alliance between king and *ulama* by issuing a *fatva*, or religious ruling, against the tobacco concession. Invoking the authority of religion, he declared, "In the name of God, the Merciful, the Beneficent. Today the use of both varieties of tobacco, in whatever fashion, is reckoned war against the Imam of the Age [the Twelfth Imam]—may God hasten his advent." The mullahs, merchants, and intellectuals seized the *fatva*, reproduced it, and spread it across Iran with the tools of Western technology—the hectograph and the telegraph. Over every city and village, every region and class, every Muslim and non-Muslim participating in the Tobacco Protest, the *fatva* of Sheikh Shirazi flew like a battle flag. In response to its instruction, Iranians, including the wives in the *haram* of Nasir ed-Din Shah, put down their water pipes. In the face of the boycott, the shah concluded to his chief minister, "When every vermin-infested priest who so lurked in the corners of the *madressehs* . . . comes forth . . . should not some other scheme be thought of [for] . . . getting out of our troubles even if it is at great loss."[6] No longer able to pit group against group, the shah faced only one choice: cancel the concession. Twenty-two days later, on January 26, 1892, the public crier in Tehran announced that Sheikh Shirazi had lifted the *fatva*. With relief, Iranians of every class and station once more lighted up their tobacco.

This semireligious, seminationalist movement against the tobacco concession left the power of public protest as its legacy to a society steeped in the tradition of authority. Popular discontent had supplied the *ulama* with the means for a direct confrontation with Shiism's traditional enemy—secular government. But victory in the tobacco revolt also left a confusion of issues and concepts related to Islam and Iranian nationalism, religion and state, clerical and temporal authority that, each in its own way, reflected the economic, social, and political shifts occurring in late-nineteenth-century Iran as the reign of Nasir ed-Din Shah drew to a close.

After so many years on the throne, Nasir ed-Din seemed to have lost interest in governing a country that spiraled ever downward. Lacking either the application or the energy for reform, he focused his interests instead on food, drink, hunting, and the cats that accompanied him everywhere in a specially constructed cage with velvet-padded wire. His passions remained. They swirled around money and women. The money he garnered through taxes, the sale of appointments, and concessions went, in part, to support the *haram* where he exercised his infamous sexual prowess. It was populated by 1,600 wives, concubines, and eunuchs.

In 1896, the portly, aging Nasir ed-Din Shah approached the fiftieth year of his reign reckoned by the Islamic calendar. At two o'clock in the afternoon of May 1, three days before the grand celebration of his ascension to the throne was to begin, the shah visited the Shah Abdul Azim Mosque just south of Tehran. There an assassin raised his pistol and shot the Qajar king.* Fearing that word of the assassination would throw the country into chaos, Nasir ed-Din Shah's entourage sat the dead king in his carriage, wedged between his prime minister

---

*Originally the assassin, Muhammad Reza of Kerman, was assumed to have been a Bahai. Later interrogation revealed that he was a Muslim obsessed with the idea of reuniting the Sunni and Shia branches of Islam and checking the encroachment of the West into the Islamic world.

and the brougham's tufted silk side. Thus Nasir ed-Din Shah rode back to Tehran. It was left to a rather poor poet to write an epitaph:

When the night was young, the King contemplated plunder
At dawn, his body, head and crown were all asunder.

Muzaffar ed-Din, at the age of forty-three the oldest of Nasir ed-Din Shah's many sons, inherited a backward, disgruntled realm with an empty treasury. Lacking great intelligence or drive, the fifth Qajar shah reigned rather than ruled. Under his nose, nobles and courtiers amassed fortunes while the clerks in the bureaucracy often went unpaid. Irrigation systems fell into ruin, turning fields and villages back to the desert. And the Russians and the British persisted in their strategic games with Iranian territory and treasure. In 1900, the shah relinquished some more of Iran to foreigners when he financed a royal tour of Europe by borrowing twenty-two million rubles from Russia. Iranian customs receipts served as collateral. And the terms included a restriction on Iran's right to borrow money elsewhere without Russian consent while any portion of the loan remained unpaid. The last drop dripped into the bucket of grievances. The Qajars had laid their incompetent and corrupt rule on apathetic Iranians for over a hundred years. At the beginning of the twentieth century, a people abused by their king and dishonored as a nation rose up to demand a voice in the government.

Between 1905 and 1911, Iran would rumble with popular revolt. What became known as the Constitutional Revolution wound together two threads, political oppression and national sovereignty. In its headiest days, it was a broad-based movement for Iranian independence and governmental accountability. But what the revolution meant in the specific nature of government took different forms for different groups. For the secular intellectuals, it translated into the adoption of some form of Western liberalism. For the merchants, it equaled economic redress. For the reformist clerics, it converted into strength for the Shia state. For the traditionalist mullahs and their followers, it stood for reestablishing the Koran as the legal, political, social, and cultural model for society.

Before Muzaffar ed-Din Shah had settled on the throne, secret societies composed of intellectuals, bureaucrats, merchants, members of craft guilds, and clerics organized in political cells to discuss the level to which Iran had fallen. None seriously spoke of revolution, only despotism and imminent enslavement to foreigners, just government and independence. Protest broke into the open in 1905 when the director of customs, a Belgian, began to enforce with bureaucratic rigidity the tariff collections that underlay the Russian loan to Muzaffar ed-Din Shah. Other incidents, following no logical order or necessarily connected to larger events, tumbled one upon another—bread riots by the hungry and poor in Mashhad; a local political dispute in Kerman; government appropriation of land in Shiraz; a plague of locusts in Sistan; and a dozen other happenings fed into the accumulation of grievances against Qajar rule.

Intellectuals railed from speakers' platforms, and the clergy drawn to political action preached from the pulpit against the sins of Qajar Iran. Discontent and agitation jelled when the prime minister, Ain ed-Dawla, raised the price of sugar. A company of merchants took sanctuary, or *bast*, in the Royal Mosque in Tehran. Reform clerics followed on their heels, denouncing the intolerable tyranny of the king. Driven from the mosque on orders of the prime minister, the core of *bastis* took refuge in the Shah Abdul Azim Mosque, the site of Nasir ed-Din Shah's assassination. More mullahs came, bringing their flocks of religious students. Together the demonstrators claimed only one goal: the dismissal of Ain ed-Dawla, the reigning symbol of all that was wrong with Qajar Iran. Flanking a road blockade erected by government troops, intellectuals, students out of the secular schools, craftsmen, and anyone else who chose to protest poured in. When the merchants closed the bazaar, the equivalent of a massive flight from the currency, a humbled Muzaffar ed-Din Shah agreed to dismiss his prime minister. He also promised to surrender absolute power by convening the "house of justice" advocated by intellectuals influenced by Western ideas.

On January 12, 1906, the *bastis* returned to Tehran led by high-ranking *ulama* riding in royal carriages provided by the shah. A jubilant crowd lined the road to hail their returning heroes. It was at that moment that political minds realized that only the *ulama*, from their position of religious authority and relative impunity to royal wrath, could mobilize the masses, perhaps 60 percent of the population. Both the bureaucrats and the landowning class were too closely identified with the government. The merchants and tradespeople possessed material resources but lacked respect and prestige. And those who looked to the liberal West for their political ideals stood on the opposite side of a gulf of understanding with the peasant and the laborer. The intellectuals might provide the movement with a new ideology, but that ideology could only be grasped by the masses in terms of Islam. Thus in the interest of an uprising against tyranny, the men who carried the ideas of the West momentarily surrendered their ideology in order to win the street power of the *ulama*. One of the intellectuals admitted, "Because the Iranian people need fanaticism, if we receive assistance from the half-alive group of the *ulama*, we probably will achieve our goal much sooner."[7] But they would find that their alliance of convenience could not reconcile the irreconcilable secular admirers of the West and the religious defenders of Islam.

Although the intellectuals instigated revolt against absolute Qajar rule and the bazaar financed it, the *ulama* ultimately determined the revolution's course. It was the clergy that mobilized the masses in the name of justice. And it was the clergy, driven by both the grand issues of theology and the petty rivalries of men, that called a halt to reform. How the Shia clerics divided on the issue of constitutional government, what motivated various individuals and groups within the clerical establishment, and the manner in which each reacted to the unfolding events are relevant not only to the Constitutional Revolution but also, in general terms, to the era of Muhammad Mossadeq, the Islamic Revolution, and the future of the Islamic Republic.

Three clerics holding different theological views, possessing divergent personalities and ambitions, and representing competing factions within the *ulama* fought, won, and finally castrated the Constitutional Revolution. They were Muhammad Tabatabai, Abdullah Behbahani, and Fazlollah Nuri.

With piercing eyes that reflected his passion for country and religion, Muhammad Tabatabai created an imposing presence with a great white beard that connected his black turban to his black cloak. A midlevel *mujtahid* rather than a grand ayatollah, he fervently believed that in order to survive the political, economic, and cultural onslaught of foreign powers, Qajar Iran had to reform. Like other clerics who preached that Iran's future lay in education, he harbored no fear about opening Shiism to the ideas of modern science. In some ways, Tabatabai represented that which is best in the Shia clerical tradition—the incorruptible man of religion who saw in theological inquiry and discourse the strength of the faith and the welfare of the Shia state.

Tabatabai's philosophical ally was Abdullah Behbahani, another midlevel *mujtahid* who seemed to compensate for his modest clerical rank with an enormous black turban. A more worldly man than Tabatabai, Behbahani balanced his ideological commitment to reform with his own interests and ambitions. Self-serving and corruptible, Behbahani proved to be a shrewd political operative who could extol the popular will and, at the same time, promote the agendas of any number of benefactors.

The third man in the clerical triumvirate that made and then broke the Constitutional Revolution was Sheikh Fazlollah Nuri. Nuri stood lower on the social and religious ladder than even Tabatabai and Behbahani. For a man who loved power, the constitutional revolt proved a rare opportunity to move up in the world. But Nuri also fiercely held a theological point of view that placed him in the mass of the *ulama* who defined constitutional government only in terms of the sharia.

By February 1906, all groups agitating against absolute monarchy concentrated on two issues—the removal of the shah's hated prime minister and the establishment of a house of justice. But as the clock ticked, the shah neither removed his minister nor convened the house of justice. In response, the radical content of Muhammad Tabatabai's sermons grew more strident. The large crowds that flocked to his mosque to receive his message of national redemption shouted slogans at the shah's resistance to political reform. With the mullahs as the only force capable of keeping the masses mobilized, Tabatabai and Behbahani organized the *ulama* into a united front while the rest of the reformers went after tribal leaders, merchants, wealthy Zoroastrians, and even women to join the crusade to limit the power of the shah. Together they papered the walls of buildings, mosques, and *madresehs* with posters and marched in mass through the streets. Meanwhile, mullahs whispered in the neighborhoods that the Qajar tribe had assisted Yazid in his war against the sons of Ali, and Tabatabai thundered in the mosques, "We want justice, we want a majlis in which the shah and the beggar are equal before the law."[8]

The detested Ain ed-Dawla responded by calling in the shah's Cossacks, Iranian troops trained by the Russians, to impose a curfew on Tehran. On June 17, 1906, soldiers of the shah fired into a crowd of demonstrators protesting the arrest of a mullah. One of their bullets struck and killed a *talabeh* by the name of Sayyid Abdul Hamid. Suddenly, the movement had its martyr. Abdullah Behbahani led the Shia mourning rituals. Behind him, a procession of weeping men wound through the streets flagellating themselves while they held high the dead man's bloodied shirt. Women and children followed, wailing and lamenting.

"Once more Husayn hath died to please Yazid;
May God accept anew, O Prophet mine,
A thousand fold this sacrifice of thine!"[9]

The bazaar closed once again. And ranking *ulama* along with Fazlollah Nuri took sanctuary in Qom.

Abruptly, center stage of the political drama shifted to the grounds of the British embassy, where the merchants appealed for British protection against an order to open their shops or face confiscation of their goods. The British, intent on protecting their geographical position in Iran and increasingly alarmed about the growing disorder over the shah's refusal to honor his pledge of reform, agreed. Hundreds of Iranians flocked into the walled British legation to claim sanctuary.* Before the week ended, anywhere between thirteen thousand and twenty thousand men massed behind the gates of the British embassy to demand the recall of the religious leaders from Qom, the immediate dismissal of the prime minister, and a house of justice representing the people. Outside the thick brick walls of the British legation a Qajar prince shouted that the *ulama* had fallen prey to a dangerous Bahai-inspired plot to hand the nation and the religion to the British and the Russians. Inside, men of letters scribbled the words of the cause to send out to newspapers waiting to print them. For probably the first time in Iranian history, Muslim mullahs and Christian clerics stood side by side against tyranny. And everyone, rich and poor, lined up to eat from the big cauldrons of food sent in by rich merchants.

For eighteen days, the *bastis* waited out the shah. A member of the British diplomatic corps later described the atmosphere. "Perhaps the scene was most picturesque at night. Nearly every tent used to have a *rawza-khwan* [rowzeh-khan], and it was really an admirable tableau, these tents with their circles of listeners and the *rawza-khwan* at one end, relating the old, old stories of Hasan and Husayn. At the tragic parts, the audience would weep in that extraordinary Persian manner, and beat their heads in a sign of grief."[10]

Almost ninety years later, I went to the scene of the great *bast.* The same wall of brick so red that it is almost black encompasses several square blocks of scattered buildings and gardens. The area is large,

*The Russians, fearful that an alliance between the British and the revolutionaries would threaten their position in Iran, invited a small crowd to take sanctuary in the Russian embassy.

yet it is difficult to imagine how in the heat of summer thousands of people crowded into its space day after day. But images and echoes of the past cannot be hurried, they must be coaxed. So I sat down alone on a bench by the lily pond and waited. Slowly from the old clock tower and the thick, aged wisteria wound around the balustrade of the ambassador's residence and from the former stables that front the straight, narrow road where the *bastis* marched into sanctuary, the summer of 1906 came back. The multitudes of people, the cacophony of sound, and the smells of steaming *chelo kabab* floated just on the other side of reality. It was enough to sense the ferment of the time when Iranians, humiliated by others, disgusted with their own government, and touched by the West, tried to chart their future.

After the first week on the embassy grounds, the *bast* passed into the hands of the teachers and students from Tehran's few secular schools who taught and studied the knowledge of the West. They transformed an exercise of protest into an open-air political seminar. In it, the loathing of corruption, injustice, and national impotence took form in the demand for a written constitution to limit the power of the shah.

With pressure mounting from all quarters, Muzaffar ed-Din Shah finally bowed before his subjects. He dismissed Ain ed-Dawla, recalled the *bastis* from Qom, and agreed to both a constitution ensuring the equality of all before the law and a national assembly to share power with the king. The royal carriages went to Qom to once more bring religious leaders triumphantly back to Tehran. In the name of the reformers, the *mujtahid* Abdullah Behbahani proclaimed the victory of national unity and the ideal of justice. On August 10, 1906, the bazaar opened and most of the *bastis* left the British compound. By August 16, the popular uprising was over, exactly a month after it had started.

On October 7, 1906, the ailing Muzaffar ed-Din Shah, in one of his last acts as king, attended the inauguration of the Majlis, or parliament.* Before it lay the task of drafting the constitution. In the deliberations that were to follow, the distinctions between secular and religious, European and Islamic, blurred in the name of unity against the shah. As a result, the Majlis produced a document whose fifty-one articles set forth the duties, limitations, and rights of an auxiliary branch of government. Again the shah dallied and delayed signing the

---

*Membership in the assembly was restricted to males of at least thirty years of age who owned land or business property.

instrument ending absolute rule in Iran. Finally, as Muzaffar ed-Din Shah lay dying, a delegation of clergymen gathered around his bed to remind him that he was about to meet God. Going into that omniscient presence, he would be well advised to take with him some deed of great goodness to counterbalance his many sins against his people. The shah signed the constitution, the Iranian Magna Carta.

Muzaffar's son, Muhammad Ali, the sixth Qajar shah, succeeded to the throne in January 1907. An American adviser at court described him as "perhaps the most perverted, cowardly, and vice-ridden monster that had disgraced the throne of Persia in many generations."[11] Counseled by evil advisers to regain absolute power, he moved to exploit the divisions within the ranks of the reformers, now known as the Constitutionalists. Excluding members of the Majlis from his coronation ceremonies and ignoring the *mujtahids* who led the revolution, the shah lavishly entertained compliant ayatollahs and other high-ranking clerics, draining the meager resources of the state treasury to purchase expensive gifts for the compliant custodians of Shia Islam. But the real challenge to the constitution brewed among the Constitutionalists themselves.

Although supported by most of the leading *ulama,* the Iranian constitution of 1906 signified a victory for the Western-influenced reformers over the religious leaders who had mustered their followers against despotism and national shame. Written by the intellectuals captivated by Western ideas, the constitution contained a range of institutional changes that, if implemented, would shrink the authority of the *ulama.* Almost immediately, the front that staged the revolution began to crack. Beneath the commonly adopted rhetoric of popular revolt, beyond the mutually held ideal of a house of justice charged with restricting the absolute power of the king, lay the great divide between the secular-clerical reformers and the clergy-led traditionalists who hewed to the sacred rules and precisely defined precepts of Shia Islam.

Sheikh Fazlollah Nuri assumed the leadership of the traditionalists in the Majlis. Regarding himself as the most brilliant thinker in the Shia world, Nuri bitterly resented the clerical stars of the revolution, Tabatabai and Behbahani. By this stage of the revolution, Tabatabai and Behbahani had undertaken different, if complementary, roles. Lacking the temperament, organizational skills, or political savvy to lead a popular revolution, Tabatabai provided the revolution its clerical voice. Frankly admitting that he scarcely understood constitutionalism, Tabatabai still propagated its promise of security and prosperity.

Abdullah Behbahani, a natural political animal who cleverly maneuvered through the expanding labyrinth of Tehran politics, reigned as the operational leader of the reform clerics. But always at his heels was Nuri, demanding government by the sharia. Because he demanded what was in essence Islamic government, Fazlollah Nuri ranks as one of the heroes of the Islamic regime that presently governs Iran.

Nuri insisted that the constitution contradicted the sharia, the divine blueprint for a just order. Sovereignty belonged to God, the Prophet, and his family, and, in the absence of the Twelfth Imam, to the *ulama*. It could not be bestowed on the people through a man-made constitution. The liberals answered. There was no contradiction in the values of liberalism, nationalism, and Islam. The conservative clerics lashed back by branding the liberal, nationalist leaders as lackeys of the infidels bent on betraying Islam and the nation.

While Nuri pressed his virulent attack on the constitution as a Western document, the Constitutionalists within the Majlis loaded shell after shell into his cannon. From early 1907, the secular Constitutionalists unabashedly copied Europe. When they wrote the constitution for Iran, they all but duplicated the 1831 Belgian constitution. They injected into the political dialogue surrounding the Shia concept of man-made law European words with no Farsi equivalents. They even sought to replace the traditional Persian rugs on which members of the Majlis sat with European-style chairs.

For eight months, a fierce war raged over supplementary provisions to the constitution which would define the parameters of legislative authority. In its intensity, it would create a political rift that eventually drained the lifeblood from the revolution. The fiery debate swirled around two broad issues: the precise limitations on the shah's authority and the explosive sociocultural questions concerning institutional and legal reforms aimed at the modernization of Iranian society. Not the least of these was the erosion of clerical authority threatened by the secularization sought by the Constitutionalists. Although every member of the Majlis looked after his own interests and often hid his real opinions and motives by practicing *taqiyeh*, the traditionalists generally lined up against the modernizers. Included among these modernizers were the Constitutionalist clerics who wrapped their novel ideas in traditional religious rhetoric and continued to wear their cloaks and turbans.

Nuri, adamant in his effort to ensure the supremacy of Islamic law, proposed an addition to the constitution to ensure just that. In a compromise forged to save the constitution from total destruction, Nuri won concessions for the *ulama*, including a council of five *mujtahids* to sit at the gateway of legislation. The Supplementary Laws of 1907 decreed, among other things, that all legislation passed by the Majlis be reviewed by a council of five *mujtahids* who as a committee "shall discuss and thoroughly investigate the bills brought in by the National Assembly and reject every one . . . that is contrary to the sacred precepts of Islam in order that it not become law."[12] But the provision never went into effect because the Constitutionalists refused to concede so much power to their clerical rivals in the Majlis, who lacked the unity to force the issue. It was not until the constitution for the Islamic Republic of Iran was written in 1979 that the clerics won veto power over legislation.

Nuri kept up the attack. Gathering power from money provided by the shah and an alliance with the royalists, he and his followers verbally assaulted the constitution in mosques, *madresehs*, and public squares, charging that European emulators schemed to destroy Islam by eradicating the sharia. These same followers of the West who held European knowledge superior to the knowledge of the Prophet would divert government money from religious pilgrimage sites to construct factories and railroads. These "infidels and Bahais" would legalize alcoholic beverages, houses of prostitution, and schools for women. As each side fired charge and counter-charge, the religious centers trembled with virulent political-theological debate that pitted the clerics following Nuri against those following Tabatabai and Behbahani. The Majlis finally delivered fragile peace by way of a written promise that the constitution would limit monarchial tyranny, not undermine the principles or spirit of Islam.

Now it was time for the Constitutionalists to split. The issue was the proposal to guarantee equal rights under the law to non-Shia. Realistically looking at a population that was over 90 percent Shia, Tabatabai saw no danger to the Shia state from non-Shia. But for Behbahani, liberalism which recognized the Zoroastrian, Christian, and Sunni as equal to the Shia went too far. On this issue, the master of clerical politics swung over to Nuri's argument that the Constitutionalists intended to destroy the exalted position of the sharia and the prerogatives of the clergy. Behbahani and some of the clerics, without whom the revolution could not have succeeded, had come to understand just what the Constitutionalists' stress on secularism meant to the Shia state and to themselves.

But they were not the only ones to desert the revolution. In a culture which demands a charismatic leader, the constitutional movement had failed to produce one magnetic personality capable of sustaining reform. The Western-tainted Constitutionalists could speak the language of the West but not the language of the masses. No *mujtahid* commanded the reverence to wield the authority of the just jurist. Without a charismatic religious leader, the merchants felt no compulsion to continue the fight for reform once their economic demands had been met in the initial revolt. Coming full circle, the intellectuals with no tradition of participatory politics drifted back to their parlors, where words constituted all political action.

During the wrangling between the Constitutionalists and Nuri, Muhammad Ali Shah succeeded to the Qajar throne. Taking advantage of the bitter dissension in the ranks of the Constitutionalists, he sent anti-Constitutionalist preachers, protected by hired ruffians and the shah's Cossacks, to set up tents in Tupkhaneh Square on one of Tehran's main thoroughfares. From there, they marched toward the Majlis, chanting, "We want the Koran; we do not want a constitution." However, it was the West that delivered the coup de grâce to the Constitutionalists. The preceding August, the 1907 Anglo-Russian agreement had divided Iran into a Russian zone in the North and a British zone in the South. (See chapter 6.) With no further need to counter each other, both powers were positioned to militarily intervene in Iranian affairs. Deciding that the shah rather than the Constitutionalists could give Iran order, the British, in contradistinction to 1906, deserted the reformers. Russia, with troops on the ground in northern Iran, supported the shah's ambitions to destroy the Majlis and with it the restrictions on his power. In terms of force, the shah and his foreign allies seemed to hold all the cards. But in terms of emotion, the collusion of shah and foreigner called back many who had waged the revolution.

With the shah and the Majlis locked in combat over power and appointments, protestors gathered in the Sepahsalar Mosque on June 23, 1908. Guns under the control of Russian officers ringed the mosque and the nearby Majlis building. For six hours, attackers and defenders exchanged fire. When they ceased, the building that had for almost two years represented the people's stand for justice lay in ruins. Most of the protestors holed up in the Sepahsalar Mosque went to jail, including Behbahani, Tabatabai, and a cousin of the shah. Those who escaped the initial sweep were later arrested and, in some cases, put before the firing squad.

Still the revolution refused to gasp its last breath. Resistance to
the shah's coup against the Majlis came from Tabriz. For four months
after guns silenced the voice of the parliament, Tabriz stood alone in
defense of the constitution. The Mujahedin, the proconstitution forces,
fought bloody skirmishes against the shah's soldiers. In October 1908,
the opponents of the shah won. But on April 29, 1909, Tabriz's heroic
resistance ended when Russian troops put the city under siege. While
many Tabrizis starved or subsisted on grass in early 1909, other Iranians revolted in Rasht in the North, Mashhad in the East, Bandar
Abbas in the South, and Isfahan and Shiraz in the Persian heartland.

Help for the surviving Constitutionalists arrived from an unexpected source—the sacred Shia religious center at Najaf, in Iraq. Despite the attacks by Nuri and the other conservative clerics, three of
Shiism's most respected scholars gave religious sanction to the constitution as a religiously acceptable means to check the tyranny of the
king. One among them went so far as to bestow on the individual,
along with the *mujtahids*, the responsibility for supervising government in the absence of the Twelfth Imam. He, in effect, sanctified the
political concept of authority of the people.

With religious cover and the European powers shifting their interests once more away from the shah, the Constitutionalists began to
move south from Tabriz toward Tehran. From the Isfahan region, an
army of Bakhtiari tribesmen massed to march north. On July 15,
1909, Constitutionalists in Tehran seized the city's south gate, leading
a frightened Muhammad Ali Shah to take refuge in the Russian legation. Considering this an ipso facto abdication, the reconstituted Majlis deposed Muhammad Ali. As the revolution had aimed at limiting
the power of the king, not abolishing the monarchy, the Majlis chose
as his successor his corpulent twelve-year-old son, Sultan Ahmed, the
last Qajar shah.

In the aftermath of the Constitutionalist victory, a court tried and
condemned Fazlollah Nuri to death as a traitor to the constitution. He
came to the gallows in his turban and cloak, showing no emotion or
fear. Refusing even in death to surrender to his rivals, Tabatabai and
Behbahani, Nuri shouted to the gathered crowd, "On the Day of
Judgment these men [i.e., my judges and executioners] will have to
answer to me for this. Neither was I a 'reactionary' nor were Sayyid
Abdu'llah [Behbahani] and Sayyid Muhammad [Tabatabai] 'constitutionalists': it was merely that they wished to excel me, and I
them, and there was no question of 'reactionary' or 'constitutional'
principles."[13]

The second Majlis lasted until 1911 before internal dissension, apathy of the masses, antagonisms from the upper class, and open enmity from Britain and Russia combined to extinguish the spirit of reform and independence that had begun to sweep Iran in 1905. As the constitutional movement edged toward its final collapse, few stepped forward to save it. The intellectuals, never succeeding in convincing the population of the real promises of modernization, had retreated. The *ulama*, never able as a whole to reconcile constitutionalism and Shiism, returned to their traditional stance against profane government. Their allies of the bazaar followed the lead of the clerics. That left the landed gentry that once sided with the shah to dominate the Majlis, checking any radical alteration of their privileged position. Law and order teetered as neither the shah nor the Majlis could provide strong central government. Periodically a little band of protestors in the provinces would march to the local telegraph office, send off a violently worded telegram to Tehran, and then melt away, disappearing down the narrow, walled alleyways to take refuge in centuries of political passivity. For the uneducated urban masses who provided the manpower of revolution, the Majlis, having failed to produce a better life for the people, could no longer claim authority.

But again it was foreigners who delivered the final blow to functional constitutional government. Reform of the state's financial structure mandated by the Majlis promised to give Iran more independence from foreign control until Russia, supported by Britain, issued an ultimatum against the plan. The shah accepted that ultimatum, the Majlis rejected it. With the parliament once again facing extinction under foreign guns, it fell to women to make the last dramatic gesture for the constitution.

During the constitutional struggle, a small but dedicated group of women, including the daughters of several prominent *ulama*, acted as couriers for the Constitutionalists. Utilizing their veils as a tool of concealment, they transferred messages and arms between various revolutionary hideouts. Despite the fact that the Majlis had refused to consider bestowing the vote on females, several hundred women surrounded the entrance to the parliament to protest the Russian ultimatum. Reprimanding men for being "unworthy sons of our fathers," a few of the demonstrators broke through the door of the Majlis, crying, "Independence or death." Holding their chadors closely around them, they walked through the deputies. At the front of the chamber, they turned to face the assembly, tore away their veils, and announced their intention to kill their husbands, their sons, and themselves if just rule and national independence died before them. It was to no avail. On December 24, 1911, the shah's cabinet, backed by twelve thousand Russian troops in northern Iran, executed a coup d'état against the Majlis. The Constitutionalists could only watch as the shah's forces roughly expelled the deputies, threatening them with death if they returned. It was a sordid end to what had been a heroic effort to bring justice to Iranian society and autonomy to the Iranian nation.

The Constitutionalists lost the revolution because the traditionalists of the *ulama* refused to allow the Iranians to adopt ideas and methods that could help address the monumental problems that stood between Iran and the twentieth century. At the other extreme, the modernizers who so enthusiastically embraced Western ideas failed to recognize that modernization in an exclusively Western mode demanded the same values and attitudes that underlay Western culture and advancement. In the Iran of Persia and Islam these did not exist. Thus, in trying to impose on Iran an alien culture, the modernizers unwittingly robbed the Iranians both of their sense of identity and their chance to build a new social order from their own traditions. For their part, the foreigners, Britain and Russia, tragically denied the Iranians the time needed for the political maturing process that should have occurred with the establishment of the Majlis. Consequently, they left unfilled the Iranian desire to limit the power of the monarchy and the demand for national sovereignty. As a result, the Iranians in the aftermath of the Constitutional Revolution focused their attention and their emotion on the negative goal of destroying foreign interference rather than on the positive task of sifting through traditional attitudes and institutions to build a modern nation.

The irony is that despite the foreigners and the Iranians themselves, the central core of the Constitutional Revolution, the concept of a Majlis representing the authority of the people, survived. Battered by events beyond its scope, wounded by those who sat on the throne, the idea of constitutional government burrowed into Iranian culture. It did so because authority of the people rose out of the traditions of both Persia and Islam. In the concept of Persian kingship, the shah earns the allegiance of his people by ruling on the side of right. Those who choose to follow the path of darkness and injustice give to their subjects the right to depose them. In Shia Islam, the *mujtahids* gain their position through their followers. As representatives of not only the Twelfth Imam but of those who look to them as spiritual guides, the just jurists according to the theology of Shiism make their decisions in the interests of the people. Thus through the combinations of the Iranians' two cultural traditions, the constitution which began as a Western-inspired idea found a cultural home among the Iranians, who carried it through the dynasty of the Pahlavis and into the Islamic Republic.

6

Reza Shah:
To the Glory
of the Nation

A SHORT STRING OF PASSENGER CARS, THEIR PAINT OXIDIZED by time to a dull gray, waited on the track of Tehran's Central Train Station. It was already half an hour past departure time and the doors refused to open. On an average of every thirty seconds, some self-appointed deputy of the waiting passengers thrust forward, pounded on a locked door with one or both fists, and yelled, *"Bazkon!"* ("Open!") Nothing happened. At last, when the big hands of the dirty old station clock approached the hour mark past the posted departure time, a squadron of conductors folded back the barriers. Everyone rushed forward, pushing me and my basket of food up the high steps and into an aged, worn coach. By the ratio of seats to people and baggage, it looked like a significant percentage of us was going to stand on the trip over the Alborz Mountains to Sari on the Caspian Sea's coastal plain. But with that uniquely Iranian talent of stacking bundles, children, and themselves, everyone wedged into some kind of sitting position.

An abrupt blast from the whistle pierced the noise in the coach. I peered around the crack in the window and saw great puffs of steam escape from beneath the train, rise, and disappear in the early spring sky. The big engine strained forward, then slowly gathered speed before beginning the climb into the Alborz. Snow blown down from the peaks during the winter surrounded little villages tucked against the mountains. Behind stands of half-naked poplar trees, flat-topped houses composed of pale yellow walls climbed like stair steps up the hills. We had reached the heart of the Alborz and were laboring on toward their summit.

I have always loved trains. But as we twisted through the steep, narrow passes, I rather uncomfortably concluded that I had never been on a railroad that challenged such steep terrain. I took my eyes away from the window long enough to pour the last glass of tea out of my thermos when the stout woman sitting next to me tapped me on the shoulder and nodded. I looked out to see a series of stone bridges carrying track zigzag up the mountain. Conscious of how slowly the straining train was already moving, I pictured the cars dragging the engine backward into the deep ravine. By the look on her face and her grip on the hold bar in front of her, my seatmate obviously thought the same thing. Yet inch by inch, the train conquered the six bridges and four tunnels that lay within a radius of nine hundred feet. Once over the summit, we plunged down toward the town of Sari, eighty-five feet below sea level. As we pulled into the station, I concluded that the Iranian National Railroad, completed in 1938, is more than a means of transportation. It stands as a steel, stone, and mortar testament to the will of Reza Shah, the first Pahlavi.

The short-lived Pahlavi dynasty that began in 1925 with Reza Shah and ended in 1979 with his son, Muhammad Reza Shah, ascended out of the chaos of Iran following World War I. Ruptured by its own internal divisions and denied control over its destiny by alien states, Iran hovered near the nadir of its long history. In 1921, a little-known military officer by the name of Reza Khan grasped the debilitated nation. Over the next four years, he crushed rebellion against the rule of Tehran and rode the changing political tides of Iran's foreign tormentors. Declared Reza Shah by the Majlis in 1925, he began his task of building a nation to his personal specifications—a revitalized Iran freed from the rapacious hands of foreign powers. Committed to a model of modernization structured on Western education and Western technology, he judged Shia Islam to be the major obstacle to his vision. As a result, the institutions and symbols of Shia Islam, the second element in the Iranians' dual identity, underwent the onslaught of the Pahlavi king. While elevating the Iranians' Persian identity in support of a modernized Iran, Reza Shah laid an authoritarian hand on the ideal of just rule, the critical underpinning of Persian kingship. Reza Shah succeeded in delivering Iran from near extinction. But in doing so, he violated core values in both the traditions of Persia and Islam.

* * *

In 1919, two years before the future Reza Shah declared his presence, Iran lay bruised and bloodied in the wreckage of the Constitutional Revolution and the backwash of World War I. The Qajar capital
composed of low, dust-colored buildings collected behind earthen walls
had lost the thin glitter applied in the late nineteenth century by Nasir
ed-Din Shah. Tehran was a backwater, untouched by the waves of
change engendered by the industrialized world. Every item in the
stream of commercial goods trickling into or out of the city moved on
the backs of pack animals. Boxes and bales strapped on the humps of
camels traveled six, eight, or ten weeks from Baghdad to the west or
Karachi to the east. Communication with Europe came in small packets
of mail that arrived every two or three weeks in dispatch cases lashed
to the running board of a muddy motorcar belonging to the British legation, guarded by an Indian soldier riding shotgun.

Within the city's maze of narrow, crooked streets, the population
of three hundred thousand had been reduced by a sixth in the epidem-
ics of typhus and typhoid that invaded during the Great War. More
disease lurked in the trash-filled *jubes* that served the common people
as drinking fountain, wash trough, and toilet. In every season, the air
hung heavy with smoke from the thousands of dung fires over which
the poor to the south and east of the old bazaar cooked their small
daily portions of rice. In this squalor, where superstition flourished as
a substitute for knowledge, dervishes with long matted hair and
patchwork cloaks traded cures for infertility or recitations of poetry for
a few nearly worthless coins.

In a sense, Tehran was Qajar Iran. The gutted Qajar monarchy
controlled only the capital and a few other large towns. Outside their
boundaries, central authority vanished. On the dirt tracks that comprised the main roads, no signpost pointed directions and no policeman or soldier provided protection. That meant that the caravans
moving goods across the spaces of Iran could travel for hundreds of
miles in any direction without meeting anyone remotely attached to
the shah's government. For every area of Iran belonged to whoever was
strong enough to enforce his rule. Often the enforcers of order were
the provincial governors, who wielded power through their private armies, and the great landlords, who held as fiefdoms the tens of thousands of villages where 90 percent of the population lived. Yet on the
roads, governors and landowners proved as vulnerable as anyone else.
Tribes in pursuit of power and booty disrupted transportation and
communication between Tehran and the provinces, rendering the vil-

lages isolated oases in a desert of social chaos. And in every far-off corner of the land, it was the tribes that ruled—the Kurds in the Northwest, the Turkomans in the Northeast, the Bakhtiaris and Qashqais in Fars, the Baluchis in the Southeast, the Lurs in the mountain ranges of the West, the Arabs in Khuzistan, and on and on.

The promise of national revival that the Constitutionalists held aloft in 1905 had smothered in the internal dissension among both secular and religious intellectuals over what the revolution actually meant. Among the uneducated masses, the concept of constitutional law never permeated their ignorance. By 1919, the word *mashruteh*, or constitutional government, meant to the nomad, peasant, or laborer only disorder. The Majlis still survived, but within its councils, landlords, courtiers, and bureaucrats who controlled the parliament squabbled like an estranged family over the spoils of government. Cabinet succeeded cabinet, each voicing high-sounding aims and executing corrupt deeds. The shah, twenty-year-old Sultan Ahmed, was still young and inexperienced. He was also cowardly and corrupt, concerned only with his personal well-being. It all left Iran wallowing in its old factionalism, where the sense of nation beyond culture and faith remained a half-finished creation.

Feeding the turmoil and benefiting from the results were the foreigners, specifically Britain and Russia. In the heart of Tehran, the enormous embassies representing the lion and the bear faced each other across Nofl Leshato Street as brooding reminders of foreign dominance over Iran.

Russian lust for Iranian territory had begun when Peter the Great envisioned in the collapsing Safavid dynasty the promise of warm-water ports. Yet it was not until the Qajars sat on the throne that Russia and Iran actually engaged in territorial competition.* At the time, Iran considered that its northern border corresponded roughly to the current border between Georgia and Russia. But between 1804 and 1828, that changed. Iran lost to Russia Georgia, Armenia, and northern Azerbaijan, as well as all the territory between the Caucasus Mountains and the Caspian Sea.† These were the territorial losses that ignited interest in Western learning which fed the Constitutional Rev-

---

*Iran also contended with the Ottoman Empire for territory. After a series of conflicts spanning several decades, the two countries established a mutually acceptable boundary in 1639 which protected Iran against further Turkish incursion.
†In later engagements, Russia took Tashkent, Samarkand, and other cities Iranians considered as part of historic Iran although not part of Qajar territory.

olution of 1906. But it would be Britain, not Iran, that stopped Russia.

By the middle of the nineteenth century, Britain saw Iran as a sentry before the jewel in the crown of the British Empire—India. Chosen by geography, Iran formed the gateway to the invasion routes through the northern tier of the Indian subcontinent; straddled the communications lines between mother country and colony; and bordered the Persian Gulf, the outlet to the Indian Ocean and the sea lanes to Bombay. When Nasir ed-Din Shah foolishly tried to reclaim the Afghanistani city of Herat for Iran, Britain forced entry into the Qajar kingdom through the Treaty of Paris of 1857. For the rest of the nineteenth century and into the twentieth, imperial Britain and imperial Russia, each in pursuit of its own interests, stalked Iran. Yet because neither power could significantly advance without risking a major war with the other, feeble Iran hung on to life, a pawn to the ambitions of Russia and the concerns of Britain. In 1889, Lord Curzon, architect of British policy in the East, actually put territorial competition into the context of a game. "Turkestan, Afghanistan, Transcaspia, Persia—to many these names breathe only a sense of utter remoteness or a memory of strange vicissitudes and moribund romance. To me, I confess, they are pieces on a chessboard upon which is being played out a game for the domination of the world."[1] So it was that as year followed year, the Iranians, embroidering harsh reality with a degree of exaggeration, came to believe that the hand of the foreigner manipulated every element of Iranian life. Too often, events confirmed perception.

In 1907, during the drama of the Constitutional Revolution, the rivalry between Britain and Russia that kept Iran marginally independent ended. Adversaries turned into allies when Britain perceived new danger to India in the German plan to build a railroad across the Middle East to the Persian Gulf and Russia grappled with the aftermath of its losing war against its Asian rival, Japan. In the face of new challenges to both, logic demanded the elimination of Iran as a zone of conflict between the two. The Anglo-Russian Agreement of August 1907 paid lip service to Iran's independence and territorial integrity before dividing the country into British and Russian spheres of interest. Russia took the North, Britain the South, leaving Iran with the neutral zone in the middle, which included Tehran. On the floor of the British House of Commons a member shamed by the actions of his nation stood to protest: "Persia is the ghost at the feast which we are celebrating with Russia in honour of this convention. This small nation

... is lying between life and death, parcelled out, almost dismembered, helpless and friendless at our feet."² But the British weekly the *Spectator* voiced the majority opinion. "When a country cannot manage its own affairs, and cannot keep order among its own people, it has already lost its independence; and in that sense Persia has long ceased to be an independent State."³

A year after the Anglo-Russian Agreement, Britain acquired another interest in Iran beyond blocking Russian expansion toward India. It was oil.

Even before the dawn of the twentieth century, it was a known fact that petroleum lay at the head of the Persian Gulf. The Bakhtiari had long skimmed black film off puddles of water along the coast to smear on sores and wounds and had traded pitch to the Arabs to caulk the giant reed boats that plied the Tigris and Euphrates. In 1901, the Australian William Knox D'Arcy secured from Muzaffar ed-Din Shah the right to search for, obtain, exploit, carry away and sell all Iranian oil save that in the five northern provinces jealously guarded by Russia.* Seven years later, British geologists discovered great pools of petroleum under the British concession in the British sphere of influence. Ironically, the precise spot where the first drill bore into the bountiful Masjid-e-Sulemain Field once held an imposing terrace of Cyclopean stone built by the ancient Persians. By 1913, the year the British Admiralty decided to convert from coal to oil, Britain had essentially claimed southern Iran. After Iranian oil helped fuel the Royal Navy to victory in World War I, Britain drove its stakes even deeper into Iranian soil.

The government of Iran realized little from its rich natural resource. Arab and Bakhtiari tribal chiefs who controlled the remote oil-producing areas of Khuzestan negotiated independent agreements with the British oil company as though the Iranian central government did not exist. When the British decided to build one of the largest refineries in the world at Abadan, it struck its deal with the sheikh of Mohammara. Controlling management, ownership, and operation of the oil company, it was the British who set the price of oil, the amount of output, and the destinations to which it was sent. And it was the British who applied their own formulas in determining revenues to the Iranian government.

The ghost of oil-based colonialism still lives in Ahwaz on the

---

*The British defused Russian opposition to the concession by presenting the Russian delegation in Tehran a text written in Farsi at a time when its translator was out of town.

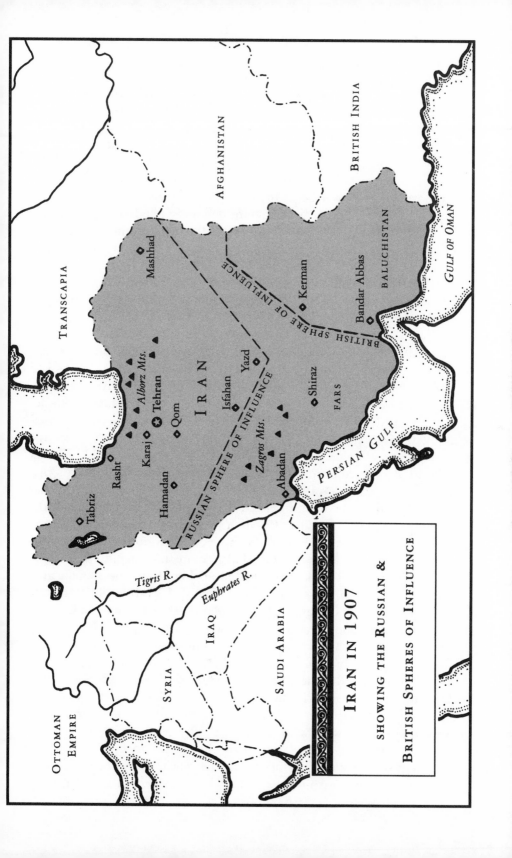

IRAN IN 1907

SHOWING THE RUSSIAN &
BRITISH SPHERES OF INFLUENCE

Karun River ninety miles northeast of the Abadan refinery. On the fringe of the oil field outside of town, a little wad of flat-topped stucco houses battered by years of sun and humidity await their inevitable decay. No one lives in them now. Perhaps that is why they still retain a peculiar English flavor. Lined up precisely, one next to the other, each is connected to the deserted street by a broken walk bordered by what were once flower beds. In style, the front door and the windows are not exactly English but they are definitely not Iranian. Therefore it is easy to imagine that within the small sitting rooms behind those doors and windows a scrap of curtain from the mills of Birmingham or a broken piece of Sheffield flatware lies on the dusty floor. Yet it is the fence, tumbled and broken, that once physically divided the British who ran the oil fields from the Iranians whose oil they pumped that so precisely puts this place in the history of impotent Iran.

In 1911, the Majlis, in an attempt to give the Iranian government authority and financing, summoned an American named W. Morgan Shuster to reorganize Iran's chaotic and corrupt tax system. Young and naive in the ways of Iran and its foreign intruders, Shuster organized a gendarmery and began collecting back taxes from delinquent taxpayers in the upper echelons of Iranian society. In his efficiency, Shuster's great error was his refusal to recognize the prerogatives of Iran's foreign interlopers. In November 1911, Shuster ordered his tax collectors to take possession of the house of a Qajar prince living in exile in Russia. The contingent of Russian troops that stopped them at the door, in effect, denied the government of Iran the right to exercise its authority in the Russian sphere of influence. Shuster ignored them and took his tax police in. But neither the fearless American nor the sinewless Majlis could stand against Russia. In two ultimatums, Russia demanded an apology from the Iranian government and the dismissal of Shuster. The shah's cabinet immediately yielded to Russian demands. But the Majlis refused, responding to the words and emotions of a Shia cleric within its membership: "It may be the will of Allah that our liberty and our sovereignty shall be taken from us by force, but let us not sign them away with our own hands."[4]

Thousands of Russian troops accompanied by their menacing artillery poured into northern Iran by land and sea. From the Caspian port of Enzeli, they began the 220-mile march toward Qasvin, near Tehran. The Iranians resisted with the most effective weapon they commanded—religion. The *ulama* called the people to boycott Russian and English goods and businesses. In the south, an ayatollah declared the notes of the British-owned Imperial Bank of Persia unclean, causing mass conversions to Iranian-minted coins. In Tehran, mullahs led huge demonstrations that wound through the capital shouting "death or independence." Meanwhile, the Majlis with its clerical contingent steadfastly refused to give in to Russian demands. All proved impotent gestures. On December 24, 1911, Russian troops shelled the parliament building, destroying the Second Majlis and with it the Constitutional Revolution. The same day, Russian troops began to massacre the inhabitants of Tabriz. On New Year's Day, they hung the chief cleric. A week later, W. Morgan Shuster resigned.* The defeated American later charged, "It is in the pursuit of 'Russian interests' or 'British trade' that innocent people have been slaughtered wholesale. Never a word about the millions of beings whose lives have been jeopardized, whose rights have been trampled under foot and whose property has been confiscated."[5]

The Majlis dispersed by Russia in 1911 reconvened in November 1914, three months after World War I began in Europe. Although it declared its strict neutrality in the war, Iran, at its end, found itself occupied piecemeal by the Russians, the British, and the Ottomans. The nation's finances were so bankrupted that the government paid its civil servants the only way it could—with bricks from the rubble of old buildings. Iran had remained intact and marginally independent only because the Russian revolution took Russia, for a time, out of contention for Iran. With Germany defeated and Russia in the throes of civil war between the democrats and the Bolsheviks, Britain's routes to India and its Iranian oil fields seemed secure. The time appeared ripe for Britain to turn Iran into a docile and well-run British protectorate under the Anglo-Persian Treaty of August 19, 1919.

Britain imposed its will on rotting Qajar Iran, where the moribund social, economic, educational, and judicial systems cried for reform. In response to foreign intrusion and domestic chaos, the Iranians whispered *harj-o-marj*, a Farsi term suggesting the worst thing that can happen to a nation. Into this abyss, a charismatic leader fitting Persian mythology came forth to restore the nation. His name was Reza Khan, the man who became Reza Shah of the Pahlavi dynasty.

Reza Khan was born March 16, 1878, into a family one step above the ordinary. They lived in the little village of Elasht in the heart of

---

*The departure of Shuster also resulted from Iranian domestic politics. The aristocratic members of the cabinet opposed Shuster because the reforms threatened their vested interests.

the Alborz Mountains, historically the least accessible part of Iran. Perhaps this is why the inhabitants of Elasht's humble stone and plaster cottages prided themselves on their pure Persian ancestry and boasted that they had accepted Islam only after it acquired a Persian patina. Around the fires on winter nights they told the stories of Ferdowsi, who set many of the scenes of the *Shahnameh* in these valleys.

The scion of a military family, Reza Khan as a tall teenager of fifteen or sixteen joined the old Cossack Division, a Russian-trained force originally organized to protect the Qajar shahs. With his six-foot, three-inch frame, bushy karakul hat, and long tunic laced with rows of cartridges, Reza Khan created an imposing figure not easily forgotten by his superiors. Possessing a savage temper and a passion for mechanized warfare, the boy from Elasht became known as "Reza Khan-e-Maximi," Machine Gun Reza. Gradually the colorful figure rose through the ranks, becoming a brigadier in command of the detachment stationed at the city of Hamadan. He strode onto the stage of Iranian history at the age of forty-three, a huge, scowling, iron-jawed man with a large nose and piercing eyes who emitted a magnetic presence.

Reza Khan might have remained what he was, a midlevel military officer, if the Bolshevik Revolution had not washed up on the Iranian side of the Caspian Sea in the form of the Soviet Republic of Gilan. In February 1921, the British, reacting to the Bolshevik presence in northern Iran, demanded command of the Cossack Division. But officers within the Cossacks, led by Reza Khan, acted before the Iranian government could say yes. In the name of freedom from foreign interference, the division marched from Qazvin to Karaj, about thirty miles from Tehran. There Sayyid Zia al-Din, a journalist turned political activist, joined them. Together the military and political wings of a nascent movement of Iranian nationalism moved on to Mehrabad, the present site of Tehran's airport. A frightened Sultan Ahmed Shah, at the moment more afraid of the insurgents than of the British, bowed by appointing Reza Khan the Cossack commander. Later the same day, Reza Kahn issued his first order. "Fellow soldiers! You have offered every possible sacrifice in the defense of the land of your fathers. All of us have, in the forests and marshes of Gilan, with empty stomachs and ragged uniforms in the pelting rain, together exposed our breasts to the bullets of the Bolsheviks and the rebels. But we have to confess that all our loyalty has served merely to preserve the interests of a handful of traitors in the capital. . . . These insignificant men are the same treacherous elements who have sucked the last drop of the nation's blood. . . ."⁶

At half past midnight on February 21, 1921, Reza Khan led three thousand Cossacks into Tehran to take up positions at key points. He and his men moved on to arrest the entire cabinet before forcing the quivering Sultan Ahmed Shah to appoint him commander of all the armed forces and to install Sayyid Zia al-Din as prime minister. Although laying no claim to a ministerial post for himself, Reza Khan, from the dawn of the coup until 1941, would impose his will on Iran.

Reza Khan harbored a soldier's contempt for Tehran's bungling, self-seeking politicians willing to surrender themselves and their country to foreigners. His own creed, molded from his experiences as an ordinary soldier under the command of Russian officers, held as a sacred tenet that no foreigner, however well intended, would ever put the interests of Iran before those of his own country. As a consequence, Reza Khan invested Iran's salvation in a wholly Iranian military force, armed and trained to the maximum of the country's resources. Through this military power created by its own citizens, Iran would free itself from foreign exploitation and restore a measure of the greatness it had once known. Therefore, while the politicians maneuvered along their well-worn course, Reza Khan pulled the Cossack Division, the ceremonial palace guard, and a motley collection of provincial levies into one force wearing a common uniform. Then he began to quell his chaotic country.

When Reza Khan looked across Iran, he saw Gilan in the control of the Bolsheviks; Azerbaijan and Khorasan seething with separatist movements; and oil-rich Khuzestan functioning as an autonomous, British-sponsored sheikhdom. Elsewhere the tribes operated as virtual masters of their own territories. Beginning in December 1921, Reza Khan and his new army crushed the leader of the Gilan rebellion in its center of Rasht before driving the Bolsheviks across the Soviet border. In like manner, he quelled the rebellions in Azerbaijan and Khorasan, completing the recovery of Iran's three most economically important provinces. He then turned to the tribes, pacifying the Kurds in the Northwest by brute force and reigning in the banditry and the mayhem of the Qashqai and Bakhtiari in the South. By the middle of 1923, only one part of the country remained outside the control of Tehran—the semiautonomous sheikhdom of Sheikh Khazal Sardar-e Qadas of Mohammara in the province of Khuzestan.

To the intellectual and the merchant, the peasant and the laborer, the Zoroastrian priest and the Shia cleric, Reza Khan assumed the position of mythic hero. In stark contrast to the rotating cabinets of professional politicians and the whining shah who constantly complained of the contempt with which his army commander treated him, Reza Khan personified patriotic pride and national resurgence. Nonetheless, his all-consuming crusade to revive his nation had required the help of the same foreign powers who had done so much to debilitate Iran in the first place. By 1921, the year Reza Khan seized military control, Bolshevik Russia had overreached itself. Accepting cooperation rather than domination, the Communist government canceled the Iranian debt and transferred ownership of both the Imperial Bank of Russia and the Julfa Railway in the north to the Iranian government. With the Bolsheviks no longer threatening to extend south, Britain reevaluated its own position in Iran. Official British policy danced around the ways in which His Majesty's government might gracefully withdraw from Iran without leaving behind chaos to stalk the oil fields and woo back the Bolsheviks. In Reza Khan, the British beheld the strongman capable of taming Iran. To this end, Britain was willing to sacrifice Sheikh Khazal Sardar-e Qadas of Mohammara.

The sheikh of Mohammara lived under the protection of the British government, bent on keeping His Majesty's oil interests out of the hands of Tehran. But the sheikh miscalculated the tensile strength of his British shield when plunged in the fire ignited by the compatible interests of Britain and Reza Khan. At the time he began to intrigue with the Iraqi government on the annexation of Khuzestan, the British stepped aside to allow Reza Khan to throw down his gauntlet. Having moved into the political realm when he assumed the office of prime minister on October 28, 1923, Reza Khan announced that he would use his new authority to personally lead a military campaign against the sheikh and his tribal allies. Immediately the Bakhtiaris and Lurs, who as nomads had already suffered Reza Khan's wrath, deserted the sheikh. Consequently, when Reza Khan arrived in Shiraz on November 15 en route south, he found a groveling telegram of surrender from the sheikh of Mohammara. The victory of Iran's prime minister exceeded the defeat of one man or one region. By force and stealth, Reza Khan had crushed rebellion among his own people and escaped the power of Britain to unite the nation.

It was Sultan Ahmed Shah who gave both Reza Khan and the British the opportunity to complete their agenda aimed at stabilizing Iran. Equally deficient in bodily health and moral strength, the grossly overweight shah left Tehran on November 3, 1923, to seek medical treatment in Europe. When he had yet to return by March 1924, sections of the Iranian press began to cautiously advocate the creation of a republic with Reza Khan as president.

That republic would jettison almost 2,500 years of Persian kingship. Drawn by the example of Turkey, where Mustafa Kemal Ataturk had recently swept away the sultanate, Reza Khan considered with a degree of pleasure the idea of becoming the father of the Iranian republic. Yet he hesitated. He knew the Iranians, in one of their great cultural traditions, demanded from their leaders evidence of breeding and culture. That raised the question of whether Reza Khan, a self-educated man who did not read, write, or speak with ease and grace, could successfully exercise authority in a republic. Even more, Reza Khan understood the mystique of kingship which came out of Iran's pre-Islamic past. Instinctively, he knew that an Iranian head of state stripped of the aura of monarchy might not survive in the first instance and, in the second, might rule in the shadow of authority exercised by the clerics.

While Reza Khan vacillated about a republic, the clergy rose in opposition. The *ulama* feared above anything else the example of secular Turkey, where Ataturk sent the power of religion into exile with the sultan. Consequently, the mullahs in the cities and the villages began to present the republic to their illiterate followers, who viewed the shah as a vague father figure, as akin to patricide. The mob formed. The bazaar closed. Reza Khan rushed to the Majlis to disperse the crowd only to be met by boos, shoves, and a few stones thrown by those protesting the end of monarchy. Having flexed their political muscle, the Shia clerics decided the future of Persian kingship.

Reza Khan answered a summons to Qom. There he heard the clergy's unyielding stand against a republican form of government. In the centuries-old balance between the temporal and religious arms of the state that had existed since Ismail set the foundation of the Safavid dynasty on Shia Islam, a deal was struck. If Reza Khan rejected a secular republic, the Shia authorities would endorse a change of dynasty. So it was that on April 1, 1925, Reza Khan called his countrymen to monarchy and Shia Islam:

> I and every man in the armed forces has held before him the high ideal of the preservation of the splendor of Islam. We have always striven to ensure that Islam thrives and spreads, and that the status of our religious leaders is respected and honored. Recently, I visited Qom and spoke with the divines of that holy city. . . . We came to the decision

to recommend to our fellow countrymen that they should cease all talk of a republic and instead devote all their energies to removing the obstacles to reform, and cooperate with me in strengthening the foundations of our faith, the independence of the country and the national government.[7]

Once again the religious leaders, as they had done in 1891 and 1906, proved their united strength. Now it was time for Reza Khan to prove his.

Reza Khan withdrew to the little mountain village of Rudehen, thirty miles east of Tehran. From there, he sent telegrams to the Majlis and the army announcing his resignation as prime minister and commander of the military. Then he waited. The population panicked. In an environment in which Reza Khan and public order had become synonymous, the country laid itself at his feet. In mid-September, when the absent Sultan Ahmed Shah announced his intention to return to Iran, the Majlis deposed the Qajar dynasty. On October 31, 1925, it gave the Peacock throne to Reza Khan and his Pahlavi dynasty. Paradoxically, in accepting kingship, Reza Khan, the man obsessed with modernizing Iran, symbolically accepted the whole traditional power structure, including the duality between secular and religious authority.

Yet the new shah remained an outsider, a man without roots in any of the social networks that traditionally provided Iran's elite. But he possessed the essential element to kingship—charisma. As soon as Reza Khan assumed the title of shah, a collection of suppositions and facts assigned to him the credentials of Persian kingship. He came from stock assumed always to have spoken Farsi, making him the first Persian king since the Sassanians. Whispers passed from person to person claiming that royal blood flowed in his veins. He chose as his dynastic name Pahlavi, the Persian language Iranians spoke before the Arabs destroyed independent Persia. Most of all, the man who left behind the name Reza Kahn to accept the title Reza Shah commanded the dignity and air of aloofness expected of a man who occupied the throne of Iran. It all played to the ancient idea that true kings are born into difficult circumstances, hidden away until the moment they are needed, and then emerge to save the nation.

April 25, 1926, the day of Reza Shah's coronation, dawned clear, bathing the newly leafed Judas and locust trees along the *jubes* in warm sunshine. Tehran, shorn of its surrounding walls by order of the new shah, also seemed to exhibit fresh life. Across the city, drab brick and stucco was transformed into color and pattern as people hung carpets on buildings edge to edge. Dingy, mean streets became dignified by garnishes of green, white, and Persian red applied to lampposts and doorways. The principal thoroughfares marked a triumphal parade route where Reza Shah's glass coach and six prancing horses passed under towering scaffolding covered from top to bottom with bunting, mirrors, candelabra, and hundreds upon hundreds of pictures of the new king.

But at Gulistan Palace, the reality of Iran of 1926 exposed itself. Ugly holes in garden walls revealed rubbish heaps where chickens scratched and soldiers hung their ragged wash on frayed lines stretched between trees. Dead leaves filled the fountains, and once graveled paths mired in mud. On the palace itself, the facade's broken tiles clung to the frames of shattered windows, and a loose iron railing wandered aimlessly across a terrace. At the end of that terrace, a rusted staircase led up to an enormous room lined with glass cases containing the artifacts of Iranian history, from Sassanian pottery to the toothbrushes of Nasir ed-Din Shah.

Within that room, an Armenian priest garbed in purple velvet, a Turkoman wearing a rose red coat, Bakhtiaris defined by domed felt hats, and Kurds wrapped in turbans of fringed silk awaited the arrival of Reza Shah. Clustered together in an inconspicuous corner were sullen princes of the Qajar dynasty, compelled against their will to give public support to the usurper. Near the center of the room a figure in black satin and an Arab headdress stood engaged in pleasant conversation. It was the stately old sheikh of Mohammara, the last of the independent chieftains broken by Reza Khan.

At 3:30, the diminutive six-year-old Crown Prince Muhammad Reza, in his miniature military uniform, solemnly walked down the long aisle to take his place at the right of the Peacock throne.* The emblems of Iranian kingship followed—the scimitar of Nadir Shah, the shirt of mail worn by Abbas the Great, and the new Pahlavi crown. When Reza Shah stepped into the room, he wore his military uniform, a cloak of heavy cashmere edged with pearls, and a khaki hat to which he had fixed the Daria-e Nur, the great diamond once belonging to the Moghuls. Walking slowly through the assembled guests, he positioned himself before the Peacock throne. There the ministers bearing the appurtenances of Persian history formed a semicircle in front of

*Reza Shah acknowledged eleven children. Muhammad Reza and his twin sister, Ashraf, were born to Reza Shah's second wife, Taj ol Molok.

the new king. Into its center stepped the green-turbaned Imam Juma, the leading ayatollah of Tehran, to remind Reza Shah where ultimate royal authority resided. "Oh, praise be to Allah who created the universe, who gives kingdoms to him whom He chooses . . . who makes the prophets and the kings the protectors of the rights of His slaves, who orders them to act with justice and kindness. . . ."8

With a hint of defiance, Reza Shah leaned forward, picked the emerald-and-diamond Pahlavi crown set with a white-plumed aigrette from its red velvet cushion, and placed it on his head. It was the act of a man who recognized no rival, secular or clerical. Outside, a salvo of gunfire proclaimed the King of Kings, the Center of the Universe, while inside the prime minster intoned, "The people of Persia are celebrating, not because a new Shah has come to the throne, but because the event has created the impression that Persia is resuming her historic glory and prosperity. . . ."9

Reza Shah passionately believed that ignorance, incompetence, selfishness, treachery, lack of confidence, and subservience to foreigners had stripped Iran's national character of its fiber. By the force of his will, he intended to grab the Iranians by the scruff of the neck, lift them out of the lethargy dragging at society since the Middle Ages, and thrust them into the twentieth century as citizens of an independent, self-reliant state. In essence, Reza Shah ranked as the ultimate Iranian nationalist whose ambitions for Iran were intensely personal. Like Charles de Gaulle, he perceived himself and his country as virtually synonymous.

Because the people of the Western world had achieved in a material sense many of the things that he desired for his own country, Reza Shah seized aspects of the West as tools with which to build Iran into a modern, sovereign country. Essentially, the old ways of the East, no longer applicable to the requirements of the twentieth century, had to give way to the new ways of the West. It was from this premise that Reza Shah began to tear away at Iranian society from the substantive to the cosmetic. He mandated Western-style dress in order to erase forever the provincial, tribal, and religious distinctions that eroded national unity. Dress also became a symbol of modernization by rejecting relics that recalled the old way of life with its passivity, sense of inferiority, and subservience to alien interests. But not all Iranians shared the shah's commitment to a new era via new style. The headman in the village of Rahmat Abad in Khuzestan took up a community collection to buy a pair of trousers and a pair of shoes. When any peasant found it necessary to deal with a government bureaucrat in the administrative center of Dezful, he borrowed the communal clothes, wore them for his brief contact with officialdom, and returned them to the headman for someone else to use. If the shah did not understand in this repeating scenario why his people resisted change, the villagers did not understand just how much their shah abhorred the number of peasants and donkeys in his kingdom.

To gain status as a modern nation, Reza Shah ripped down whole sections of Tehran, Shiraz, Tabriz, and other cities, ruthlessly destroying edifices with the mellowness and charm of age. He replaced them with broad but sterile boulevards accessible to motorized vehicles. To give his new streets beauty, he sent his soldiers out with poplar seedlings and watering cans, warning them, "If the tree dies, you die." Determined that Iran be seen as a modern nation to an increasing number of visitors, he removed beggars from the streets and banned the use of camels for commercial transport. He followed up with a law forbidding photographing old parts of towns that extracted from the pictures Europeans took home the manifestations of religion which Reza Shah regarded as symbols of backwardness.

Reza Shah's hopes and dreams for Iran took form in the Iranian National Railroad that took me from Tehran to Sari. Railways could have crossed Iran in the Qajar dynasty had it not been for the rivalry between Britain and Russia, which ruled out a concession to either competitor. In a new dynasty and a new time, Reza Shah cut the first sod at the site of the Tehran station on October 15, 1927. The centerpiece of the shah's plan of progress and prosperity for Iran, the railroad would be built without foreign loans, by foreign technicians from countries with no historic interest in Iran—principally Germany, Scandinavia, and the United States. Over a span of ten years, 1928 to 1938, 865 miles of track went down, linking the Persian Gulf with the Caspian Sea. These parallel ribbons of steel crossed bridges and deserts, crawled up steep mountains, and plunged into dark tunnels in unique feats of engineering. To ensure that his foreign labor force did its job well, Reza Shah put the families of his European workers under the bridges their husbands and fathers had constructed the first time a train passed over. At last, it was finished. On August 26, 1938, the Pahlavi king tightened the last golden bolt at the mountain station of Saif Chashmeh, forty-two miles south of Arak. As the first train moved off, Reza Shah stood alone on the tracks, tears of fulfillment running down his cheeks. It did not matter that his rejection of foreign loans to finance the $125 million to construct the railroad put a crushing economic burden on his people. To Reza Shah, the Iranian National Railroad meant more than an economic or military asset. It was the representation of the new Iran.

In the first ten years that Reza Shah worked his will on his nation, Iran made remarkable progress in physical terms. A standing army of one hundred thousand men ensured stability, and a rational system of administration staffed by ninety thousand civil servants delivered order. Yet in pursuit of rapid modernization, Reza Shah came to rule Iran as the all-powerful despot characteristic of the centuries-old institution of Persian kingship. By the early 1930s, the shah's personal vision of the Iranian nation required the sacrifice of all traditional organizations and groups on the altar of the state. For as long as any potential organized opposition existed, Reza Shah saw an intolerable obstacle to his radical modernization program, which held as its sacred goal a strong, vibrant nation. In an age when Mussolini of Italy and Franco of Spain clasped their iron hands on their own countries, Reza Shah qualified as a Persian Fascist, pulverizing the elements of Iranian society group by group to ensure the omnipotence of the state.

The tribes represented not only a challenge to Reza Shah's policy of centralization but an anachronism to the modern state. Consequently, throughout his reign, Reza Shah employed every means at his disposal to bend the tribes to his will. Sending armored cars and German planes against nomads armed with nothing but rifles, he decimated the most lawless of the tribes. For the rest, he ordered his army to fan out along the new road system to push into settlements those who knew nothing but the nomadic life. Dumped on land often unsuitable for cultivation, the nomads watched their arms confiscated, their young men conscripted for the national army, their language banned, and their leaders removed to Tehran, where they lived as hostages for the good behavior of their people.

This forced settlement of the Bakhtiari, Qashqai, Lur, Kurd, Baluchi, and a host of other tribes shattered tribal economics and undermined the traditional social structure. To compound the problems, Tehran provided the new settlements with little in the way of financial or technical help. Consequently, people and herds, ill adapted to a sedentary lifestyle and dependent for hygiene and health on moving campsites from time to time, died in terrible numbers. None have forgotten.

I rang the doorbell embedded in the wall next to a metal gate painted the palest of yellows. Within a few seconds, a man in his mid-sixties with skin leathered by the sun ushered me through a small garden heavy with the scent of flowers and into a rectangular room furnished almost entirely with *poshti*, Persian sitting pillows. The tea and fruit appeared and we settled back to talk. My host is a Qashqai now settled in an area on the outskirts of Shiraz. As a child in the 1930s, he heard his parents describe Reza Shah's assault on the tribe. "The army came. They took my family out of the historic Qashqai region, pointed at a spot, and told them they had one week to build a mud house. Every few days several soldiers came from the army post nearby to make sure they were still there. What else could they do? My father no longer had any sheep or goats, much less a horse or camel. He had to learn to farm, just like a villager." He spat out his last words like poison. "Every season when the Qashqai moved, the army would be there to take their animals and force them into settlements like the one where my family now lived. The Qashqai had never reached such a point of destruction before." He looked into space, tears flowing from his eyes. Mentally returning to the present, he reached for a wooden flute. Out of it came a mournful phrase and then another and another. In a while, he put the flute aside to recite some lines by the Qashqai poet Maazoon:

> *"I was sleeping, you woke me up.*
> *My memories were resting, you agitated them.*
> *My heart is burning and wants to leave the body.*
> *Oh, friends come and gather to see what is happening."*

As the bottom of the social order paid its price to Reza Shah's state, so did the aristocracy. Titles of nobility that had multiplied exponentially under the Qajars vanished by government decree. Everyone became simply "mister" except the shah and his immediate family. Gradually members of the Thousand Families found themselves moved out of their government positions to be replaced by men with modern education and professional training. Finally Reza Shah attacked the landowners directly, stripping many of their land and executing those who protested unduly. Tragically for the future, Reza Shah in this assault on the landed elite did nothing to hoist the peasants out of servitude. Land reform, the cornerstone of economic development for an agricultural society, never happened. Instead, Reza Shah expropriated land in his own name. By the end of his reign, he ranked as the largest landowner in Iran, protective of a new aristocracy that lived in his shadow.

The bazaar class also watched its power drain away as Reza Shah incorporated the economy in the name of the state. Superseding the network of bazaar merchants that had manipulated trade for centuries, the government took over the initiative, organization, and administration of economic activity. Through state control of production and prices, the merchants, in essence, became a class of government employees. By the same token, every citizen found himself a subject of state monopolies that reached into the most ordinary aspects of daily life by way of rice, tea and sugar, tobacco and matches.

In Reza Shah's new order, the Majlis established by the constitution of 1906 stayed in place. But in the political reality of absolute monarchy, the Majlis existed as little more than the chosen and obedient instrument of Reza Shah's regime, asking timid questions and eulogizing the shah's decisions. Those who refused to betray the ideals of 1906 went to prison, into exile, or, in one instance, committed suicide. Most, however, took their assigned place, where they became cooperative adjuncts to the man who believed that only authoritarian government kept Iran from sinking back into the chaos from which he had rescued it.

At his best and at his worst, Reza Shah relentlessly pursued his supreme goal—a modern, powerful Iran grounded in secular society fashioned on Western models. Holding Islam responsible for the major failings of society, which he saw as the lack of a modern educational system, an outmoded legal system, the seclusion of women, and the passive acceptance of fate, the Pahlavi shah intended to do no less than cut the knot between church and state tied by Ismail. It was for this reason that the institutions of Shia Islam bore the brunt of the Pahlavi reforms.

Understanding the potential power the *ulama* wielded, Reza Shah launched his attack on Islam by painting the religious leaders as symbols of the old, impotent Iran and himself as the great deliverer of the nation. Freeing Iran from the stultifying influence of Islam, the shah would gain his authority as the leader of a modernized state protected by a mechanized army, not as the "Defender of the Faith" or the "Shadow of God on Earth."

But Iran could not be simply disengaged from Islamic traditionalism. Nor could Islam be relegated to some unobtrusive corner of society. Since Islam is at once a religion, a state, and a way of life, Reza Shah needed to create an alternative definition of Iranian culture. The ideology of modernization wearing its coat of Western education and Western technology would not do because it threatened to undermine Reza Shah's own authority rooted in the tradition of Iranian kingship.

As important, he recognized that the strength of their own culture precluded Iranians from assuming the ideologies, traditions, or even symbols of the West. Nor did he want them to. The West could provide education and technology for national survival. But Iranian language, art, and history gave reason to that survival.

Reza Shah decided to bypass Islam by connecting the notion of modern Iran to a glorified image of ancient Persia. To this end, he summoned the impotent nation once more to the great days of Iranian history, to the age of the Achaemenian kings—Cyrus, Darius, and Xerxes; to the Sassanians—especially Shapour the Great, the king who humbled the Roman Empire, and to Khosrow I, the "Immortal Spirit." This recall of memory ended before Abbas the Great, for he belonged to the Iran of Shia Islam. In his resurrection of pre-Islamic Iran, Reza Shah fertilized the deeply planted idea that the Arabs humiliated Iran in the seventh century and plowed up images of ignorant camel herders compelling the highly civilized Iranians to accept a new religion. He fed it all with a systematic resuscitation of Zoroastrian symbols, congenial to the spirit of denying the relevance of Islam. Reza Shah, in essence, attached the might of the new Iran straight to the cloak tails of Cyrus the Great as if thirteen hundred years of Islam and a national identity shaped by Shiism never existed.

Drawing inspiration from Persepolis and Susa, the architects of the many new buildings rising in Tehran and other cities followed designs and repeated decorations of the Achaemenians. They are still visible. The police headquarters and the Central Bank in Tehran recreate the architectural style of Persepolis, including the sun disk symbol of Ahura Mazda. The Archaeological Museum nearby echoes the Sassanian palace at Ctesiphon. But the most obvious architectural linkage between Pahlavi Iran and pre-Islamic history and culture is Ferdowsi's tomb at Tus, in far northwestern Iran.

The white marble mausoleum was built in 1934 on the order of Reza Shah to celebrate the millennium of Ferdowsi's birth. There is little about it which even hints that Ferdowsi was born into Islamic Iran. The calligraphy on the tablets that create the tomb's facade are Ferdowsi's words, not the Prophet's. Inside, the long stone reliefs tell the story of the Persian kings, not the Shia imams.

Beyond Tus, every schoolchild in Reza Shah's Iran learned by rote memory extracts from the *Shahnameh* that emphasized Iran's Persian past and its dependence on kingly rule. Language also bent to the new order when Farsi underwent a process of purification by which ancient Persian words replaced words from Arabic. On a new calendar that replaced the Islamic version with a modernized form of the ancient Zoroastrian calendar the names of the months changed from Arabic to Persian. Cities also dropped their Arabic names, transforming Mohammara to Khorramshahr and Soltanabad to Arak. When the order went out for people to take family names in order to simplify government administration, Reza Shah let it be known that Iranian rather than Arabic or Islamic names were preferred. As a result, the politically astute chose names of ancient kings and heroes of pre-Islamic Iran. So pervasive did this glorification of the pre-Islamic past become that even Bayer aspirin chose to advertise its product through an appeal to Achaemenian symbols.

In 1935, Reza Shah changed the name of the country from Persia to Iran. According to the Pahlavi king, Greek and other classical writers assigned his country the name of Persia and the countries that subjugated the Iranians perpetuated it. In the illustrious days of Cyrus and Darius, the homeland was called Iran. And so it would be again in Reza Shah's new era of Iranian glory. Yet no matter how aggressively the shah redefined history and language, it was not enough to break Shiism's hold on the Iranians. So from the time he conceded the republic to the *ulama*, Reza Shah conducted war against the power of the clergy. He fought his major battles over law, education, land, religious ceremonies, and women.

One of the most hated symbols of foreign influence in Iran was the system of "capitulations" or extraterritorial privileges granted to foreign nationals living on Iranian soil. Britain and others, including the United States, claimed these privileges for their citizens largely on the basis of overlapping jurisdictions between the religious courts and the state courts that reflected the intertwined nature of secular and religious law. This made reform of the judiciary the vital prerequisite to the abolition of the capitulations, a stone in the craw of the nationalist Reza Shah. The imperfect process of refining and amending over four hundred years of customary law in order to divide the secular from the religious went on almost continuously through Reza Shah's reign. In it, each successive step further eroded the power of the *ulama*. In 1927 a new civil code sought to reconcile the Koran and the Code Napoleon. Its result reduced the influence of the sharia in criminal proceedings and property titles, restricting the jurisdiction of lower-level mullahs to personal matters such as marriage, divorce, and wills. In a turning point in the evolving definition of the Shia clergy, Reza Shah restricted the turban and cloak in 1928 to those truly knowledgeable in the law. In 1936, he stripped the state judicial system of most of its clerics when he required that all judges presiding over government courts hold a law degree from the secular Tehran University Faculty of Law or from a foreign university. From that point on, any cleric serving as a judge within the Justice Ministry worked as an employee of the state. Gone was the clergy's right to interpret the law totally under the precepts of the Koran and Islamic tradition. Gone also was the function of the jurist, who, by his own authority, settled disputes among the faithful. With most of their courts abolished, the majority of clerical judges retreated into the religious schools to write opinions which seldom circulated outside religious circles.

Reza Shah's attack on education paralleled his assault on the law. For a thousand years, elementary education resided in the *maktab*, the Koran school, where the pious, in exchange for the modest fees they collected from their students, taught the rudiments of reading, writing, and arithmetic in the context of religion. But religious education could claim no place in Reza Shah's Iran. To attain its nationalist goals, his new state required modern, technical education. As a result, Islamic schools, Christian missionary schools, and schools of the religious minorities closed their doors under Reza Shah's orders. All Iranians—male and female—went into free, compulsory education. By the end of Reza Shah's reign, only one form of primary and secondary education remained. It was secular and it belonged to the state. Within it, students acquired knowledge of the glories of the vanished Persian Empire and learned to be loyal, patriotic citizens of the equally glorious Pahlavi state.

The crown of educational reform was University of Tehran, located in view of Damavand, the snow-capped volcano that symbolizes the age and strength of Iran. Reza Shah decreed its mission: turn out the Western-educated Iranians that he needed for his state. Although the voice of the clergy branded those who studied a foreign language infidels and forbade the dissection of human bodies in the medical school, males and females entered the university seeking a share of the new order in Iran.*

At the same time that he was dismantling the Islamic systems of law and education, Reza Shah went after clerical wealth. The great shrines of Mashhad and Qom, as well as a covey of smaller shrines, disposed of huge incomes derived from raw land and developed real estate. With one stroke of the pen, the state appropriated this wealth

---

*In defiance of the Koranic ban on necropsy, Reza Shah forced his cabinet members to accompany him to the university's pathology lab to view two cadavers in a vat.

for its own use. In Mashhad, the revenues of the sanctuary of Imam Reza now helped finance secular education, build a modern hospital, improve the water supply of the city, and underwrite industrial enterprises. As a consequence, the clergy connected with these shrines lost not only their independence but a potent means of influencing the masses. Like clerical judges and teachers, the guardians of the holy sites became government employees and state functionaries.

Through these reforms in the courts, education, and ecclesiastical holdings, Reza Shah had accomplished what no other shah in Shia Iran had succeeded in doing—disrupting the financial status and self-administration of Shia Islam. The final blow to clerical autonomy came when Reza Shah made every mullah liable for two years active duty in his military.

Yet while Reza Shah plowed aside one prerogative of the clergy after another, he never lost sight of Shiism's latent power in Iran. Much of the clerics' ability to mobilize that power rested in the mullahs' control of the traditional symbols of the faith with all their accompanying emotion. Unable to declare total war on the Shia faith without undermining the monarchical component of the traditional power structure, Reza Shah chose to systematically attack Shiism's forms of expression.

In 1924, two years before he became shah, Reza Khan had strewed straw on his bare head and walked in the Muharram procession like a pious Shia. But in case anyone thought the minister of war submitted to traditional Shiism, Reza Khan's military band followed him, playing its version of Chopin's funeral march in honor of the murdered Hussein. When he took the throne, Reza Shah began to shut down the rich and picturesque rituals of the Shia creed whose expressions of justice and martyrdom so deeply appeal to Iranian sentimentality. The number of pilgrims to Najaf, Karbala, and Mecca dwindled in the bureaucracy of the passport office. More important, an edict from the shah in 1929 forbade the practice of self-flagellation during Ashura. In this one move, Reza Shah tore the emotional heart from Shiism, reducing the observance of Hussein's death at Karbala from the passionate to the mundane. The *taziehs*, the passion plays that keep alive the Battle of Karbala, also disappeared under police scrutiny. That left the *rowzeh-khans* to re-create the pain of Hussein in private homes. Even the dervishes, a component of Shia religious life for centuries, disappeared from the streets and country roads.

Of all Reza Shah's moves against the institutions and practices of Shiism, none elicited the same level of public response as did the changes in the status of women. In an act pregnant with symbolism, Reza Shah put women on the frontline of his social revolution against Islam. His motives rested in nationalism rather than in an engagement with the questions of religion and patriarchy. Illiteracy among women denied skills needed for nation building. Child brides and the practice of *muta*, or temporary marriage, brushed Iran with the stain of backwardness. Finally, the chador of funereal black that enveloped women spoke not only of the subordination of females but the subordination of Iran. By tearing away the veil, an emblem of religious traditionalism, Reza Shah announced his intention to enlist women in the resurrection of Iran. But the unveiling of women enraged the religious establishment.

The confrontation between Reza Shah and the clergy over the veil began almost by accident. In March 1928, the shah's wife came to Qom to pray at the shrine of Fatima. While in an upper gallery, changing from a heavy chador designed for the street to a lighter one for prayer, she momentarily exposed her face. A mullah happened to see her. With a chorus of students behind him, he poured shame upon her. The next day, Reza Shah pulled up in front of the gold-domed shrine accompanied by two armored cars and four hundred troops. He strode through the gate in his heavy military boots and across the graves of Shiism's holy men. Finding the offending mullah, he knocked off his turban, grabbed him by the hair, and thrashed him with a riding crop. Then he turned and left, leaving Qom and Iranian Shiism stunned.

Throughout 1928, hints surfaced that the chador would be banished to the trash heap of the past. Although angry demonstrations did nothing to deter Reza Shah from his chosen path, he proceeded with caution. Women's groups composed of educated, middle- and upper-class women organized to beat the drum of support. In 1934, government policy first allowed, and then ordered, women teachers and female students to appear in school without the chador. At the same time, cinemas, restaurants, and hotels, on pain of heavy fines, unlocked their doors to both sexes. Finally, a 1935 government decree banned the veil entirely.

That same year, the moral authority of Shiism and the military power of Reza Shah clashed over the twin issues of the veil and the requirement that men wear the billed Pahlavi cap that prevented a Muslim from touching the ground with his forehead during prayer. In Mashhad, angry clerics and equally angry laymen turned the main courtyard of the sacred shrine of Imam Reza into a platform from which to denounce the shah's assaults against Shiism. For a day, demonstrators ebbed and flowed inside the cavernous courtyard while the governor of Khorasan waited for instructions from Tehran. When they came, they were short: restore order even at the price of leveling the shrine. In the evening of the third day, Reza Shah's soldiers poured into the blue mosaic shrine, climbed up the iron staircases leading to the roof overlooking the principal courtyard, fixed machine guns to their mounts, took aim, and fired. Somewhere in the neighborhood of a hundred people died.* So did public protest. That a massacre within the most holy site in Iran could pass without provoking at least a local uprising in the devout province of Khorasan measured, as nothing else, the intimidating power of Reza Shah and his instrument of coercion—the army.

With religious opposition quelled, Reza Shah continued his war on the chador. After 1936, cinema houses and public baths closed to women wearing the veil. Law forbade bus and taxi drivers to accept veiled women as passengers. To enforce the regulations, the police roamed the streets to snatch scarves from the heads of women still trying to observe *hejab* or Islamic dress. While women of the educated elite rejoiced in a type of liberation, the majority of women felt disgraced and stained with sin. Those who refused to abandon the chador retreated into their homes, never leaving for fear of being attacked by the shah's police.

Ignoring the self-imposed seclusion of women neither emotionally nor culturally ready to embrace modernization, Reza Shah pushed on to extend the rights of citizenship and higher education to the female half of the population. As always, his sole purpose was to build the country. While men retained the exclusive right to vote, run for political office, initiate divorce, and retain custody of their children, the shah, in 1936, told a class of graduating female students, "We must never forget that one-half of the population of our country has not been taken into account, that is to say, one-half of the country's working force has been idle."[10]

Bloodied and bruised in its battles with Reza Shah, the *ulama* essentially retreated from politics. There is no one explanation of why the mullahs stayed largely quiescent as the first Pahlavi shah picked apart the institutions and traditions of Shia Islam. In part, modernization in pursuit of nationalism appealed to more than a small segment of the clerics. And there was the shah's military power, which proved

*Some estimates place the number at between four hundred and five hundred.

in the brutal murder of the poet Farrokhi Yazdi that it would punish anyone who challenged the tyranny of Reza Shah. But an army of tens of thousands cannot completely subdue a nation of 16 million that refuses to be coerced. Reza Shah succeeded in removing Shiism as co-partner in the state largely because no authority figure existed capable of summoning the faithful to resistance. The model of imitation was not there, nor was there a *mujtahid* possessing enough moral authority to mobilize the faithful against the shah. In effect, the clergy was suffering the legacy of the Constitutional Revolution, during which the depth and range of clerical divisions had destroyed unified leadership under one man acknowledged by his followers and his peers as "most learned." The clerics, like everyone else, were forced to recognize that only the king, a secular man, ran the country. Isa Sadiq, a leader in education and a servant of Reza Shah, wrote what many Iranians accepted: "The whole history of Persia bears out . . . [that] whenever there has been a great leader . . . Persia has risen to the pitch of glory and zenith of power. . . . The regeneration of Persia under the leadership of Reza Shah Pahlavi is another striking fact that proves that only great men have been able to lead the Nation toward its destiny."[11]

Reza Shah reigned as the charismatic leader who, according to Iranian tradition, emerged to save the nation. Even so he differed markedly from the shahs of both pre-Islamic and Islamic Iran. He made no claim to be a quasi-divine person. And he held the state separate from the person of the ruler. Nevertheless, the first Pahlavi shah shared with his predecessors the intense desire to make of himself and his dynasty the great symbol of the nation. In pursuit of personal and national power, Reza Shah acted as the ultimate father, snuffing out the lives of Iranian sons who refused to do his bidding for the good of the nation. For twenty years, Reza Shah succeeded in maintaining order and defending the nation. But during most of those years, Iranians lived as they had lived under too many shahs—with injustice, corruption, insecurity, and autocracy. Holding nationalism like the sword of Shapour, Reza Shah drove Iranians with unflagging demands that often exceeded their capacity or willingness to comply. When his people did rise to his demands, Reza Shah failed to restore to them the equivalent of their efforts and their means. Instead he continued to take, expecting total submission to his will. In the pattern of ultranationalists, he concentrated on the independence of his country rather than on the freedom of its people, requiring his compatriots to be proud of their fatherland rather than of their liberties.

It was within this repressive political climate that Reza Shah built a railway, founded a modern educational system, instituted programs of public health, and attacked the entrenched interests of the clergy. It was also within his one-man rule that society split between the new Westernized middle class and the traditionalist masses. Yet in Reza Shah's Iran both felt a sense of homelessness in an environment where the normal laws of evolution did not apply. Change that should have slowly evolved was crowded into a few years in which the twentieth century sometimes appeared overnight, sometimes came in fragments, and sometimes not at all. As a consequence, life resembled a madly eclectic time machine that shocked the Iranian people into a deep confusion about their values and identity.

For all his efforts, Reza Shah, in the end, failed to shred the fabric of traditional society. He wrested control of the army, parliament, and other instruments of power but he never completely subverted the clergy. In some instances, the shah's blows against Shiism produced the opposite effect of what he intended. For instance, in the uniformity-of-dress law passed in December 1928, everyone except Shia jurisconsults who had passed a special examination were required to wear Western clothes. The self-styled mullahs disappeared, leaving any man in clerical garb a learned scholar of the faith, someone deserving the respect of the faithful. Even more, none of Reza Shah's laws changed the reality that true religious leadership generates among the clerics themselves. With the hundreds of thousands of religious titles conferred by the Qajars stripped away by Reza Shah, those within the faith once more exclusively conferred the titles of "jurist" and "model of imitation."

Although Reza Shah put Muslim jurists and religious teachers on the public payroll and claimed much of the income of the shrines for the state, the clergy remained, to a significant degree, self-financed. For nothing Reza Shah did interrupted the flow of money from ordinary Shia to the cleric of his or her choice. Due to this money, the important *mujtahids* continued to pay the basic student stipend to the *talabehs* at Qom, thereby maintaining both the tradition of learning and the network of loyalties undergirding the *ulama* of Shia Islam. It all proved that Reza Shah, the ultimate Iranian nationalist, never came to grips with how deeply Shiism is ingrained in the Iranian national character and to what degree Shiism contributes to national identity. No matter how much the shah touted Iran's Persian past, Islam remained the other strand of the Iranians' intertwined identity. In the end, Reza Shah, the man who drove Iran like a Bismarck, fell to those very same foreigners who had manipulated Iran during the dynasty of the Qajars.

Through the 1930s, Reza Shah had applied the time-honored technique of protecting Iran's territorial integrity by balancing powerful predators. As the Qajars juggled Turkey, Britain, and Russia, using one as a third party against the others, Reza Shah checked Britain and Stalin's Soviet Union by calling in Germany as that third force. Because of Nazi ideology and the military force Adolph Hitler released on Europe in 1939, it proved to be the wrong country at the wrong time. When Germany invaded the Soviet Union in June 1941, Reza Shah's carefully constructed tripod collapsed. Suddenly Reza Shah's cherished railroad became the lifeline for Allied supplies to Russia. Just as in World War I, when Iran's enemies joined forces, Iranian neutrality meant nothing as the vice of the new Anglo-Russian alliance closed on Iran.

On August 25, 1941, the British navy sailed into Khorramshahr and the Red Army took Azerbaijan under the British-inspired pretext that the man on the Peacock throne was a German collaborator. Before the military machines of countries far larger and stronger than Iran, Reza Shah's proud army of 127,000 faded. Had the Pahlavi shah bowed to the Allies he might have survived. But the prickly old nationalist refused to become a vassal to the masters of his nation. With British and Russian troops closing in on the capital, Reza Shah watched his railway confiscated; his tiny navy wiped out; his army, the extension of himself, disbanded. Large quantities of small arms and ammunition that he had bought with taxes pounded out of his people flowed into the hands of the tribes ready again to challenge the authority of the state. In the wreckage, the man whose consuming passion was to secure independence for Iran abdicated. In his resignation statement on September 16, 1941, he told his countrymen, "I cannot be the nominal head of an occupied land, to be dictated to by a minor English or Russian officer."[12] With a vacant throne a foregone conclusion, the British cabinet had considered restoring a Qajar to the Peacock Throne. Unfortunately, the favored choice could not speak one word of Farsi, a fact that even London recognized as a liability. So the British and the Soviets decided on Reza Shah's son, the twenty-two-year-old Muhammad Reza. Known as a weak playboy, he could be replaced if he refused to do as he was told.

With his great power evaporated, his vast wealth abandoned, his revitalized state subjected to foreign domination, Reza Shah left Tehran on his long, sad journey into exile. Accompanied by his fourth wife and eight of his ten children, his melancholy course took him through Isfahan, Yazd, Kerman, and finally Bandar Abbas. When he arrived on the Persian Gulf, the SS *Bandra*, a 3,194-ton steamer registered in Glasgow, waited at anchor. The deposed shah sent his family on board while he stayed ashore to spend one last night on Iranian soil. The next morning, as the little ship plowed its way down the Persian Gulf, the once-mighty Reza Shah stood on deck gazing back at the fading coastline of his beloved nation. He lived in exile on the Indian Ocean island of Mauritius for five months before being allowed to move to Johannesburg, South Africa, where he died in 1944. His body returned to the Middle East for burial in Cairo.

Iranian history, as recurrent as it is ageless, had repeated the pattern of two and a half thousand years. A dynasty declines and some young soldier seizes power,

> taking for himself the diamonds, the rubies and the peacock throne. A renewal of Persian nationalism ensues, the young soldier becomes an emblem of regeneration, he frees his country from foreign influences, he founds a new dynasty, he amasses enormous wealth, and he imposes upon his people such particular forms of progress as suits his personal tastes. But then, as the pleasures of his sultanate begin to pull and the chill of older age creeps upon him, his days become darkened by suspicion; the companions of his early adventures, the architects of his central success are alienated, exiled, murdered; enraged and sullen the potentate stalks alone through the frail palaces which he has built for forgotten loves; the crude parquet creaks at his passage, the chandeliers tinkle as he lumbers by.[13]

Reza Shah accomplished much for Iran. But in attempting to forge a modern, independent nation, Reza Shah lost touch with the Shia aspects of Iranian culture and violated the Persian expectation of just rule. In the end, the *farr* of Reza Shah lived only in his nationalism. His son would repeat the father's mistakes of cultural alienation and absolute rule while failing, at the same time, to secure the nation against foreigners.

7

The Shah and
the Prime Minister:
Iran's Second Revolution

A FULL MOON TOUCHED THE DARK NIGHT WITH A GENTLE glow. And the soft air of late spring dismissed winter as if it had never been and ignored summer as if it would never come. I sat within a group assembled in the garden of a 1960s contemporary house of stone and glass that hid behind a wall on a busy thoroughfare in north Tehran. The underwater lights of a modest swimming pool added their own ethereal sense to the night. The conversation that flowed among people who had belonged to the upper classes of prerevolutionary Iran was political. But it was of the politics of the early 1950s, when a young, powerless Muhammad Reza Shah vacated his throne for the first time. A lawyer, perhaps sixty years old, talked on and on in a voice quivering with passion about the short era between 1951 and 1953 when the intellectual heirs of the Constitutional Revolution grabbed for the golden rings of national independence and constitutional monarchy. One name wove in and out of his soliloquy—Muhammad Mossadeq. On the opposite side of the misshapen circle of chairs, an elegant, raven-haired woman just past middle age drew impatiently on a cigarette. Stamping its filtered end into a heavy ashtray, she broke into the monologue with a vengeance. "Your idol Mossadeq created chaos for something he called nationalism. Then he alienated his own supporters, let loose the Communists, ushered in the United States, turned the shah from a mouse into a lion, and left the opposition to the monarchy to the mullahs. And you say this was Iran's moment in history? If it hadn't been for Mossadeq, the Islamic Revolution might never have happened." The object of her attack suddenly became speechless.

Between 1951 and 1953, a charismatic figure named Muhammad Mossadeq rose out of the Iranian parliament to lead Iran in its second revolution against national subjugation and absolute monarchy. The British-owned Anglo-Iranian Oil Company was his sword and a broad spectrum of Iran's population his soldiers. For over two years, the weak and vacillating Muhammad Reza Shah, king for almost a decade, played a passive role as leadership moved from the Peacock throne to the magnetic Mossadeq. Finally, the second Pahlavi shah fled Iran for the first, but not the last, time. It was Mossadeq's own mistakes and the intervention into Iran of yet another foreign power—the United States—that placed Muhammad Reza Shah back on his throne. The Pahlavi dynasty survived in large part because Mossadeq's Nationalist Movement, which found its ideology in Western political thought, could gather but not hold the great masses of Iran to its cause. Like the first revolution of twentieth-century Iran, the second faded when it failed to connect with the soul of the Iranians. In the end, the Nationalist Movement of 1951 to 1953 by engaging the United States in Iran, exhausting the middle of the political spectrum, and largely destroying the left, bequeathed to Shiism the emotional issue of nationalism and the leadership of the opposition against absolute monarchy.

At 3:15 P.M. on September 16, 1941, the day the iron-willed Reza Shah abdicated, his son Muhammad Reza presented himself to the Majlis to swear "to reign accordingly and in conformity with the established laws." With that pledge he crawled onto the throne of Iran in a time of national humiliation.

In 1941, heavily armed troops belonging to the Soviet Union and Britain occupied northern Iran in the interest of war against Nazi Germany.* With no military power of his own, the young, timid shah could do nothing but wait while the Allies held open the rail line to the Soviet Union. For four years—1941 to 1945—the shah watched in the wings as his country struggled with the grim products of wartime—occupation, shortages, hunger, and chaos. When the war at last ended, the Soviet Union made a naked grab for Azerbaijan. Again

---

*It was not until 1942 that the United States sent forty thousand men into Iran to facilitate the transfer of ammunition to the Soviet Union.

forced to the sidelines of events crippling his country, the Pahlavi king watched as the United States countered Soviet ambitions in one of the opening moves of the cold war. (See chapter 9.) Yet war and occupation only played accompaniment to Muhammad Reza Shah's domestic problems.

The young shah had ascended the throne dragging the legacy of Reza Shah. Starkly different from his despotic father in both temperament and authority, Muhammad Reza Shah in 1946 faced all the elements of opposition suppressed over twenty years of Pahlavi rule. Reza Shah's army, fearful of the wrath of those it had oppressed, had quickly faded away. In the vacuum of power, the tribes dug up their long-buried guns. Supplementing their small arsenal with weapons bought or stolen from the deserting army, they declared their freedom from Tehran. The Qashqai I visited in Shiraz told me, "When Reza Shah announced his abdication we tore down our mud houses, destroyed our plows, and uprooted the trees settlement forced us to plant. Since we had no animals for transportation, we took our children by their hands and began walking toward the mountain to rejoin the tribe."

Motivated by the need to strengthen his fragile hold on the throne, the shah turned back to the state much of the fortune his father had amassed and restored to the former owners a large portion of the property his father had confiscated. At the same time, he freed political prisoners, reduced taxes, and bowed to constitutional rule. In the first month that Muhammad Reza Shah ruled Iran, the American magazine *Time* approvingly commented, "The beginning of his reign looked fine, where it would end nobody knows."[1]

Muhammad Reza Shah also made concessions to the *ulama.* He annulled his father's ban on the Shia passion play and lifted restrictions on pilgrimages to Najaf, Karbala, and Mecca. He instructed government offices to once more enforce Islam's prohibition on food and drink during the day-long fast associated with the month of Ramazan. Tearing away the blanket of repression that Reza Shah had spread over Shia Islam, his son allowed women to emerge from their houses wrapped in the chador and men of religion exiled for their defense of Shiism to come home.

For the first decade of his reign, Muhammad Reza Shah survived as much as ruled. He gingerly moved from year to year carrying his burden of negatives: his wartime cooperation with the Allied occupation; the legacy of his father's autocratic rule; a dismantled army unable to defend his throne; the hostile *ulama*, still scalded by Reza

Shah's secular policies, refusing to sanction his rule; and the splintered Majlis, where each of a multitude of new parties grabbed for its own power. If this were not enough, the already politically frail shah possessed neither the charisma of a Persian king nor the air of Shia piety beneficial to secular authority.

Muhammad Reza Shah had first walked onto the stage of public life in 1926 as a six-year-old shyly toying with the pearls sewn on the hem of Reza Shah's coronation robe. He had been born October 26, 1919, as the second baby in twins delivered by Reza Shah's second wife, Taj ol Molok.* Ironically, it was Muhammad Reza's twin sister, Ashraf, older by an hour, who proved to be the stronger personality. Self-assured and assertive, she began as a child to weave an almost mystical bond with her brother that she used to advise, direct, badger, and drive him as long as they both lived.

However, not even Ashraf was strong enough to protect the child Muhammad Reza from his overpowering father. Although he loved his son with the possessiveness of an Iranian father, Reza Shah feared that the meek little boy given to daydreaming and tears lacked the fiber to be king. While the father drilled the principles of power—control everything, trust no one, hit first, show no mercy—the son escaped into his secret reveries. At the age of seven, the crown prince had survived typhoid, diphtheria, and malaria. Seven was also the age he was taken from his mother's care and put into a separate household under the charge of a governess. His education proceeded in a specially created military school of rigid rules where the sons of twenty high-ranking military officers deferred to the crown prince as the future king. By the time he turned eight, Reza Shah's heir began to attend meetings of the high council and take the salute of the troops at his father's many military parades. But in the palace, Muhammad Reza cowered under the same whip that his father used to drive the nation. The second Pahlavi shah once reportedly said about his indomitable father, "[He] was a very great character but we were all frightened of him. He only needed to fix his piercing eyes upon us and we went rigid with fear and respect."[2]

At the age of twelve, the heir apparent to the Pahlavi throne entered the LeRosey School in Lausanne, Switzerland. Over the next five

---

*Reza Shah was a thirty-seven-year-old widower when he married Taj ol Molok. He subsequently took two other wives but as the mother of his firstborn son, Taj ol Molok remained the senior wife and a power within the family well into the reign of Muhammad Reza Shah.

years, he absorbed the Western education that added its own dimension to his Iranian identity rooted in Persia and Islam. Muhammad
Reza returned to Iran for military school at the age of seventeen. At
nineteen, he accepted an arranged political marriage to Fawzia, the
favorite sister of King Farouk of Egypt. Two years later, he found
himself the shah of Iran. Before he turned twenty-six in 1946,
Muhammad Reza Shah confronted the storm of political dissent arch-
ing Iranian society from the Marxist left, across the democratic center,
to a cluster of clergy on the right anxious about secularization and
Westernization. The most virulent opposition came from the Tudeh,
the Iranian Communist party.

Officially formed in 1941, the Tudeh had expanded rapidly
through the mid-1940s. Advocating a Marxist solution to Iran's rig-
idly stratified society and inequitable economic system, the party
gathered followers from among middle-class intellectuals and lower-
class laborers in industrial cities such as Tabriz and Isfahan and in the
oil fields of Khuzestan. From its inception, the Tudeh drew strength
from economic and political support provided by the Soviet Union. In
1945, the Tudeh and its labor affiliate, the Central Council of United
Trade Unions, claimed over four hundred thousand members. Showing
its strength on May Day 1946, the Tudeh paraded eighty thousand
marchers in Abadan and another fifty thousand in Tehran.

The party's vigor grew out of its uniqueness in Iranian politics.
Unlike the usual political group that clustered around the personality
of one man, the Tudeh operated as an authentic party advocating
clearly defined social and economic goals articulated through newspapers by writers who reached into every interest group except the landowners. Yet the Tudeh contained flaws that would ultimately prevent
it from capturing the Iranian government. First, since its ideology and
tactics tended the global agenda of the Soviet Union more than Iranian nationalism, the Tudeh existed more as a cog in international
communism than an indigenous Iranian phenomenon. Second, the energy of the party was generated by young intellectuals who spoke the
language of socialism but largely remained captives of Iran's hierarchical social structure. Consequently, few among them ever genuinely
embraced the Marxist idea that the common people held salvation for
a corrupt and decadent society. Instead, the intellectuals disdained
ordinary workers and peasants, regarding them as despicable rabble
unworthy of political and economic redemption. Last, atheistic communism lacked the spiritual force necessary to mobilize the masses of
Shia Iran. As would be proved in 1979, it was Iranian nationalism and

the promise of social revolution articulated by the mullahs through the theology of Shia Islam that would raise the lower classes to revolution. But in 1949, it was the Communists under the banner of the Tudeh that made war on Pahlavi rule.

Shortly after 3:00 P.M. on February 4, Muhammad Reza Shah's Rolls-Royce pulled to a stop in front of the University of Tehran's Faculty of Law. Iran's monarch stepped onto a red carpet rolled out over the snow, adjusted his perfectly tailored jacket, and walked toward the building's entrance. Less than six feet from the door, four shots fired by a follower of the Tudeh hidden in a group of photographers hit the shah. One penetrated his cheekbone and exited under his nose. The other three passed through his hat. Miraculously escaping death, the shah was wounded psychologically more than physically. From that day on, he seldom mingled with his people. But perhaps more crucial to the nature of his rule, Muhammad Reza Shah added the assassination attempt to his survival of a near-fatal bout with typhoid as evidence that he lived under the protection of a higher power. As a result, an aura of mysticism seemed to engulf the psyche of the shah, casting him, in his own mind, as a divine person in the tradition of Persian kingship. To confirm his personal link with the godhead, the shah put the bloodstained uniform that he wore on that February day on reverential display at the Military Officers Club in Tehran. It stayed there until it was torn to shreds in the 1979 revolution.

Under the pressure of the Communists and other dissident elements, the embattled Muhammad Reza Shah employed compromise and concession to win over enough elements in the military, the old aristocracy, and the *ulama* to hold the throne. In the period prior to 1950, help came from the United States in the form of H. Norman Schwarzkopf, the father of the American general in the 1991 Gulf War. As head of the New Jersey State police in 1932, Schwarzkopf headed the investigation into the sensational Lindbergh kidnapping. From 1942 to 1948, he served as a colonel in the U.S. Army detailed to Iran to organize the shah's national police force. Drawing on his own experience as a West Point cadet, Schwarzkopf instilled an esprit de corps in the poorly trained and provisioned rural police force. As a result, he created a gendarmerie that provided the shah what he needed the most—some military muscle. But it failed to provide political stability.

In a string of quixotic episodes of political intrigue, the shah's minister of court died by assassination, prime ministers and ministers constantly circulated in and out of the cabinet, and the Majlis churned with political and personal rancor. Perhaps the shah could have tamed the tides lapping at his throne if the emotional power of nationalism had not swept the charismatic Muhammad Mossadeq to prominence.

Mossadeq rode to power on the wave of the Anglo-Iranian Oil Company (AIOC). AIOC had emerged from the Masjid-e-Sulemain oil field discovered in southwest Khuzestan in 1908. After the admiralty converted from coal to oil in May 1913, the British government acquired 51 percent ownership of the company and a direct partnership in the sixty-year concession that the Qajar shah, Muzaffar ed-Din, had granted in 1901. Nonetheless it was not until the oil of Khuzestan helped fuel the Allied victory in World War I which prompted the construction of the oil refinery at Abadan on the Shatt al-Arab that British national interests locked onto Iranian petroleum, adding another dimension to the British intrusion into Iran.

Before 1980, when Iraq invaded Iran, the oil refinery at Abadan was among the largest in the world. Twenty-four hours a day its tall flaring towers sent up flames of orange-red gas into air heavy with heat and humidity. Abadan itself was a company town supported by the black gold beneath its soil. Except for the weather, which one Iranian described as three months of summer and nine months of hell, life was good for those who lived among the palm trees that shaded the housing compounds.

In all the company towns of the Anglo-Iranian Oil Company, policemen in white ducks directed traffic along roads that wove between employee houses, the school, and the company store, all of which looked as if they had mysteriously lifted themselves out of the English midlands and plopped down in the Persian oil fields. Within the fields, secrecy attended the business of dragging oil up from its cache. The wellheads rhythmically worked in plain sight and the roustabouts barked orders for all to hear, but the results stayed invisible. The black, glutinous treasure of Masjid-e-Sulemain disappeared into a great pipeline that writhed over the plains of Khuzestan to be carried away to Abadan and the sea.

Sensitized by a century of imperialist intrigue, Iranians chafed at British control of one quarter of the world's proven oil reserves and Iran's major source of income. Because of this control, Iran earned more from the export of carpets than from the sale of oil. By the late 1920s, Iranian anger over British control of AIOC broke through the dam of economics to seep into politics and culture. According to AIOC's own history of the time, "The Company had become a double scapegoat. On ideological grounds it was caricatured as an imperialist bogey, a capitalist bloodsucker. In religious circles it was characterized as being a partner in an unholy alliance with the [British] Government in overturning traditional values and introducing alien princi-ples."[3] This perception of Britain as a nation of satanically clever manipulators intent on plundering Iran led every villager to believe with certainty that locusts, drought, and crop failure resulted from nothing less than the evil designs of the British. The city dweller skipped natural disasters to assign to Britain blame for the impotence suffered by the Iranian nation.

In 1932, Reza Shah raised the sword of Iranian nationalism to strike at the power of Anglo-Iranian Oil. In one stroke, he canceled the original oil concession that paid Iran only 16 percent of AIOC's profits on Iranian crude.* The shah won a bigger percentage of the profits but lost on the central issue—prices. In the only deal he could seal if he wanted to keep oil flowing during the Great Depression of the 1930s, Reza Shah agreed to freeze the price AIOC paid for Iranian crude for a period of thirty-two years. Thus in 1950, the Anglo-Iranian Oil Company, under the terms of the 1932 agreement, paid Iran royalties of $45 million for its oil and paid the British government taxes of $142 million on profits from that crude and its downstream products. Nineteen fifty was also the year that the Anglo-Iranian Oil Company found itself in the center of Iranian politics.

The issue pitting Iranian nationalism against AIOC was not just British exploitation of Iranian resources; or the company's refusal to al-low Iranian officials to audit company books to verify the accuracy of Iran's percentage; or the resistance of company officials to bringing Iranians into management positions. It was not even those signs hang-ing over drinking fountains in the oil fields that read NOT FOR IRANI-ANS. Ultimately, the building clash between the Iranian nationalists and the British over the terms by which Anglo-Iranian Oil would op-erate in Iran focused on national sovereignty. Personifying Iranian na-tionalism, Muhammad Mossadeq picked up the flag of Iran trampled in the dirt for centuries by Turks, Russians, and British and carried it into battle against the Anglo-Iranian Oil Company and the British presence in Iran. From 1951 to 1953, the magnetic Mossadeq pushed Muhammad Reza Shah aside to reign as the de facto ruler of Iran.

*Iran's share of the profits came only from crude oil. AIOC shut Iran out of a percentage of its highly profitable refining and distribution activities created by that crude.

Contrary to the long tradition of Persian kingship, he, not the shah, shone as the flaming sun in the sky, pulling millions of Iranians for a time into his orbit. For many among the educated, Mossadeq is still the sun king who ruled in that brief moment when Iran lived under neither Persian kingship nor Islamic theology.

When 1951 began, sixty-nine-year-old Muhammad Mossadeq sat as a member of the Majlis. Even to his supporters, the bald man with a long neck and large, beaklike nose resembled a vulture. And like a vulture, he had peered into Iranian politics for decades, waiting to devour those willing to sacrifice the interests of Iran.

In the hierarchy of Qajar Iran, Muhammad Mossadeq was an aristocrat, the son of a high-ranking bureaucrat and a great-granddaughter of the Qajar king, Fath Ali Shah. The prominence of his family provided him an appointment as treasurer of the large, rich province of Khorasan at the ripe age of fifteen. In 1909, the twenty-seven-year-old Mossadeq, like others of his class, climbed the Alborz Mountains, sailed the Caspian, and rode the railways to Paris to acquire the learning of the West. But almost immediately upon arrival, stomach ulcers, which Mossadeq reveled in describing as the creation of the most "irregular and disorderly" stomach secretions ever observed by a famed French physician, sent him back to Iran. He returned to Europe in 1910 to study law in Lausanne, Switzerland. Over the next four years, he produced a thesis entitled *The Will in Muslim Law (Shia Sect) Preceded by an Introduction on the Sources of Muslim Law* that wound together Shia tradition, Western constitutional law, and Iranian nationalism. Once more returning to Iran, he served in several government posts before being elected to the Fifth Majlis, where, in 1925, he stood almost alone in opposition to the creation of the Pahlavi dynasty. As Reza Shah gathered power in the 1930s, Muhammad Mossadeq paid the price for his dissent. Hounded from public life and periodically imprisoned, he retreated behind the walls of his estate in Ahmadabad, not far from Tehran. In 1941, when Reza Shah abdicated, Mossadeq emerged as the popular hero of the moral drama that Iranians call politics. It is a drama in which Iranians obey, and sometimes even admire, the ruling royal despot but still hold the eternal hope that somewhere there is a mythic hero who will defend justice against the autocrat. It was as the martyr of Reza Shah that Muhammad Mossadeq again entered the Majlis in 1944. From there he put together a coalition of nationalists that bridged Iran's broad and complex political spectrum to incorporate almost all political groupings except the Communists.

From an ideology grounded in the inequities of capitalism and imperialism rather than in Iranian nationalism, the Communists organized into the Tudeh party had long beat the drum on the Iranian left.
The loud and aggressive Tudeh had been outlawed in 1949 after its
implication in the attempt on the shah's life. Nevertheless it was the
Tudeh, operating through a variety of front organizations, that continued to provide the ideology and power of the political left. Wedded
to the Soviet Union and the vision of Marxism which united workers
across national boundaries, the Tudeh never shared the nationalist ideology of Mossadeq's broad-based movement.

At the center of the nationalist coalition clustered the National
Front, a large, variegated, and vociferous collection of political groups
dating to the late 1940s. Overwhelmingly members of the middle
class educated in the Western mode, they regarded themselves as the
true heirs to the Constitutionalists of 1905 to 1911. Consequently,
their collective agenda echoed that of the Constitutional Revolution:
a shah that reigned rather than ruled; freedom of the press and assembly; open and honest parliamentary elections; and civilian control of
the military. Most of all, they demanded that Iran be released from the
grip of Britain. That the National Front organized itself as a coalition
rather than a party reflected the divisions of personality that characterize Iranian politics. Although every faction held to its leader, the National Front as a whole derived much of its energy and ideology from
young intellectuals such as Mehdi Bazargan, Shahpur Bakhtiar, Karim
Sanjabi, and Allahyar Saleh, all of whom would surface again in 1979
as secular leaders of Iran's third revolution against absolute monarchy
and foreign domination. But in 1951, they stood with other nationalists behind Muhammad Mossadeq on the emotionally charged issue
of oil.

On the right of the nationalist coalition, the guardians of the institutions and traditions of Shia Islam reflected the diversity of opinion which so often characterizes the Shia establishment. In contrast to
1905, when the clergy united, the upper echelons of the clerical hierarchy included two men who saw religion and government from radically different perspectives. Ayatollah Borujerdi of Qom, the most
exalted Shia cleric of the day, reigned as the sole model of imitation
in the Shia world. In important ways, the highly learned and quietly
dignified Borujerdi represented the traditional Shia attitude toward
secular authority: all governments are profane in the absence of the
Hidden Imam. At the same time, Borujerdi found no sin in engaging
in practical politics for the benefit of the faith. In the wake of Reza

Shah's assault on Shiism's organization and customs, Ayatollah Borujerdi struck a deal with Muhammad Reza Shah. According to its terms, the secular realm of the shah and the religious realm of the ayatollah would live in a state of peaceful coexistence advantageous to both king and faith. In a period of accommodation and stability between the mullahs and the throne, Borujerdi kept himself and Shiism aloof from the affairs of state and the shah traveled to Qom from time to time to publicly pay his respects to Shiism by way of its most revered cleric. Consequently, when nationalist passions began building around the personality of Muhammad Mossadeq, Ayatollah Borujerdi kept silent. So did most of the other clerics who obediently followed the model of emulation. The conspicuous exception was Ayatollah Sayyed Abol-Qasem Kashani, a man regarded as a shallow intellectual by his peers and a dynamic leader by his followers.

In 1951, the sixty-six-year-old Ayatollah Kashani radiated a charismatic personality composed in equal parts of cleric and nationalist. Short, pudgy, but handsome, Kashani had built his reputation opposing British influence in the Middle East. During World War I, he led uprisings against the British in Iraq. In World War II, he went to prison in Iran for collusion with German agents. He emerged in 1945 as a hero in command of an army of followers. He parlayed his popularity into a political organization called Mujahedin-e Islam that demanded the application of the sharia as stated in the 1906 constitution and the reintroduction of the veil for women. Between 1945 and 1950, Ayatollah Kashani's campaigns for a variety of popular causes distasteful to the throne slotted him into the shah's revolving door of prison and exile. Yet each time the ayatollah suffered royal wrath in the name of religion or nationalism his following grew until it spanned the social spectrum. When Borujerdi convened a conference of two thousand clerics in Qom on February 20, 1949, to instruct Shiism's clerical establishment to stay out of the issue of oil, Kashani refused, arguing that he was following the hadith of the Prophet which says, "He who upon waking does not concern himself with the affairs of Muslims is not himself a Muslim." Then he pointed to the example of Sheikh Shirazi, who issued the *fatva* in the Tobacco Protest. Ignoring both Shia tradition concerning secular government and the religious leadership of Ayatollah Borujerdi, Kashani wrapped Islam and politics together in a revolutionary theology that ultimately changed the future of Iran. For it was the idea of religion as politics that Kashani fashioned and executed in the early 1950s that profoundly influenced Ayatollah Ruhollah Khomeini's own version of politicized Islam that would come in the 1960s.

In 1951, the soft-spoken Kashani handed his political theology and his huge following to Mossadeq's crusade against Anglo-Iranian Oil. Virtually alone among the leading *mujtahids* in joining Mossadeq, Kashani provided a crucial ally to the nationalists. As an ayatollah highly respected in religious circles, he could influence clerical members in the Majlis to give their votes to Mossadeq. Outside parliament, he possessed the ability and the authority to arouse support for the nationalist cause among the normally apolitical traditionalists composed of the merchant class and the masses. To them, he said, "Islamic doctrines apply to social life, patriotism, administration of justice and opposition to tyranny and despotism. Islam warns its adherents not to submit to a foreign yoke. This is the reason why the imperialists are trying to confuse the minds of the people by drawing a distinction between religion and government and politics."[4]

Factions within the nationalist coalition represented by the National Front and the followers of Ayatollah Kashani shared only one common denominator: opposition to British power in Iran symbolized by the Anglo-Iranian Oil Company. Otherwise each group held conflicting ideologies and philosophies that cut to the very core of government—what constitutes authority and legitimacy in the political system of Iran. This fundamental question dividing the secular and the religious was no more apparent than in the personalities and philosophies of Muhammad Mossadeq and Ayatollah Kashani. One was a lawyer and the other a clergyman. One thought in terms of man-made law, the other in terms of God-given law. But these conflicts stayed hidden for the moment as the center and Kashani's right gathered as one behind the charismatic Muhammad Mossadeq. Each contributed its own particular power, the National Front in the Majlis and Kashani in the mosques. Absent from the campaign of Iranian nationalism was Muhammad Reza Shah and most of the hierarchy of Shia Islam.

The events which coalesced in the Nationalist era had begun in September 1949, when Iran wrung from the Anglo-Iranian Oil Company the Supplemental Agreement that granted somewhat better terms than those negotiated by Reza Shah in 1932. But a commission established by the Majlis and chaired by Muhammad Mossadeq rejected it on November 25, 1950. By early 1951, AIOC indicated its reluctant willingness to discuss the same fifty-fifty profit split which Saudi Arabia had just reached with its own foreign-owned oil company, the Arabian-American Oil Company (ARAMCO). Nonetheless there was a caveat. The Supplemental Agreement must be approved first. By then, profit share no longer propelled Mossadeq and the nationalists. They wanted nothing less than the destruction of British influence in the affairs of Iran. That meant nationalization of Anglo-Iranian Oil. The sides lined up, with Muhammad Reza Shah and the old aristocracy on the side of accommodation with AIOC and virtually everyone else with any interest in politics, including the Tudeh, gathered on the side of nationalization.*

On March 3, 1951, the shah's prime minister, Ali Razmara, came before the Majlis to ask for support of the Supplemental Agreement as a path toward further negotiations. Four days later, he was killed by an assassin.† Immediately, Muhammad Mossadeq filled the political void, relegating the shah to the sidelines as little more than an observer. With Mossadeq leading the charge against Iran's economic master, the Majlis, on March 15, boldly nationalized the Anglo-Iranian Oil Company, making Iran the first Third World country to defy the economic interests of a major power.‡ On April 29, the same Majlis elected Muhammad Mossadeq prime minister. While the shah sat on the throne as a mere shadow, Muhammad Mossadeq basked in the acclaim of the vast majority of Iranians, who for the first time in decades gave their genuine respect, devotion, and loyalty to their recognized national leader.

Much of Mossadeq's great appeal came out of personal characteristics that struck chords deep in Iranian culture. In a patriarchal and authoritarian society that puts great emphasis on family, education, and age, the aristocratic, highly educated, elderly Mossadeq fulfilled the requirements of the strong father figure. He was also the heroic leader defending the Iranian homeland against the hated foreigner. By accident or fate, elements of the ancient mythology concerning the founder of a new dynasty encircled the prime minister—his relationship to the preceding Qajar dynasty; persecution by Reza Shah, the

---

*Tudeh supported nationalization of the British-owned AIOC but opposed nationalization of oil concessions held by the Soviet Union in northern Iran. The National Front, on the other hand, insisted that all oil resources and facilities in Iran be brought under the control of the Iranian government.

†The accused killer of Razmara was a member of an organization called Fadaiyan-e Islam, which was created in the first half of the 1940s to "fight all forms of irreligion." (See chapter 10.)

‡It was not until 1956 that Egypt's Gamal Abdul Nasser nationalized the British- and French-owned Suez Canal Company using Iran and the AIOC as his model.

reigning authority of the day; years of exile in his Ahmadabad estate; manifestations of greatness in time of national peril; and possession of the quixotic charisma that bestows the *farr*. Finally, Muhammad Mossadeq was an Ali figure, a man of integrity and commitment willing to take upon himself the sorrows and burdens of imperfect mankind. Wrapped in all the elements of Iranian leadership that had escaped Muhammad Reza Shah, Mossadeq, in 1951, claimed the indisputable right to rule.

As paradoxical as Iran itself, Muhammad Mossadeq would prove to be a man of great success and enormous failure. Possessing a magnificent courage to challenge, he sadly lacked the capacity to construct. Consequently, between 1951 and 1953 Muhammad Mossadeq slid from the pinnacle of power to the humiliation of imprisonment. The Iranians and their shah rode with him all the way.

In the euphoric days following the nationalization vote, Mossadeq and the nationalist coalition operated with the certitude that the West's need for Iranian oil provided Iran a sure lever in the battle with AIOC. They just as strongly believed that exclusively Iranian labor and management could produce and market the black gold of Iran's oil fields and refineries. Sounding the cry of "self-sufficiency" in July 1951, Muhammad Mossadeq ordered all British employees of AIOC home. In this exercise of nationalistic panache, neither Mossadeq nor the nationalists grasped the technological and financial complexities of oil. Nor did they really care in their heady gratification of booting Britain out of Iran. They should have. For the oil fields, the international petroleum markets, and British resistance ultimately determined not only the outcome of Iran's defiant nationalization of the Anglo-Iranian Oil Company but the future of Iran.

Although Mossadeq's declaration of self-sufficiency played to national pride, it demonstrated once again the Iranian propensity to make the grand gesture at the expense of reality. Iranian engineers, long denied hands-on management experience by AIOC, proved incapable of operating either the wells or the refinery. Maintenance workers, always the recipients of orders rather than the initiators, allowed complex installations to stall and pipelines to choke. Rapidly Abadan, whose refinery with its orange-crested flaring towers symbolized the Iranian oil industry, took on the milieu of a ghost town. Concurrently, AIOC engineered a boycott of Iranian oil in international markets and Britain battled the nationalization order in the International Court of Justice and within diplomatic circles composed of countries worried about the security of their own assets abroad.

As the reality of economic stagnation took hold, the enthusiasm of 1951 transformed into despair. Oil export income dropped precipitously from the 1950 level of $400 million. Seeking a solution to the crisis, Mossadeq did what Iranian kings had done since the nineteenth century—looked for a third power to strengthen Iran by neutralizing Britain. He chose the United States. When the U.S. agreed to undertake the role of mediator, the American novices in Iranian culture confronted the full range of Muhammad Mossadeq's perceptions and personality. At their first meeting, Mossadeq displayed the Iranians' consistent proclivity for blaming all Iran's ills on the foreigner. In conspiratorial whispers, he confided to U.S. envoy Vernon Walters that "Iran's problems have always been caused by foreigners. The whole thing began with that Greek Alexander."[5] It was only the beginning of America's bewildering relationship with Muhammad Mossadeq.

To the utter confusion of the West, Mossadeq exhibited an extravagant sense of drama that exceeded even the standards of Iran. Something of a mystic, he claimed that as a young man an angel came to him in a dream to command him to devote his life to driving the British from Iran. In this self-defined role of the weak David fighting the giant Goliath, the Iranian prime minister ranted, shrieked, moaned, and frequently laughed. When excited and exhausted by one of his two-day speeches to the Majlis, he fell into a dead faint to be carried from the floor feet first. When deeply moved, he publicly wept. Playing on his age, he leaned on the cane that was part of his persona to emphasize his age and threw it away to prove his vigor. But his great forte was poor health. His celebrated stomach ulcers tolerated only a little tea, milk, and cakes. And his self-defined frail body required foreign ministers to often pay their official calls at a plain iron bed where "Old Mossy" lay in gray woolen pajamas, propped on a pile of pillows, claiming that his last ounce of life dripped into the welfare of his nation. It all played well to an Iranian public steeped in the tradition of the *tazieh*. But to the West, the "blanket prime minister" looked like a buffoon. *New York Times* reporter Albion Ross wrote, "In London clubs, the dashed fellow was regarded as a confounded maniac. . . . The world marched through Mossadeq's bedroom and left shaking its head. Iranians loved it. To them the show was worth the price."[6]

Deprived of both oil income and financial and political allies capable of putting Iranian petroleum back in the market, Mossadeq's position as the mythic hero steadily eroded. The National Front still controlled the Majlis and the Tudeh held the streets. But in the bazaar, a dark cloud of doubt about Iran's ability to survive without foreign exchange invaded every corner. The police and the gendarmerie, schoolteachers and the lower ranks of the civil service, worried about survival as their salaries turned into IOUs from the Iranian government. In a move to contain the growing unrest, Mossadeq demanded absolute power for himself for a period of six months dating from July 13, 1952. Illustrative of the dictatorial powers the Majlis agreed to bestow on Mossadeq was a list the prime minister issued containing topics banned from mention in the press. Number 19, the last, simply read "et cetera." Suddenly authoritarianism had moved from its traditional place on the throne to the prime minister's office. However, Muhammad Reza Shah mounted no credible opposition. In the building crisis over emergency powers and the authority of the shah, the prime minister feared the women of the royal family more than the king, hiding in his palace in Shemaran in northern Tehran. Exercising more of his new powers, Mossadeq ordered the shah's mother and his formidable sister Ashraf to leave the country within twenty-four hours or face arrest on charges of "treasonable intrigue." But Mossadeq's greatest enemy had become himself. Obsessed with his struggle against foreign imperialism, Mossadeq had done nothing to put together a constructive plan of attack on Iran's chronic internal problems and divisions. In an important sense, he could not devise specific proposals on the economy or administration without sacrificing his coalition of liberals and traditionalists held together by nothing more than the negative goal of ridding Iran of Britain.

By the end of May 1953, Muhammad Mossadeq huddled under siege. Externally, the attempt to employ the United States as leverage against Britain had collapsed in Mossadeq's rigidity and America's misunderstanding of the melodramatic prime minister. Internally, the economic crisis coupled with conflicting personalities, political philosophies, and an increasingly suspicious and authoritarian Mossadeq tore at the nationalist alliance. The powerful merchants, much of the army, and some of the court—all elements of the National Front drawn to Mossadeq solely on the basis of his mortification of Britain—deserted. With the rest of the center weakening over the issue of emergency powers and the erosion of the monarchy, the Tudeh party now ranked as the strongest organized political force in the nation. The party's power came in part from organization and in part from the hard-knuckle tactics that employed thugs to cower the Tudeh's ideological adversaries through lies and libel, intimidation and terror. Mossadeq initially tolerated the Tudeh's lawlessness in order to frighten the

United States into backing the nationalization of the Anglo-Iranian Oil Company by raising the Communist threat to the Iranian government. But the Tudeh now threatened the National Front. Intent on keeping Mossadeq from compromising with Britain in the interest of starting Iran's oil flowing again, mobs organized by the Tudeh roamed Tehran waving the hammer and sickle and shouting slogans that smeared Mossadeq as a feudal landlord playing stooge for the United States. Yet despite the noise and chaos created by the Communists, it was Ayatollah Kashani who quietly inflicted Shiism's mortal wound on Muhammad Mossadeq.

Mossadeq had always presented the mullahs a knotty problem that they never completely untangled. The prime minister made no secret of the fact that he was a secular intellectual who cherished his European education. A true descendant of those Iranians who emerged in the nineteenth century, he believed Iran could only be strengthened through reform of religious tradition. But he was also an ardent nationalist. The clerics who entered the National Front had done so precisely because they saw Mossadeq as the defender of Shia Iran against non-Muslim foreigners. To their profound disappointment, they discovered that Mossadeq was willing to defend Shia Islam, not as the divine faith, but as an element of Iranian national identity. This is the reason Ayatollah Borujerdi and the senior mullahs never trusted Mossadeq. He talked of Islam but he seldom prayed; he was an Iranian but his education and many of his values came from the West; he sought the support of Shiism's clerics but he also appealed for tolerance of the Communists, the atheistic enemies of religion.

Sayyed Abol-Qasem Kashani, the most visible and influential cleric within the nationalist coalition, backed Mossadeq only until the nationalization of oil seemed to rid Iran of British influence. At that point, Kashani and Mossadeq stood on opposite sides of the chasm lying between their contradictory philosophies of religion and government. Mossadeq's concept of the state came from the West, Kashani's from religion. Kashani demanded the restoration of Islamic law as the core of Iranian government. Mossadeq insisted on law by man, written by elected representatives under the rule of the constitution. While Mossadeq saw Iran in terms of secular, liberal nationalism, Kashani saw it as a nation of believers. As the prime minister gathered extraordinary political powers for himself and allowed the Marxist Tudeh party to run unchecked, Kashani joined the Shia establishment in opposition to Mossadeq.

The royalist coalition that had been building against Mossadeq despite the timidity of the shah quickly inducted the disenchanted Kashani into its ranks along with Ayatollah Behbahani, another nationalist cleric who controlled his own extensive network of followers in south Tehran. Although they were never more than junior partners in a political movement led by the modernized middle class, the loss of the political clerics effectively cut Mossadeq's connections with the lower middle classes and the Iranian masses which are crucial to any popular movement. Conditions were ripe for a foreign power to end the era of Muhammad Mossadeq. Unlike the Constitutional Revolution, when Russia and Britain filled that role, this time it was the United States.

Deprived of his sword of oil by the international marketing consortium, Mossadeq boldly seized another weapon to save what remained of his nationalist movement. In a May 28, 1953, letter to American president Dwight Eisenhower, in which he intended to solicit desperately needed financial and moral assistance, Mossadeq boldly drew the picture of an economically deprived Iran heading toward communism. Already alarmed by the strength of the Tudeh, Washington began to view the situation only from the narrow perspective of the cold war. With Iran lying between the Soviet Union and the Persian Gulf, any sympathy the United States might have had for Iranian nationalism evaporated in the heat of global politics.

During the summer of 1953, Allen Dulles, the head of the CIA, U.S. ambassador to Iran Loy Henderson, and Princess Ashraf, the banished sister of Muhammad Reza Shah, mysteriously turned up in Switzerland at the same time. Concurrently, Brigadier General H. Norman Schwarzkopf, the man who presided over Muhammad Reza Shah's national police force from 1942 to 1948, embarked on a tour of the Middle East which he described simply as a "private visit." As later events proved, they were all characters in a plot to rid Iran of its troublesome prime minister by restoring the authority of the shah.

In the twenty-seven months since Muhammad Mossadeq became prime minister, Muhammad Reza Shah had stood by, confused, vacuous, and afraid, as Mossadeq wielded absolute authority. The prime minister and the Majlis he dominated had disbanded the Senate, suspended the functions of the Supreme Court, extended martial law, forced the shah to transfer some of his property to the government, set up a committee to examine ways to curtail the monarch's power, and finally presented a bill to the Majlis to limit those powers. Unable to challenge the enormously popular prime minister and his nationalist cause from his fragile base of power composed of an unreliable army and unarmed bureaucracy, the shah cowered in his palace. It was not until the anti-Mossadeq forces—domestic and foreign—needed a figure to rally around that the shah became relevant to events.

The external and internal forces arrayed against Muhammad Mossadeq swung into action in the second week of August 1953 following a referendum on the tenth that gave the prime minister the authority to dissolve parliament. When Ayatollah Kashani formally deserted Mossadeq and twenty-five deputies of the National Front joined those who had already broken with the prime minister over emergency powers, Muhammad Reza Shah was wheeled on stage for the finale of the nationalist movement. Following directions dictated by his court and its American conspirators, the shah, on August 13, sent Colonel Nematollah Nassiri to inform Mossadeq that he had been removed as prime minister. But instead of relinquishing office, Mossadeq arrested the messenger. As the news spread of the prime minister's defiance of the shah, the streets of Tehran filled with Mossadeq supporters who joined members of the Tudeh shouting over and over, "Yankee go home!" The army, nervously waiting in the barracks, pondered its options.

On the day Muhammad Mossadeq refused to bend to monarchical authority, the shah waited at Kalardasht in the mountains above the Caspian Sea, safely out of reach of the swirling political events. A radio linked to his palace in Shemaran provided his only contact with Tehran, where others decided his political fate. According to Soraya, the shah's wife at the time, no messages regarding the unfolding situation in the capital came through on either the fourteenth or fifteenth. At 4:00 A.M. on August 16, word crackled over the radio that an attempt by the right wing of the army to unseat Mossadeq had failed. Immediately, the frightened shah went into the bedroom of his wife, shook her out of a deep sleep, and told her to prepare to flee the country.

Muhammad Reza Shah took the controls of the small two-engined Beechcraft plane that had brought the royal couple to Kalardasht and headed toward Baghdad, the limit of the craft's gas tanks. In the Iraqi capital, the tired and disheveled royal couple deplaned in the torrid heat of summer carrying nothing but a few clothes hurriedly stuffed into a bag and a leather box containing Soraya's jewels. Two days later a relieved Iraqi government watched them go on to Rome, where they became meat for the hungry international press corps. Denied accommodations by his own embassy, the shah took up residence in a suite at the Excelsior Hotel borrowed from an Iranian industrialist. With little ready cash and no official recognition from Iranian officials in Rome, Muhammad Reza Shah and his wife were what they appeared to be—political exiles. The beautiful Soraya wandered the shops, looking but not buying, and the shah held one press conference after another denying, again and again, that he had abdicated.

Meanwhile in Tehran, thirty-seven-year-old Kermit Roosevelt, the twelve-thousand-dollar-a-year head of the CIA's Middle East operations and grandson of Teddy, had released the trigger on "Operation Ajax." Employing bribery and contacts provided by British intelligence in the police, armed forces, and the bazaar, he deftly wove together a royalist coalition of the aristocracy, industrialists, major merchants, disillusioned members of the National Front, and the handful of political clerics who had joined Mossadeq in 1951. On August 18, the day the shah arrived in Rome, the Iranian army, reacting to the possibility that the Tudeh might form the next government, came out of the barracks to crush street demonstrations in the name of the shah. With the army secured, Roosevelt sent a throng hired in south Tehran for one hundred thousand dollars marching toward Mossadeq's office in the heart of the city.

Exchanging their gymnasium for street politics, members of a *zur khaneh*, or "house of strength," turned handsprings, twirled iron bars, and flexed their biceps behind their leader, Shaban Bi Mokh (Shaban "the Brainless"). Waves of unskilled laborers followed, punching the air with little Iranian flags made of paper distributed through the clerical networks of Kashani and others. As spectators along the sidewalks grew in number, the bizarre assortment of performers with their supporting cast began shouting in unison the name of Muhammad Reza Shah. The crowd, motivated by ten-riyal notes passed out by gangs of young men employed by Roosevelt, took up the chant. In one precarious moment, the balance of public psychology seemed to swing against the once heroic Mossadeq. But the war for the streets had yet to be won. For nine hours, the pro-shah army, utilizing American-style military strategy and logistics, battled pro-Mossadeq demonstrators. At least three hundred people died. By nightfall, the Mossadeq partisans had drawn into a tight cordon around the premier's palace. Inside, the aged and always ailing prime minister threw a coat over his pajamas, leaped over the garden wall, and went into hiding. Forty-eight hours later he was arrested. The brief euphoric moment when the followers of Mossadeq believed that he held Iran's destiny in his hands evaporated. With their leader tarnished and deposed by a foreign power, the remaining nationalists accepted the futility of fighting on.

The coup triumphed with a speed that surprised even its most ardent supporters. With nine hundred thousand of the million dollars originally set aside for Operation Ajax remaining, Kermit Roosevelt and the royalist coalition surveyed the realm of Muhammad Reza Shah cleansed of those who threatened the throne. In Rome, the man under whose name the coup was staged sat with his wife at lunch in the dining room of the Excelsior Hotel. They were ignorant of events in Tehran until a young reporter from the Associated Press rushed to the table and handed the shah a piece of paper ripped from the wire. "Mossadeq overthrown. Imperial troops control Tehran." Soraya burst into tears. Muhammad Reza Shah went pale and reportedly whispered, "I knew that they loved me."

Operation Ajax succeeded with such ease because Muhammad Mossadeq had lost the *farr*. In his misguided pursuit of national sovereignty, he divided the intellectuals of the National Front between those who remained loyal to the man and his cause to the end and those who suffered disillusionment over their leader's dictatorial methods that threatened not only the authority of the shah but that of parliament. For the Shia clerics of the nationalist coalition who put the government of God before the government of man, Mossadeq fell because he denied the faith. He remained a hero only as champion of Iranian sovereignty. That might have saved him. In the last two days that he held the office of prime minister, Mossadeq could have commandeered the radio to send out an appeal for help. And, like many times before, tens of thousands of Iranians would have poured into the streets to overwhelm the hired mob from south Tehran. But he declined. In the end, "Mossadeq was not only the battling hero Rostam, the son of Zal, and the brilliant commander Ali, the Lion of God, he was also Hosain, the Prince of Martyrs."[7]

The drama did not end when Muhammad Reza Shah arrived back in Tehran to reclaim his throne. Seeking revenge through the humiliation of the grand old man, the shah put Mossadeq on public trial before the nation. But the wily Mossadeq turned his own trial into yet another stage where he performed his last act. In one of the most impressive performances of his theatrical career, he assumed the role of symbolic leader who, if he had not been overthrown, would have led Iran toward the millennium. As a result, millions of Iranians emotionally flocked back to the deposed prime minister. Yet Mossadeq's resurrection came as much from culture as performance. For the paradox of power in Iranian culture is that once stripped of authority, a leader can once more be trusted. In this sense political defeat gave Muhammad Mossadeq permanent claim to a special martyrdom reserved for nationalists.

Condemned by the shah's court, Mossadeq went to prison for three years before disappearing into his estate in Ahmadabad. He neither left his village nor received visitors for the rest of his life. In 1967 he died, at the age of eighty-five, killed by the stomach ulcers that had sent him home from Paris in 1909. Still fearing Mossadeq's magnetism, Muhammad Reza Shah denied him all public rites of mourning.

Today in Iran the people of the villages and the crowded urban slums tell the tales of the Iranian Revolution. But many of the educated who still hold the ideals of secular, representative government and national honor tell the tale of Mossadeq. The man I listened to in the garden in north Tehran that warm spring night talked about the National Front and the ideals of Mossadeq as if the shah had never returned and the Iranian Revolution had never happened. For him and uncounted others like him, Muhammad Mossadeq and his National Front still represent the promise of the Iranian nation. Whether viewed as a hero or a villain, Muhammad Mossadeq left Iran two legacies—one external and one internal.

The bitter recriminations thrown at the United States during the 1979 Iranian Revolution can be comprehended only by understanding the role the United States played in the ouster of Mossadeq in 1953. To Iranians, British control of Iran's petroleum resources represented the same national impotence inflicted by the Mongols, the Turks, and the Russians.* Regardless of his subsequent failings, Mossadeq for a brief moment gave Iran its sovereignty. That ended when the United States restored Muhammad Reza Shah and enrolled him in the West's containment of the Soviet Union. So it was in 1953 that the U.S. embassy in Tehran was labeled a "nest of spies" and the acronym CIA became the most defamatory term in the lexicon of both secular and religious nationalists. Over the next twenty-six years, the sore caused by Operation Ajax would fester. In 1979, it ruptured.

Internally, the fact that the United States so easily ensured the political survival of Muhammad Reza Shah confirmed just how deeply

---

*In the galaxy of conspiracy theories of the time, many Iranians supposedly in the know said it was Britain that had brought Mossadeq to power. Certain that he would nationalize oil, Mossadeq would rid the British of the purportedly uneconomical Abadan refinery and, at the same time, award British Petroleum millions of dollars in compensation.

the roots of kingship dug into Iran's culture and political life. For most of the people of Iran in 1953, a king represented the only constant of political life. After so many centuries, any other form of government other than absolute or constitutional monarchy seemed inconceivable. Still it was the other lessons of 1951 to 1953 that would prove even more true when the Iranian Revolution came in 1979. First, the coalition that followed Muhammad Mossadeq formed by a segment of clerics and the diverse political groups of the National Front certified the passionate power of Iranian nationalism. Second, the ability of Mossadeq to draw vast numbers of people to his cause demonstrated the power of public opinion, which in the future revolution would serve as the major weapon against Muhammad Reza Shah. Finally, the Tudeh party's catastrophic failure to mobilize a mass movement among the downtrodden of society bore out the reality that alien ideologies such as communism, translated and executed by leaders whose interests lie beyond Shia Iran, could not deliver vast numbers to a cause. Marxism, with its call to class war led by political cadres committed to world revolution, proved to be an unacceptable substitute for the deep and pervasive beliefs of social justice in Shiism supported by loyalty to clerics who acted as its primary custodians. The same held true for Western liberal thought that had challenged the traditions of Shiism in the interest of national revival since the nineteenth century. The collapse of Mossadeq's government from its own internal contradictions created confusion and self-doubt across the breadth of the political center. As in 1906, only religion had proved able to direct the masses. As a result, the thinkers who had long followed the Persian tradition of inquiry and assimilation of Western political thought abdicated their frontline position in Iranian politics. No man, group, or ideology took their place until 1963, when nationalism and opposition to Muhammad Reza Shah revived under the flag of Islam. But for the moment, Shiism remained contained in its traditional mold.

When the shah resumed his seat on the Peacock throne, he strengthened his ties with Ayatollah Borujerdi, whose policy of political quiescence had denied Mossadeq the full benefit of Iran's masses. The *ulama*, for their part, entertained no interest in challenging the monarchy as long as the shah allowed them to exercise religious authority in relative peace. In this atmosphere of coexistence of crown and turban, the fiery old Ayatollah Kashani slipped into political obscurity. Sharing the shah's fear of and contempt for communism, the *ulama* quietly supported the brutal two-year campaign to crush the

Tudeh. Ayatollah Borujerdi, the apolitical model of emulation, claimed only one reward for the clerical hierarchy's refusal to follow Mossadeq. It was official tolerance of a campaign against the Bahais. In 1955, the shah sent his own chief of staff to swing the first pick that destroyed the dome of the Bahai temple in Tehran. In the ensuing months, he remained silent as death and destruction descended on the Bahais in what was whispered to be Borujerdi's attempt to destroy the faith. Before that goal was realized, the shah became alarmed that public order might slip beyond the control of his army. For perhaps the first time but not the last, the shah saw the raw power of religion. In response, he began to shut down the assault on the Bahais. And Borujerdi acquiesced, for he had already forced the shah to swallow a large bite of Shiism. In the interest of accommodation with clerical authority, the shah delivered to Borujerdi more religious instruction in the public schools; tighter control of cinemas and other offensive secular entertainment; and public acts which confirmed the monarch's obedience to Shiism. Although never recognized as a pious man, Muhammad Reza Shah visited Iran's Shia shrines and put on the simple white seamless garment of the pilgrim to make the Haj to Mecca. He broke ground for a mosque on the campus of the University of Tehran, Iran's temple of secular education. And he publicly described his visions, in which he saw Ali bestowing on him the spiritual link to the divine force of Shia Islam and its imams. But Muhammad Reza Shah never succeeded in convincing either the Shia establishment or pious Iranians of his religious commitment. When Ayatollah Borujerdi died on March 30, 1961, the mutually beneficial arrangement between the Shia hierarchy and the shah began to unravel. The way opened to the politicization of the deeply religious middle and lower classes in response to the drive toward absolute power by a shah who fulfilled neither the Persian nor the Islamic requirements for authority.

8

The Shah and
the Ayatollah:
Persia and Islam

THE RUINS OF PERSEPOLIS ARE HAUNTED BY GHOSTS OTHER than those of Darius and Xerxes. Also lurking in the great ceremonial city of the Achaemenians is the spirit of Muhammad Reza Shah, the last Pahlavi. Unlike Darius, who chose to leave his image as a king locked in mortal combat with the forces of evil, the representation of the shah does not adorn a towering portal. Nor is his name attached to any grand building where the delegates of nations paid him homage. For only once did representatives from the world beyond Iran's borders come to Persepolis to salute the Pahlavi king. Little is left to commemorate that event, only several rows of rusting iron chairs linked together like bleachers that sit just beyond the two majestic winged horses that compose the Gate of Nations. About them hangs a haunting air of the past absent from the rest of Persepolis. Perhaps the broken columns, portals, and reliefs of ancient Persepolis resonate grandeur because they evince true greatness. What the corroded relic of a day in October 1971 represents is Muhammad Reza Shah's plastic resurrection of Achaemenian Persia. When kings and princes, presidents and prime ministers came to Persepolis to pay tribute to the Pahlavi king, Iran possessed neither an authentic empire nor a celebrated monarch who ruled hand in hand with either Ahura Mazda or Allah.

After the events of 1953, the weak, vacillating Muhammad Reza Shah disappeared. In his place materialized the heir of Reza Shah's authoritarianism. With this new political persona, the second Pahlavi shah began to build the apparatus that would create a supreme patriarch ensconced on an all-powerful throne. Lacking charisma and ignoring the expectation of just rule, Muhammad Reza Shah's monarchy rested on foundation blocks composed from the military, the police, and an internal intelligence organization called SAVAK. But the shah's reconstruction of his monarchy did not go unchallenged. In the second decade of the second Pahlavi shah, escalating opposition locked step with escalating control. In 1963, Muhammad Reza Shah, responding to pressure from his American ally and to his own need to broaden his base of popular support, launched the bloodless reformation of Iranian society known as the White Revolution. In it, cosmetic economic and social reform directed from the throne ran head on into the interests and traditions of Shia Islam. So it was that twelve years after Muhammad Mossadeq galvanized the secularists into defiance of Pahlavi rule, a charismatic cleric by the name of Ayatollah Ruhollah Khomeini charged out of near obscurity to challenge Muhammad Reza Shah in the name of Islam. Bereft of a complacent clergy and alienated from the nontraditional middle class that had followed Mossadeq, the shah wrapped himself in the cloak of ancient kingship to shove Iran toward the extreme of its Persian identity. The Pahlavi version of resurrected Persia was celebrated at Persepolis in 1971. In this elevation of his own rendition of ancient Persia and his repression of Islam, Muhammad Reza Shah laid the cultural foundations of the Iranian Revolution that would eventually consume him and the 2,500-year-old institution of Persian kingship.

Muhammad Reza Shah's kingship transformed in his precipitate flight from Iran in 1953. Mossadeq's referendum to dissolve the Majlis that triggered Operation Ajax, the flight of the shah into self-imposed exile, and the restoration of Pahlavi rule had all occurred over a short span of twelve days. En route home from Rome aboard a chartered KLM Constellation, the euphoric shah shed his suit coat and joined the scant dozen journalists accompanying him in one champagne toast after another. However, each mile that passed below the wings of the plane brought him physically and psychologically closer to Iran and his destiny as the shahanshah. When the man who had so nominally ruled Iran since 1941 arrived in Tehran, he was a changed man.

Reacting to the crowd that greeted him, Muhammad Reza Shah decided that he was no longer a purely hereditary king but the chosen of the people. Ignoring the part that Mossadeq's failings and American actions played in the drama, the shah chose to see in his restoration to the throne, as he saw in the failed attempt on his life in 1949, that divinely decreed link between the Iranian people and their king. Tragically for himself and Iran, the shah would never understand that the missing element in this mystical vision of ruler and ruled was the ancient Persian requirement for kingly authority—just rule. Instead, the shah had decided in exile that his preordained possession of the Peacock throne demanded absolute power. This meant that he would trust no man to remain absolutely loyal to him in all circumstances and would depend on the allegiance of no group or organization to defend his throne. Like his father, he would walk alone, suspicious of every so-called friend; of every minister professing obedience; of every servant bowing in devotion; of every shadow that crossed his path.

Between 1953 and 1960, a monarch previously known for equivocation mobilized the elements of authoritarianism. In the Pahlavi manner, Muhammad Reza Shah pressed on his fractious kingdom the organs of coercion belonging to the state—the army, the gendarmerie, the police, and SAVAK.* SAVAK's decade would be the 1970s. In the 1950s, the shah principally relied on the more conventional tools of state control.

The foot soldiers of the military, gendarmerie, and police came largely from members of the lower and lower middle classes anxious to improve their humble social status and with it the uncertain economic circumstances surrounding them and their extended families. Those in the officer corps, particularly that of the military, were products of the middle class and a segment of the upper class drawn into service to the shah by the contacts and economic rewards that service provided. By the early 1960s, Muhammad Reza Shah had tapped into other bases of support—the economic elite and the bureaucracy who shared with the throne an interest in the status quo. Still, the fledgling security forces and two groups of elites were not enough to give Muhammad Reza Shah true power. Political unrest, primarily from the remnants of the old National Front and the Communist left, erupted in a dozen ugly episodes on Tehran's streets between January 1960 and January 1962. Out of them, the sound of rebellion reverberated across the whole country, once more calling into question Pahlavi control.

The shah sought some accommodation with the opposition by permitting a degree of freedom in the areas of speech, assembly, and the

*SAVAK, formed in 1957, was the acronym for Sazman-e-Ettelaat va Amniyat-e-Keshvar, meaning Intelligence and Security Organization of the Country.

press. But these modest reforms failed to satisfy the far left wing of the political spectrum as well as those in the political center who had followed Mossadeq. It was this liberal, nationalist center, thinking in terms of Western political models, that blamed the shah for failing to deliver to his subjects some form of Western-style democracy. Below the surface of the political debate between the shah and his secular opponents gestated an embryonic cultural debate which questioned the priorities and assumptions that had fueled much of the Mossadeq era. The young and restless generation that provided the nationalist movement of the early 1950s with much of its energy had been driven by the hope for a democratic future. In their vision, they perceived democracy as the mother of all progress just as they viewed the equally amorphous past as the cause of all malice. Like most educated Iranians of the time, these young intellectuals floated between tomorrow and yesterday, yearning for one and rejecting the other. The man who began to bring the Iranian past and the future together in terms of culture was Jalal Al-e Ahmad, the giant of Iranian literature in the 1960s.

Jalal Al-e Ahmad has come perhaps closer than anyone to addressing the duality of Iranian identity. Born into a Tehran family of clerics in 1923, he spent his childhood living under the imposing shadow of two powerful authority figures—his father and Reza Shah. The dueling demands of each pulled Al-e Ahmad in two diametrically opposed directions—the faith and traditions of his father and the ideology and imagery of Reza Shah's modernizing Iran. As a consequence, Al-e Ahmad gathered his education from both. During the day, he followed his peers to the religious school dictated for sons of the clergy. At night, he quietly stole away to Dar-ul-Fonun, Tehran's polytechnic institute, where he tasted modern Western education. It was both Islamic theology and Pahlavi secularism, disguised as Persian culture, that formed the philosophical field to which Jalal Al-e Ahmad eventually called Iranians to come to examine their identity. The mirror he gave them was language. Of all modern Iranian writers, none has wielded words and ideas with the force of Jalal Al-e Ahmad. With his pen and his mind, he articulated the Iranians' deep sense of cultural alienation stemming from a dynasty all but disconnected from an essential element in Iranian identity—Islam.

Al-e Ahmad's adolescence was spent in the confusion of World War II, when foreign occupation confirmed Iran's national impotence. In that confusion, a host of ideologies floated, each promising the an-

swer to Iranian society's malaise created by the twentieth-century conflict between past and present, tradition and change, religion and secularism, nationalism and Westernization. By the end of the war, Jalal
Al-e Ahmad had renounced both his faith and his family to embrace
the Tudeh, the Iranian Communist party. With almost nothing beyond a necktie and a secondhand American suit, he joined the quest
for Iran's future. It proved to be an uneven course. By 1947, Al-e
Ahmad's Communist ideology had paled under the cloud of Stalinism
and Soviet expansionism. It was replaced by a more European-style
socialism. That was tested in 1953, when the liberals behind Muhammad Mossadeq faced disillusionment in the prime minister's assumption of dictatorial powers. In time, Al-e Ahmad's socialist philosophy
gave way, to be replaced by a deep cynicism that grew from the belief
that no political movement existed that was capable of addressing the
complexities and inequities of Iranian society. Hence as he had once
rejected his family, Al-e Ahmad now publicly renounced his leftist
politics in order to devote himself to the search for what some would
term the soul of Iran.

Jalal Al-e Ahmad might well have spent the rest of his life as a
nameless pilgrim on a pointless quest if he had not been a gifted
writer of moody, quasi-autobiographical essays and short stories that
spoke to a people accustomed to notable literature. Through his own
self-reflections, Al-e Ahmad not only challenged the failings he observed in Iranian society but began to define his particular vision of
Iranian culture. For the rest of his life, the politics of culture served
as the great subject of his work.

Between 1953 and 1960, Al-e Ahmad abandoned the intellectual
life in Tehran to immerse himself in the countryside. He was driven
by the uneasy feeling that while the politicians and intellectuals "were
trying to determine the fate of Iran in the fever of coup and
countercoup in the capital, the real Iran might be 'out there' in the
tens of thousands of villages, neglected, quietly suffering, not yet seduced by a thousand foreign objects and ideas, still somehow genuinely and unembarrassedly Iranian."[1] Instead, it was the city that
listened to the realities of the Iranian cultural dilemma.

In 1962, Jalal Al-e Ahmad published his best-known work,
Gharbzadegi, or, in a loose translation from the Farsi, "Plagued by the
West." Writing in the genre of the essay, Al-e Ahmad attacked the
rapid Westernization that Muhammad Reza Shah, in the pattern of
Reza Shah, was inflicting on the country. Although an all-out verbal
assault on the Western intrusion of Iran, the real message of *Gharb-*

zadegi was the Iranians' own deep cultural alienation. In the words of the author, "Today we stand under that [Western] banner, a people alienated from ourselves; in our clothing, shelter, food, literature, and press. And more dangerous than all, in our culture. We educate pseudo-Westerners and we try to find solutions to every problem like pseudo-Westerners."[2]

Dwelling at the core of Jalal Al-e Ahmad's anxiety about the Westernization chased by the Pahlavis was the fear that the Iranians stood in danger of losing their unique identity. He said, "A West-stricken man who is a member of the ruling establishment of the country has no place to stand. He is like a dust particle floating in space, or a string floating on water. He has severed his ties with the essence of society, culture, custom. He is not a bond between antiquity and modernity. He is not a dividing line between the old and the new. He is something unrelated to the past and someone with no understanding of the future."[3]

As counterweight to the shah's rootless Westernization, Al-e Ahmad used *Gharbzadegi* and his later writings to affirm an Iranian identity grounded in the Persian language and Shia Islam. In his mind, Iranian culture could be secured only when the vast majority of Iranians accepted that there is an essential role for Islam in Iranian culture just as there is an essential role for the characteristics of Persia. Castigating both intellectual and cleric for forfeiting their heritage, Al-e Ahmad's pen drew the maxim that Iranian society cannot rely exclusively on either half of its identity. Climaxing his years of observing Iranian politics and culture, he wrote, "Whenever clericalism and intellectualism go hand in hand or one follows the other [in Iranian politics] there is in the Social Struggle a gain, progress and a step toward perfection and evolution. And whenever these two have clashed with, or ignored, each other or have singly participated in the struggle, there has been, from a social perspective, a loss, a setback, and a step backward."[4] It was an argument that touched a broad range of Iranians. While being a Muslim might no longer be an intimate spiritual experience for the nontraditional segment of the population, professing Islam still remained an intricate part of being an Iranian.

While not necessarily accepting his call to Shia Islam, the liberal secularists consumed *Gharbzadegi*. Already angry about the shah's closed political system, they added another item to their list of grievances—cultural invasion. With stunning speed, copies of a book proposing the idea of identity as a rallying point for social grievances circulated among intellectuals. When the shah's censorship machine, operating as the Committee for the Guidance of Iranian Culture, banned its publication, Al-e Ahmad's devotees passed smudged, dog-eared photocopies hand to hand. In this manner, *Gharbzadegi* joined his other writings circulating in the literary underground from earlier years of the shah's reign.

During the first two decades that he sat on the throne, Muhammad Reza Shah's personal life seemed at times as tumultuous as his political life. After a childhood in his father's forbidding shadow, there had been his 1939 marriage to Fawzia, the sister of Egypt's King Farouk.* The ceremony itself proved difficult when Reza Shah and the bride's mother wrangled over whether the dowry stayed in Iran or went to Egypt. The shah won, causing Egypt's dowager queen to storm out of Tehran before the five-week-long festivities ended.

Despite its rocky start, the first year of the union of Muhammad Reza and Fawzia seemed happy. At least happy enough to produce the princess Shahnaz in 1940. In 1941, the crown prince suddenly became shah and Fawzia his queen. Through World War II, the restrictions on travel imposed by global conflict locked the ruler of a poor, isolated country and the cosmopolitan sister of the Egyptian king in Tehran, in the palace with Ashraf, the shah's dominating twin sister. By the end of 1947, Fawzia had had enough. Because she was a princess in her own right, she possessed the power and the means to leave the heir of the Peacock throne and return to Egypt with their child. All that remained of the marriage was the formality of divorce.

By 1949, Muhammad Reza Shah had reverted back to his earlier pattern of playboy. Seeming to be engaged in a psychological battle against his own weaknesses, he barreled through life as a pilot, sports-man, and womanizer. In sight of the Western gossip columnists, he danced the night away in the nightclubs of London and romanced such actresses as Yvonne De Carlo, Gene Tierney, and Silvana Mangano. But on February 12, 1951, the philandering shah took as his second wife Soraya Esfandiari, the European-educated daughter of a Bakhtiari tribal chief and his German wife. Fate stalked the marriage from the beginning. The wedding had to be postponed once because the bride contracted typhoid. A second date set at her recovery tottered when she relapsed. Regardless of the state of his bride's health,

---

*In arranging the marriage, Reza Shah demonstrated just how little he regarded the Shia faith in public affairs by wedding the crown prince to a Sunni Muslim.

the anxious bridegroom would wait no longer. The weak, feverish Soraya was pulled from her bed, dressed in thick woolen underwear to protect her from the cold, and buttoned into her forty-pound Dior wedding gown. When she almost fainted while sitting for the wedding picture, the shah ordered her ladies-in-waiting to lighten the weight of the dress by cutting away its heavy petticoats. Relieved of some of her burden, Soraya crept into the waiting Rolls-Royce, rode to Gulistan Palace, and endured the wedding and grand dinner for three hundred guests. Three months into the royal marriage, Muhammad Mossadeq became prime minister of Iran.

Only nineteen when she married, Soraya weathered the political turmoil of 1951 and 1952. In 1953, she fled Iran with her husband and returned to spend five more years in the shah's palace. The marriage broke under a crisis that was more political than personal. The shah needed a male heir to the shaky Peacock throne. His only full brother, Ali Reza, had died in a plane crash in October 1954, leaving the Pahlavi dynasty without a successor. This conjured up the unhappy prospect that in the event of Muhammad Reza Shah's untimely death the throne might go back to the Qajars through Reza Shah's children by his third and fourth wives. In seven years of marriage, Soraya had yet to conceive. Again finding himself unable to wait, the shah divorced his second wife on March 14, 1958.

Muhammad Reza Shah was now thirty-nine years old. Lacking a male heir, he had ruled as the uncrowned king of Iran for seventeen years. Time demanded another wife, one who could give him the son he so desperately needed. It was his daughter by Fawzia who found the beautiful Farah Diba, the product of a respectable Iranian family who was studying at the Ecole Speciale d'Architecture in Paris. They married on December 21, 1959, two months after Farah's twenty-first birthday.

Within a few months, Farah had undertaken her expected role. The palace announced that she was pregnant and "following a careful regime to insure that her baby would be a boy."[5] Prince Reza, the long-awaited heir, arrived October 31, 1960. Across Iran, cannons boomed the news of a male heir. In the Pahlavi capital of Tehran, airplanes swooped low to drop flowers over the city while outside the hospital where the new prince slept, wild rue, a sweet-smelling herb, burned day and night to ward off the evil eye.

Farah and her son gave Muhammad Reza Shah a sense of security he had never experienced before. Yet it was an illusion. To vast numbers of Iranians, an heir to the throne could not satisfy the expectation of just rule by the sitting king. But the shah listened less and less to the voices inside Iran. He preferred to hear those from the West. To Westerners fed a constant stream of articles in the popular press about the making of modern Iran, the shah, his charming wife, and their infant son created their own fairy tale. A 1962 *Saturday Evening Post* article accompanied by pictures of the royal family on the lawn of the summer palace proved to be more prophetic than most. "There was no hint, in the quiet garden, of the greater crises which lurked like ogres beyond the garden walls, nor of the dynamic forces of change which could, if uncontrolled, destroy this happy family and all it represented."[6]

In the summer of 1960, the shah, in accordance with the 1906 constitution, had announced the results of the election for the Majlis. Like everything else in Pahlavi Iran, the Majlis elections mimicked a puppet show in which the shah functioned as the sole puppeteer. Although no one had expected a completely honest election, that of 1960 was so blatantly rigged that even some of the winners were embarrassed. A usually lethargic electorate rose up in protest. When the bazaar closed, the shah canceled the election and with it the new parliament. In the end, the election, rather than creating a defining moment for political reform, served only as another symptom of the shah's increasingly autocratic rule.

Muhammad Reza Shah worked his will through favor and force, cooperation and coercion. In a system that promoted complete loyalty to his person, the Pahlavi king presided as the shahanshah. He brooked no criticism and tolerated no dissent. Within the shah's autocratic state, a generation of young intellectuals confronted the issues that Jalal Al-e Ahmad articulated—corruption of the Pahlavi regime, Westernization and modernization, Iranian identity and national integrity. In January 1962, the University of Tehran, one of the shah's institutions of modernization, became the scene of noisy student demonstrations against the king. After the military went in to crush the protests, the chancellor of the university wrote, "I have never seen or heard so much cruelty, sadism, atrocity, and vandalism on the part of the government forces. Some of the girls in the classrooms were criminally attacked by the soldiers. When we inspected the University buildings we were faced with the same situation as if an army of barbarians had invaded enemy territory."[7]

Fretting as the Eisenhower administration had fretted about the Communist threat in Iran, the administration of John F. Kennedy prodded the shah to institute basic political reform. Bluntly stated, that was the price of continued American support. Consequently in January 1963, Muhammad Reza Shah unfurled the banner of his White Revolution, the bloodless transformation of Iranian society. Although its multiple components included the reorganization of government, privatization of a certain class of government-owned factories, profit-sharing plans for some workers, and the enfranchisement of women, the thrust of the White Revolution was land reform.

In 1963, roughly 75 percent of Iran's total population toiled as peasants. With 80 to 85 percent of all cultivatable land in the hands of a few hundred families, they lived within Iran's own particular form of feudalism. Into the second half of the twentieth century, some rural areas remained so economically underdeveloped that they still operated on a barter economy. In too many villages, there was no school or hospital, no sanitation or electricity. At times, there was not even a match.

But the difficulty of village life was not the reason why Muhammad Reza Shah decided to distribute the property of the landed aristocracy to the landless peasants. Despite his efforts to build a political base in the military, the industrial elite, and the bureaucracy, the shah in the early 1960s faced both a resurgent National Front still demanding democracy and national independence and a kinetic Communist left energized by Soviet propaganda that maintained a constant barrage against Iran's "rotten monarchical regime." In addition there lurked, as it had always lurked in the minds of the Pahlavi shahs, the power of Islam. In the grand scheme known as the White Revolution, the shah would sacrifice the large landholdings that gave the aristocracy its income and the clergy an important part of its funding to secure the loyalty of the peasants. With their massive numbers and traditional loyalty to Persian-style kingship, the peasantry would, in turn, counter the forces lined up against the shah. For a while, the White Revolution seemed to give the shah what he sought.

A few months after declaring land reform a covenant between the king and his subjects, Muhammad Reza Shah arrived in an impoverished village in Khuzestan. Erect and regal in a pin-striped suit, he mounted the steps of a podium covered by a deep red Persian carpet to take his place next to a leather box holding rolls of heavy white paper tied with strands of dark blue ribbon. Each was a deed to a plot of land designated for a peasant who had always tilled the land of others. One by one, sun-baked men climbed three steps, bowed to the shah, and took their document. Halfway through the ceremony, a peasant, dressed in a loose green-and-white striped robe cinched with a bright green sash, fell to his knees. Tears of gratitude washed down his face as he kissed the shah's feet again and again. A king who craved public adoration looked embarrassed. Reaching down to touch the prostrate man on the shoulder, he indicated that he rise. The humble peasant slowly got to his feet, wiped his eyes, took his deed, and returned to his newly granted land to join the peasants in support of Muhammad Reza Shah. Unfortunately for the future of Iran, neither the peasants nor the shah fulfilled the expectations the one had of the other.

The White Revolution never constituted a real revolution. Rather, it represented an exercise in political expediency dictated by the man who sat at the top of Iran's social order. While it gave the peasants hope, it also alienated most of the other groups on the Iranian political spectrum. The old aristocracy, the "thousand families," opposed the White Revolution because land reform eroded their wealth and position. The middle class dismissed it as nothing more than a political palliative designed to impress the Western press and an American administration. And the clergy resisted, first, because land reform threatened to take ten thousand villages that helped finance the clerical establishment and its religious mission, and second, because it hit the landowning families from which a large percentage of the upper echelon of the clergy came. To his later regret, the shah ignored them all. He dismissed the landowners as small fish in the shah's new political order. He refused to placate the middle classes with real political reform, thereby losing his most effective allies in modernization. And he invited the wrath of Shia Islam. The White Revolution did nothing less than put Muhammad Reza Shah and the guardians of Shiism on a collision course over its two most celebrated elements—land reform and the initial steps toward the emancipation of women.

Although united in recognizing the reality of the White Revolution's threat to established religion, the Shia clerics divided between those who agitated against the shah's program and those who, in the tradition of Shiism and personal gain, chose to stay quiet. Rather than seeking accommodation with the dissidents, the shah attempted to exploit the division by defining who among the clerics legitimately exercised authority. From the holy city of Qom, he declared that only those religious leaders who did not oppose his land reform "are indubitably our religious leaders . . . and by the blessings of this sacred shrine they will serve Islam, the Shah and their country."[8] He dismissed the rest of Shiism's clerics as "black reactionaries" and "lice-ridden mullahs."

With the benefit of hindsight, the direct, overt challenge that some of Shiism's clerics threw at the shah over core elements in the White Revolution marked the beginning of the Iranian Revolution that erupted sixteen years later. Central to those later events was an ongoing revision of religion's role within the state generated by a tiny core of Shia theologians. This new strand of Shia thought asserted the importance of Islam as a way of life to a society increasingly pressured by state-mandated policies of modernization based on Western ideas and technology. Its revolutionary aspect lay in the call to the religious establishment and its followers to engage in active political opposition to the Pahlavi regime.

For almost thirteen hundred years after Hussein's stand against the usurpers of authority at Karbala, Shiism had stayed disengaged from politics. Although political men such as the Safavids employed Shiism as a tool of nation building, the learned scholars of Shia Islam had kept themselves and the faith removed from the secular world. Even during the Constitutional Revolution and the era of Mossadeq, the political clerics who participated in the Nationalist Movement came almost exclusively out of the middle tiers of the religious hierarchy. But by the early 1960s, the theological opinions of several renowned religious leaders had come together in the argument that the *mujtahid* must move out of the isolation of religious rituals and practices to grasp the whole range of society and politics as the Prophet had done. The most celebrated figure in this revolutionary reconstruction of religion as politics was Ayatollah Ruhollah Khomeini.

Ruhollah Khomeini seems fatefully intertwined with twentieth-century Iran. The man who would destroy the Pahlavi dynasty in the name of Shia Iran was born in 1902 in a mud brick house in the backwater town of Khomein during the prelude to Iran's first revolution. In material terms, his family lived in neither poverty nor riches. Nonetheless, it claimed wealth in its religious credentials bestowed by the claim of descent from the Prophet and a procession of mullahs produced through its bloodlines. It was in this religious tradition that the child was named Ruhollah, meaning "soul of God."* Denied a fa-

*The man the world knows as Ayatollah Ruhollah Khomeini was simply "Ruhollah" until 1926, when Reza Shah required all Iranians to adopt a last name. At that time, he became Ruhollah Mustafavi. He acquired the name Khomeini when he became an aya-

ther by murder, the boy grew up with the Koran, completing his first reading of Islam's holiest text at the age of seven.*

Seeming to follow the plotline of a grand drama, Khomeini became a mullah the year Reza Shah ascended the throne of Iran. In the years that the first Pahlavi shah drove Iran toward Western-style modernization and warred with Shia Islam, Ruhollah Khomeini built a reputation as a teacher and Islamic scholar. Although he observed the introduction of Western technology, the unveiling of women, and the establishment of the secular University of Tehran with foreboding, Khomeini's political consciousness awoke in Reza Shah's brutal suppression of the popular revolt in the Shrine of Imam Reza in 1935. Nonetheless in both his instruction and his writing, which began to appear in the late 1920s, he accepted monarchy as an integral part of Iranian tradition and, therefore, a legitimate form of government for Iran. In 1941, the year Reza Shah abdicated, Ruhollah Khomeini was established as a teacher at Qom. In 1944, the year the exiled Reza Shah died, Khomeini published his most important theological work to date—*Secrets Exposed*—which reflected his rising concern about a society and a regime pervaded with Western secular ideas.

During the early 1950s, when the Nationalist Movement confronted the second Pahlavi shah, Ruhollah Khomeini identified with Ayatollah Kashani's political stance. But he absented himself from the political trenches in compliance with Ayatollah Borujerdi's apolitical philosophy. As long as Borujerdi lived, Khomeini refused to defy his superior, keeping his political opinions in writing, stored away within the pages of his advanced Arabic textbooks. When Borujerdi died in 1961, the clerical climate in which Khomeini lived changed dramatically. Khomeini's political behavior changed with it.

After the watershed year of 1953, Ruhollah Khomeini had continued to build his reputation within Qom's clerical circles as an exceptional legal talent. The tall, forbidding man moved through the halls of the *madresehs* never smiling at anybody or anything. Rather than his personality, it was his intellect that pulled the *talabehs* to his public lectures on Thursday afternoons, where his practice of ignoring

tollah. According to tradition, a cleric adopts the name of his place of birth when he reaches the highest station in Shia Islam. For the sake of clarity, Ruhollah Mustafavi will be consistently referred to as Khomeini.

*Khomeini's father was the chief cleric of Khomein. In that position, he ordered the execution of a man who defied the Islamic injunction of fasting between sunrise and sunset during the month of Ramazan. His own death came at the hands of a friend of the executed man.

his audience while he taught contributed to his charisma. In private, Khomeini wrote *ghazals* in the style of Hafez and taught to a select group of students the controversial philosophy of *erfan*, Shia mysticism. As a respected cleric through the 1930s, 1940s, and 1950s, he had attracted followers as well as requests for religious rulings from Shia all over Iran. In 1960, the year Muhammad Reza Shah's heir was born, he collated these opinions into a book titled *Towzihih-e Masail*, "Explication of Problems." Containing over three thousand rulings on everything from the correct way to face while defecating to the relationship of religion to the state, its publication gave Ruhollah Khomeini the status of ayatollah.

In retrospect, the most significant chapter in *Towzihih-e Masail* concerned the resistance to oppression. In it, Khomeini argued that Islam's mission extends beyond the establishment of rules of worship and morality. Indeed, the divine mandate of the religion delivered by the Prophet is the regulation of all the affairs of society, including the secular realm of politics. Breaking centuries-old Shia tradition, Khomeini argued that Islam cannot divide the state from society, the secular from the religious. So it was that over thirty years after he became a mullah, Ruhollah Khomeini stepped forward to give religious sanction and clerical leadership to political opposition to Muhammad Reza Shah.

It was Ayatollah Khomeini who threw the White Revolution like a gauntlet before the shah. Pointing his long finger at the announced distribution of clerical lands to the peasants and the emancipation of women, Khomeini damned the White Revolution as the final Pahlavi assault on the remaining powers of the clergy and the place of religion in Iranian society. Portraying himself as the conscience of a nation, Khomeini denounced the White Revolution as deviation from God's will and a violation of the faith. During the ancient Persian holiday of No Ruz in March 1963, he urged all believers to boycott celebrations of the new year "in order to warn the Muslim community of the imminent dangers facing the Koran...."[9] His admonition ended with the prophetic words, "Oh Allah, I have performed my first duty and if you allow me to live longer and permit me, I shall shoulder other tasks in the future."[10]

In his denunciation of the White Revolution, Ayatollah Khomeini had changed the format and leadership of political opposition in Iran from liberal secularism to religion. But while the cleric waved moral authority, the shah commanded secular power. Through a series of orders from the throne aimed at stemming the rising tide of religious dissent, more than sixty mullahs went into detention; hundreds of theology students, normally exempt from national service, reported to the army; government funds to targeted clergymen disappeared; and security around Qom tightened. On March 22, 1963, the shah's soldiers stormed through the doors of the revered Faiziyeh Theological School in Qom. In the claimed defense of state security, they arrested dozens of students. Unsheathing their weapons, the agents of the shah repeatedly struck the *talabehs*, ultimately killing two students of Shiism armed with nothing but their Korans. Those who managed to escape ran directly to Ayatollah Khomeini.

The house where Khomeini lived in 1963 is located on a narrow alley within walking distance of the Shrine of Fatimah. Like the typical Iranian house, it is surrounded by a high stucco wall bisected by wide iron gates. They open into a garden where the water from a small fountain plays against the desert heat. The house itself is modest—a small reception room, a sitting room, a narrow kitchen, and a few bedrooms to the back. Except for a recent coat of paint, little about it has changed since 1963, when Ayatollah Ruhollah Khomeini lived within its walls. Even the same tea boy who served the great teacher of Qom is still there. He is now grayed and wrinkled. But wearing the same style white skullcap, baggy pants, and vest, he gives life to that moment in history when the events surrounding the invasion of the Faiziyeh Theological School transformed Ayatollah Khomeini from a highly respected clergyman into a political icon.

Positioning himself to confront Muhammad Reza Shah on the political battlefield, Khomeini led the traditional mourning ceremonies for the dead students of Faiziyeh forty days after the raid. From the Great Mosque of Qom, he spoke of martyrdom and politics with a passion and courage never before seen in twentieth-century Iran. Four days later, on the afternoon of June 3, Khomeini returned to the theological school to preach again. It was Ashura, the tenth day of the Shia month of Muharram, when the faithful mourn Hussein's martyrdom at Karbala. Students and townspeople filled the courtyards around the school and spilled into those of the buildings around, including the Shrine of Fatimah. Loudspeakers stood ready to carry the ayatollah's message to the ears of the person in the farthest corner. Khomeini himself sat in a tall archway, his turban unwound and draped across his shoulders as a symbol of deep mourning. When he began to speak, officials of the shah cut the electricity all over Qom. Demonstrating the ability to frustrate authority which would characterize the 1979 revolution, Khomeini supporters quickly uncovered a generator, hooked up the speaker system, and returned to their places to hear the words of the ayatollah. At the age of sixty-one, Ruhollah Khomeini hurled politicized religion at Muhammad Reza Shah, charging that the king opposed Islam. And then he issued a warning. "You miserable wretch, forty-five years of your life have passed. Isn't it time for you to think and reflect a little, to ponder about where all of this is leading you, to learn a lesson from the experience of your father? I hope to God that you did not have in mind the religious scholars when you said, 'The reactionaries are like an impure animal,' because if you did, it will be difficult for us to tolerate you much longer, and you will find yourself in a predicament. . . . The nation will not allow you to continue this way."[11] Finally his passionate words labeled the shah the modern-day Yazid, the ruler who ordered Hussein slain. It was the most vile accusation any Shia could direct at the man on the throne. As much as its boldness, Khomeini's condemnation of Muhammad Reza Shah carried with it the authority of religion in Shia Iran.

Before the dawn the next day, agents of the shah arrested Ayatollah Ruhollah Khomeini. The news spread with the light of the rising sun. By the following day, June 5, mullahs, theology students, and guild leaders had plastered the walls of Tehran with Khomeini's picture and organized thousands of tradesmen, craftsmen, vendors, and anyone else willing to join in mass demonstrations against Pahlavi power. Out of the southern slums, the mullahs sent the poor surging northward shouting, "Down with the shah!" In the center of the city, mobs utilizing young boys as shields stormed toward the radio station and key government buildings. Defending the Pahlavi capital, troops of the shah sent in to quell the mayhem opened fire at point-blank range. In place after place, the crowds fell back, regrouped, and charged down another main street. Armed with clubs, rocks, and torches, they demolished stores and set fire to part of the bazaar. Unable to contain the violence, helmeted troops screened by the menacing bulk of tanks carrying the mark Made in the USA sealed off the royal palaces and hid the whereabouts of the shah. For three days, all the pent-up rage that had been festering since the shah returned to power in 1953 unleashed its fury.

The days of rioting in June 1963 engulfed Mashhad, Isfahan, Shiraz, and Qom, killing at least eighty-six people and destroying millions of dollars' worth of property. In the end, it took seven thousand troops wielding the club of martial law to restore order in the mass outpouring of support for the man one American expert on Iran identified as someone named "Abdullah" Khomeini.

If Westerners did not yet know the man whom they would one day bitterly call "the ayatollah," the Iranians did. Ruhollah Khomeini had catapulted into national consciousness as the man who dared to publicly oppose the authoritarianism of the shah. His imprisonment at the hands of secular authority only amplified his demand for justice. Attracting *bazaaris*, teachers, workers, and professionals, Khomeini essentially took up the reins of the struggle against Muhammad Reza Shah and his foreign patrons snatched from the hands of the nationalists in 1953. With the secular political parties discredited since the overthrow of Mossadeq, he poised to take charge of a mass political movement, cutting across lines of class and ideology, that was defined in terms of Shia Islam. It was a movement in which many failed to question just what Khomeini's political philosophy, if carried to its conclusion, really meant. According to one dissident lawyer who had stood with Mossadeq but now lined up behind Khomeini, "We have not been allowed to form political parties. We have no newspapers of our own. But the religious leaders have a built-in communications system. They easily reach the masses through their weekly sermons in the mosques and their network of mullahs throughout the nation. That is why so many non-religious elements cloak their opposition in the mantle of religion."[12] For those who still sought the promises of the Constitutional Revolution, the bloody riots of June 1963 brought to a final close the Mossadeq era, in which the secularists led the opposition to the shah. With Khomeini and his religious following now in the lead, they began the long march toward the 1979 Iranian Revolution.

In the spring of 1964, the now celebrated Ayatollah Khomeini walked out of jail, freed by his monarch. Various emissaries sent by the shah tried to persuade the cleric to leave politics to the politicians, but his reply was always the same: "All of Islam is politics."[13] He would confront the shah again later that same year on another issue that would send him into exile, leaving the shah, for the moment, alone on the political playing field. (See chapter 12.)

At the end of the June riots, Muhammad Reza Shah emerged from seclusion. Repression of his political enemies lockstepped with the promises of the White Revolution. In Hamadan, the shah told twelve thousand new landowners clutching deeds personally bestowed by His Imperial Majesty, "We will not retreat one millimeter [on land reform]."[14] To its credit, the White Revolution did fitfully extend the government's authority outward from the bureaucratic warrens of Tehran into the remote and neglected countryside. Roads and airfields, radios and telephones came to areas previously connected to the world outside by camel tracks and dirt paths. As a result, teachers and rural health workers established themselves among those who knew no authority other than that of the landlords, the mullahs, and the tribes. But instead of infrastructure and government employees delivering a measure of economic and political freedom, one type of authority simply replaced another. On the road from Shiraz to Pasargadae, as well as other points in Pahlavi Iran, forts standing six to ten miles apart combined the past and the present. Stone towers with loopholes and battlements represented the past. Fifty-caliber machine guns mounted on armored cars tended by full crews in helmets and battle dress defined the present.

Regardless of the realities of Pahlavi rule, the Western press slavishly embraced the shah as a benevolent king compassionately tending his people through his White Revolution. The royal presence graced covers of *Life* and smiled from the pages of most of the major magazines of Western Europe. It all tended to confirm the truth that the White Revolution was little more than the shah's glitzy quest for Western approval. In truth, all of the lofty rhetoric and all of the public ceremonies starring shah and peasant never addressed the root causes of popular dissatisfaction with the Pahlavi regime—one-man rule in the absence of social justice. Like a bad melodrama, some of the changes prompted under the shah's reform program actually increased rather than decreased opposition to Pahlavi rule. For instance, women won the right to vote in 1962, feeding their voice into the affairs of the patriarchal system that undergirded the philosophy of Persian kingship. Government-sponsored adult literacy classes initiated within the larger factories accomplished an almost 100 percent literacy rate among long-term employees but also sparked a new curiosity about politics. Even land reform politicized the masses by sharpening their expectations and drawing them into the political arena as self-interested observers.

Ironically, land reform, the centerpiece of the White Revolution, largely created the urban masses that would propel the Iranian Revolution in 1979. In the redistribution of land, illiterate peasants who for centuries had lived under the benevolent or brutal control of landowners were suddenly cut loose without capital or knowledge to become modern farmers. Quickly the loan shark who could provide money for seed or survival replaced the old landowner as a new and far less beneficent master. Not so quickly, the *qanats*, vital to irrigation, often went to ruin because that organizing force that ensured their maintenance no longer existed. When the *qanats* failed, they took thousands of productive villages with them. Even in areas with adequate water, the plots of land distributed with so much fanfare typically proved too small to yield a living. The possibilities of cooperative farming and the maintenance of equipment to make those cooperatives work had passed to people suffering the fatalism, fear, superstition, and suspicion of illiteracy. Consequently millions of eager, able-bodied farmers watched new tractors they could not repair rust in small fields they could not work because they were deprived of water from the *qanats* they did not maintain. The litany of cause and effect went on and on. By the late 1960s, the cumulative effects of poor management and bloodsucking economics had sent thousands of new landowners and their families to the slums of the cities looking for a means of survival. Jalal Al-e Ahmad pronounced the final verdict on the shah's program of land reform in his story "The White Revolution," in which the writer portrayed a village targeted for land reform. At its end, the villagers, forced to migrate to the cities, have lost not only their land but the taproot attaching them to their traditions and sense of identity.

In the mirror game of myth and reality, Pahlavi rule experienced its golden autumn at the end of the 1960s. Benefiting more from the caprices of short-term luck than the results of long-term development, the Iranian economy surged forward as much as 10 percent a year with little inflation. With the shah's image in the West as the stimulus, Iran reached for stardom as a tourist attraction. Restaurants and public rest rooms to accommodate tourists went up adjacent to the ancient sites of Persia. In Tehran, the Museum of Modern Art and an architecturally distinct theater built in the round beckoned Westerners. As hoped, the tourists came, booked by some of the biggest names in the tourist industry. The first-class tours stayed in northern Tehran in the Hilton Hotel with its spectacular view of the Alborz Mountains. The economy groups went to hotels like the modest five-story Kosar, tucked into a narrow side street off what is now Vali-ye-Asr Square. In some ways, the Kosar remains a monument to the period. The fanned tail of a peacock created from thick pieces of tinted mirror surrounded by heavy plaster still overwhelms the lobby with a poor imitation of the mirrored walls of Gulistan Palace, while two huge urns flanking what was once the concierge desk ineffectually suggest Isfahan. Although the Kosar is now shabby, even seedy, it is easy to imagine the droves of Western tourists who came through its door to be suitably impressed by the artificial face of Pahlavi Iran.

Beneath the incessant propaganda touting the shah and his White Revolution, the populace seethed at the inequalities existing between the sliver of privileged who sat atop the political order and the rest of the population. In 1965 that anger erupted twice. Prime Minister Hassan Ali Mansur died at the door of the Majlis building on January 21, 1965. His assassin proved to be a twenty-one-year-old ironworker who belonged to an activist religious group called Hezb-e-Millat-e-Islami, the Islamic Nations party. It was a little-known group hidden deep within the recesses of lower-class Iranian society. In its very existence, it expressed the milieu of discontent that came from economic deprivation and cultural alienation from a regime that increasingly distanced itself from the Islamic component of Iranian identity.

Less than four months later, on April 10, 1965, a twenty-two-year-old member of the shah's own Imperial Guards turned his submachine gun on the monarch as he entered the Marble Palace. This would-be assassin came from the secular intelligentsia. Taken together, the two men charged with the assassination plots of 1965 represented the range of opposition building against Muhammad Reza Shah. On the right grouped the religiously oriented lower class, and on the left clusters of secular liberals and radicals within the middle class who, through their assimilation of the ideas of the West, adhered more to the Persian strand of Iranian identity. Divided by ideology and community, the religious right and the political left could challenge but not topple Pahlavi rule.

By 1967, Muhammad Reza Shah had survived the wartime occupation of Iran, the Mossadeq era, two assassination attempts, and the first challenge of Ayatollah Khomeini. He had produced an heir to follow him to the Peacock throne. The time had arrived to officially claim the crown of Iran, twenty-six years after Reza Shah abdicated. For seven days before Muhammad Reza Shah's coronation, planes of the Royal Iranian Air Force bombed Tehran with 17,532 roses—one for every day of the shah's life. The same week cannons pounded out 101-gun salutes and the Tehran Symphony premiered the coronation hymn, "You Are the Shadow of God." On October 26, 1967, his forty-eighth birthday, Muhammad Reza Shah and his empress rode through streets strung with a multitude of lights in a seventy-five-thousand-dollar gilded Austrian coach drawn by four pairs of white Hungarian

horses. Their destination was the same as that of Reza Shah on his coronation day—Gulistan Palace.

At the door, the shah stepped down from his coach wearing a
gold-embroidered cloak draped over a military uniform heavily encrusted with gold braid. Farah wore white under a magnificent black
sleeveless coat embroidered in a jeweled paisley design and trimmed
in white ermine. Six-year-old Crown Prince Reza, the same age as his
father at Reza Shah's coronation, wore a miniature military uniform.
In 1992, he told me of his memories of the event. They emphasize the
mythical link between Muhammad Reza Shah and Persian kingship
the ceremony was intended to promote.

> I hated to come and have to practice for consecutive weeks for the cer-
> emony and wearing tight and uncomfortable clothes. . . . That day I
> had a fever from a cold. [Still] I did understand . . . to some degree the
> concept of the crown prince and the Pahlavi dynasty. For Persians . . .
> kingship was one of the most fundamental concerns of their life. It af-
> fected them. It's in their blood. They really responded to that institu-
> tion with heart and soul. Being part of the scene it is hard for me to
> say, but speaking to other Iranians it was like my father was the father
> of the nation. Or for my mother—like the mother of the nation. And
> that's the way people really reacted. It's like they could go easier to
> sleep at night knowing that the shah is there. . . . The shah embodied
> everything—he embodied national pride, he embodied progress, he
> embodied development, he embodied—you know—people feeling
> happy.[15]

The actual ceremony was brief. A strutting private of the Imperial
Guards brought the shah a copy of the Koran, which he brushed with
his lips and touched against his forehead. He fastened on the sword
and golden belt of Nasir ed-Din Shah. And then pausing a moment
for dramatic effect, he lifted the diamond-studded Pahlavi crown and
placed it on his head. Outside, guns saluted Muhammad Reza Pahlavi,
King of Kings. Breaking all the traditions of patriarchal Iran, the shah
crowned his wife, Farah, empress with a 1,480-gram emerald, ruby,
diamond, and pearl crown designed by Van Cleef and Arpels.* From
the Peacock throne, the shah delivered a coronation speech riddled
with the Iranian dichotomy between kingship and religion. "Firstly,

---

*In addition to the title of empress, Farah also became designated regent for the crown
prince in the event of the early death of Muhammad Reza Shah.

my particular attention has been and always will be directed to the preservation of the principles and foundations of religion, for in my opinion one of the most effective means of ensuring national unity and strengthening the spirit of community of the Iranians, is fortifying the basis of religious faith. . . . Secondly, my imperial government must remember without fail the duty of carrying out the fundamental reform of the country."[16]

In all its pomp and grandeur, the coronation of Muhammad Reza Shah symbolized ancient despotism more than either religion or the rising, modern nation he proclaimed. The crown jewels in the basement of the Central Bank constituted the only solid backing for the national currency. The average per capita income strained to reach $250 a year in a skewed system of income distribution where the rich around the shah became richer and the poor separated from the shah became poorer. The budding infrastructure that promised economic development struggled in the drought of trained engineers and skilled workers. The projects that did reach completion often evidenced more show than substance. As an example, one-fifth of the land under the huge dams built for irrigation possessed no distribution systems. That represented one reason why agricultural production increased only 2 percent per year while the population rose by 3 percent and the cost of living by 6 percent. Social peace held because state security services from the military to SAVAK acted as the eyes, ears, and booted heel of the king.

Meanwhile, Muhammad Reza Shah turned nationalism, one of the Iranians' great emotive forces, into a cult of monarchy. In his coronation, showy development projects, and even repression, the shah reached for the glory of the ancient Persian kings. The second ruler in the Pahlavi dynasty had acquired what Jalal Al-e Ahmad described as the "delusion of grandeur syndrome." It occurs

> because an insignificant individual sees his own greatness in grandeur which is falsely ascribed to him in national pageants, extravagant festivals, tinsel victory arches, crown jewels . . . and the grand uniforms, saddles and equipage of cavalry! It is also ascribed in the gold braid of military brass, in the huge buildings and even huger dams, the building of which, they say, has involved squandering of national wealth. In short in anything that will please the eye and that will pump up an insignificant man so that he will imagine himself to be great . . . Pretentious bragging—foolish self-glorification—Cyrus the Great and Darius!—self-aggrandizement based on irrelevant past glories.[17]

Jalal Al-e Ahmad's voice stilled in 1969 when he suddenly died at the age of forty-six. Although a heart attack was the official cause of death, many of Al-e Ahmad's followers laid the death at the feet of SAVAK.

With the death of Jalal Al-e Ahmad and the increasingly tight lid SAVAK kept on political dissent, religion rose as the only voice of opposition capable of making itself heard. Writings and sermons couched in politically acceptable language as well as underground messages and murmurs uttered by clergymen to followers, continued to ripple through the population that found its Iranian identity in Shia Islam. In 1969, a book entitled *The Eternal Martyr* postulated that Hussein had not gone to Karbala to seek martyrdom but rather that martyrdom came to him as a consequence of his political acts in the cause of justice. But it was Ayatollah Ruhollah Khomeini, exiled from Iran since 1964, who delivered the opponents of the shah a new, systematic ideology of dissent.

Between January 21 and February 8, 1970, the great teacher of Qom who had led the demonstrations against Pahlavi power in 1963 delivered in Najaf, Iraq, a series of nineteen lectures in which he laid out the theological framework of the *Velayat-e Faqih,* the Guardianship of the Jurist. The amplification of a theme first delivered in Qom in the early 1960s, Khomeini's *Velayat-e Faqih* developed two major and interrelated concerns of Shia Islam in Iran: the economic, political, and cultural invasion of the West, and the issue of justice. Its conclusion called for an Islamic government to replace the unjust Iranian monarchy.

In perhaps the most revolutionary document in Shiism, Ayatollah Ruhollah Khomeini broke one of the sect's core tenets—all government in the absence of the Twelfth Imam is profane. Contradicting this sacred tradition, Khomeini's arguments for an Islamic state proceeded from a simple premise. Divine will established Muhammad's just and sacred community on earth. Upon his death, the future of that divinely inspired community fell to the Twelve Infallible Imams beginning with the just and righteous Ali. In the absence of the Twelfth or Hidden Imam, divine will permits neither injustice nor ungodly rule. Thus, until the Twelfth Imam physically reappears, it is the most just and the most knowledgeable among the *mujtahids* who possesses the religious as well as the political authority to direct the Muslim community.

Khomeini went on to categorically condemn the entire monarchical history of Iran, denying legitimacy to the very idea of Persian kingship. To Muhammad Reza Shah's resurrection of royal glory, the ayatollah sneered, "Kingship from the day it started to this very day has been the shame of history."[18]

Fascinated with Aristotle and Plato, Khomeini took the Greek model and applied it to an Islamic Republic in which a Shia theologian rather than the philosopher-king would rule. This "just jurist" is charged with the supreme task of ensuring the rule of justice. Based on the prototype of Ali's short-lived caliphate, this justice is as complex as establishing the equality of all believers or as simple as the jurist going to bed hungry when all his people are not fed. Khomeini's *faqih*, the supreme jurist, is nothing short of the learned and righteous caretaker of the community of the faithful who follows as his models the Prophet and the Twelve Imams. All other authority, including kingship, is illegitimate, requiring the mandatory opposition of the believer. In the *Velayat-e Faqih*, Ayatollah Khomeini delivered to the Iranians a new political ideology. From that point on, opposition to the shah by the faithful wrapped itself in all the images of Shia Islam and grasped the promise of justice held within the concept of the Islamic state filled with the spirit of Ali.

Muhammad Reza Shah refused to bow. Prompted by Khomeini's denunciation of Muhammad Reza Shah's authority and SAVAK reports of the ayatollah's messages passing through the network of his followers, the shah struck directly at the religious power structure. In May 1970, the security services arrested and tortured to death *hojjat ol-eslam* Muhammad Reza Saidi, a leading *mujtahid* and Khomeini disciple. Legend says that in death he told his tormentors, "I swear to God if you kill me, in every drop of my blood you can see the holy name of Khomeini." But with Ayatollah Khomeini in exile, no cleric with sufficient stature or courage to challenge the throne came forward. So in early 1971, the shah launched a bold frontal attack across the spectrum of the Shia religious establishment. Tactics ranged from economic measures that eroded clerical power to the forced closing of the Husseiniyeh-e-Ershad, a gathering place in north Tehran where thousands of Iranians came in the evenings to hear sermons delivered by esteemed religious leaders.

As he zealously suppressed Islam, Muhammad Reza Shah energetically elevated the image of ancient Persia in his quest to create what he termed the "Great Civilization." Essentially aiming to develop an Iranian identity independent of Shia Islam, the shah grafted a mix of myth and history of ancient Persia onto a society that also claimed an

Islamic past and an Islamic present. Radio Tehran began each day with verses from Ferdowsi. First-grade Persian school textbooks described Muhammad Reza Shah as the descendant of the ancient Persian kings who commanded the unquestioning obedience of their subjects. As in Reza Shah's time, Iranians again found it politically expedient to give their children names that dated back to the Medes and the Persians— Darius, Cyrus, Jamshid, Shapour, and Khosrow. Yet the more tightly the regime wrapped itself in Iran's newly reconstructed history, the more irrelevant ancient Persia became.

For centuries, Iranians had honored their cultural heritage that came from the Persians and other peoples who wound through pre-Islamic Iran. They did so in nonreligious settings, reserving religious occasions to invoke their Islamic identity. The custom was typified by the Safavids, Iran's Islamic rulers, who paraded their crowns and their royal parasols within their lavish courts in imitation of the Sassanians. But in the mosque, they proclaimed their role as defenders of Islam and patrons of the mullahs. Muhammad Reza Shah intended to change the formula.

In the fall of 1971, the second Pahlavi shah summoned all Iranians, rich and poor, intellectual and illiterate, to Persepolis to identify themselves exclusively as heirs of Cyrus in the 2,500th anniversary of the Iranian nation.* For Muhammad Reza Shah, the commemoration, on one level, constituted a symbol of nationalism, a grand and glorious statement that Pahlavi Iran lived as no nation's vassal. On a more significant level for the future of Iran, it testified to the Pahlavi vision of Persian kingship and an Iranian identity centered on Muhammad Reza Shah as the direct heir of Cyrus. A Western scholar of Iranian studies present at the celebration wrote, "What we are celebrating, I suggest, is a 2,500-year-old continuing historical and cultural tradition in which the institution of the monarchy has played . . . an essential part: an historical and cultural tradition so strong that not all the political vicissitudes which Iran has experienced and military catastrophes which Iran has suffered . . . have succeeded in destroying . . . . What we are dealing with is, quite simply, the theory of the Divine Right of Kings as slightly modified by the Persian Constitution of 1906.[19] To confirm that he had indeed inherited the "kingly glory," the shah commissioned a special hymn composed for the celebration entitled "Our Everlasting Happiness and Prosperity Derive from Your

*The celebration was nine years late if it was to observe Cyrus's capture of Babylon.

Kingly Glory, O King!" But in the end, the extravaganza at Persepolis only separated the king further from his subjects.

The preparations consumed months and cost somewhere between $50 million and $300 million depending on whether or not the infrastructure costs of airports, sanitation facilities, and roads built for the celebration are included. The money came from government employees forced to contribute one day's pay, businessmen needing to protect themselves from royal displeasure, cronies of the shah, and a government treasury faced with all the unrelenting demands of a poor country. By some unhappy coincidence, 1971 was a year of drought and poor harvests. In Baluchistan, Sistan, and Fars, the location of Persepolis, famine stalked. And in the cities of Isfahan, Tabriz, and Tehran, hundreds of thousands of the shah's subjects lived in want. But hostility to the shah's extravagance lapped over the walls of poverty. Months before the scheduled opening of the festivities, university students struck in protest. Within intellectual circles, an event treated as high camp by the international press evolved into a symbol of national humiliation. What was taking root among these educated classes was a deep resentment at the shah's effort to legitimize the brief Pahlavi dynasty by placing it on a par with the Achaemenians and Sassanians. The resulting anger took form in escalating student unrest and a nascent urban guerrilla movement that raided banks, attacked police posts, and attempted to kidnap Prince Shahram, son of the shah's twin sister, Ashraf. Among the masses of the uneducated, the mullahs quietly passed the word that the glorification of Persian kingship amounted to the shah's repudiation of Islam.

At the heart of all dissent lay the issue of Iranian culture. Ultimately, the shah's grand spectacle overwhelmed both the Persian and Islamic aspects of Iranian culture with the trappings of the West. It began with the tent city that went up on the 160 acres directly in front of Persepolis's massive platform. It required forty-three thousand yards of European-manufactured beige and royal blue flameproof cloth. The fifty air-conditioned private apartments created for invited heads of state were equipped with American plumbing fixtures, European furniture, and set in a modern oasis designed by the French landscape artist Truffant. At its center stood the Imperial Reception Hall. Beneath the twenty chandeliers of European crystal and the Louis XIV decor, only the carpets came from Persia, the object of the whole celebration.

The master French hotelier, Max Bouet, came out of retirement to supervise a staff of 159 chefs, bakers, and waiters flown in from Paris.

Except for Iranian caviar, the shah's guests ate French food and drank five thousand bottles of fine French champagne from special crystal by Baccarat. They slept on linens of Porthaut, bathed with special oils by Guerlain and medicated themselves with Alka-Seltzer wrapped in gold foil by Fauchon of Paris.

Only a few Iranians from the upper echelon of the elite received invitations to Persepolis. To the Iranians sealed off from the festivities by the tight security ring erected for miles around the site and the thousands of suspected troublemakers sitting in jail, the shah gave a short prayer for the nation. Mentioning the shahanshah or Persian kingship six times, it began, "O God Almighty, creator of the Universe and Man, The bestower of intelligence, wisdom and thought on Man, The Creator of countless blessings in our Noble Land, Thou who has appointed the Just Aryamehr [the Light of the Aryans] as the Custodian of the Land of Iran."[20]

From the site of Ali's tomb in Najaf, Iraq, Ayatollah Ruhollah Khomeini thundered his wrath. "Anyone who organizes or participates in these festivals is a traitor to Islam and the Iranian nation."[21] Reiterating a basic premise in the *Velayat-e Faqih*, he declared that Islam is fundamentally opposed to the whole notion of monarchy and denounced the title King of Kings as "the most hated of all titles in the sight of God. . . ."[22]

In the wake of Khomeini's denunciation of the events at Persepolis, Shia mullahs and *talabehs* within Iran gathered in clandestine organizations. Their purpose no longer restricted itself to the reintroduction of Islam into Iran's legal system or state education. The guardians of Islam sought the destruction of the monarchy itself. Shadows on the left—a selection of intellectuals and the surviving cadres who had clustered around Muhammad Mossadeq in 1953 and the Communist Tudeh—shared the same goal of toppling the monarchy if not the same philosophy of Islamic government. Together they asked the profound question, Did Muhammad Reza Shah possess the spiritual charisma of the King of Kings?

After the foreign dignitaries went home and the lights dimmed on the shah's spectacle at Persepolis, the splendid tent city passed into the hands of Club Mediterranean. It lasted as a tourist attraction only until 1979 and the Iranian Revolution. Yet the tired and dusty tents of 1971 have survived. The trees planted over two decades ago have grown, partially obstructing the view of the great reception tent. The lighted fountains that gave the elaborate encampment an ethereal beauty no longer glow. And the gardens are nothing more than weeds growing between blue cubicles encasing outdoor latrines. At times since the revolution, the royal camp has been occupied by the Revolutionary Guards, Ayatollah Khomeini's foot soldiers, and by the army of the Islamic Republic of Iran. Now, despite the presence of a few scattered military trucks and other languid signs of life, the shah's magical encampment is a ghost town. Breezes ruffle the squared-off scallops that trim the rooflines and stir the layers of dust that have dimmed the brilliant blues and gold. The Persepolis of Muhammad Reza Shah is decaying as his dynasty decayed in the wealth of the 1970s oil boom.

9

The Persian Empire
of Muhammad Reza Shah

T WAS 1974, THE YEAR AFTER THE QUADRUPLING OF OIL PRICES
gave Muhammad Reza Shah the wealth to create his version of
the modern Persian Empire. In the New Year tradition of his self-
proclaimed predecessor, Darius, the shah of Iran was receiving the
homage of his people and the world. Inside the sparkling, mirrored
halls of Gulistan Palace, His Imperial Majesty, Light of the Aryans,
King of Kings, stood stiffly in a white military tunic encrusted with
gold and bisected by a broad blue sash pinned with the medals of
state. Although the elevator shoes added a couple of inches to his five-
foot, seven-inch frame, they failed to raise the shah high above his
subjects in the manner of the ancient throne at Persepolis. But the
same subjugation of subject to ruler that characterized Achaemenian
and Sassanian Persia presented itself in Pahlavi Iran. One by one, cabinet ministers, provincial governors, senior civil servants, and a pha-
lanx of military men, costumed in gold-embroidered tailcoats, white
gloves, and plumed hats, bowed low to kiss the hand of their monarch. The Shia clerical establishment in their traditional robes and turbans followed in the yearly ritual that required a delicate balancing
of an acceptance of Persian kingship with the authority of religion.
Finally, the ambassadors of countries around the world paid their
respects to the man who controlled 70 million barrels of crude
oil crucial to the economic survival of the industrial world. The
shahanshah accepted the homage of each with an air of condescension,

smiling briefly and bleakly. It all amounted to a pompous display of power presided over by the man who thirteen centuries after Persia fell to the Arabs saw himself establishing Iran once again among the elite of nations. However, beneath the pageantry lurked the issues of justice, nationalism, and culture that were gathering to destroy Muhammad Reza Shah and the Iranian monarchy.

The nation of Iran that the second Pahlavi shah inherited in 1941 controlled neither empire nor its own autonomy. Rather, it lived under wartime occupation. When World War II ended, rich and fertile Azerbaijan could not escape the grip of the expansive, aggressive Soviet Union. In 1946, Muhammad Reza Shah solicited the United States to free Iranian territory, and the United States enlisted the shah as an ally against the rising power of Stalinist Russia. It was the beginning of an almost four-decades-long linkage between Iran and the United States in which the shah would use the Americans to secure his throne and promote his visions of grandeur and the United States would use the shah in its contest of power with the Soviet Union. In this mutually beneficial alliance between the lion and the eagle, both the shah and the Americans ignored the dual threat to Iran's values and cultural identity posed by Muhammad Reza Shah's reach for absolute power.

Through most of the 1970s, Iran lived under the cult of personality created by the second Pahlavi shah. Every aspect of Iranian life—economics, politics, and culture—moved to the dictates of the man on the Peacock throne. In pursuit of what he termed the "Great Civilization," Muhammad Reza Shah opened Iran's doors to vast numbers of Westerners who invaded Iran in a manner in which it had never been invaded before. Western products and pop culture washed over proud Iran. In addition, too many Westerners who came to deliver the technology that the shah demanded carried with them no understanding or sensitivity to the Iranians' ancient, complex culture. In the economically and socially disruptive years of the post-1973 oil boom, opposition to Pahlavi rule and Western intrusion came from the intertwined resentments of secularists cut out of the economy and politics of Pahlavi Iran and pious Shia drawn by a collection of writers and theologians who redefined the relationship between Shiism and the state. Together they built the Iranian Revolution of 1979.

The core of the Iranian Revolution would contain the issues of absolute monarchy and cultural definition. It also would contain nationalism. Even before the storm of 1979, nationalism evoked among large segments of the Iranian population a powerful, visceral anger engendered by the symbiotic relationship between Muhammad Reza Shah and the United States. The roots of this anger extended back to 1941, when Iran's newly enthroned king failed to secure an alliance with the United States that would give Iran a third force against the historic incursions of Britain and Russia. Two years later, Franklin Delano Roosevelt and the other giants of World War II, Winston Churchill and Joseph Stalin, came to Tehran to cement their personal relationship and to plan for a second front in Europe by way of the beaches of Normandy. While the three sat for those historic pictures on the lawn of the British embassy, the site of the great *bast* of the Constitutional Revolution, the American president all but ignored Muhammad Reza Shah. Iran seemed inconsequential to great-power strategy until the war ended and the grand alliance split between the Soviet Union and the Western democracies.

With Nazi Germany defeated in May 1945, the United States and Britain set March 1, 1946, as the date to pull their troops out of Iran. But Joseph Stalin, the iron man of the Kremlin, held firm in Azerbaijan. Spreading his military umbrella over an indigenous Communist movement sprouting in northern Iran, he demanded, in addition to the occupied territory, a slice of Iranian oil resources. For both the shah and his subjects, the Soviet grab for Azerbaijan conjured bitter memories of czarist Russia. With Britain still holding Iran in the noose of the Anglo-Iranian Oil Company, the young shah again solicited the United States to serve as the third power in the triad that he judged essential to Iranian independence. This time the Americans responded in the first crisis of what became the cold war. Under the threat of U.S. military action, Soviet tanks, artillery, and troops moved back north, patching the hole in the 1,200-mile-long border separating Iran and the Union of Soviet Socialist Republics. The United States, once known as *yengeh donya*, the land at the end of the earth, had moved into Iranian affairs as the active partner of Muhammad Reza Shah. Until 1979, influence flowed between the two, reciprocal but not necessarily equal, as the shah charted his own course in tandem with or independent of American national interests.

From the beginning, the shah drew the United States into Iran not only to guard Iranian independence but to buttress the Pahlavi throne. As it had freed Iranian territory in 1946, the United States rescued Muhammad Reza Shah from the nationalists in 1953. Through the rest of the 1950s and the 1960s, the shah milked his American alliance by playing a shrewd game with both superpowers. By the time the great pageant at Persepolis ended in 1971, the shah had set out on the road of national and dynastic grandeur. The United States went along as arms supplier and consort.

The new Persian Empire had begun in 1969, when Muhammad Reza Shah challenged Iraq's exclusive claim to the 160-mile-long Shatt al-Arab, the broad, marshy channel of brown water connecting the confluence of the Tigris and Euphrates to the head of the Persian Gulf. Fifty miles upstream from the Gulf's northern shore lies Abadan, the southernmost port of Iran. Historically, the Iranian side of the Shatt al-Arab marked the Iraq-Iran border. Consequently, access to Abadan's great oil refinery required Iran to secure right of passage from Iraq. Declaring the thalweg, or the center of the main channel, as the new boundary, the shah sent an Iranian ship, escorted by Iranian naval vessels, upriver without Iraqi permission. In retaliation, Iraq moved troops to the river, and Iran answered. Although the two sides fought sporadic border clashes over the next six years, internal subversion by both sides constituted the grist of the conflict. Iraq egged on Arab separatists in Khuzestan and Baluchi separatists in Baluchistan while periodically dumping Iranians living in Iraq across the border. Iran stirred the Iraqi Kurds in revolt against a government controlled by Arabs.

The Shatt al-Arab represented only one of Muhammad Reza Shah's territorial ambitions. In 1968, the financial and military drain of World War II coupled with the rise of nationalism among people living under colonialism caused the sun to set on the British Empire east of Suez. For a hundred years, Persian Gulf politics had ebbed and flowed around British money and naval power. But as of 1971, the British would withdraw, leaving the countries and sheikhdoms along the Gulf's shores on their own. In the three years between the British announcement of withdrawal and the execution of that withdrawal, Muhammad Reza Shah prepared to inject Iran into the power vacuum. Consequently when the last British soldier and naval vessel left the Gulf on March 1, 1971, the shah pounced, snatching hegemony in the Gulf away from would-be rivals. Diplomatic recognition of the government of the island state of Bahrain with its majority Shia population meant that any Arab state making a claim on its territory faced Iran. Six weeks after the celebration at Persepolis, the shah revived Iran's claim to the forlorn but strategic islands of Abu Musa and Greater and Lesser Tunbs, located at the mouth of the Strait of Hormuz. The following day, Iraq severed diplomatic relations with expansionist Iran. The day after that, December 2, 1971, Muhammad

Reza Shah watched with satisfaction as the seven oil-laden, defenseless sheikhdoms along the western shore of the Gulf that lay in the shadow of Iraq joined together to become the United Arab Emirates (UAE). Claim to the Shatt al-Arab, Abu Musa, and the two Tunbs; recognition of Bahrain; and the formation of the UAE all seemed to contribute to the shah's goal of making Iran the preeminent force in the Persian Gulf.

Rather than an expansive area of open water, the Persian Gulf is more like a big, shallow lake. On both the Arab side and the Iranian side, its flat shores steam with a heat that drains the last ounce of energy out of the humans who walk them. Yet the Gulf's tremendous value becomes obvious when the mammoth hull of an oil tanker silently moves through the steam of a hot, humid afternoon. It carries as much as 250,000 tons of Persian Gulf crude southward toward the 170-mile-long and 21- to 80-mile wide Strait of Hormuz and on into the open waters of the Indian Ocean. If Achaemenian and Sassanian power depended on controlling the Iranian plateau, Pahlavi power lay in the Persian Gulf.

In November 1972, Muhammad Reza Shah extended his ambitions beyond the specific confines of the Persian Gulf when he announced that he considered the Indian Ocean also vital to Iran's national security. Yet nothing energized the shah's vision of a new Persian Empire as much as the explosion of oil prices in 1973. The shah himself had placed the dynamite on February 14, 1971, at the Tehran Conference of the Organization of Petroleum Exporting Countries (OPEC). Correctly reading the West's increasing need for imported oil, Iran's king engineered a new structure of oil pricing that, for the first time in history, favored the producers. But it was the Arabs who lit the fuse that blew up the existing oil market. On October 6, 1973, Egypt's Anwar Sadat, in collusion with King Faisal of Saudi Arabia, sent eighty thousand Egyptian troops across the Suez Canal to attack Israeli positions on the Sinai Peninsula. For Egypt, the October War came as a desperation move to force peace talks with Israel. For the oil producers, including Iran, it created the golden moment to force up oil prices. In retaliation for American arms flown to Israel during the second week of the war, Saudi Arabia and the other Arab producers slapped an oil embargo on the United States and any other country held responsible for aiding and abetting the Jewish state. Muhammad Reza Shah harbored no quarrel with Israel, the blood enemy of his Arab competitors in the Gulf and the ward of his American ally. Although Iranian oil continued to flow West, Iran, as much as the Arab oil producers, reaped the benefits of the embargo. Before 1973 ended, oil prices leaped in giant strides from $3.01 per barrel to $5.12 to $11.65. In this sudden and dramatic shift of the international oil market, the shah garnered the cash to construct his version of the new Persian Empire. Through hegemony in the Persian Gulf, influence in the Indian Ocean, and the imagery of military power provided by a menacing arsenal of sophisticated weapons, the shah vowed to give Iran a place in the world denied it since the time of the Sassanians. Like the tableau of Shapour at Naqsh-e-Rustam in which the Sassanian king accepts the surrender of the Roman emperor Valerian, Muhammad Reza Shah would command the supplication of lesser men and nations.

In 1973 alone, the shah invested $3 billion in military hardware. By 1974, when Iran's oil revenues rocketed upward on OPEC's pricing policy, the shah's proliferating arsenal included laser-guided bombs, a hundred-plus F-4 Phantoms, KC-135 aerial tankers to refuel the Phantoms, nearly 1,800 state-of-the-art tanks, a fleet of American C-130 transport aircraft, and the largest military Hovercraft fleet in the world. At the same time, a naval base at Bushehr on the Persian Gulf and a vast new military complex at Chah Bahar on the Indian Ocean were rising out of sand and virgin jungle. With the capability to patrol the sea as far south as Madagascar and the skies as far west as Cairo coupled with the economic clout to influence the Western powers through oil prices, Muhammad Reza Shah declared the new Persian Empire.

Still the shah's ambitions multiplied. In successive interviews given at the time, Muhammad Reza Shah's imagination moved Iran from an industrialized country on par with Switzerland to competing with France economically and militarily by the year 1993 to reaching parity with Germany in 1996 to becoming the second Japan by the end of the century. In his obsession for national power in support of this vision, the shah poured more and more money into his military buildup. By 1975, he was spending approximately $5 billion a year on arms and matériel. It seemed to pay off.

Nineteen seventy-five was the year that Muhammad Reza Shah secured his claim to the eastern side of the Shatt al-Arab. In the Algiers Accord, Iraq's Saddam Hussein agreed to accept Iran's definition of the Iraq-Iran border in exchange for the shah's withdrawal of armed support for the dissident Kurds. Although the Islamic Republic would pay the price of Hussein's vengeance in 1980, the shah chalked up one more piece of territory for his empire.

By 1977, the shah was gathering weapons at a level that equaled a major power preparing for war. The combination of conventional military forces and his internal security apparatus consumed $9.4 billion, over 40 percent of the Iranian budget. Much of it was wasted. The logistical, maintenance, and training demands of the shah's vast, sophisticated arsenal exceeded the size and capabilities of Iran's thirty-one thousand professional military men and its seven hundred thousand reservists. Consequently, Iran's extravagant military functioned more as an ornament for the Pahlavi dynasty than a valid use of national resources. Every year at the mid-December celebration of Azerbaijan Liberation Day, the Pahlavi shah staged the equivalent of May Day in Red Square. With television cameras poised to capture every moment, the shah descended from the sky in a helicopter, mounted a fine horse, and led a military parade to the reviewing stand. There he dismounted to take his place on a gilded chair. Over the following hours, the parade passed in front of him—the Imperial Guards, the elite of the air force, army regiments marching under their regimental flags, and frogmen in wetsuits—all accompanied by the latest in military hardware. The irony was that except for the television coverage, no one saw the parade except the shah's restricted list of guests for the reason that imperial security could not risk a public event.

Muhammad Reza Shah had built his extravagant military through his own personal will and with the profits from Iran's oil resources. But neither would have been enough without the cooperation of the United States, which saw in Pahlavi Iran a strategic ally against the Soviet Union.

Historically, U.S. interests in Iran largely restricted themselves to missionaries, educators, and trade. Even the 1946 liberation of Azerbaijan represented a tactical maneuver rather than a decision to nest the American eagle in Iran. That changed in 1951 when Muhammad Mossadeq's Nationalist Movement became for the United States "one of the worst calamities to the anti-Communist world since the Red conquest of China."[1] With the tidy coup against Mossadeq completed, the United States engaged Iran in America's global contest with the Soviet Union for resources, allies, and strategic position.

In 1955, the Baghdad Pact, an American-sponsored, British-led alliance sought to tie together countries lying south and east of the Soviet Union—namely Turkey, Iran, Iraq, and Pakistan. Of the four, Iran ranked as the prize. According to a Joint Chiefs of Staff intelligence report dated April 13, 1955, "From the viewpoint of attaining US military objectives in the Middle East, the natural defensive barrier provided by the Zagros Mountains must be retained under Allied control indefinitely. Because Western Iran includes the Zagros Mountains barrier, geographically, Iran is the most important country in the Middle East."[2] The United States desperately wanted Iran in the Baghdad Pact and Muhammad Reza Shah, despite domestic opposition based on nationalism, wanted to join in order to curry favor with the Eisenhower administration.

In 1957, the Eisenhower Doctrine, which promised military and economic aid to countries whose independence and integrity were threatened by armed Communist invasion from without or by subversion from within, also snared the shah. Or viewed from the Iranian side, the shah snared the United States. Muhammad Reza Shah had begun to covet extraordinary power for himself and his nation. One way to achieve it was with American arms. Understanding the link between the shah's ambitions and U.S. military hardware, the U.S. ambassador to Tehran issued a warning to the State Department. "[The] Shah personally appears under psychological compulsions which lead him to desire military forces well over and above what might be objectively required for internal security, prestige, or a rational contribution to regional collective security."[3] Eisenhower's foreign policy team might have listened better if a left-wing revolution had not convulsed Iraq.

On July 14, 1958, revolutionaries friendly to the Soviet Union shot King Faisal, the pro-British king of Iraq, rolled the body in a carpet, and whisked it away for a secret burial. Almost overnight, the Baghdad Pact minus Iraq transformed into CENTO, the Central Treaty Organization. Iran sat at the geographic center of CENTO. And CENTO linked Pakistan, the westernmost country of the South East Asia Treaty Organization (SEATO), to Turkey, the eastern anchor of NATO's defensive line. According to an American diplomat describing its strategic importance at the time, "Iran is like the stopper in the bathtub. Pull it out and the Caspian Sea, which is a Soviet lake, will pour down into the Persian Gulf, create a political vacuum there, and the Russians will seize the warm water ports they've been wanting ever since the time of Peter the Great. They'll be in striking distance of 181 billion barrels of mideastern oil."[4]

By 1960, Muhammad Reza Shah had captured not only the U.S. government but the American media. The slick magazines, the image makers of the day, lauded him as the glamorous king modernizing his country while acting as the steadfast American ally in the war against sinister communism. News magazines, women's magazines, and travel magazines all ran article after article on the shah, the beautiful Farah, and the rebirth of Iran. In 1963, *Life*, in a multipage, color spread extolling the shah, raised the specter of Iran at the end of World War II. "Just when the name of Iran seemed about to disappear from the list of free nations, there rose a worthy son of this ancient land who was destined to extricate this nation from its plight."[5]

The brief moment when the Kennedy administration questioned the level of Iran's arms purchases and pushed Muhammad Reza Shah toward economic and social reform passed. Accepting the shah's decade-long argument that Iran alone could protect Western oil and Western strategic interests in the Gulf, Lyndon Johnson, in 1964, offered the shah American military advisers and $200 million in credits for the purchase of more American-made military weapons. He added one caveat—Iranian acceptance of the Status of Forces Agreement (SOFA). On this issue, the avenging form of Ayatollah Ruhollah Khomeini rose to challenge Muhammad Reza Shah for the second time.

U.S. global strategy against the Soviet Union during the 1950s and the early 1960s deposited colonies of American military personnel in friendly countries from Morocco to Turkey. According to a pattern, the host country granted U.S. military advisers, their support staffs, and families immunity from the national laws of the host country. In most of these countries, immunity for Americans produced little political fire. But this was Iran. With bitter memories of the capitulations granted by the Qajars, public opinion exploded, searing SOFA as a Pahlavi capitulation to the United States. Indicative of the intensity of the opposition, the shah's handpicked Majlis passed the measure by a narrow vote of seventy to sixty-two. The victory came only through the convenient absence of sixty-eight deputies. After the vote, the voice of Ayatollah Khomeini rose out of Qom to denounce the "document of enslavement of Iran." On October 26, 1964, the cleric who had condemned the White Revolution in 1963 delivered a fiery, passionate sermon in which he spoke as much as an Iranian nationalist as a Shia cleric. Beginning with a quote from the Koran which says, "Never will God give the unbelievers a way [to triumph] over the Believers," he poured venom on the Status of Forces Agreement:

Does the Iranian nation know what has happened in recent days in the Assembly [Majlis]? Does it know what crime has occurred surreptitiously and without the knowledge of the nation? Does it know that the Assembly, at the initiative of the government, has signed the document of enslavement of Iran? It has acknowledged that Iran is a colony; it has given America a document attesting that the nation of Muslims is barbarous, it has struck out all our Islamic and national glories with a black line.

By this shameful vote, if an American adviser or the servant of an American adviser should take any liberty with one of the greatest specialists in Shiah law . . . the police would have no right to investigate. If the Shah should run over an American dog, he would be called to account but if an American cook should run over the Shah, no one has any claims against him. . . . I proclaim that his shameful vote of the Majlis is in contradiction to Islam and has no legality. . . .[6]

For the seventeen months between June 1963, when riots against the White Revolution erupted and October 1964, when the Majlis approved the Status of Forces Agreement, Ayatollah Ruhollah Khomeini and Muhammad Reza Shah had mobilized every material, ideological, and symbolic force at their command to challenge each other's legitimacy, even existence. In this contest of power, the duality of authority between the crown and the turban that had been part of the Iranian political character since the Safavids came to an end. This time only one could win—kingship or Islam.

As hastily printed leaflets and scratchy cassettes of Khomeini's sermon clandestinely circulated through Iran with the speed of the telegraph, the shah arrested the fiery cleric for the second time. Rejecting advice to execute his turbaned nemesis, the shah decreed exile. So it was that on November 4, 1964, police escorted the eminent ayatollah to a lonely military airport, put him on a plane, and sent him to Turkey. He went like the martyred Hussein, bearing the symbols of religion and nationalism. He would not see Iran again until he returned in triumph in February 1979 as the charismatic leader who ended the reign of Muhammad Reza Shah.

Khomeini left behind in Iran followers ready to take up his cause against Muhammad Reza Shah and the United States. One is a humble-looking man in khaki working clothes with cropped hair and black stubble that seems to resist growing into a full beard. I met Muhammad Qavam in a Tehran apartment belonging to friends. A shy, simple man, he seemed intimidated by an American pressing him for the reasons why he chose to follow Khomeini. Looking at the floor instead of me, he finally provided an answer. "Before Ayatollah Khomeini raised his voice, we had lost our identity. We had to bow our heads down to American dogs that had as much right in Iranian courts as Iranians." He hesitated, locked and unlocked his hands. Then haltingly, he said, "You see, we had lost our cultural *hejab* [innocence] inside and outside. We had also lost social justice. Ayatollah Khomeini had the bravery to fight for our Islamic culture and to stand up for justice. I tried to have bravery like him, to put my life in danger."

With Khomeini gone, the shah and the United States, one seeking personal and national pride and the other strategic advantage, went on their way, locked in step. In 1970, Richard Nixon and his national security adviser, Henry Kissinger, pressed by the ever-escalating military demands of the Vietnam War, searched for an alternative to American power to defend the Persian Gulf. Like the apparition of some shining knight, Muhammad Reza Shah appeared, anxious to assume guardianship of the Gulf in return for American military equipment and American training of his army and security forces. Nixon and Kissinger embraced the deal. Consequently, in May 1972, the United States essentially made the shah a partner in American global strategy. The Nixon doctrine that entrusted certain key American allies with the defense of their own regions elevated the shah to the position of policeman of the Gulf. Therefore, thirty years after he first crawled to the United States begging for any kind of alliance, the shah ranked as an equal in the eyes of the American superpower. Only the Defense Department questioned the Nixon decision to open the American arsenal to Iran. Nonetheless, Henry Kissinger, besotted by the shah's personality and self-drawn image, issued a July memorandum encouraging unlimited weapons sales to Iran. In the four years that followed, the shah would spend $4 billion on American weapons, making Iran the largest importer of American-produced arms in the world.

American support of the Pahlavi king held firm in 1973, when the shah led as much as followed the quadrupling of oil prices. Although he never denied his oil to his American partner, the shah did nothing to spare the United States any of the pain associated with the jolt of the oil market from the buyers to the sellers. As a result, 1973 posed the question to the U.S.-Iranian relationship of who was using whom. The shah's lust to dominate the Persian Gulf had come to exceed the strategic role the United States had assigned to him. Regardless, the Nixon, Ford, and Carter administrations would continue to provide the military and diplomatic support Muhammad Reza Shah demanded for his new Persian Empire. They all bought the shah's argument, laid out in a 1977 interview, that American security in the Gulf depended on a militarily strong Iran. "If you didn't have . . . a strong Iran capable of securing its own security and providing security in the region and eventually the Indian Ocean how will you replace that? With the presence of one million American troops? Do you want several more Vietnams? In Vietnam, you had only 550,000 American boys. But the Persian armed forces have more than that. And they are not smoking grass."[7]

For the greater part of a decade, the United States essentially anchored its national interest in the crucial Persian Gulf in the absolute monarch of a relatively small, underdeveloped nation. Beginning with Richard Nixon's appointment of the shah as the vanguard of the Gulf in 1972 until 1978, when the clouds of revolution gathered over Iran, the two countries fused. Like interlocking pyramids topped by the heads of state and resting on a base of CIA and SAVAK agents in the field, the United States operated in Iran as an appendage of the shah. And with the aid of the shah, the American community resident in the Pahlavi kingdom functioned as a privileged colony removed from Iranian culture.

The historically limited American presence in Iran began to expand in 1963, when the White Revolution's call for economic development drew U.S. corporate giants such as Allied Chemical, Amoco, and BFGoodrich. The invasion proved cultural as well as economic. Tehran, in the Persian tradition of assimilation, took on the trappings of the West. Elizabeth II Avenue, which ran from the airport through the central city, roared with American, French, British, and German cars. Above them, neon signs flashed the constantly changing tactics in the soft drink wars between Coca-Cola and Pepsi. A building boom created monotonous concrete box apartment buildings and repetitive public structures that imitated the mediocre in Western contemporary architecture. By the mid-1970s, the upscale shops of north Tehran overflowed with Helena Rubenstein cosmetics, Vicks VapoRub, Marlboro cigarettes, and skimpy California-style bathing suits. Along with the sidewalk cafés, cinemas, and astronomical rents, they identified a visible subculture within Iranian society.

Although Europeans formed part of the Western mix, it was the influx of hundreds and eventually thousands of American civilians and military personnel that created a level and type of foreign presence totally new to Iranians. Unlike invaders mounted on horses or imperialists carrying documents confirming territorial and economic concessions, the new aliens came to Iran to tend the machines of industrialization and war. Too few of the technologists knew or cared about old, self-esteeming Iranian culture. And too many, particularly those with limited education, took pride in calling highly developed Iranian culture "camel culture" and deriding Iranians as "sand-niggers," "rags," "stinkies," and—perhaps worst of all from an Iranian perspective—"Bedouins." As early as 1958, a perceptive British resident of Iran had written, "It is the misfortune of so many foreigners in Iran that they have gone there in a superior, even patronizing role. The business man with his glossy Western products, the technical expert with his higher knowledge, even the missionary with his unspoken condemnation of the country's faith, all run the risk of evoking in those with whom they have to deal the reaction of the 'underdog.'"[8]

The Americans congregated in their own little suburbia, where the movie theaters showed Hollywood films, fast-food restaurants served pizza and hamburgers, and shops sold only American-produced goods priced in dollars. This is where the journalists and pseudojournalists who came to describe the new Iran to the West stayed to write as the American feminist Betty Friedan wrote in 1975, "My first few days in Tehran were strictly caviar and jet lag and a sense of being strangely at home. Tehran, a Middle Eastern city, seems like an American Western boom town—buildings going up overnight, international banks next to a Persian Wimpy stand, and no beggars."[9]

What Iranians saw as American arrogance came in part from the simple fact that most Americans lived far better in Iran than they did in the United States. Some of the military technicians who had fought in Vietnam left behind army pay for a $120,000-a-year salary in Iran. They were not unique. For almost all Americans, a combination of dollar salaries and employee perks provided large houses and luxury apartments, servants and drivers to people who in the United States lived a middle-class life. But it was insensitivity to the culture as much as economic differentiations that fed the poisonous Iranian hatred of America that erupted in the Iranian Revolution.

In the mid 1970s the number of Americans living in Iran approached fifty thousand, making them among the largest minority communities. Their presence was ubiquitous. On July 4, 1976, the United States' bicentennial, Americans flocked to the campus of the Tehran American School for a massive celebration. With the permission of the shah, it ended with an elaborate fireworks display. Below, in the city, Iranians saw the American flag ablaze on a mountain of the Alborz. The next day, the newspaper *Kayhan International* commented that in celebrating their country's birth the Americans "all had that air of flippancy, streak of irreverence, or whatever, which is typically American, and has brought praise and reproach alike."

About this same time, Americans had become involved in recurring episodes of public rowdiness, drunkenness, and physical violence that were reported by Iranian newspapers. Although they could, and did, happen anywhere that Americans concentrated, the ugly incidents seemed to center in Isfahan, a conservative city where both the Bell helicopter plant and a large American military contingent were located. In October 1975, three American women clad in skimpy shorts and halters strolled through the ancient Friday mosque talking and laughing while Muslims prayed. On other occasions, American teenagers drove motorbikes through the venerable Royal Mosque; several well-dressed women turned over a table in a popular restaurant because service was slow; and an American in a taxi shot the driver in the head in a dispute over a fare. Every year the holidays associated with Ashura, when Hussein is mourned, became to many Americans an occasion for large parties where rock music blared from stereos and drunks staggered from house to house. In city after city, month after month, other incidents great and small offended and enraged the Iranians. Almost all the culprits went unpunished because the twenty-four thousand plus members of the U.S. military enjoyed immunity under the Status of Forces Agreement, and the rest possessed their American passports backed by the two-thousand-member embassy in the heart of Muhammad Reza Shah's Tehran. In that embassy, the diplomats assiduously stayed away from the villages, the urban slums, and, on the orders of the shah, the clerics. They talked almost exclusively to the English-speaking elite of Pahlavi Iran, who themselves rejected the illiteracy, poverty, and religious traditions of their country.

Almost everywhere in Iranian society, an obsessive unease about the American presence and the effects of the shah's program of rapid modernization gripped wide segments of the population. Although most educated Iranians accepted modernization as the only path to economic advancement, it was the heavy emphasis put on Westernization as synonymous with that advancement that raised the cultural and nationalistic hackles of the Iranians. They listened again to the advice of the ancient sage: "To foreign culture open both the windows of thy house—then let foreign culture seep in through one window and leave from the other." In essence, the same sense of nationalist pride and cultural uniqueness that characterized Iranian resentment of the incursions of the Arabs, Mongols, Turks, Afghanis, Russians, and

British transferred to the shah's promotion of Western-style modernization. In this meeting of two highly developed but very different cultures, the Iranians could not seem to absorb the West and make it their own as they had absorbed previous invasions. This invader brought not only himself but Western quantative thought, rationalism, certitude, mass-produced uniformity, a linear view of history, and the assurance of secularism, all of which clashed with the characteristics and values of Iranian culture. Consequently, the West and Iran failed to meet as equals. The West was technological, Iran mystical; the West was rich and powerful, Iran, despite the oil boom and the shah's massive militarization, was poor and weak. On these unequal terms with the West, the Iranian collective consciousness feared "the drowning of our ancient Persian culture in a mindless imitation of the West."[10]

Perhaps the Iranians could have coped better if the engine of modernization chosen by Muhammad Reza Shah had not been the American superpower. Feeling themselves held under the foot of a giant, opponents of the shah became suspicious of everything attached to the United States. In 1977, the dissident intellectual Reza Baraheni wrote in the *Nation*, "The American passport, the yellow card of immunity, the job for Grumman, Northrop, Lockheed, Rockwell International, Bell Helicopter and tens of other U.S. corporations in Iran, the Shah's petrodollars pouring into the pockets of the stockholders of these corporations, his policy of oil for arms, and the participation of Americans in the Shah's oppressive measures—all these, in sum, are what is called American-Iranian relations."[11] Echoes of Jalal Al-e Ahmad's warnings of Westoxication welled and raged in the consciousness of the educated, who saw themselves as part of the enforced barter that Al-e Ahmad had described in the early 1960s.

The United States loomed as such an imposing threat because Muhammad Reza Shah allowed it. And he allowed it because he needed American weapons to sustain Pahlavi Iran. Without the military strength provided by American arms and training, the shahanshah believed that neither his new Persian Empire nor the social, economic, and political development necessary to realize his dream of a "Great Civilization" were possible. As a consequence, there developed in the last two decades of the shah's reign what might be called the Iranian syndrome. "At the heart of that syndrome lay the interplay between the Shah's personality traits . . . and the deep-rooted problems of social, economic, political, psychological and cultural continuity and change of the Iranian society."[12]

* * *

Ultimately, the seeds of destruction of the Iranian monarchy lay within Muhammad Reza Shah. Beneath the pomp and ceremony that surrounded his person hid a tangle of unresolved conflicts produced by his father, his sister, his early years on the throne, and his own imagination. More humorless than Charles de Gaulle, he permitted himself no friends and few pleasures beyond the exercise of power. Going back to the Sassanian concept of the king as a semidivine figure separated from the people, his self-defined dignity and imperial majesty demanded that he rule alone. In many ways, the pompous shah was a sad, insecure figure who constantly needed to convince himself as well as others that "before being a man, I'm a king."[13] Whether through his own psychological needs or an exaggerated sense of history and custom, Muhammad Reza Shah had assumed all the trappings of Persian kingship.

Confessing an abiding mysticism, the shah, in the tradition of the king blessed by Ahura Mazda, asserted his claim to divine ordination. "I believe in God, and that I have been chosen by God to perform a task. . . . My reign has saved the country, and it has done so because God was on my side.[14] But Muhammad Reza Shah did not stop with Ahura Mazda. He wrote extensively about dreams and visions in which he saw and talked with great Islamic figures such as Ali and the shah Abbas. He even described meeting the Hidden Imam on a Tehran street. It all buttressed the shah's possessed vision of the monarchy as a spiritual catalyst, the unifying force which gathered up and coordinated the forces of the Persian psyche. In a 1971 interview, he said it all: "No foreigner can really understand what the monarchy means to Iran. It is our way of life. We could not be a nation without it."[15]

Although Persian-style kingship served as his ideal, Muhammad Reza Shah practiced to perfection the techniques and tactics of the Iranian patriarch. He was the king who ruled by emanation, the source of all ideas and the fount of all good. In the spirit of noblesse oblige, he saw his subjects as children receiving the beneficence of a knowing and divinely inspired leader. But they were children viewed with little affection, an ungrateful lot incapable of appreciating his services to them.

The shah held the throne for as long as he did because he proved a master at balancing ambitious men against one another. Within the cabinet, minister vied with minister and within each department deputies maneuvered against one another for the favor of the monarch. All the while the shah, like a juggler, kept his eye on a hundred balls moving in complex patterns of motion, making sure that none fell to the ground to disrupt his authority. It worked in part because the shah excelled at intrigue. It also worked because every officeholder in Iran served at the sufferance of the king. Muhammad Reza Shah hand-picked all military leaders above the rank of major and all members of the bureaucracy above the middle tier. At the same time, a minor official in some provincial office could also be there by way of personal appointment by the shah. Once chosen, these servants of the king performed their jobs under the close personal scrutiny of their monarch. They did as they were told while flattering the man who gave them their orders. Individuals of integrity and independence who dared tell unpleasant truths or challenge the ideas of the sole decision maker in Iran found themselves quickly and unceremoniously cut out of the system. The only place the shah failed to keep the lines of personal rivalry in fine tune was in his own household, where the powerful Ashraf locked in perpetual conflict with the shah's wives—first Soraya and then Farah.

In this totally centralized monarchy, Muhammad Reza Shah manifested everywhere. "Salaam to Shahanshah" was the title of the national anthem. The eleven-foot-tall coronation portraits of the shah and Farah in the grand lobby of Tehran's opera house resembled the murals in Abbas's pavilion in Isfahan. In a poor imitation of the reliefs the Achaemenians left at Pasargadae and Persepolis, great, dignified pictures of the shah adorned government offices, railway stations, billboards, and business establishments intent on protecting their right to operate. Statues of the shah stood at crossroads, in the middle of villages, in city parks, and at the top of a few mountain peaks. Sculptured shrubbery in public gardens spelled out his name, thousands of strings of colored lights heralded his birthday, fine Persian carpets wove his image, over seventy-five different sets of Iranian postage stamps carried his portrait, and the currency bore his face set in a high-collared uniform. It all constituted a grand scheme to legitimize the rule of a man who commanded no real sources of authority other than the military and the omnipresent SAVAK. In the glorification of the monarchy, the shah's principle residence at Niavaran stands as a paradox.

In the 1950s, Niavaran Palace went up in a quiet village in the foothills of the Alborz Mountains. Its location is now on the curve of a busy street where Tehran's relentless traffic roars by. Inside the gates, the noise of motors dies in old, towering trees and expansive gardens that create a sense of grandeur. The palace itself is hardly extravagant.

Rather it plays to Muhammad Reza Shah's reconstruction of Persia. The two-story, flat-roofed stucco-and-brick structure rejects the architecture of Islam and the pseudo-European style so favored by the Qajars. In the simplicity of design and the retractable roof which can turn the whole structure into an outdoor pavilion, Niavaran imitates classical Persian architecture. It was here that the shah and his family lived in dignified, if rarefied, informality. The shah saw his ultimate glorification not in palaces but in the modernization of Iran. However while the king drove his people toward his own concept of modernity wrapped in Western packaging, he confronted the defenses of Iranian society constructed from the raw material of cultural norms. He met them with repression.

In the early 1970s the shah abandoned his policy of the previous decade, when he had balanced coercion with cooperation, repression with reform. In its place, SAVAK, the internal security force trained by the United States CIA and Israel's Mossad, took control of internal politics. Like the organization that attended Darius, SAVAK served as the eyes and ears of the king. And like the kings before him, Muhammad Reza Shah took note when a lone sparrow fell in his kingdom. Everywhere the agents of the shah, seen and unseen, spied and reported, arrested and tortured. Evin Prison, spread out over a series of hills in northwest Tehran, stood as the most infamous symbol of SAVAK's menacing authority. It was all compatible with the authoritarian values of Iranian kingship that wound through pre-Islamic and Islamic Iran. The only difference in the reign of Muhammad Reza Shah was that modern tools rather than crude weapons inflicted ancient cruelties on the forces of political opposition that possessed no protection of the law.

In addition to coercion, the shah commanded another source of power—oil. In the explosion of petroleum prices in 1973, Muhammad Reza Shah, in a modern-day replay of Cyrus at Lydia, captured sudden wealth. Between 1972 and 1974, Iran's oil revenues multiplied ninefold, from $2.4 billion to $17.4 billion, while per capita income shot up to $2,000 per year, the highest in the Third World. In the flood of dollars, public-sector investment doubled. Imports also doubled to a staggering 30 percent of GNP. With little accompanying inflation, most of the population experienced real gains in their standard of living.

With Iran's oil reserves predicted to begin a decline as soon as 1990, the shah declared it his duty to prepare for the future by applying petroleum assets to a crash program of development. When oil did run out, the nation would possess an infrastructure of roads, communication links, power plants, and an educated population capable of exporting to the Third World at prices cheaper than the United States, Europe, or Japan. But the window of opportunity was narrow and once the wells began to run dry it would close. Lavishly funding his vision of development, the shah thrust his people toward the greatness he had decreed for them.

Iran's golden years created by high oil prices and little inflation proved even more brief than expected. By late 1974 inflation raged, and by 1975 petroleum revenues leveled off as the industrial world learned to cut consumption. The shah pushed on, determined to lead his nation by force if necessary to his "Great Civilization." Months or years could not be spent fighting opposition or suppressing sedition from dissidents he classified as either "red" or "black"—Communists or reactionary mullahs. In one bold stroke, the shah stripped away the last feeble vestiges from the fragile democratic ideal established by the 1905 to 1911 Constitutional Revolution. Stating that he filled the role of political parties, the shah declared Rastakhiz, the National Resurgence party, the only legitimate political voice allowed the people of Iran. For those who refused to surrender the democratic process, SAVAK served as the court of last resort. But neither Rastakhiz or SAVAK possessed the ability to combat Iranian culture. The ambitions of Muhammad Reza Shah, dependent on the secularization of society and the all-encompassing power of the king, refused to flow through the arteries and veins of Iranian life. The Iranians, as they had at the time of Reza Shah, bowed down to monarchical power but refused to rise to their king's great expectations. For the second Pahlavi shah, like the first, had placed himself on only one side of Iran's cultural heritage. To Muhammad Reza Shah, Islam existed only as a resented religion, not as a way of life which demanded respect for values the shah found noxious to his concepts of modernization to be achieved under his own form of Persian kingship. Regardless of the shah's refusal to recognize those values, their origins traced back to the Achaemenians, when the concept of justice entwined itself in the culture. This ancient expectation that the king rule on the side of right began forcefully to assert itself in the oil boom of the mid-1970s.

Criticism of how the shah used Iran's single most important perishable natural resource festered across a broad spectrum of Iranians as the people watched oil revenues go into grandiose economic projects, massive arms purchases, and the grotesque corruption of the royal family and their cronies. Concurrently, the choices the shah made in

spending oil revenues magnified every weakness in the Iranian economy. The misdirected economic development plans, the massive
imports of food and consumer goods, the neglect of agricultural pro-
ductivity, and the maldistribution of wealth only added to the historic
miseries of the Iranians. At a time when the gap between the rich and
poor widened rather than diminished, little money proportional to
what was spent on the glamour projects went into basic human services such as rural electrification, agricultural development, or public
health. Representative of the critics, a pediatrician bitterly denounced
the shah's skewed priorities: "Millions were spent to build big [gam-
bling] casinos . . . while kids died because they drank contaminated
water."[16]

With few resources going to the countryside, the promises raised
by the oil boom pulled the peasants out of the villages into the cities,
especially Tehran. By 1976, the capital held at least 13 percent of
Iran's total population. These migrants found jobs easier than they
found housing in a city where real estate speculation had made the
rich richer for forty years. Families of one, two, or sometimes three
generations crowded in miserable apartments in south Tehran. The
even less fortunate squatted in scrap-metal huts surrounded by garbage and vermin. Those who did find jobs also found that employment for manual laborers seldom proved permanent. Too often, in too
many places, hungry job hunters from the provinces slept on the
ground like animals and beggars haunted the unswept streets. Regardless of the flood of oil money, the lowest of the social order made apathetic by ignorance, poverty, and disease still lived in the squalor
they had endured for two thousand years.

In a milieu of profligate spending, corruption, and galloping inflation, the abject poverty of uncounted millions passed unseen before
the eyes of the Westernized upper class of Pahlavi Iran. This new class
of Iranians made rich by the oil boom fed the same cultural alienation
as the presence of so many Americans. They, too, lived in north Tehran, which spread out over the tree-shaded foothills of the Alborz
Mountains to proclaim itself in form and culture more a province of
the West than of Iran. Pahlavi Avenue, the long, sloping street lined
with poplar trees, reigned as Tehran's Champs-Élysées. Behind its *jubes*
in which cold, clear water produced by melting snow flowed over narrow stair-step terraces, intimate cafés played host to a clientele that
spoke English as often as Farsi and read the American novel *Love Story*
rather than Persian poetry. It was here in the north that Iranians in the
tradition of ancient Persia eagerly sought assimilation with the West-

erners they lived beside who influenced most aspects of Iran's public and commercial life. Floating back and forth between Iran and the West, they left their country with little except money to deposit in their foreign bank accounts and returned carrying Western material-ism, mores, and attitudes. Like the shah, they invested absolute faith in modernization according to the Western model. This insensitivity to the deeper problems of their society rendered them alien Iranians, or, as it was expressed in Persian, "They were neither here, nor there," neither Eastern nor Western. In some ways, the Americans in Iran knew more about the Iranian masses than many members of the Ira-nian elite for the simple reason that Americans were more willing to leave the comfort of their homes to travel through rural Iran. These beneficiaries of Pahlavi rule largely clustered in north Tehran refused to recognize that cosmopolitan Iran racing toward Western-style mod-ernization constituted only one side of the Iranian character. The other side huddled in south Tehran, divided from the north by culture as well as distance.

South Tehran boasted no Pahlavi avenues, boutiques, or discos, no luxury apartment buildings, or chic cafés beckoning to a clientele fas-cinated by the West. Only the Arab belly dancers performing at the Club Shekufeh-no drew people south of the bazaar. They avoided south Tehran because it was, and is, poor, crowded, and traditional. Crumbling apartment blocks leaned one against the other, broken only by small dwellings that were hardly more than hovels. In the streets, scrawny horses pulled overloaded carts through throngs of laborers and chador-draped shoppers dodging the ancient electric streetcars. Away from the major thoroughfares, plodding donkeys led by peasants in from the villages carried produce and milk from door to door in the warren of intersecting alleyways in which most people were born, lived, and died. Here people spun out lives void of all dignity except for that provided by religion. And it was in the square, squat neigh-borhood mosque presided over by a turbaned mullah that those steeped in the traditional life of Iran found meaning and purpose. This is why the traditional south so angrily watched as Muhammad Reza Shah in the name of modernization turned Iran further and further away from its Islamic heritage.

By the latter half of the 1970s, Iran's hierarchical society, which had divided for centuries into landowners and peasants, now divided again between the urban elite and the urban poor. Unlike the past, when the welfare of landowners had depended on the men and women who worked their land from generation to generation, the new elite derived its wealth from its privileged position in an oil-rich economy directed by Muhammad Reza Shah. Members of this new elite were often the most ruthless members of SAVAK, the highest-ranking military officers, the most ambitious bureaucrats and ministers, and the most avaricious businessmen gathering enormous fortunes in the oil boom.

This private sector that the shah created with his oil revenues encompassed a small group of import-export agents, selected *bazaaris*, and some landowners who had lost most of their holdings in the 1963 land reform. As newly born industrialists, they benefited from a government eager for import substitution and generous with concessions and subsidies for domestic manufacturing. Hiding behind high tariffs, they gathered industrial licenses, tax privileges, and huge bank loans. Concurrently, they gained technical know-how and management skills from foreign corporations given the choice in the Iranian economy of a joint venture or nothing. Together with the tiny number of manufacturers who preceded the boom years, they represented the concentration of economic power that accentuated the extremes of wealth and poverty. While the villagers and the slum dwellers struggled to feed their children, the elite bought their eleven-year-old sons new cars equipped with a driver old enough to operate it.

Fifteen years after the revolution, I walked in Jangali-ye-Lavizin Park on the edge of the Alborz Mountains in north Tehran. Sahar, a striking woman in her late thirties, had just arrived on her first visit to Iran since the rage of 1979 had forced her into exile. She had belonged to the elite of the shah's Iran and had lived the upper-class lifestyle of the 1970s. Now she was just another person within the Islamic Republic.

The park was crowded. The laughter of children darting between the trees rang off the bold, jagged mountains that formed a majestic backdrop. We followed a steep path for a while before we stopped at a bench and sat down. Sahar lit a cigarette. Through the smoke that curled around her head, she looked at the families clustered around their picnic baskets and watched people in the dress of the working class pass by on their way up the rutted path. Deep thought furrowed her forehead and she seemed to remove herself mentally to a realm where she did not want to be disturbed. Finally she spoke. "We never came to places like this. We didn't need to. Our houses were surrounded by gardens that created our own private parks." She dropped her half-smoked cigarette and ground it out with the toe of a fine leather shoe before leaning back on the wooden bench. Then she spoke again. "Maybe if we had come to places like this the revolution would never have happened."

Between 1975 and 1977, economic hardship pressed on everyone but the very rich. Gross national product that had soared by 43 percent in 1974 grew by 14 percent in 1975. That same year inflation reached 25 percent. In 1976, the budget deficit topped $2.4 billion. An attempt to rein in galloping inflation led government banking institutions to shut down credit for everyone but the elite. Still the shah continued to buy his American arms and build his showy, empty development projects. By 1977, the budget deficit totaled $6 billion. In the four years since the oil boom had given Iran undreamed-of riches, the revolution of rising expectations had turned into a revolution of rising alienation.

Culture joined economics in the growing opposition to a system imposed by a select elite and an alien presence. Nothing demonstrated the bizarre nature of Pahlavi modernism better than the Shiraz Arts Festival, the personal project of Empress Farah.

The festival claimed to mix the traditional music and theater of the East with avant-garde mutations from Europe and America. In 1972, it featured the music of Karlheinz Stockhausen as well as an immense play entitled *Ka Mountain and GUARDenia Terrace*. Stockhausen wrote atonal music and injected the synthesizer into his symphony compositions.* *Ka Mountain and GUARDenia Terrace*, a drama about a family going through stages of change, worked itself up a mountain over a period of eight days. In the process, it hospitalized the director with exhaustion. But Shiraz's great public outrage occurred in 1978, when a Brazilian dance troupe performed sex on stage.

Also deeply stirring the cultural cross-currents was the issue of women. In 1967, women had benefited from the Family Protection Bill. Under its provisions, a woman could, under certain circumstances, sue for divorce; deny her husband a second wife; and win custody of her children in a dissolved marriage. It also abolished the Shia practice of temporary marriage and raised the legal age of marriage for girls from nine to fifteen. It was all laudable. But the shah's efforts in behalf of women's rights had little to do with any principle of equality of the sexes and everything to do with his policy of modernization. Thus, while the modernizers within the elite applauded, the vast majority of the population sullenly complied with rules interpreted as

---

*When asked if he had ever heard Stockhausen's work, the conductor Sir Thomas Beecham replied, "I've not only heard it, I've stepped in it."

threatening hallowed patriarchy and, by extension, the family, which forms the foundation of Iranian society. Even among leftists and intellectuals, rights for women ran into opposition. Just before the revolution, a Marxist academic wrote a pamphlet arguing that the wearing of *hejab* and the barring of females from certain professions actually enhanced the freedom of women by preventing them from becoming the sexual playthings of men. Ironically, women themselves sometimes resisted their own liberation. In concrete terms, the wages of working-class women never reached a level that provided enough financial independence to enable them to moderate or escape the constraints of the patriarchal family. Consequently, females who had been declared forces of production by the shah also were required by their families to function as traditional homemakers and mothers. In the hard economic times of the mid-1970s, many women of the lower and lower middle classes debated the doubtful benefits of liberalization for what they perceived as the certain protection and security of Islamic ideology.

For the illiterate and the educated, the poor and the middle class, the fabric of traditional Iranian society first torn by Reza Shah shredded under his son Muhammad Reza Shah. Over two generations of Pahlavi rulers, Iranians had been pulled from their cultural roots through the manipulation of Iranian identity that diluted Islam and overemphasized Persia. Their yearning for identity found expression in the words of the poet Ahmad Shamlu:

> I am bothered by a pain
> which isn't mine,
> I lived in a land
> which isn't mine,
> I have lived with a name
> which isn't mine,
> I have wept of grief,
> which isn't mine,
> I was born out of joy
> which isn't mine,
> I die a death
> which isn't mine.[17]

Delivering little social improvement to the masses and denying political expression to the middle class, Muhammad Reza Shah had pushed the pace of progress to the edge of the Iranians' psychological ability to adjust. The shah should have listened to his own words. "In a world which is falling apart, it could be constructive to build a society of social justice, adapting modernization to our own traditions."[18] Instead, cultural confusion and alienation joined the lack of justice to bond the poor of the country and city to the not so poor among the educated, resentful of their exclusion from the privileges of Pahlavi Iran. In a one-party state ruled by the iron hand of an absolute monarch, the only political voice reaching disaffected millions was the implicit message of Islam.

Until the early 1970s, opposition to Pahlavi rule was led from the left of the political spectrum. But as plots to kidnap the shah, the empress, and the crown prince unfolded, bombs exploded, and members of the shah's government and the American community died by assassination, the religious right as well as the Marxist left swam in the waters of political protest. Paradoxically, the Pahlavi assault on Shiism had served to draw people back to the traditional values espoused in Islam.

In the Iran of the Pahlavi dynasty, the ordered life of prayer and lecture, commentary and interpretation, had retreated into the realm of the esoteric. The number of *talabehs* in the *madresehs* fell from a reported 5,532 in 1930 to 1,341 in 1974. In the intervening years, the children of prominent mullahs, often as not with the blessing of their fathers, partook of the new government-financed education and joined the shah's administrative elite. It all represented a shift in the role the jurist had played in Shia Iran.

Traditionally, application of personal, independent reasoning by the jurists of Shiism smoothed the interaction between the demands of the original teachings of Islam and the social, political, and economic conditions of any given time. But the rapid pace of modernization forced by the shah rendered the religious leaders unwilling to provide innovative leadership to their followers caught in a topsy-turvy world driven by the alien ideas of the West. Still, they could not avoid the truth that the eternal questions of light and dark, goodness and evil, justice and injustice remained embedded in Iranian culture. Frustrated by the failure of imported Western ideologies and institutions to satisfy either their social and political aspirations or their deep interior needs, the educated products of religious families began to exert pressure on their religious leaders to provide direction to the faithful lost in a world of corruption and injustice. Among several writers and teachers, two men particularly would follow the path first charted by Jalal Al-e Ahmad. They were Ali Shariati and Morteza Motahhari.

Ali Shariati, the most furious revolutionary among the ideologues of rebellion led by Islam, was not a cleric. Rather, he was an academic who studied sociology and religious history in Paris between 1960 and 1965. Returning to Iran, he taught at Mashhad University before moving in 1967 to Tehran, where he became part of the Husseiniyeh-e-Ershad, an ad hoc lyceum in north Tehran where some of Shia Islam's major intellects taught. There Shariati attracted droves of young, estranged students who formed part of the massive migration from the villages to the city. They came to hear him speak because they had read page after page of a new revolutionary ideology that poured from his pen. As Jalal Al-e Ahmad had awakened the young, educated Iranian to his cultural alienation, Shariati prepared him for revolution.

The powerful theme of cultural disjunction labeled "Westoxication" underlay all of Shariati's writings. Although his frame of reference, his conceptions of history, society, class, economics, and institutions of state all came out of classic Marxism, his vehicle of revolt against the power and privilege of Pahlavi Iran was Islam. Shariati himself bore witness to the failure of radical ideologies transplanted from the West to take root in the political consciousness of the masses of deeply religious Iranians. Consequently, Shariati conducted his revolutionary discourse against Muhammad Reza Shah and the Westerners who undergirded his power in the language of Iranian culture. Essentially rewriting the entire Islamic history of Iran, he stripped Islam of the moribund *ulama* and shaped it into a systemized ideology of revolt. According to Shariati:

> The problem which is now at hand is the thirteen-hundred-year-old complex of the misery of a people, the intellectual hopelessness of an umma, the metamorphosis and going astray of an emancipating and consciousness-giving belief, the wasting, passivity and going to sleep of a people with tyranny, ignorance and poverty; and that with the most sacred, the most exalted, and the most progressive belief and eternal divine values that we possess, and that with the dearest personalities and epic-making figures that each one of them is enough for the awakening, self-consciousness, movement and freedom of a nation of a people.[19]

Shariati's Islam dismissed the individual standing before his God, seeking salvation through his *marja-e taqlid*. His Islam no longer resided in the seminaries, held hostage by its guardians to either the tradition of quietism or collaboration with the shah. Instead, Shariati's Islam envisioned collective salvation of the Iranian people through the ideology of liberation and emancipation. Like Ayatollah Khomeini's *Velayat-e Faqih*, Shariati saw politics and piety, ideology and faith as interchangeable. And it was this interpretation of the divine faith that captured those who rejected Marxism because of its Western character and its absence of God.

Shariati did not live to see the revolution he helped spawn. In June 1977, the exiled Ali Shariati suffered the same kind of unexpected heart attack that removed Jamal Al-e Ahmad from the lines of confrontation with the shah. Again the whispered accusations implicated SAVAK in political assassination.

If Shariati used Islam to redefine Marxism for Iranians, Morteza Motahhari employed Islam to counter it. And if Shariati disdained the *ulama*, Motahhari reigned as the quintessential cleric. A product of Qom, he studied with both Ayatollah Borujerdi and Ayatollah Khomeini. It was as a certified cleric that he met the challenge thrown at Shia Islam by leftist, secular ideologies; he did so by confronting the same political issues of Pahlavi Iran using the ideological and intellectual discourse of Islam. The result was to undercut the powerful appeal of Marxism based on economic justice and to establish the credentials of Islam as the legitimate force of political protest against an unjust monarch.

Motahhari's importance to the Iranian Revolution came in part from a rare ability among intellectuals to speak to the masses. Through two small volumes, he retold the hallowed stories of Shia Islam. His style—simple, concise, and anecdotal—created a common and compelling folklore that celebrated the virtues of the faith— learning, patience, humility, magnanimity, benevolence, and, above all, justice. Paradoxically, it was the shah's regime that helped popularize Ayatollah Motahhari's religious tales when the National Radio broadcast them to the illiterate during Ramazan in 1963. Gathered around cheap receivers, the peasant and the laborer visited the mythical utopia of Shia history, where the imams and the just jurists enforced public virtue, interceded in the miseries of man, and confirmed for the believer the value of the Islamic way of life.

Motahhari also spoke as forcefully to the educated. Seeing Islamic Iran besieged by two forces—the tyrannical Pahlavi regime burdened with the ideas of the West and the Marxists gathered behind the Godless label of secularism—Motahhari began to redefine Islam for contemporary Iran. By addressing the stresses imposed by Western-style modernization, including the issue of women, Motahhari injected Islam into the politics of Iran.

Among the essential questions he addressed was authority in the Shia community. Ali, the first imam, served as the source for Motahhari's argument that no Muslim should accept the authority of an unjust ruler. And since secular kings were inherently unjust, as demonstrated by Muhammad Reza Shah, they should be replaced at the top of the political ladder by a *marja-e taqlid*, the supreme judicial authority of Shiism. Motahhari argued that only the *marja-e taqlid* possessed Shia Islam's concerns for the just distribution of wealth, social justice, and freedom from foreign control. As he wrote, "One of the responsibilities of the Islamic *ulama* is that where they face a society in which some eat too much that they explode, and others cannot even get a decent meal, in such conditions it is incumbent upon them to revolt, and to fill this gap, to eliminate this discrepancy."[20] By insisting that the *marja-e taqlid* act as the Shia Muslim's guide for politics as well as religion and by basing his authority on the Koran, which enjoins the good and forbids the evil, Motahhari prepared Iranians for the epic battle against Muhammad Reza Shah conducted by a charismatic religious figure.

During the years when Ayatollah Khomeini lived in exile, it was Motahhari who kept alive the flame of revolutionary Islam. His light drew followers from groups that ranged from urban intellectuals to businessmen to bureaucrats to high school students. All listened as Motahhari unflinchingly confronted the established monarchical order, the secular left, and that portion of the *ulama* willing to coexist with the status quo. No issue of contemporary relevance remained untouched as he renovated, updated, and presented Islam as a new, competitive political ideology.

Unlike Shariati, Morteza Motahhari did live to see the revolution. But on May 1, 1979, five months after Muhammad Reza Shah fell, he was assassinated by a group engaged to the death against an Islamic state. (See chapter 11.)

In the rising tide of politicized Islam, Muhammad Reza Shah adhered to Shia traditions in public. In private his hostility to the clergy increased exponentially with the spread of revolutionary Islamic ideology. Refusing to accept the validity of its call for justice and cultural cleansing, the shah rejected the dissenting mullahs as "ragheads" while he drew his collaborating clergy around him. The repression of Shiism that reached a crescendo in the 1970 murder of Ayatollah Muhammad Reza Saidi increased again in volume and tempo. The government took charge of the wealthy Endowments Organization (Sazman-e Awqaf), an important cog in the economic system of the *ulama*. This sacred network of donations from the faithful and distributions to the needy passed into the hands of secular politicians, some connected to SAVAK. The clergy and its followers saw the move as nothing less than a noose dropped around the neck of the clerics. As it tightened around traditional religious practices of Shia Iran, it came to represent an intolerable assault on the spiritual bonds between Shiism and the people.

In 1974 the shah closed down the publishing houses that produced religious books; sent SAVAK clandestinely into the mosques to detect political activity; disbanded religious student organizations on campuses throughout Iran; and arrested, interrogated, imprisoned, and tortured large numbers of clerics, including Ali Akbar Hashemi Rafsanjani, Hussein Ali Montazeri, and Ali Khamenei, leaders of the coming revolution.

The tighter secular authorities turned the screws, the more inflexible Shiism became toward the government. The shah completed the cycle by promoting with equal determination the ideology of his new Persian Empire. In 1976, in the boldest gesture in two generations of the Pahlavi resurrection of pre-Islamic Persia, the shah abolished the Islamic calendar and replaced it with the Pahlavi calendar, which was based on the assumed date of the foundation of Iranian kingship by Cyrus. Suddenly the Iranians catapulted from 1355 of the Islamic era to 2535 of "the era of the King of Kings." It was one more cosmetic move in the shah's strategy to destroy the clergy's existence and influence. But neither the clergy nor Shiism could be restrained. The ideological appeal of revolutionary Shiism began to sweep up the alienated millions disaffected and disenchanted with the rule of the shah. As the 1970s inched toward their end, Iranians increasingly found in religion refuge from economic and political repression and affirmation of an identity battered by Pahlavi policy and American presence.

The explosive strength of religious revival asserted itself at the University of Tehran on October 9, 1977, when two dozen masked students, demanding the segregation of women on campus, went on a rampage, smashing windows and burning buses. Elsewhere, the street demonstrations, firebombs, guerrilla attacks on police posts, and political assassinations which stained the 1970s were no longer the exclusive work of the leftists.

On November 15, 1977, the United States glimpsed the religious and secular rage against Muhammad Reza Shah on the lawn of the White House. President and Mrs. Carter, the U.S. marine band, a contingent of pro-shah Iranians, and twenty-one guns had assembled to welcome the shah and his empress to the United States. Hundreds of anti-shah Iranians massed across the street in Lafayette Square. Mostly part of the seventeen thousand Iranian students studying in the United States, they wore crude white cloth masks made from pillowcases that shielded their identities from SAVAK. In their hands, they held placards reading Shah: Fascist Murderer and Shah Is a U.S. Puppet. The welcoming ceremony was under way when the sea of white faces washed over the lines of startled policemen. In a desperate tactic of crowd control, the police let off canisters of tear gas. The wind picked up the gas and blew it toward the South Lawn. The shah and Mrs. Carter pressed handkerchiefs over their eyes and nose and Farah hurriedly pulled sunglasses out of her purse while the president, his eyes streaming tears, extolled the "wonderful opportunity for us to share experiences."[21]

The Carters and the shah met together again a month later, this time in Tehran. Jimmy Carter was on a tour of the Middle East, pushing another American peace initiative between the Arabs and Israel. He had stopped in Tehran to spend New Year's Eve with the Pahlavis. Although Carter had left the United States with a statement signed by twenty-nine prominent Iranian dissidents, he raised his champagne glass to toast Muhammad Reza Shah. "Iran under the great leadership of the shah is an island of stability in one of the more troubled areas of the world. This is a great tribute to you, Your Majesty, and to your leadership, and to the respect, admiration, and love which your people give to you."[22] A short time later, the clock struck midnight. It was 1978—the year the charismatic cleric Ayatollah Ruhollah Khomeini, carrying the symbols of nationalism and Islam, led the revolution against Muhammad Reza Shah and the alien presence of the United States.

PART IV

10

The Double Revolution

O N FEBRUARY 1, 1979, HUNDREDS OF THOUSANDS OF PEO-
ple scanned the clear, cold sky above Tehran, eagerly
searching for the Air France 747 bearing the exiled Ayatollah Ruhollah Khomeini back to Iran. They already had
waited hours while negotiations went on in Paris between Air France
officials and Khomeini's entourage. The French expressed the legitimate fear that their aircraft would be shot down by an Iranian air force
loyal to Muhammad Reza Shah, and Khomeini's representatives loudly
insisted that all Iran awaited the revered ayatollah. The plane had
eventually taken off but only half-loaded. If the caretaker government
installed when the shah left Iran fifteen days earlier denied permission
to land, there would be enough fuel to return to Paris. Now, five hours
later, it entered Iranian airspace, approached Tehran, and circled three
times while a fragile government made a decision of politics and destiny. Finally, the sleek aircraft began its descent. Below, horns belonging to the hundreds of cars surrounding Mehrabad Airport trumpeted.
In Tehran's streets and squares jammed with people the word went
out—"*agha amad* (the respectful one) has come."

The big 747 rolled to a stop on the tarmac. Its whining engines
shut down. Suddenly the moment was at hand. The seventy-eight-
year-old man who had fought Muhammad Reza Shah for a decade and
a half appeared at the plane's open door. Wrapped in the cloak of the
clergy, crowned by a turban, he slowly descended the wide aluminum

steps on the arm of an Air France steward. At the bottom, he knelt to kiss the ground of Iran. Ayatollah Ruhollah Khomeini had returned from exile to reclaim Iran's Islamic identity.

The Iranian Revolution began in early 1978. Following the Constitutional Revolution of 1905 to 1911 and the Nationalist Movement of 1951 to 1953, it was Iran's third popular uprising against absolute monarchy and foreign intervention. Coalescing around the charismatic personality of Ayatollah Ruhollah Khomeini, the secular descendants of the Constitutionalists and the National Front joined the masses of peasants and laborers inspired to political action by religious leaders who had altered the lower classes' most basic notions about themselves and their roles as citizens of Iran. Together the secularists and the pious drove Muhammad Reza Shah from the throne in January 1979. With the collapse of the centuries-old institution of kingship, Ayatollah Khomeini returned to Iran to complete the revolution. In its initial phases, that revolution reordered Iran's social hierarchy and renounced the alien presence of the West. This was the revolution powered by the political, economic, and social inequities of Pahlavi Iran and driven by nationalism. But another revolution followed. Bridging mid-1979 to mid-1981, Iran's revolution within a revolution pitted group against group in a violent struggle for the right to define the culture of the Iranian state. From that struggle, Iran emerged as the Islamic Republic committed to the preservation of traditional Shia culture, governed by a new elite composed of the Shia clergy, and ultimately ruled by a Shia authority figure—Ayatollah Ruhollah Khomeini.

In the years leading up to 1978, Muhammad Reza Shah and his opponents had engaged in sporadic battles beneath the outward luster of Pahlavi Iran. The Tudeh led the challenge from the left. Less visible Islamic groups proved just as effective on the right. One, called Fadaiyan-e Islam, assassinated the shah's court minister in 1949 and the prime minister Ali Razmara in 1951. Beginning in 1971, the opposition to Muhammad Reza Shah escalated its militancy. Both Marxist and Islamic groups sent guerrillas against isolated government targets, and most university students engaged in political protest in what amounted to a rite of passage. The shah's military along with SAVAK clandestinely fought the guerrilla war but the war with the students could not be hidden. In one of the most notorious acts of government repression during the 1970s, security forces in June 1974 invaded Shiraz University, a hotbed of left-wing activism. Men deputized by the shah flailed police batons against the backs and limbs of hundreds of students and hauled both the political agitator and the passive bystander into the bowels of the SAVAK detention system. By the end of 1974, student protests against the incarceration of political prisoners had shut down almost every university in the country and engaged many of the forty thousand Iranian students the shah had sent West to school. In Europe and the United States, the secular left-ists freed from the shah's censorship feasted on Western liberal thought and Socialist ideology while devout Muslims consumed the writings of Ali Shariati, Morteza Motahhari, and the other Islamic ideologues. Inside Iran, Marxist and mullah shared the dark, hot cells of Evin Prison, where they plotted the destruction of the Pahlavi throne. As the discontent, anger, and violence built against Muhammad Reza Shah through the last years of the 1970s, the secularists and the pious found a voice in Ayatollah Ruhollah Khomeini, the exiled cleric who had led both the 1963 uprising against the shah and the 1964 protest against American privileges in Iran. More than anyone else, Khomeini symbolized opposition to absolute monarchy. Equally, he stood as the great avenger of Iranian nationalism.

Khomeini the nationalist materialized when he denounced the 1964 Status of Forces Agreement, which exempted United States military personnel from Iranian law. In passionate words that captivated the nation and burned the United States with the brand of colonialism, Khomeini declared that the agreement put the Iranian nation under American bondage. A furious Muhammad Reza Shah sent the offending Khomeini into exile in Turkey. Turning expulsion into allegory, the ayatollah summoned images of the Quraysh driving the Prophet Muhammad from Mecca and the evil Umayyad usurper Muawiya denying authority to Ali, the true heir of Muhammad. A month less than a year after he arrived in Turkey, in November 1964, Khomeini moved to Najaf, the great theological center of Shia Islam where tradition holds that Ali, the first imam, died.

Najaf squats on a low ridge above a marshy lowland in south-central Iraq, a hundred miles due south of Baghdad. It is an ugly town of drab stucco buildings set down in a hard, oppressive environment. The summer is hot and humid, the winter cold and dank. In 1965, when Khomeini arrived, mud walls still surrounded the town's few streets and maze of alleys. What little charm Najaf exuded came from wooden lattice windows that projected from the second story of small houses. From what amounted to shuttered porches, sequestered women watched pilgrims from the most distant places of Shiism pass on their way to the gold-domed shrine of Imam Ali, the man by which the Shia concept of justice is measured. In the shadow of that shrine, at the center of Shia geography, Ayatollah Ruhollah Khomeini took command of the symbols of the faith.

Already sixty-three years old, Khomeini lived simply in a small house with his wife and elder son, Mustafa. Like the Prophet and Ali, he ate a meager diet of yogurt, cheese, lentils, and fruit. He slept on an ordinary rug spread on the floor. Day in and day out for almost thirteen years, he walked for twenty minutes; ate lunch and dinner; taught a small corps of students; received visitors; wrote his correspondence; and went to bed on a precise schedule that never varied. Through this asceticism and regimentation, he held himself aloof from any hint of corruption bred of materialism and worldly power. By the late 1960s, this compelling combination of nationalism and religious imagery had made Ayatollah Ruhollah Khomeini the model for imitation for thousands of Iranians.

Yet between the mid-1960s and the mid-1970s Khomeini lacked the critical mass of followers necessary to change the political structure of Pahlavi Iran. At best, his followers exhibiting a willingness to risk a verbal or physical challenge to the power of the shah concentrated in Qom, in the Tehran bazaar, and a few other old commercial centers scattered around the country. For the rest of his devotees, the bond between the white-bearded ayatollah and themselves existed on a mystical plane. In the context of the Shia psyche, Khomeini's otherworldliness gave him a potent appeal. Because he lived in exile, he was both absent and present—the paradox in which the Shia collective memory remembers its last figure of cosmic authority, the Hidden Imam. This suggested parallel between Khomeini and the Twelfth Imam did not need to be absolute to be compelling. It did not even need articulation. Religious symbolism, on one hand, and social and political realities, on the other, drew numbers of Iranians to the man in Najaf. There, year after year, Khomeini seemed to hover over Pahlavi Iran, an ethereal figure who was absent but present, persecuted but powerful.

Khomeini's influence grew precisely because he lived in exile. From the safety of Iraq, he could speak fiery words with a freedom denied those resident in Pahlavi Iran. In the presence of the security forces, the secular opponents of the shah voiced their protests in symbolic language hidden in poetry and prose. And the Islamic ideologues like Ali Shariati and Morteza Motahhari penned their works within the narrow margins of censorship. But Khomeini, able to pour his venom and wrath on the shah from his sanctuary in Najaf, became the champion of "justice," the single most important concept in Iranian political culture. Conceived by Cyrus, exemplified by Ali, the ideal of justice had absorbed the Iranians for 2,500 years.

Khomeini attacked the kingship of Muhammad Reza Shah by charging that the king and his government were in a state of armed rebellion against the righteous people of Iran. Raising Islam's concern with justice like a sword, he called the faithful to seek the revenge of the just on the unjust. He also spoke to a nation historically trampled by the alien. Exhibiting the ingrained xenophobia of the Iranians, which always sees foreigners secretly plotting against them, Khomeini identified "the West" as the cause of Iranian suffering in the twentieth century. Employing Jalal Al-e Ahmad's celebrated term, he indicted "Westoxicated" Iranians for cooperating with Western colonialists to rob Iran of its resources and its culture. In so doing, the elite of Pahlavi Iran had denied the religious authorities their historical responsibility to guide government and society toward the perfection demanded by the Prophet. Khomeini warned in terms as dark as the Day of Judgment that at stake in Pahlavi Iran was nothing less than the elimination of Islam as a faith and a way of life.

While Khomeini issued his messages in Iraq, his network delivered them in Iran. The *mujtahids* that the ayatollah helped educate during his years in Qom composed the center of that network. And the thousands of students who had flocked to his famous Thursday class at the Faiziyeh Theological School formed the web. This loose organization of mullahs recruited pious men and women committed to the culture of Shia Islam into the ayatollah's campaign against Muhammad Reza Shah. Like a giant communications system, Khomeini's network received his pronouncements from across the border, mimeographed them on cheap paper, and covertly distributed them through the shrines, mosques, bazaars, and lower-class urban neighborhoods. Those caught proselytizing for Khomeini went to prison, where they gathered more recruits, often among the leftists also imprisoned for political crimes. Bit by bit, an organization built toward 1979.

As early as 1967, Khomeini sensed the possibility of a political revolution against the Pahlavi dynasty. In 1968, he began to prepare his army. He renounced those within the *ulama* who declined to join ranks against the shah and issued an edict designating Morteza Motahhari to collect religious taxes from his followers. In 1969, he called secular and religious Iranian students studying abroad to a "sacred Islamic movement that, God willing, [will] lead to cutting off the hands of the instruments of foreigners, those who advocate colonialism and the Westoxicated."[1] In May 1970, after his confidant, Ayatollah Muhammad Reza Saidi, died in a SAVAK prison, Khomeini at last called for an end to the Pahlavi monarchy. During the Persepolis spectacle in 1971, the ayatollah, wielding authority bestowed by Islam, denied the very legitimacy of the institution of kingship. Muhammad Reza Shah had barely ended the ceremony at the tomb of Cyrus the Great when Khomeini thundered that Iranian monarchy "from the day it started to this very day has been the shame of history."[2]

When the shah began to spend his oil millions in 1973 to create a state stripped of the weight of religion, the aged ayatollah sat cross-legged on a rug before his tiny desk writing letters, issuing edicts, and dispatching telegrams. He stayed alive in the mass consciousness because he possessed a charisma not seen in Iran since Ismail rode out of Gilan in the late fifteenth century and Muhammad Mossadeq strode over the oil fields of Khuzestan in 1951. This force of personality radiated from his impassioned moral commitment and the aura of absolute integrity that surrounded him. Appropriate to the literary tradition of Iran, Khomeini was a master of words. A highly educated man, he could also speak with the tongue of a village mullah. Through language, the ayatollah reached deep into the collective consciousness of his followers to grasp their pain and alienation. And through language, he gave the learned and the unlearned a sense of dignity and self-respect delivered with the promise of a better tomorrow. In the process, he turned their silent anger into an articulate voice of dissent, stamped with God's approval.

By the mid-1970s, Khomeini as cleric and nationalist appealed to a spectrum of ideological persuasions: moderate, conservative, and militant seminarians in Qom and Mashhad; secular and religious students in American and European universities; liberal and radical intellectuals. Without ever moderating his stance against Marxism, Khomeini pulled the divergent opponents of the shah under his clerical robe. There the martyrdom of Hussein transformed into the struggle of the people against the throne. In the Iranians' emotionally charged realm of symbols, the shah stood as evil incarnate.

By now, the audiocassette had outclassed the mimeograph machine as an instrument of revolt. Spools of magnetic tape containing sermons and instructions in Khomeini's own voice came from Iraq, circulated through the ayatollah's underground, and crossed oceans to the student opponents of the shah. In these messages, the absent cleric wove together imagery and tradition to strike at the shah. Khomeini named the conscripts to the shah's army the "soldiers of the Hidden Imam" and prohibited membership in the shah's 1975 National Resurgence party as an act of "forbidding the evil." By 1977, a broad spectrum of Iran's population had retrieved an old Shia saying attributed to the Imam Musa al-Jafar. Prior to his death in 799, he prophesied that "A man will come out from Qom and he will summon people to the right path. There will rally to him people resembling pieces of iron, not to be shaken by violent winds, unsparing and relying on God."[3]

In metaphorical terms, the Iranian revolution of 1979 would pit Ayatollah Ruhollah Khomeini's characterization of Shia Islam against Muhammad Reza Shah's version of Persian kingship. The overture began in October 1977 with the death of Mustafa, Ayatollah Khomeini's elder son. The brilliant forty-nine-year-old cleric died suddenly in Najaf of a reported heart attack less than twenty-four hours after being visited by two men described as "strangers." Immediately whispers implicating SAVAK in another political assassination buzzed among Khomeini's followers. As befitting a culture steeped in martyrdom and death, the traditional Shia memorial service held forty days after Mustafa's death proved a defining moment for the revolution. Ayatollah Khomeini, the father at whose side Mustafa had stood so long, had been the most visible leader of the opposition to Pahlavi rule since 1963. His name and his dramatic image were recognizable to a large percentage of the population. But it was not until rumor, innuendo, and collective experience hung on SAVAK the responsibility for the death of his son that Khomeini finally became the essential symbol around which the disparate elements would gather in revolt against Pahlavi rule.

A revolution that would thrust the power of the spoken word against the might of loaded machine guns began in 1978. In important ways, it joined the 1905–11 Constitutional Revolution and the 1951–53 Nationalist Movement as a revolt against absolute monarchy and the influence of foreign powers. But unlike its predecessors, this revolution engaged every stratum of society and every region of the country. Its preparatory stages had been paved by the secularists, particularly the old National Front and the Marxists. They were followed by Jalal Al-e Ahmad and Ali Shariati, who built crucial bridges between the intellectuals and Islam. But it was the clerical leaders, masters of the art of rhetoric, who disseminated a revolutionary ideology

that placed the spiritual at the center of the political stage and produced the masses that drove the revolution. In its passion and power,
politics of the street touched something far deeper than the desire for
a more equitable share of Iran's political system and economy.

Khomeini's portrayal of the shah as an illegitimate ruler who had
betrayed his hierarchical role by failing to protect the physical and
spiritual needs of his people went to the very core of Persian kingship.
In essence, Muhammad Reza Shah had lost the *farr*. In terms of Islam,
Khomeini rhetorically juxtaposed legitimate religious authority
against illegitimate secular authority. Once most of the population accepted this symbolic model, the shah was virtually removed from the
Iranian cultural universe. The lines of the poet Saadi echoed across the
vast breadth of Iran: "I am not mounted on a camel, nor, like an ass,
am I saddled with a load; I am not the lord of subject people, nor am
I the slave of my monarch."

Ironically, it was Muhammad Reza Shah himself who lit the fuse
of the revolution. On January 7, 1978, a slanderous letter planted in
the newspaper *Ettelaat* accused Ayatollah Khomeini of the double sin
of homosexuality and serving as a British agent. The next day, a group
of *talabehs* in Qom gathered to protest the scurrilous attack on the
cleric. Marching toward the hospital crossroads, the exit point from
the shrine area to the south, they met the police, who commanded
them to disperse. When they refused, the police opened fire. At least
twenty died.

Tensions mounted. Less than ten days after Jimmy Carter toasted
the stability of Pahlavi Iran, all the pent-up hostilities toward the
Pahlavi dynasty ignited. For the next year, the flames of revolution
moved toward the Peacock throne, inch by inch.

The students killed at Qom became instant martyrs. Forty days after their deaths, the leading cleric of Tabriz called the people of the
city to perform the mourning ritual. As the procession wound through
the city, one of the shah's soldiers shot a mourner. Thirty-six hours of
rioting followed, in which the enraged mob smashed stocks of liquor
stores, burned billboards carrying sexually suggestive advertising, and
broke the blue-and-gold emblems of the Iranian monarchy hanging in
government offices. The shah's troops stormed the city, killing 19 and
injuring 100 by official figures. The opposition claimed 432 dead and
1,500 injured. On the fortieth day, the mourning ceremony held for
the martyrs of Tabriz incited more riots that rolled across Iran as the
Shia mourning ritual again turned into an act of rebellion.

The shah's security organizations flailed against revolution gathering momentum from the bottom reaches of society. But neither the shah nor his highly touted secret police sensed the power of the movement. The United States, primarily dependent on the shah's elite for its information, remained mystified by the social and political realities of Iran. Despite the escalating violence, the shah and President Carter continued their arms deals as if Iran remained the Iran of 1972. In March 1978, the shah pressed ahead with his plans for a massive naval expansion worth more than $5 billion. And Carter allowed the sale of nearly $600 million worth of American arms to go ahead.

By the end of March, the breadth and depth of the disturbances became obvious. The intellectuals who had originally fed revolutionary ideology centered their revolt in the universities, particularly the University of Tehran, Reza Shah's monument to Western education. There female students wearing hip-fitting blue jeans and T-shirts wrapped themselves in the chador as a banner of national identity. The black drape once banned by Reza Shah as a symbol of Iran's backwardness now "showed that women are chaste; the family's honor is intact. The women are in their traditional place; society has been cleansed of corrupting foreign influence."[4] Outside the campuses, the peasants and the urban poor who had created neither the strategy nor the ideology of the revolution provided gigantic numbers willing to die under the treads of army tanks in defiance of the shah. All the while, the clerics, Friday after Friday, used their sermons as a vehicle of politics. Following the lead of Khomeini, they preached that Karbala was not one day, it is always.

Spring budded in violence in Shiraz, Tehran, and Tabriz. In Qom, three busloads of armed and helmeted commandos arrived on May 10 to quell large demonstrations. Led by their commander, a squad of soldiers burst into the home of Ayatollah Kazem Shariatmadari. In the presence of the most influential cleric inside Iran, they shot one of his followers dead on the spot. At that moment, Shariatmadari left behind Shia Islam's traditional abhorrence of politics to join the opposition to Pahlavi rule. Most of the religious moderates followed him. For centuries a faith of lament and submission, Shiism had suddenly become the vehicle of ecstasy and rebellion.

On through the summer, demonstrations, strikes, and riots convulsed the country. Sometimes the government reacted with great force, sometimes with unexpected, almost apologetic, conciliation, especially toward Shia Islam. During the year, the shah abolished the imperial calendar commencing with the reign of Cyrus along with the Ministry of Women's Affairs. He closed the casinos and gambling clubs; began to rid the government of Bahais; and tried to restore some of the royal family's Islamic credentials. Empress Farah went on pilgrimage to Mecca and the shah touted the amount of money he had spent on the beautification of the shrine at Mashhad. As the shah attempted to shore up his throne, the elite kept telling themselves and the Americans that everything would be all right. After all, the shah had the army and the army would never crack. That was before the fire at the Cinema Rex in Abadan.

On August 19, people packed the theater for an Iranian-made film entitled *The Deer*. Without warning, flames engulfed the building. Screams of dying people trapped in the inferno by locked exit doors carried into the street. Those who heard them were rendered helpless by the intensity of the fire. When it finally died, four hundred charred bodies, mostly women and children, lay in the ruins. Fed by the symbolism that August 19 was the anniversary of the American-led coup against Mossadeq, another day of national disaster, rumors raced faster than the fire. Distilled, they all said the same thing. SAVAK had pursued several Islamic militants into the theater. When informed of the situation, the shah personally ordered the burning of the building. Regardless of a history among Muslim militants for torching theaters, thousands upon thousands of Iranians who so far had stayed neutral in a struggle they saw as between the shah and the mullahs suddenly shifted to the opposition.

In the first week in September, the shah imposed martial law after marchers in religious processions at the end of Ramazan shouted for the return of Khomeini. That Friday, September 8, somewhere between five thousand and twenty thousand people moved through south Tehran toward a squad of armed soldiers assembled in a square named Jaleh. Under orders to break up demonstrations, the men of the shah's military pumped round after round of bullets into a defenseless crowd. A dark, sticky red from the dead and wounded covered the square as if the asphalt itself bled. The deaths of innocent people in the cause of justice raised again the potent symbolism of Karbala, turning "Black Friday" into a national outrage. With it, the last remnants of support for the monarchy collapsed and the Pahlavi dynasty teetered on the brink of the abyss.

In October, the resistant shah unsheathed another weapon against his great nemesis, Ayatollah Khomeini. Exerting pressure on Saddam Hussein, Iraq's de facto ruler, the shah forced Khomeini out of Najaf. The cleric with his family and entourage found sanctuary in the Paris suburb of Neauphle-le-Chateau. In the despised West, not far from the home of Brigitte Bardot, Khomeini resumed his assault on Muhammad Reza Shah. Once more technology aided the battle. Unlike Najaf, France boasted a multitude of international telephone lines, allowing Khomeini's lieutenants to direct-dial the ayatollah's instructions to the combat troops on the ground in Iran. Equally important, Khomeini gained access to the international press. In repeated press conferences, the ayatollah's spokesmen, who were men educated in the West, related in the languages of the West Iranian grievances against Muhammad Reza Shah. Over and over, they insisted that Khomeini himself would not administer post-Pahlavi Iran but rather would guide the state on the path of Islam.

On through October and November, the masses who had failed the Constitutional Revolution and Muhammad Mossadeq rammed against the barricades of Pahlavi rule. The mullahs, bankrolled by the bazaar, urged them on.* The liberal secularists and the Communists joined them. In the escalating revolt, the foot soldiers of the shah's army, the conscripts from the villages and urban slums, stood back and watched. Deprived of shock troops, an increasingly desperate shah grabbed for control. Through government orders and coercion, the doors of schools and universities slammed shut, the presses of the newspapers ground to a halt, a scattering of striking oil workers and government employees trudged back to work, opposition leaders went to jail, and parliament recessed. On December 2, the beginning of Muharram, the holy month in which Hussein was martyred, a curfew descended on all the cities.

But with a thousand men a day defecting from the military, the shah had lost his teeth. During the first few days of Muharram, young men wrapped in white burial shrouds symbolizing a willingness to die paraded by an army unable to stop them. When Ashura dawned, 2 million people running the social gamut from the president of a leading bank to the newest arrival to the slums of Tehran surged through the streets in an eight-hour-long procession that ended at the Shahyad. In the shadow of the monument built in 1971 to celebrate the kingship of Muhammad Reza Shah, an enormous chorus of voices called, *"Allahu akbar, Khomeini rahbar,"* God is great, Khomeini is our leader.

---

*The *bazaaris* acted from mixed motives. This was the traditional middle class that had always maintained strong ties to the clergy. But they also had a powerful economic motivation. The *bazaaris* had lost status as well as suffered the repercussions of a modernizing economy. They believed a revolutionary government influenced by the clergy would restore the traditional economy and the *bazaaris'* place in it.

To the pious, Khomeini was Ali. To the secularists, he was Mossadeq. The same imagery extended to the goals each group sought in political revolt. The secularists saw an end to Pahlavi kingship and national subjugation as constituting the revolution. But the pious regarded the abolition of kingship and the Western presence in Iran as only the beginning of the revolution of Islam. Nonetheless in that moment at the Shahyad, the secularists and the pious stood together surrounded by a powerful sense of oneness voiced in poetry.

> *How glorious is our night*
> *when bullets*
> *tattoo it*
> *and cries of "God is Great"*
> *bring together*
> *our hearts*
> *our anxious hearts*
> *from the two sides of the night*
> *when darkness*
> *unites the town.*[5]

The country spun toward anarchy. American employees of Bell helicopter wore T-shirts emblazoned with the slogan Keep a Low Profile, underlined with a row of bullet holes. The Iranian rich fled West carrying billions of dollars vital to the Iranian economy. Arms passed out of supposedly impregnable military arsenals into the hands of ragtag militias. Meanwhile strikes so effective that they cut off heat to the shah's palace made everyday life difficult, if not impossible. And always, there was the seemingly incessant sound of marching feet and chanted slogans.

The sycophants hovering around the Peacock throne insisted that the shah hang on. But behind the throne, they growled that Muhammad Reza Shah was instinctively weak, that he lacked the killer instinct of his father, that Ashraf was the only one "with balls." Even American ambassador William Sullivan observed that the shah "was truly not cast to be a leader of men or the nation in times of crisis."[6]

Before the new year of 1979, the shah concluded that he could not survive politically. To his credit, Muhammad Reza Shah refused to sit on a throne floating in the blood of his own people. Regardless of his many mistakes, he understood better than his pompous military commanders, arrogant cabinet, and privileged elite the reality of failed legitimacy. After thirty-eight years on the throne, perhaps the shah finally grasped the true essence of Persian kingship. Now all that was left was the manner of his departure.

Shapur Bakhtiar, a weathered veteran of the National Front, agreed to become prime minister on the condition that the shah hand authority over to a regency council before leaving the country on a "vacation" of undetermined length. The sooner the departure date the better.

January 16, 1979, dawned cloudy and cold. Muhammad Reza Shah had spent the preceding day saying good-bye to his palace staff, the Immortals, his corps of Persian-style bodyguards, and the high-ranking officers of his cherished military establishment. Now it was time to say good-bye to Iran. The fifty-nine-year-old monarch accompanied by a fur-clad Farah told Shapur Bakhtiar and others gathered at Mehrabad Airport, "I am going on vacation because I am feeling tired. I hope the government will be able to make amends for the past and also succeed in laying the foundation for the future."[7] Carrying a small box of Iranian soil in his jacket pocket, the departing shah passed under a Koran held over his head as a wish for a safe journey and walked toward his silver-and-blue Boeing 707. Before he reached the plane, a colonel of the Imperial Guard threw himself at his monarch's feet, kissed his shoes, and pleaded with him to stay. The shah bent down and spoke a few words. When he rose, the face of the King of Kings held the agony of the moment.

Muhammad Reza Shah had been king of Iran since the age of twenty-one. He had dealt with every American president from Franklin Delano Roosevelt to Jimmy Carter; sparred with every Soviet leader from Stalin to Brezhnev; talked international affairs with Churchill, de Gaulle, Chiang Kai-shek, Tito, Jawaharlal Nehru, and Anwar Sadat; and dined with Britain's King George VI and Elizabeth II, Princess Grace of Monaco, King Hussein of Jordan, and the Philippines' Imelda Marcos. He knew them all, it seemed, better than he knew his own people. Over the last three decades of his long reign, Muhammad Reza Shah had wanted different things for the Iranians than they wanted for themselves. In a culture where spirituality exceeds materialism as a value, the shah had pursued physical development at the expense of religious heritage. Much like his father, he gave his people infrastructure and his own vision of modern Iran. But he took from those same people their freedom and their faith.

Fifteen years beyond that January day in 1979, I strolled through a date grove in Kerman Province with a man who had marched with one of the Islamic student groups in demonstrations against the shah.

I asked him if, in retrospect, he saw the shah as an evil man. He pondered a moment before replying. "No, not evil. He was corrupt. He was corrupt because he had too much power. I have often thought that without all that power, he might not have been a bad king."

Before the plane in which Muhammad Reza Shah departed Tehran reached its destination of Cairo, the headlines screamed *Shah Raft!*, The Shah Is Gone. Along with the newspapers, a line borrowed from Hafez circulated through the streets—"When the demon departs, the angel shall arrive." But few asked what the angel would bring.

The Iranian Revolution of 1979 was in a profound sense a work of imagination. The destruction of the Pahlavi dynasty not only meant a sudden radical transformation of the political and economic structures of society. It also created the need to construct a society able to live in peace with itself. But like the Constitutional Revolution, the forces of change had only one thing in common—the destruction of the Pahlavi dynasty. Beyond that, no two groups agreed on the very source of government—legitimacy and authority. The extreme left of the political spectrum wanted communism, the Khomeini right wanted Islamic government. The rest of the Iranians more or less cut the umbilical cord to their monarchical history without contemplating its replacement. What most expected from a revolution laced with the rhetoric of Islam was the creation of some political entity capable of integrating the diverse ideals of freedom and modernization in the context of traditional values and customs.

For the moment, Shapur Bakhtiar headed the caretaker government left by the shah. Probably no one appointed by the Pahlavi king could have survived, but Bakhtiar proved a particularly poor choice. Almost a comic caricature of the "Western struck" dandy lampooned by Iranian literature for three decades, Bakhtiar seemed to mock a revolution carrying the torch of Iranian identity. While the rhetoric of the revolt had spoken powerfully to the great symbolic issues of Iranian civilization—the internal versus the external, hierarchy versus equality—Bakhtiar spoke largely in Western terms—modern versus traditional, democracy versus dictatorship. From the beginning, he and his government were out of sync with a revolution that in many ways had risen from the very soul of the Iranians.

But the preordained failure of the Bakhtiar government also included the Khomeini factor. In reality, only Khomeini could lead Iran. Over a decade and a half, he had grown into a mythical figure of absolute authority ready to receive the Iranian Revolution as an offering to his indomitable will. Thus, once the shah departed, Khomeini announced his intention to return to Iran. Bakhtiar's fragile government begged for a delay of three months to give order a chance to gel. Khomeini refused. Stalling tactics assisted by a French air controllers' strike and bad weather kept the ayatollah at bay until the end of January. It was then that Khomeini gave notice that he would delay no longer. Boarding his chartered Air France jetliner, he arrived in Tehran in the bitter cold of February 1, 1979.

As soon as the aged Khomeini rose from his poignant act of kissing Iranian soil, a welcoming committee swept him into Mehrabad Airport's special Haj terminal, the departure and arrival point of pilgrims to Mecca. Before several hundred mullahs, the man revered as a tower of strength showed a human weakness—he fainted. Reviving quickly, he climbed into a blue Chevrolet Blazer for the twenty-mile trip to Behesht-e-Zahra Cemetery, where many of the estimated ten thousand to twelve thousand people killed in the course of the revolution are buried. Progress was slow in a car that could barely move through thousands of cheering, weeping followers waving portraits of Khomeini captioned, The Light of Our Life. Recognizing the impossible, the marshals appointed to direct the parade called in a U.S.-made Iranian air force helicopter and put the ayatollah aboard. It landed at Behesht-e-Zahra's plot 17. Rushing admirers engulfed Khomeini, knocking his turban off his bald head. Behind them, women clutching their black chadors close around them sang, "May every drop of martyr's blood turn into a tulip." Finally seated on a podium before a microphone, Khomeini sounded the death knell on the Bakhtiar government. "This parliament and government are illegal. If they continue, we will arrest them. I will shut their mouths. And I will appoint a government with the support of the Iranian people."[8]

Khomeini did appoint his own Provisional Revolutionary Government. During the early days of February, the two governments—one official, the other de facto—played a game of power in which the prize was the shah's once formidable military. On every military base, loyalists of the shah and defectors to the Khomeini government skirmished as orders and counterorders flowed from the two centers of command. In the showdown at Doshan Tappeh Air Force Base, the defectors established dominance as the pride of Pahlavi Iran surrendered to the Provisional Revolutionary Government. At Niavaran Palace, the last remnants of the Imperial Guard, the famed Immortals, stripped to their underwear and piled their gold-encrusted uniforms on a flatbed truck. Shahpur Bakhtiar went into hiding. A few days later, he boarded a commercial airliner in heavy disguise and flew to exile in Paris.*

The flight of Bakhtiar bore witness to the reality that the revolution as a unified, multiclass movement had reached its conclusion with the fall of Muhammad Reza Shah. Black chadors, mass prayer meetings, and ritual funeral processions were no longer instruments meant to cleanse Iran of economic, social, and political impurities. Instead, they represented the cultural essence of the revolution around which the new state had already begun to organize itself. Secular Iranians who during the drama of the revolution chose to ignore Ayatollah Ruhollah Khomeini's political philosophy laid out in the *Velayat-e Faqih* found themselves face-to-face with the concept of Islamic government.

In "the guardianship of the jurists," Khomeini had carefully constructed an argument for Islamic government led by religious authorities. In the absence of the Hidden Imam, it is they who stand guard against injustice and ungodly rule. But while the *mujtahids* might exercise leadership over the community collectively, ultimate authority is vested in a single jurist superior to all others—the *faqih*, the vice-regent for God. Holding absolute religious authority and political power, he is to guide society toward its potential perfection. In Khomeini's words, "If a deserving jurist is endowed with these two qualities [justice and knowledge of Islamic law], then his regency will be the same as enjoyed by the Prophet in the governing of the Islamic community, and it is incumbent on all Moslems to obey him."[9]

Acknowledging the Iranians' twentieth-century expectation of constitutional government, Khomeini postulated that Islamic government is constitutional. But rather than legislating laws according to the will of the majority of the electorate, Islamic government adheres to the standards and demands specified in the Koran and in the traditions of the Prophet. Because of its divine nature, the mandate of Islamic government exceeds that of secular government. Thus the clerical guardians of the community in Khomeini's Islamic government are responsible for the whole society, in contradiction to secular governments, which the ayatollah held are concerned only with the social order. According to Khomeini, secular government leaves an individual alone as long as he is socially harmless. "What he wants to do in the privacy of his home, drinking wine, . . . gambling, or other

*Shahpur Bakhtiar was assassinated in Paris by unknown assailants in August 1991.

such dirty deeds, the government has nothing to do with him. Only if he comes out screaming, then he would be prosecuted, because that disturbs the peace. . . . Islam and divine governments are not like that. These [governments] have commandments for everybody, everywhere, at any place, in any condition. If a person were to commit an immoral dirty deed right next to his house, Islamic governments have business with him."[10]

Except for the few months he spent in France when his opponents claimed that he practiced *taqiyeh* before the Western press, Khomeini made no secret of his goal of establishing Islamic government. The secularists simply did not listen. Khosrow, a Western-educated Iranian of about thirty, was typical of the liberal, democratic center of the revolution who so totally believed in Khomeini. I encountered him at passport control in Kathmandu, Nepal, during the final days of Pahlavi Iran. The line was long and slow, creating an atmosphere in which total strangers drift into conversation. Naturally Khosrow and I talked about Iran. He was enthralled with the unfolding events. I asked him what he thought was going to happen. He happily replied, "The shah is finished. Khomeini did it. He will come back to Iran and make everything right." Somewhat surprised at his enthusiasm, I asked him if he had considered what it would be like to live in a theocracy. He looked startled. "A theocracy? That isn't what this revolution is about. Iranians would never tolerate a theocracy. And Khomeini would never try to establish one." But he was wrong.

For a while after his tumultuous welcome home, Khomeini went back to the simple house at 61 Kuche Yakchal Ghazi in Qom, where he had lived before his exile. On the surface, he seemed content to act as guide or counselor, leaving his handpicked prime minister, Mehdi Bazargan, in charge of the Provisional Revolutionary Government. Below the surface, the polarization process between the left and center, on one side, and Khomeini and his followers on the other had already begun.

Bazargan, a scrupulously religious man, came out of the National Front. One of Iran's Western-educated, he was another of the prerevolutionary writers who had reshaped Marxist ideology in terms of Islam. For him, there was no conflict between the faith and his deeply held belief in the rule of law, parliamentary democracy, basic freedoms, and respect for the individual. Yet all were rooted in Western political thought, which Khomeini viewed as secularism, that despicable cultural import from the imperial West. Vowing to avoid a repeat of the

Constitutional Revolution, Khomeini braced to stop the Western-tainted intelligentsia from pushing the *ulama* aside.

Ignoring his philosophical differences with the ayatollah, the short, balding, and bespectacled Bazargan harnessed his reputation for piety and integrity to the political and economic havoc created by fourteen months of demonstrations and crippling strikes. Unfortunately for the liberals, Bazargan proved too ineffectual and too naive for his time. Void of charisma that bestows authority in Iranian political culture, he could not collect the taxes, utility bills, or even bus fares that Iranians had refused to pay during the shah's final months. What support he commanded came from the educated middle class. Too small and too late to the revolution, it provided him no leverage. Real power resided with the mullahs, who wrote Bazargan off. Benefiting from the collapse of the monarchy and Khomeini's immense popularity, the *ulama* had converted from a decaying institution into a formidable force capable of wielding potent political power.

As the Provisional Revolutionary Government had challenged Bakhtiar's transitional government, the clerics now challenged Bazargan through the Revolutionary Council. With a membership of sixteen to nineteen, the Revolutionary Council was originally organized by Khomeini during his final weeks in France. A secret body, it brought together the ayatollah's most trusted supporters from his years of exile. Although among those in its original membership, Bazargan was a layman within a group dominated by clerics. However, with credentials as a Khomeini revolutionary, he managed to pull the Revolutionary Council and the Provisional Revolutionary Government into tandem for a while. In general, the Revolutionary Council made policy and the Provisional Government carried it out.* But it could not last. Bazargan wanted to govern the nation, the Revolutionary Council wanted to remake society. It was during Bazargan's stewardship of Iran—mid-February to early November 1979—that the political revolution began to give way to the cultural revolution.

The fault lines of the political-cultural contest appeared during the March 30 referendum called to determine the nature of the postrevolutionary state. Pulling together several secular groups as well as a collection of moderate mullahs, Bazargan argued that the electorate should be given a choice between at least two forms of government—secular or religious. Khomeini said no. The voters would vote yes or

---

*In the interest of clarity, the Provisional Revolutionary Government will be referred to as simply the Provisional Government.

no on whether Iran should become an Islamic republic. Supposedly 90 percent of the voters went to the polls amid charges of voting irregularities to cast their ballots in overwhelming numbers for an Islamic republic. Consequently in the first showdown with the secularists, the Islamic militants had won. Ayatollah Khomeini declared the first day of a government of God. Over the next fifteen months, institutions possessed by the militants ensured that the vote for the Islamic republic turned into reality.

The first of these were the *komitehs* (committees), organized around neighborhood mosques and within groups of students and workers. During 1978, they formed the front lines of the anti-shah strikes and demonstrations. After Khomeini's return, the *komitehs* established themselves as a rival authority to the police. Basically vigilantes determined to prevent a counterrevolution, they arbitrarily arrested men, women, and even children on charges ranging from suspected prostitution to undefined antirevolutionary activities. Although a few came from the political left, the overwhelming number of *komitehs* were Islamic. As guardians of a revolution they saw only in terms of Islam, they invaded private homes to seize Western music, pour out liquor, and confiscate anything that offended their Islamic sensitivities. Loyal to a local mullah, they multiplied like bacteria in a medium of newfound power.

Karim is fortyish, a product of the Iranian middle class who now lives in Los Angeles. "I supported the revolution. After all, being educated but without good connections, I was one of the ones who expected to benefit from the fall of the shah. I even supported Khomeini. I believed all that garbage about the 'just society' freed from American domination. That didn't last long. You know why— the *komitehs*. One night about eleven o'clock some of my friends were at my house. We were having some beers and listening to some music. Someone who had just come in from Europe brought one of those silly 'girlie' magazines. We were just having some laughs. All of a sudden—bam! The front door flew open and here came the bearded fanatics. They took us all to jail. I stayed there for ten days. That's when I decided to leave Iran."

The Revolutionary Guards Corps, the military arm of the Revolutionary Council, constituted the second institution undercutting Bazargan's government. It was born in the aftermath of the May 1979 assassination of Ayatollah Morteza Motahhari, the powerful Islamic voice of the revolution. Fearing for their own safety, the militant clerics organized a private army to act as a counterweight to both the regular army and the parties of the left. Recruitment began immediately through the mosques. It drew zealous volunteers from the poor and the humble empowered by the revolution. As the soldiers of Islam, the men of the Guards wore plain green fatigues without insignia, medals, or ranks. Although they played a crucial role in quelling some of the ethnic uprisings that had erupted against a weakened central government, the Revolutionary Guards belonged to the mullahs, not the state.*

The revolutionary tribunals composed the third institution created and controlled by the Islamic militants. The product of Shia Islam's legal tradition, which entrusts enforcement of the sharia to Islamic judges, these tribunals operated beyond the scope of government. The first convened secretly on February 15, 1979, in the Alawi Girls School in Tehran, where Khomeini set up headquarters immediately after his return. With the approval of the ayatollah, hojjat ol-eslam Sadeq Khalkhali pronounced sentence on four high-ranking commanders in the shah's military. In an act of grim efficiency, lackeys of the court led the condemned to the roof, ordered them to lie down spread-eagle, and shot them through the head. Trials and points of execution spread. By the middle of March maybe seventy people, mostly members of SAVAK, the army, and the cabinet, had faced the firing squad. On April 7, Amir Abbas Hoveyda, the shah's longtime prime minister, was found to be a "doer of mischief on earth" and shot. These executions proceeded from the assumption that if no senior army officers and no political personalities from the old regime remained alive, there could be no counterrevolution. But they also flowed from the fountain of revenge. Hojjat ol-eslam Kermani, a foreign-policy specialist in the Islamic Republic who had spent ten years in the shah's prisons, told me, "After the victory of the revolution, many of the same people who tortured me in prison came begging for favors. The same happened to other clerics. None of us was tolerant of these people who were torturers and executioners. We tried them and we executed them."

Bazargan pleaded for an end to the bloodletting, and Khomeini, the accepted guide of morality, ruled in May 1979 that capital punishment was the exclusive fate of those responsible for actual killing during the shah's rule. But the executions continued unabated and Khomeini remained quiet. During the revolution's first nine months,

---

*Ethnic uprisings linked to the demand for political autonomy represented a major threat to the new government.

almost six hundred Iranians, ranging from the elite of Pahlavi Iran to prostitutes and brothel managers, went before the firing squad. Although death sentences were pronounced in many places by many clerics, hojjat ol-eslam Khalkhali personified the revolutionary tribunals. A short, fat man with eyes wildly magnified by thick, dirty glasses, he scribbled execution orders on scraps of paper and rushed the firing squad or the hangman to action before anyone in real authority could hear appeals. A man known for the pleasure he took in strangling cats, Khalkhali defended his actions. "There is no room in the Revolutionary Courts for defense lawyers because they keep quoting laws to play for time, and this tries the patience of the people."[11] Khalkhali was tolerated as a convenient tool of militant Islam's political campaign. When he was eventually forced to resign as an Islamic judge, it was because he was unable to account for nearly $14 million collected in drug raids, property confiscations, and fines.

In the months following the shah's departure, these three revolutionary organizations strengthened their positions through edicts from the top of the clerical order and harassment and terror inflicted at the street level by zealots. While Bazargan dueled with a sword lacking a blade, the *komitehs*, the Revolutionary Guards, and the tribunals evolved into a rival state apparatus capable of engaging the Provisional Government in a full-scale power struggle.

In the third week of April 1979, the power exerted by the Revolutionary Council split the ranks of those who had waged the revolution. Karim Sanjabi, one of Mossadeq's disciples in the 1950s and foreign minister in Bazargan's government, quit in protest over "disorders created by government within government."[12] That same week, Mahmoud Taleghani, the prayer leader of Tehran, a philosophical soulmate of Ali Shariati and one of the few clerics with ties to the Marxists, warned that Iran was in danger of slipping back into dictatorship. In response, the Revolutionary Council arrested Taleghani's Marxist sons and drove the father into hiding. Thousands of his followers went into the streets chanting "Taleghani, you are the soul of the revolution. Down with the reactionaries." Suddenly the centrists and leftists glimpsed the possibility of taking charge of the revolution through Taleghani. But they lacked the critical element—Khomeini. Abhorring the "nonbelievers" of the left, Ayatollah Khomeini summoned Ayatollah Taleghani to Qom. There he heaped scorn on the cleric's head before he called in the press. Denying him respect as an ayatollah, Khomeini announced, "Mr. Taleghani is with us and he is sorry for what happened."[13]

In August 1979, the liberals and the leftists chose to stand and fight rather than abandon their place in Iran's new order. Ten thousand protestors massed at the gates of the University of Tehran to protest new restrictions on the press that essentially ended the Prague Spring of the Iranian Revolution. The mullahs' street toughs dispersed them and Khomeini issued a stark warning to his challengers: "When we want we can throw you into the dustbin of death."[14]

Thus as the summer of 1979 ended, Khomeini's version of the revolution took shape. Censorship of "certain things that would lead to the corruption and demoralization of man" was in place; four clerics close to Khomeini, including Ali Akbar Hashemi Rafsanjani and Ali Khamenei, joined Bazargan's cabinet; and the Assembly of Experts charged with finalizing the new constitution had been elected.

The Bazargan government had unveiled a draft constitution on June 18. Although paying lip service to an Islamic state, it resembled the 1906 constitution minus the monarch. The document had been approved by the cabinet, the Revolutionary Council, and Khomeini, after he added provisions barring women from the presidency and judgeships. On August 3, an election chose the Assembly of Experts to act as a constituent assembly to finalize the basic law. Debate centered on the role of religion in the Islamic Republic declared by the votes of the masses fulfilling Khomeini's will.

Khomeini charged the militant clerics dominating the assembly to review the draft constitution from an Islamic perspective. According to the ayatollah, "This right belongs to you. It is those knowledgeable in Islam who may express an opinion on the law of Islam. The constitution of the Islamic Republic means the constitution of Islam. Don't sit back while foreignized intellectuals, who have no faith in Islam, give their views and write the things they write."[15] So the battle was joined as the militant clerics dissected the draft constitution article by article. And article by article, the secularists and clerics who recognized Islam as integral to Iran but who opposed fusing religion and the state grappled with Khomeini supporters who wanted only one thing—government defined in the *Velayat-e Faqih*. Unlike their predecessors in 1906, Khomeini's men in the Assembly of Experts suffered from neither an inferiority complex toward the West nor intellectual confusion about government and religion. With no apologies to anyone, they translated Islam into constitutional principles which guaranteed the privileged status of the *ulama* as Iran's new rulers.

The 1979 constitution that emerged from the Assembly of Experts created a Majlis, modeled on that of the 1906 constitution, and a president. Together they formed the legislative and executive wings of government, much like those found in the secular West. But real power resided in the parallel religious branches—the Council of Guardians and the Supreme Jurisprudent or *faqih*. In essence, the constitution created a republic while repudiating popular sovereignty. Although the Majlis passed all legislation, the twelve-man Council of Guardians was empowered to veto all laws—civil, penal, economic, administrative, cultural, military, and political—which failed to meet the exacting laws of Islam. In turn, the Council of Guardians, along with the president and the Majlis, submitted to the authority of the *faqih*. Just as it defined the powers of the executive and legislative branches of government, the constitution recognized the *faqih* as possessing a special mystique and aura of infallibility which sanctified politics and required obedience as a religious obligation. In the Shia tradition, the *faqih* serves as the powerful authority figure who distinguishes good from evil, truth from falsehood.

It came as no surprise that the Assembly of Experts on October 14, 1979, approved Ayatollah Ruhollah Khomeini as the *faqih*—the Supreme Jurisprudent. He also collected command of the armed forces and veto power over all candidates for the Majlis and the presidency. All that remained was the referendum approving Iran's theocracy. A little over a week after he became *faqih*, Khomeini warned his followers about "dissenters" plotting the destruction of the Islamic Republic through the election. Before those alleged dissenters could even vote, they would be disarmed by the seizure of the American embassy in Tehran.

It had been nine months since Muhammad Reza Shah left Iran. He had spent a brief five days in Egypt, then moved on to Morocco, where a nervous King Hassan played reluctant host for two and a half months. On March 30, the day of the referendum on the Islamic Republic, Hassan put the shah and his shrinking entourage on a plane for the Bahamas. Ever since he left Iran in mid-January, the shah had assumed that the United States would welcome him when he chose to come. But on February 14, 1979, militants staged the first attack on the American embassy in Tehran. Although Prime Minister Bazargan succeeded in calling them off, Washington trembled. When the shah expressed his wish to enter the United States in the early summer of 1979, the nervous Carter administration found him refuge in a villa in Cuernavaca, Mexico.

Muhammad Reza Pahlavi was a sick man. In 1974 he had been diagnosed with lymphoma, cancer of the lymphatic system. For five years, Dr. Georges Flandrin of the Hospital St. Louis in Paris secretly flew into Tehran every five or six weeks to treat the man so many believed indispensable to Iran. Incredibly, the secret stayed within the palace. Despite its ties to the court and all of its CIA agents, the United States remained as ignorant of the shah's health as the Iranians. But now everyone knew.

Henry Kissinger and Chase Manhattan Bank's David Rockefeller led a battalion of the shah's American friends to pound on the doors of the White House, Congress, and the media demanding that the United States honor its commitment to its old ally. Finally, Jimmy Carter, the man the shah accused of throwing him out of Iran like a mouse, caved in. The shah could come to New York for medical treatment and then return to Mexico.

The news flashed to Iran. Immediately the xenophobic fears rooted in 1953 took charge of the Iranian imagination. In popular perception, the deposed shah in New York meant nothing less than the intention of the United States to overthrow the revolution and restore the Pahlavi dynasty. The royal patient had hardly settled into Cornell Medical Center on the East River when some eighty students, mostly from Tehran's Polytechnique University, gathered to formulate a spectacular act of protest over both the shah's presence in the United States and Bazargan's recent contact with President Carter's national security adviser, Zbigniew Brzezinski. They began planning a sit-in at the United States embassy, the imposing symbol of American power in Iran.

Occupying twenty-three acres in the heart of downtown Tehran, the property on which the American embassy sat had been purchased in 1928 for sixty thousand dollars from a family forced to sell to pay off a gambling debt. By 1979, the walled compound bordered by Roosevelt and Takht-e Jamshid avenues resembled a small town protected by thirteen U.S. Marines and a handful of Iranian policemen.

At midmorning on November 4, the group calling itself Students Following the Imam's Line sent chador-clad women to parade around the embassy's perimeter. Over and over, they shouted, "Death to America." Ironically, two top U.S. envoys were at the Foreign Ministry at about the same time requesting diplomatic immunity for the embassy's military personnel, the same issue on which Khomeini had attacked the shah in 1964. With the chanting women pulling attention to the street, a second contingent of students, following directions provided by inside information, found a basement window in the main chancery. Slipping inside, they seized every American in the building.

With pistols pointed to their heads, blindfolds covering their eyes, and cords binding their wrists, the Americans were marched out into the open for the world to see. Aware that the embassy had been invaded, staff members in the two adjacent buildings frantically shredded documents. Before they finished, they too were overpowered and herded to the circus outside. The American envoys at the Iranian Foreign Ministry pleaded with the Bazargan government to intervene as it had in February. But it was too late for the Provisional Government.

By the next day, the scene outside the embassy had turned into an orgy of hatred. The students ran a succession of press conferences in which they held up documents found in the "nest of spies" and displayed the latest photographs of bound and blindfolded hostages to crowds roaring their approval. Others wielding cans of spray paint continued to turn the high brick walls surrounding the embassy into billboards for anti-American slogans printed in English and Farsi. During the day, a string of mullahs, including Khomeini's son Ahmed, passed through the barricades to inspect the great prize of the revolution. However once that prize was captured, the militants had no idea how to use it. Khomeini did. An act of outrage against the United States would serve to ensure the adoption of the new constitution.

The ayatollah had not instigated the seizure of the embassy. But once he saw that it played to most Iranians as a high-profile act of nationalism, he embraced it. Khomeini the nationalist and Khomeini the Muslim laid the United States on the rack while Khomeini the politician whipped the fifty-two American hostages to win his definition of the Iranian state. Again Khomeini reached into Shia tradition for the symbol he needed for his revolution within the revolution. In Shiism, it is believed that Satan exerts his influence by acting within a person. Although it may appear that the person is the wrongdoer, it is, in fact, Satan. Khomeini applied the same concept to the United States. Satan dwelled within the global superpower, directing his power against Iran. From this premise of invisible evil exerting its will, America became the Great Satan. According to R. K. Ramazani, the preimminent authority on Iranian foreign policy, "The taking of American hostages was a supreme example of the continuity of past Iranian behavioral patterns, namely, to manipulate foreign powers or their nationals in domestic struggles for power."[16]

Bazargan, stripped of the last shred of his authority, resigned. The Provisional Government went with him, leaving the Revolutionary

Council to take over as the third steward of the state since the revolution.

The Revolutionary Council scheduled the vote on the proposed constitution for the Islamic Republic for the following month. In the intervening weeks, the Islamic radicals used the American hostages and the state's radio and television network to deftly twist together opposition to the constitution as collaboration with the United States. In the final manipulation of Shia symbols, the vote came the day after Ashura in the holy month of Muharram. By a 99.5 percent margin, almost 16 million voters approved the twentieth century's only theocracy. For the moment, Iranians shed their Persian past to become an Islamic society in which the principles of social order and personal life strictly conformed to the limits set in scripture, interpreted by the *ulama*.

While the masses might have approved the idea of the *Velayat-e Faqih*, the secularists did not. However, they proved less a threat than official Shiism. Among six grand ayatollahs, not one totally concurred with Khomeini on the key issues of Islamic government, including the whole theory of the supreme spiritual guide. Opposition within the clergy, centering around the concern over the corrupting effect of political power, dug so deep and sparked so much emotion that followers of rival ayatollahs clashed with supporters of Khomeini in December 1979 and January 1980. In the agitation, it appeared that Ayatollah Shariatmadari, still a revered Shia scholar in Iran, might lead a rival religious movement to that of Khomeini. But never a political man, he faltered. As a result, Khomeini and the political clerics were free to unleash ridicule, intimidation, censorship, and house arrest on their dissenting colleagues.

Perhaps to head off rival clerics, Khomeini as the *faqih* forbade any clerical candidates in Iran's presidential election on January 25, 1980. As a result, Abolhassan Bani-Sadr became the first president of the Islamic Republic. Another of the Western-educated Marxists who created the Islamic alternative to secular socialism, he had joined Khomeini at Neauphle-le Chateau in France. His goals then were no different than his goals as president: equitable distribution of national resources and justice within an Iran free of foreign influence. But Bani-Sadr would fail largely because he did not embrace either the masses or Khomeini's version of Islamic government. Tall, lean, sporting a neat little mustache and European haircut, he looked like what he was—a Westernized Iranian. And like the other reform-minded intellectuals, he neither understood nor communicated with the Iranian masses. Be that as it may, Bani-Sadr's greatest political error was his attempt to hold the state separate from and superior to the mosque. That proved intolerable to the new political elite—the politicized mullahs. Unlike the senior clerics, who generally came out of distinguished families of the Qajar era, the younger clerics were predominantly products of the middle and lower class. Their prestige resulted from political activism rather than scholarly erudition. Having achieved upward social mobility behind Islamic government, they would not tolerate any compromise with secular authority. Even the name of Ali Shariati disappeared from the revolutionary lexicon. Because he had targeted the *ulama* in his writings as a cause of Iran's malaise, the clerics who welcomed his influence in the revolution against the shah now erased it from the Islamic Republic.

With the forces of politicized Islam muddying the field of government, Bani-Sadr was mired in deep political trouble from the beginning. Mistrusted not only by the clerics but by several members of his own liberal coalition, the president never really commanded authority. Instead power resided with the militant clerics clustered in a pseudo-political party called the Islamic Republican Party (IRP), essentially a reconstruction of the Revolutionary Council replaced by the new constitution.

Accepted in popular perception as speaking for Khomeini, the IRP won almost half the seats in the First Majlis election on March 14. Aided by allies, it controlled parliament, the Council of Guardians, and the Revolutionary Guards. Bani-Sadr held the fragile presidency, the dismembered army, and a slice of Iranian culture. Between them huddled the American hostages, pawns in the internal struggle for power. The president urged that the hostages be transferred to government control. The clerics insisted they stay with the students. Khomeini watched and waited for his next opportunity to push his agenda forward. It came when the United States attempted to rescue its citizens.

In the dark of April 24, 1980, eight Sea Stallion RH-53D helicopters lifted off from the elongated deck of the aircraft carrier *Nimitz*, cruising in the Arabian Sea southeast of Iran. Their orders were to fly northwest to a remote landing strip 275 miles from Tehran. There they would rendezvous with six C-130 Hercules transport planes carrying the commandos, vans, and trucks assigned to storm the American embassy in Tehran to rescue the hostages. The helicopters hit a sandstorm that disabled two and sent a third crashing into one of the C-130s. Both aircraft burst into flames. With eight servicemen dead, the rescue mission ended, leaving the hostages in place and the Iranians convinced that the United States had attempted another 1953-style coup.

Ayatollah Khomeini had long been warning the Iranian people of an impending American attack. When the invasion of Iranian airspace came and so dismally failed, Khomeini credited God. In words alive with political and religious imagery, he said God had thrown sand into the motors of the U.S. helicopters to protect a nation governed by Islam. In the circumstances, Bani-Sadr simply could not compete with God. The way opened for Khomeini and his clerics to launch their final drive for absolute power in what was a cultural as well as a political revolution. The mullahs understood as Muhammad Reza Shah had understood that culture is not politically neutral. Rather it implies who in society wields power and who enjoys legitimacy.

During the week of the ill-fated American rescue mission, supporters of Khomeini's vision of Islamic Iran launched bloody riots at universities in Tehran, Mashhad, Shiraz, and Isfahan, bases of secular opposition to the Islamic state. Militant Muslim students attacked the Marxist Fadaiyan-e Khalq (People's Sacrificers) and the Mujahedin-e Khalq (People's Holy Warriors) as well as moderate and liberal organizations judged "counterrevolutionary." (See chapter 11 for a discussion of the Fadaiyan-e Khalq and the Mujahedin-e Khalq.) The Islamic militants won. But the war for the culture consumed all of society, not just the universities. In the early phases of the revolution, mobs in the street had taken it upon themselves to force Islamic dress on women. Now the government imposed *hejab* on the entire female population. In less than half a century, Reza Shah's police, who beat women for wearing the chador, had been replaced by Khomeini's police, who beat women for not wearing the veil. Elsewhere in the new order, neckties, a symbol of the West, disappeared; restrictions on the press imposed prison terms for criticizing Islam; the Center for the Campaign Against Sin banned the sale of records and tapes of "vulgar music" from the West; and ancient punishments for the crime of adultery resurfaced.

In a reversal of the Pahlavis, the new regime tried to eradicate vestiges of Iran's pre-Islamic culture. Ayatollah Khomeini attacked Ferdowsi, discouraged the use of Persian first names, and hinted at an end to the observance of No Ruz by expressing the hope that in the future the only holiday celebrated would be the Prophet's birthday. Others took aim at the physical symbols of Persia. In Shiraz, zealots set out on the back of bulldozers intent on knocking down the Persian ruins at Persepolis. That group was dissuaded by historical preservationists, but others damaged a wall of the Apadana etched with the image of Ahura Mazda. The large Sassanian reliefs at Biston carved in 250 B.C. survived only because an ingenious guard convinced the crowd that one of the figures in stone represented the man who married the daughter of Hussein.

It is somehow ironic that Muhammad Reza Shah, the man who tried to erase Islam from Iranian culture, died that same summer of 1980. His death occurred on July 27 in Cairo, the first and last stop on a lonely odyssey that had taken him to Egypt, Morocco, the Bahamas, Mexico, the United States, Panama, and back to Egypt. There, in the words of the poet Awhadi, "he ended fearing for his life, on the pinnacle of nothingness." A horse-drawn carriage bore his coffin, covered with the flag of Pahlavi Iran, through the blistering heat of an Egyptian summer to el-Rifai Mosque, to the tomb where Reza Shah was laid to rest in 1944. In the Islamic Republic, Radio Tehran gloated, "Mohammad Reza Pahlavi, the bloodsucker of the century, has died at last." The object against which all the disparate elements of the revolution had thrown their rage was gone. But another common enemy poised ready to strike.

On September 22, 1980, Iraq's Saddam Hussein sent his army across the Shatt al-Arab and into Iran. Seeking revenge for the shah's territorial ambitions of 1975 and moving to weaken a revolution that called to his own Shia population, Saddam Hussein staged the second Arab invasion of Iran. Although the war surprised the clerics within the leadership of revolutionary Iran, they embraced it as an opportunity to test the mettle of the nation and affirm the spiritual power of the faith. To the embattled president Bani-Sadr, the war came almost as a blessing. The assault on him mounted by the political clerics paused as nationalism temporarily bonded Iranians even more tightly than during the uprising against the shah. But unity did not last long because the more basic war over the culture still had to be decided.

By the first months of 1981, the word "moderate" carried treasonous overtones for those pushing Iran to the extreme of its Islamic identity. Holding all the power, revolutionary Islam would, in time, destroy the secular president of the Islamic Republic. When the American hostages were released on January 20, 1981, it was Khomeini who made the decision, not Bani-Sadr. It came because 444 days after their seizure, the hostages no longer served a purpose in the contest with secular government. Driven by the need to end Iran's international isolation in order to better fight the war with Iraq, Khomeini solved Iran's great external crisis.

In March 1981, the Majlis officially began to restrict the president's powers. At the same time, the militant students began to push him from office by releasing correspondence pieced together from the American embassy files documenting CIA contacts with Bani-Sadr both in Paris and in Tehran. Although there was no proof that he served as an American informer, the dark shadow of the Great Satan fell across Bani-Sadr. More important, the last months of the struggle for power between the secular president and the militant clerics functioning through the Islamic Republican party unfolded against the backdrop of the war with Iraq. Bani-Sadr denounced the IRP as a "greater calamity for the country than the war with Iraq," and the IRP retorted that it was "preferable to lose half of Iran than for Bani-Sadr to become the ruler."[17] Desperate for some leverage against the IRP, the president called for a national referendum to decide the issue of who controlled the government. That constituted Bani-Sadr's final act. In a contest between a Paris-educated intellectual and the clergy, Khomeini would decide the outcome. Responding to a June rally that sent two hundred thousand secularists into Tehran's streets, Khomeini, the *faqih*, thundered, "The day I feel danger to the Islamic Republic, I will cut everybody's hand off. I will do to you what I did to Muhammad Reza [Shah]."[18] Then he stripped Bani-Sadr of the title of commander in chief.* The signal had been sent that the president no longer possessed the ayatollah's backing. On June 21, the Majlis by a vote of 177 to 1 declared Bani-Sadr "politically incompetent" to hold office. Seeing the proverbial writing on the wall, Bani-Sadr had already gone underground. Six weeks later, he escaped to France on an air force plane piloted by the same Captain Behzad Moezzi who had flown the shah out of Iran for the last time. The man who, in the Persian tradition, sought to assimilate the ideas of western democracy into Islam left behind Ayatollah Khomeini and the radical clergy at the center of Iranian politics holding high the Islamic component of Iranian culture. Thus ten years after the celebration at Persepolis, Iran had swung from the excessive emphasis on its Persian identity to the far reaches of its Islamic identity.

---

*Other demonstrations in support of Bani-Sadr occurred in Qom, Tabriz, Shiraz, Ahwaz, and Bandar Abbas.

11

The Internal and External: Wars for the Iranian Nation

THE DRY, PALE SOIL OF BEHESHT-E-ZAHRA CEMETERY HAS RE-ceived Iran's dead for generations. Day in, day out, funeral processions led by boxy hearses creep the twelve miles south from central Tehran and pass through the gates of this sprawling city of death. Bodies belonging to members of old, well-to-do families go into the private mausoleums that form the cemetery's thick outer walls. The poor and not so poor are laid in simple graves that point the deceased toward Mecca. But Behesht-e-Zahra is more than a place of burial. It is a chronicle of the turbulent and tragic 1980s in Iran.

One chapter of that chronicle is recorded by a cluster of graves that share a brick wall with a garden thick with pink roses. Each white marble sarcophagus anchors a roughly two-foot-by-three-foot framed photograph of a leader of the Islamic Republic assassinated during the summer and fall of 1981. The regularity of turbans in the photographs and the inscriptions of Koranic sayings on the tomb-stones speak only of Islam. And it was for the Islamic state that all the men buried here died.

Another chapter of the 1980s is written in the crowded acres of the cemetery where the dead of the eight-year-long Iran-Iraq War lie. Over acres and acres, row after row of graves jam one against the other. At the head of almost all is a small, shallow cabinet constructed of glass held together by aluminum strips. In each, the fading photograph of a young face hangs over a collection of small objects. In some, there is a toy from a childhood cut short by war. In others, there is candy from the wedding of the young soldier. In still others, I saw objects symbolizing the Iranians' two identities—a tiny prayer rug representing Islam sprinkled with plastic flowers depicting the Persian New Year; miniature dumbbells used in the gymnastics performance that accompanies the reading of the *Shahnameh* crossed on top of a Koran. In their simplicity, they tell the tragic story of a generation that went to war for Islam.

Iran suffered two wars in the 1980s—the internal and the external. The internal war between the clerics and groups combining Islam and Marxism raged over control of the Islamic Republic. Assassination and execution were its weapons, terror its strategy. In eighteen months of what amounted to civil war, Ayatollah Khomeini's Islamic government survived its test by fire. Gaining new strength in the deadly challenge, the clerics assumed a new mandate—the export of the Islamic Revolution.

Seeking to prove its relevancy to a broader sphere, the ideology of revolutionary Islam was pushed by Ayatollah Khomeini and the political clerics into the Persian Gulf and on to Lebanon. There it won adherents within a Shia population demanding justice and equality in a Lebanese political system shredded by war. It was the Lebanese Shia who engaged the United States in another confrontation between Islam and the West. On October 23, 1983, their passion, generated by Khomeini's politicized Islam, killed 241 U.S. Marines. In 1984, Islam as politics began to sweep civilians from Western countries off the streets of Beirut to become hostages of political agendas often inspired by Iran. With each instance of terrorism, the perceived power of Iran magnified and intimidated those it threatened. Yet neither Iran's internal war nor the export of the revolution occurred in isolation. Both unfolded against the backdrop of external conflict—the Iran-Iraq War.

That war began in 1980, when Iraq's Saddam Hussein attacked the Islamic Republic of Iran. Defense of the Iranian nation from unexpected attack also became the testing ground of the revolution and its ideology. For the next eight years, Ayatollah Ruhollah Khomeini sent Islamic Iran to destroy secular Iraq. In the terrible carnage, the goal of expanding the Islamic Revolution eventually gave way to the preservation of the Iranian nation encompassing both its Persian and Islamic characters.

* * *

In the beginning, the Iran-Iraq War threatened the political survival of the Islamic Republic less than did the clerics' internal war with their enemies. As the downfall of Muhammad Reza Shah had acted as prelude to the contest between the secularists and the clerics for dominance, the June 1981 collapse of Abolhassan Bani-Sadr's presidency sounded the prelude to a second contest over the right to define Islamic government. Although following their coup against the secularists, the clerics controlled the executive, legislative, and judicial institutions of state, ran the National Iranian Oil Company, possessed the Revolutionary Guards as the parallel of the army, and dispensed patronage simultaneously from government coffers and organizations of the revolution, they could not deliver stability. Chaos swirled out of personal rivalries and old grudges. Turmoil enveloped the technocrats and professionals desperately needed to develop the country, sending them fleeing in fear and frustration. Anarchy made itself felt in the grievances that ethnic groups and tribes hurled against a disintegrating central government. In the wild disorder, the economy stagnated; the war with Iraq bled the nation; and opposition to the clerical regime stalked the political landscape. One more phase of the revolution had yet to be fought. It would pit the political clerics against the Islamic Left, represented primarily by the Mujahedin-e Khalq.

The Mujahedin-e Khalq came to life in 1965 as a nationalistic group committed to building a radical Socialist state. It drew its ideology from a combination of Marxism and the Islamic concept of *towhid*, a divinely inspired classless society where all men are equal and all women are entitled to basic social and political rights. The Islamic Marxists collected recruits from among the poor and in segments of the middle class to turn them into soldiers through training acquired from the Palestine Liberation Organization. In 1971, the Mujahedin began to send its armed guerrillas against Muhammad Reza Shah.* Over the years leading to the revolution, they struck Pahlavi installations and SAVAK struck back with imprisonment and execution. But the Mujahedin never broke. Although judging clerics as a parasitic class that perverts Islamic values, the Mujahedin greeted Khomeini on his return to Iran and gave tepid support to the Islamic constitution. It was when Ayatollah Khomeini barred the Mujahedin leader,

*The other major Marxist-Islamic guerrilla group was the Fadaiyan-e Khalq. Splintering into three factions in 1980, it dropped out of the opposition when the largest of those factions sought protection of its existence and interests through accommodation with the Islamic Republican party.

Masoud Rajavi, from running for president in January 1981 on grounds that he was "un-Islamic" that the group went into active opposition against the clerics in control of government. In the ensuing contest, both the Mujahedin on Islam's left and the clerics on Islam's right lived by revealed truth and absolute faith. And both held within them the same passion for vengeance.

Through the first months of 1981, the Mujahedin increasingly allied itself with the embattled President Abolhassan Bani-Sadr. When Bani-Sadr escaped Iran, Masoud Rajavi went with him. In Paris, they formed the National Council of Resistance. But it was the Mujahedin-e Khalq, not Bani-Sadr, who commanded power on the ground in Iran. There, Mujahedin supporters numbered several hundred thousand. In addition, the organization possessed a seasoned guerrilla army of perhaps one hundred thousand as well as an ideology salable in an Iran largely stripped of viable political opposition. With its commitment to an Islamic-sanctioned socialism and its history of resistance to Pahlavi despotism and Western intervention, the Mujahedin provided the rallying point for those who opposed rule by radical clerics. Denied a place in the electoral process by a constitutional system in which the clerics certified who could run for office, the Mujahedin voted with terror.

That terror began only five days after Bani-Sadr received his dismissal notice. Ali Khamenei, a central figure among Ayatollah Khomeini's disciples, lost the use of his right arm when a small bomb planted in a tape recorder exploded during his Friday sermon. The following night, ninety leaders of the Islamic Republican Party gathered at their Tehran headquarters for a routine meeting. At 8:50 P.M., a sixty-pound bomb planted in a trash can next to the speaker's podium roared its destruction. Bodies and parts of bodies flew through the air to be buried under tons of rubble. Although the government placed the death toll at seventy-two to correspond to the number killed with Hussein at Karbala, seventy-four actually died. They included four government ministers, six deputy ministers, twenty members of parliament, and Ayatollah Muhammad Beheshti, the second most powerful man in Iran.

Multilingual and savvy about the world beyond Iran, the fifty-two-year-old Beheshti had served as the revolution's propagandist in the days before Khomeini returned to Iran. He also orchestrated the highs and lows of the drama surrounding the American hostages. At the time he died, Beheshti held the positions of secretary general of the IRP and chief jurist of the Islamic Republic. Unofficially he served as the major strategist of Ayatollah Khomeini's theocratic state. Turned into an instant martyr, Beheshti drew thousands of weeping mourners who followed his funeral procession to Behesht-e-Zahra. At the cemetery, the body of the ayatollah and those killed with him were washed, wrapped in white shrouds, and buried in the plot reserved for "martyrs of the revolution." Converting the Islamic Republic's loss into political rhetoric, Khomeini held the Mujahedin-e Khalq responsible for the deaths and warned "blind hearts who claimed they took part in crusades for the people. You are breathing your last breath— you are going to hell."[1]

Outside Iran, exile groups ranging from royalists to Bakhtiar liberals to Bani-Sadr's National Resistance Front were also raising their voices against Iran's theocracy. In mid-August, royalist pirates led by Admiral Kamal Habibollahi, former commander of the shah's navy, captured a missile boat belonging to the Islamic Republic cruising off the coast of Spain.* That same month, the streets of Bonn, London, Paris, Washington, Copenhagen, Los Angeles, and Stockholm served as stadiums for anti-Khomeini rallies staged by Iranian exiles. In New York, two hundred Iranian students staged a six-day hunger strike in front of the United Nations. But none of the demonstrators exerted influence on the regime in Tehran. For only the Mujahedin-e Khalq was on the ground in Iran, able to strike the political clerics.

On August 30, 1981, a dozen high-ranking officials of the Islamic Republic convened to discuss the Mujahedin's campaign of assassination that had killed two hundred government functionaries over the past two months. Among those gathered around a conference table were Muhammad Ali Rajai, the president elected on July 24 to replace the deposed Bani-Sadr, and his prime minister, hojjat ol-eslam Muhammad Javad Bahonar. Without warning, a bomb hidden in the wall behind the table exploded, burning beyond recognition Rajai, Bahonar, and six other men. Again a million followers of the radical clerics poured into the streets of Tehran. Bearing the bodies toward the martyrs' plot in Behesht-e-Zahra, where Beheshti is buried, the mourners chanted, "revenge, revenge, revenge."

Sensing the vulnerability of the regime, other left-wing groups as well as some of the tribes took up arms against the Islamic Republic. Violence rumbled from Bandar Abbas on the Persian Gulf to Astara on the Soviet border. But the Mujahedin, armed with rocket-propelled grenade launchers, machine guns, and simple knives, dealt the real

*The vessel was surrendered five days later.

damage. During the summer and fall of 1981, more than a thousand government officials, including mullahs, judges, police officials, Islamic Republican Party leaders, and Khomeini aides died by assassination. All formed links in the chain of command through which Khomeini exercised his will. When security around the remaining key officials tightened, the Mujahedin struck the minor players of the Islamic government, civil servants and Revolutionary Guards. Often they took ordinary citizens with them.

One of the Mujahedin's near victims was Farah, a woman of about forty. In 1981, she and her husband had just returned to Iran after several years of graduate study in Europe to take up residence in west-central Tehran. "Milk was in short supply. Every morning I had to get up early to get in line at the corner grocer's. Before seven o'clock, I was standing on the street with a number of other people. It was like any other day at any grocery in Tehran. All of a sudden a car squealed around the corner and something came flying at us. The next thing I knew there was a loud explosion and I was on the ground covered with blood and pieces of human flesh. I didn't know what to do so I got up and went home."

In the terrorism, the Mujahedin aimed at no less than a second revolution, this one against Ayatollah Khomeini and the political clerics. But the combination of Khomeini's immense prestige and the absolute loyalty of the clerics' private army, the Revolutionary Guards, along with other grassroots revolutionary organizations, gave the regime enough power to retaliate.

Driven by fear for their survival, the authorities visited a terrible vengeance on their challengers that included the Tudeh, the Iranian Communist party. Mullahs picked up guns to become turbaned militiamen behind the Revolutionary Guards, the shield protecting the clerics from those who would destroy them. Turned loose with unrestricted power, they ruthlessly suppressed street demonstrations, entered homes at will, made unauthorized arrests, and fed the machine of execution. By September, fifty people a day routinely went before the firing squad or were hanged from scaffolding, bridges, and, on one occasion, the crossbar of a swing set on a children's playground. Too often, courts in search of blood randomly chose their victims. Royalists already in jail, the despised Bahais, and a twelve-year-old accused of participating in a demonstration, all went to their deaths. But mostly it was those tainted by real or imagined connections with the Islamic or secular left who made up the estimated eighteen hundred people executed between June and November 1981 for "waging war against God."

Her family still talks about Leila with pain as fresh as it was in 1981. She was a nineteen-year-old college student in an American university when the Pahlavi throne collapsed. Eager to build the new Iran, she returned home to the Islamic Republic. Fate, tempted by her opposition to the right-wing clerics, directed her into a group linked to the Mujahedin. Suddenly realpolitik consumed political idealism. Swept up by the guardians of the regime, Leila went to Evin Prison and then before the firing squad. She returned home to her family in a box.

In this atmosphere in which ideological purity warred against the deviant, the government urged parents to turn their misguided children over to authorities. A film run on government-controlled television showed a mother denouncing her son as a Marxist. The son, sobbing and grabbing for his mother's hand, desperately tries to convince her that he has given up Marxist politics. The mother rejects his pleas saying, "You must repent in front of God and you will be executed." The picture fades to Ayatollah Khomeini telling the people of Iran, "I want to see more mothers turning in their children with such courage without shedding a tear. That is what Islam is."[2]

At the peak of the revolution's second reign of terror, the Islamic Republic held, on October 2, 1981, its third presidential election in a period of twenty-one months. As expected, Ali Khamenei, the militant cleric who had been crippled in one of the first acts of violence, emerged as president on the votes of the masses following the instructions of their religious guides. Below him, men of the Islamic Republican Party held government's administrative apparatus from the highest office to provincial governorships down to officials on the district and township level. But the opposition had yet to concede.

In February 1982, the Mujahedin averaged twenty raids a day leaving behind functionaries of the regime blindfolded, manacled, and shot in the head. By April, even Khomeini's inner circle frayed in the chaos. Sadeq Qotbzadeh, a man who stood at Khomeini's side during the heady days in Neauphle-le Chateau and served as foreign minister during the American hostage crisis, confessed on Iranian television his participation in a plot to assassinate Khomeini and overthrow the government.* Named as one of his forty-five fellow conspirators was Ayatollah Kazem Shariatmadari, the chief cleric of Qom and spiritual

---

*At his trial, Qotbzadeh recanted his statement that the death of Khomeini was part of the plan. He claimed that after the coup, the plotters intended to send the ayatollah to Qom to fill a strictly religious role.

leader of 5 million Azerbaijanis. The news jolted the regime. Shariatmadari had long constituted a major problem for Khomeini's inner circle. Refusing to support the concept of a Supreme Jurisprudent, differing with Khomeini on many interpretations of Shia Islam, and claiming the title of grand ayatollah, Shariatmadari posed a challenge potentially more dangerous than the Mujahedin. Unable to execute Shariatmadari as they did Qotbzadeh, the radical clerics defrocked him. From the pulpit and in the Majlis, the clerical allies of the regime accused Shariatmadari of treason. His Center for Islamic Study and Publications in Qom went under lock and key and the ayatollah himself disappeared under house arrest. Finally, in a move virtually without precedent, a collection of clerics claiming dubious authority stripped Shariatmadari of his title as *marja-e taqlid*. In the fear-ridden atmosphere of 1982, no voice sounded against this blasphemous treatment dealt an eminent religious leader.

After a year of unspeakable violence in which the extremists of the left and the right demonstrated their willingness to both kill and die for their beliefs, Iran lay in the midst of uncollected garbage, decaying public works, and a crippled civil service. Educated Iranians afraid of jittery, trigger-happy militiamen unrestrained by any real government authority continued to pour out of Iran, taking their skills and their resources with them. They left behind a nation whose social and political fabric was unraveling in ideological confrontation while at the same time it fought a bloody, losing war against Iraq along its western border. Still it took until 1982 for the wave of extremism and terror to wane. As the challenge from the Mujahedin and other left-wing groups drained away, Ayatollah Khomeini himself ended the reign of terror which had consumed many of the revolution's original supporters. An Eight Point Declaration issued on December 15, 1982, not only aimed at curbing abuses but, in some ways, sought to meet the Iranians' expectation of justice from their rulers. (See chapter 12.)

The clerical regime's willingness during 1981 and 1982 to employ any means necessary to retain power enshrined terror as a legitimate tool of government. As a result, the Islamic Republic still emits an aura of fear. It manifests itself in various ways but particularly at Evin Prison, the hated institutions of the shah's SAVAK that became the clerics' most dreaded political prison. Once in an outer suburb of Tehran, Evin Prison is now surrounded by the city. The tall, sleek Azadi Hotel, the most expensive hotel in Tehran, marks the turnoff point from a new expressway. Behind it, the street turns into the narrow lane that runs in front of the prison's main gate. Physically, Evin looks much less ominous than most prisons. Inside the barbed-wire fence, grass and scattered trees divide three- and four-story buildings that resemble dormitories more than cell blocks. But Evin's history belies its appearance. Terrible things happened within its walls in the early 1980s and they have left a scar. I noticed it among taxi drivers. As soon as the gates of Evin appeared, they most often gripped their steering wheels, pushed their gas pedals, and kept their eyes straight ahead until they passed the last guard.

It was precisely because of its excesses that the reign of terror accomplished its purpose—the dissipation of opposition within Iran to the clerical regime reigned over by Ayatollah Khomeini. When political control became reasonably assured, Khomeini again pushed the theme that the Islamic Revolution belonged to all believers, not just Iranians.

In the political theology of Ayatollah Khomeini, it was God's will that a revolution unique to Iran's own political history and cultural environment reach out to bring oppressed people everywhere into its folds. The roots of this certainty that the Islamic Republic constituted the universal model of justice for Muslims and non-Muslims lay in Iran's Persian-Islamic culture. A fundamental feature of that culture is the incessant quest for an ideal society, defined primarily in terms of universal justice. In Persia, the hope for the ideal society resided in Ahura Mazda, the cosmic "Force of Good." In Islam, it found confirmation in the tenet that religion is the primary advocate for justice. It is in this context that Khomeini declared that "Islam wishes to bring all of humanity under the umbrella of justice."[3] That umbrella, woven with stripes of both temporal and spiritual power, was to be provided by the Islamic Republic of Iran. Khomeini meant what he said. On December 10, 1982, the Foreign Broadcast Information Service for the Middle East and Asia reported that the Ayatollah told Mikhail Gorbachev in 1979, "I openly announce the Islamic Republic of Iran, as the greatest and most powerful base of the Islamic world, can easily help fill up the ideological vacuum of your system." Despite his rhetoric, Khomeini as a Muslim deeply imbued with Islamic theology, thought more in terms of *dar al-Islam*, the house of Islam, than a universality of all peoples. Moving Iran from a prerevolutionary foreign policy aimed at maximizing Iran's national interest, Khomeini and the clerics of the Islamic Republic directed foreign policy toward the creation of a new Islamic world order. They began with the new constitution, which stated the primacy of faith over nation. "All

Muslims shall be considered as one single nation and the Islamic Republic of Iran shall make its general policy on the basis of coalition and unity of all Muslim people and shall constantly make every endeavor to realize the political, economic and cultural unity of the world of Islam."[4] In essence, Iran was no longer the distinctive nation celebrated by passionate Iranian nationalism but the vanguard of the Islamic revival that would free the oppressed from their oppressors. Khomeini, as the theoretician of Muslim unity, dropped the term *mellat-e Iran*, the Iranian nation, to address Iranians as the *ummat-e Islam*, the nation of Islam. In this nation in which all believers are brothers, there was no room for nationalism, a Western creation that Khomeini charged intended to divide the Muslims.

Very early in the revolution, Khomeini and the political clerics committed themselves to the export of the Islamic Revolution. It was a policy containing an offensive strategy for spreading revolutionary ideology. But it also contained its defensive elements. Expansion of the Islamic Republic's ideological borders provided protection against the superpowers that Khomeini and others believed stalked the revolution. It also created what is called in foreign policy parlance a "congenial security environment" in which all the states of a given region share the same basic beliefs and the same worldview. Finally, revolutionary ideology presented Iran an opportunity to undermine the presence and influence of the West in the Middle East, particularly that of the United States.

Despite its ideological and security arguments, a policy to export the revolution divided the ruling clerics. The idealogues embraced it while the more realistic among the leadership understood that Iran must live as part of the international system built on nation-states. At this juncture of revolutionary history, the expansionists won the foreign policy debate. So for much of the 1980s, the government of the Islamic Republic, directly and indirectly, through persuasion and force, propagated Islamic militancy beyond the borders of Iran.

Initially Iran's message of revolutionary Islam, electrified by Khomeini's charisma, sped through the scattered Shia communities in the Sunni Arab world. Recognizing an advantage, the Islamic Republic opened camps to give military training to hundreds of young Islamic zealots largely drawn from the states on the western side of the Persian Gulf and the Fertile Crescent, the Arab arc from Iraq to Lebanon. Financed by oil income and staffed by Revolutionary Guards, the camps taught recruits the rudiments of small arms, explosives, and simple rocket launchers. With the military training came indoctrination. Islam's soldiers spent long hours studying Khomeini's thoughts and praying as a community behind men who made no distinction between religion and politics.

From the beginning of the Iranian Revolution, all the Arab states, anxious that militant Islam might destabilize the secular governments in place, had watched events in Iran with foreboding. Of these governments, it was the monarchies of the Persian Gulf states who most feared the subversive activities of the Islamic Republic, for all contained Shia populations of varying sizes. In the small island sheikhdom of Bahrain, the Shia population was 60 percent; tiny Kuwait looked at 30 percent; Saudi Arabia 15 percent; and the United Arab Emirates, the sheikhdoms strung along the coast of the Gulf, 10 percent. As important, the Gulf states were ruled by autocratic, pro-Western monarchs whose methods of governing installed them at the center of Khomeini's model of the oppressor and the oppressed. Consequently, a king, a sultan, and a covey of emirs and sheikhs cringed as the rhetoric of the revolution branded them all as despotic, corrupt, and too much in the company of the Great Satan. That same rhetoric issued dire predictions about the dark fate awaiting reactionary regimes that thwarted the will of politicized Islam.

In response, Saudi Arabia, Bahrain, Kuwait, the United Arab Emirates, Oman, and Qatar in May 1981 ringed their wagons around an economic and military alliance called the Gulf Cooperative Council (GCC). The move proved prudent. The following December an Iranian-backed plot targeted the sheikh of Bahrain. Tipped off by the providential detainment in Dubai of a group of youthful infiltrators boarding a plane headed for Bahrain, authorities uncovered stashes of submachine guns, grenades, and ammunition smuggled across the Gulf in small, high-backed dhows and communications equipment sent from Tehran to Manama via the diplomatic pouch of the Iranian embassy. Caught red-handed, the Islamic Republic made no apologies. It simply restated in words dripping with venom that monarchy, an evil and unjust system of rule, is a curse on Islam.

Kuwait became the target of the Islamic Revolution in 1983. On December 12, six bombs exploding over a ninety-minute period killed six, injured eighty, and damaged a variety of targets, including the American and French embassies. Among the perpetrators apprehended, there were no Iranian nationals. But everyone in the Gulf felt the hand of the Islamic Republic of Iran.

I was living in Saudi Arabia at the time. Ever since religious fanatics seized the Grand Mosque in Mecca in November 1979, everyone, Saudi and foreigner alike, understood the potential power of revolutionary Islam. On the night of the Kuwait bombings, I happened to be at a dinner party in a Saudi home. It was less than festive. In one room, Saudi men huddled around a television set viewing pictures from Kuwait, and in another room the women speculated on just how long it would be before Saudi Arabia became the prime target of Iran's Islamic Revolution.

The truth was that Saudi Arabia's turn had already come by way of the *haj*, the annual pilgrimage to Mecca. Every year upward of 2 million people go to Saudi Arabia to fulfill one of the obligations stated in the five pillars of Islam. The House of Saud, the masters of Saudi Arabia, preside over the *haj* in a grand style that is as political as it is religious. For the Saudi royal family draws much of its legitimacy from its guardianship of Mecca and Medina, the two holiest sites in Islam. Ayatollah Khomeini challenged that guardianship when he called the House of Saud "a bunch of pleasure-seeking mercenaries" and asked, "How long must Satan rule in the House of God?"[5]

In 1982, Khomeini had turned the *haj* into a political vehicle for revolutionary Islam. That year one hundred thousand Iranian pilgrims shouting revolutionary slogans under placards carrying Khomeini's picture clashed with Saudi police. In 1983, the year of the Kuwait bombings, Khomeini had urged the Iranian pilgrims to use the *haj* for an "Islamic uprising" against "the criminal Soviet Union and the criminal America."[6] Nineteen eighty-four and 1985 stayed relatively quiet because of restrictions nervous and shaken Saudi authorities imposed on Iranian pilgrims. But as the *haj* approached in 1986, a hundred Iranians went to jail, charged with attempting to smuggle weapons and explosives into Saudi Arabia.

The next year, 1987, Iran sent 155,000 pilgrims to Mecca. They included half the members of the Majlis and Ayatollah Khomeini's wife, Khadija. They arrived carrying specific instructions from the ayatollah. "Disavowing the pagans, one of the pre-requisites of monotheism and a political criterion of the *haj* should be carried out with as much ceremony as possible during the *haj* period in the form of demonstrations and marches."[7] The pilgrims did just that. Minutes after the Friday prayers, thousands of Iranians surged through the streets, firing from their rhetorical arsenal slogans, posters, and a banner proclaiming Victory Is Made by Waves of Martyrs. En route to the Grand Mosque of Mecca, they collided with Saudi riot police. In the ensuing melee, death filled the street as Saudi police committed mass murder—the Iranian version—or tried to control a stampeding crowd trampling helpless people—the Saudi version. Over the bodies of 402 dead, Riyadh charged Tehran with attempting to seize the Grand Mosque in order to declare Ayatollah Khomeini leader of the Muslim world. Unbowed, Khomeini answered. "We will export our experiences to the whole world. The result of this exportation will certainly result in the blooming of the buds of victory and independence and in the implementation of Islamic teachings among enslaved nations."[8] Yet despite the powerful symbolism the *haj* provided Iran's militant Islam, Lebanon was where the Islamic Revolution had found a berth.

Multicultural Lebanon proved the only country in the Arab world primed to receive Khomeini's message of political Islam. In 1979, roughly 35 percent of Lebanon's population was Shia, the largest concentration of Shia in the Arab world outside Iraq. For generations, Lebanon's Shia clerics studied in Iran and its Shia religious pilgrims trekked east to Karbala and Najaf, Qom and Mashhad. Trapped in a political and economic system dominated by Christians and Sunni Muslims, the Shia of Lebanon lived as a genuinely oppressed people. Even before the Islamic Revolution, the cleric Sayyid Musa Sadr had organized the Lebanese Shia into a political movement with religious overtones. When he mysteriously disappeared in 1978, Musa Sadr's followers already understood politicized Islam.

Since 1975, the Lebanese Shia had been part of a civil war that was reordering Lebanon's political system with guns. In 1979, they glimpsed in the Iranian Revolution the vision of an Islamic government sounding the trumpet of justice. In 1980, they grasped the promise of liberation from repression through Islamic government. But it was Israel's invasion of Lebanon on April 6, 1982, that actually put Iran's Islamic Revolution on the ground among the Lebanese Shia.

The armed forces of Israel rolled out of the Galilean hills and over the border of Lebanon for one reason—to destroy the political, economic, and military structure of the Palestine Liberation Organization operating in Lebanon as a state within a state. Although Iran never constituted a part of Israel's ill-fated plan, the movement across the borders of the Western-armed and -supported Zionist state that had usurped Jerusalem from the Muslims roused the passions of Khomeini and the political clerics. As a result, Lebanon, that small, riddled country on the shore of the Mediterranean, became the field on which the Islamic Revolution would again confront the West.

On June 12, 1982, a contingent of Revolutionary Guards arrived in eastern Lebanon's Baaka Valley to take up residence in a shabby hotel and an old barracks belonging to the largely defunct Lebanese army. Missionaries as much as revolutionaries, they began preaching their ideology in the local mosques, transmitting religious programming over a small radio station, and providing some basic social services to the war-ravaged population. Quickly Baalbek, the Baaka's major town, became "little Tehran." Beside the massive Roman ruins that attest to the West's first invasion of the Middle East, banners and posters hailing Khomeini and Islamic government covered walls, fences, and utility poles. Women donned the chador that Lebanon's pervasive Westernization had rejected. And bars closed under the law of religious vigilantes. Overshadowed by the war swirling around Beirut, this first foreign military expedition of the Islamic Republic largely escaped notice. Nonetheless, a contingent of Iran's revolution had penetrated the Arab world and soon its presence would be felt. In the East and South of Lebanon, the *mostazafin*, the disinherited poor of Shia Lebanon, answered the call to Islamic government that Iran and its *faqih* promised would deliver the justice of the martyred Ali and Hussein.

Amal, Sayyid Musa Sadr's Shia political organization, broke as the strong pro-Khomeini Islamic Amal emerged. It, in turn, associated with Hezbollah. Hezbollah, a name coming out of a Koranic verse promising triumph for those who join the party of God, provided the umbrella under which cells formed in local mosques gathered. Rather than a structured organization, it linked a panoply of Islamic groups who looked to Iran for ideological inspiration as well as financial and operational help.

In loose partnership, Iran nurtured Hezbollah and Hezbollah served Iran's Islamic Revolution. It was an arrangement that fit the extremist clerics' tactic of employing a variety of organizations that they either controlled or in which they wielded significant influence to push the revolution abroad. Ignoring the realists and even Khomeini's pronouncement that it does not take swords to export an ideology, the radicals regarded terrorism as another legitimate weapon in revolutionary Islam's arsenal. Terrorism had been deployed in the Persian Gulf. Now it would be unleashed in Lebanon.

During the summer of 1982, Israel pounded the Palestine Liberation Organization holed up in Beirut. On August 25, the United States at the head of the quickly strapped together Multinational Force (MNF) began extricating Yasser Arafat and most of his commandos in order to spare the Lebanese population of once beautiful Beirut. Completing its mission, the MNF withdrew from Lebanon. But following the assassination of the Lebanese president and the infamous massacres in the Palestinian refugee camps of Sabra and Shatila, the heavily American MNF returned to Lebanon in a naive mission of peacekeeping. In Tehran, Khomeini and the hard-liners grabbed hold of the MNF as another military and cultural invasion of the Muslim world, a repetition of the American intrusion into Iran during the shah's era. Influenced or perhaps directed by Iran, militant Lebanese Shia went into battle for Islam.

At 1:05 P.M. on April 18, 1983, an ordinary delivery van turned into the American embassy compound located on Beirut's Bliss Street. It pulled to a stop in front of the six-story building housing most of the embassy's administrative offices. And then it exploded. Fifty-eight Americans and Lebanese lay dead beneath twisted steel and crumbled cement. While rescue workers were still taking away the wounded and collecting body parts, a shadowy group calling itself Islamic Jihad claimed credit for the attack. Men conducting their own version of holy war were traced to the Baaka and tenuously linked to Hezbollah. Some evidence pointed to money and advice coming by way of Iranian diplomats in Damascus. But nothing was proved and worse was yet to come.

On the quiet Sunday morning of October 24, 1983, the sun crept out of Beirut's eastern horizon and spread its soft golden light over the war-scarred city. In a building at the airport converted from offices into a barracks, the American members of the Multinational Force slept. With reveille still ten minutes away, a big yellow Mercedes truck pulled into a gate and headed toward the makeshift barracks. In what seemed only an instant, nine tons of dynamite exploded and 241 U.S. Marines died. Again Islamic Jihad touted its might against the Great Satan.* The effect rippled across the Middle East. From Riyadh to Damascus to Cairo, massive concrete blocks designed to thwart bombs on wheels went up in front of embassies and other installations identified with the West and more particularly with the United States. Even in Washington, the White House, Pentagon, and State Department became forts against revolutionary Islam.

In death, destruction, and fear, the U.S. mission in Lebanon never recovered. In February 1984, the remaining marines struck their battle flags and waded out to landing craft that would take them to ships waiting to bear them home. The same month that the United States

---

*Islamic Jihad also hit the French contingent of the MNF, causing the deaths of forty-seven soldiers. On November 2, it struck the Israeli Defense Force at Tyre, killing twenty-nine Israelis.

pulled out of Lebanon, Frank Regier, the first Western hostage of revolutionary Islam, disappeared off a Beirut street. By the time a second bomb was delivered to the American embassy in Beirut, the 190-person staff had been reduced to a handful of envoys pressed into hazard duty. From the viewpoint of Tehran, the export of the revolution had gone from theory to reality. But the militant clerics began to discover that cultivating and releasing revolutionary groups proved easier than controlling them. In the repeating drama of political kidnapping that would grip the west for the next seven years, Iran sometimes gave the orders and sometimes acquiesced to hostage takers pursuing their own agendas. As early as 1985, Iran's high-stakes game, which had labeled it a sponsor of international terrorism, was paying diminishing returns. Consequently, the regime's commitment to the export of the revolution passed its crest. After five years of bloody war with Iraq, the interests of Iran had begun to exceed the call of Islam. That pattern would repeat in the Iran-Iraq War.

Since September 1980, both the internal war between the political clerics and their opponents and the external campaign to export the Islamic Revolution took place against the backdrop of the Iran-Iraq War. It was a war that had marched out of the chaos, opportunities, and miscalculations produced by the Iranian Revolution.

Competition and conflict between Iran and Iraq trace back to the nineteenth century and concentrate on possession of the Shatt al-Arab. In 1971, hostilities flared in the heat of Muhammad Reza Shah's territorial ambitions. Iran's seizure of Abu Musa and the two Tunbs located at the mouth of the Strait of Hormuz sat like bile in the throat of Iraq. So did the 1975 Algiers agreement by which Iran secured the eastern side of the Shatt al-Arab. Beyond mere anger and ambition, landlocked Iraq believed it needed the broad river, its only outlet to the sea lanes of the Persian Gulf. But the Iran-Iraq War would involve more than territory. In important ways, the terrible war that would span eight years and claim a million casualties boiled out of the personal vendetta between two powerful personalities who both came to power in 1979—Iraq's Saddam Hussein and Iran's Ayatollah Ruhollah Khomeini. One was a secular Arab; the other was a religious Iranian.

Saddam Hussein had just connived, kicked, and murdered his way to the top of Iraq's political pyramid when he confronted the Iranian Revolution. For Hussein, the cascading events in Iran constituted more than a political upheaval in a neighboring country. A revolution driven by a Shia Muslim religious figure posed a direct threat to

Hussein's political survival in a country where 60 percent of the population was Shia. They lived under a repressive regime in which all political and economic power resided in the hands of Sunni Muslims. In accord with the precepts of Khomeini's revolutionary ideology, Iraq's Shia fit perfectly the definition of oppressed people awaiting liberation from the infidel. In July 1979, when Saddam Hussein officially took over the presidency of Iraq, Ayatollah Khomeini went on Tehran Radio to describe the new Iraqi president as "a puppet of Satan." Eight months later, on April 8, 1980, he called the pious among the Iraqis to rise up and overthrow Saddam Hussein. When he broadcast his message, Khomeini knew an audience was already waiting for his instruction. Al-Dawa al-Islamiya, or the Call to Islam, Iraq's extreme Shia party, already breathed fire against Baghdad.* With the charismatic Khomeini providing leadership and an Islamic government in a position to provide money and weapons, Hussein feared that al-Dawa might actually launch holy war against the infidel.

Rolling up his own weapons, Hussein called the Islamic Republic's ruling mullahs "racist Persians" and stirred Iran's ethnic minorities, particularly the Arab population in Khuzestan—or, to the Iraqis, Arabistan.

As Saddam Hussein anxiously looked at Iran in 1979 and 1980, he saw a country in the throes of not one but two revolutions—the uprising against Muhammad Reza Shah and the contest between the clerics and the secularists. Furthermore, he saw the military machine built by Muhammad Reza Shah lying in shambles. The clerics, suspicious of men recruited by the shah, had dismantled the armed forces' formidable collection of arms and had ignored the consequences of desertions, purges, trials, and executions that had turned a well-manned military force into a skeleton.

In this political upheaval and military disintegration of his stronger neighbor, Saddam Hussein's ambitions exploded. The Iraqi president coveted complete control of the Shatt al-Arab for reasons beyond the waterway itself. The Shatt al-Arab carried with it power in the Persian Gulf. And domination of the Gulf gave substance to Hussein's aspiration to be the new Gamal Abdul Nasser marching at the head of the mythical Arab nation spanning from Iraq to Egypt. The Iraqi

*Al-Dawa al-Islamiya played a significant role in Saddam Hussein's ouster of the sitting Iraqi president on July 17, 1979. When Ahmed Hassan Bakr refused to sign execution orders for al-Dawa members, Saddam Hussein staged the coup that made him the undisputed leader of Iraq.

leader verbalized his vision in April 1980 when he told his cheering supporters at Nineveh, "Iraq is once again to assume its leading Arab role. Iraq is once again to serve the Arab nation and defend its honor, dignity and sovereignty."[9]

Through the summer of 1980, Saddam Hussein locked onto war as the only means to win the Shatt al-Arab and to silence the Islamic Republic's beckoning to his Shia population. Therefore at dawn on September 22, 1980, fifty thousand Iraqi troops hit four strategic junctions along the 730-mile-long Iran-Iraq border. While the infantry punched forward from the bleak mountain ranges of northern Kurdistan to the swamplands of oil-rich Khuzestan, Iraqi planes pounded Iran's air fields and military installations. In the Persian Gulf, the supertankers hauling black crude from the oil producers to the oil consumers dropped anchor to wait out what everyone assumed would be a short war. Tragically, it would not be a short war because too much was at stake: hegemony in the Persian Gulf; the test of wills between Saddam Hussein and Ayatollah Khomeini; and secularism versus Islam. Finally, the Iran-Iraq War was, in important respects, a contemporary war between Arabs and Persians. Through eight long years, both Saddam Hussein and Ayatollah Khomeini would wage war around the mythology of collective identity. For Iraq, it was the elusive and ambiguous idea of Arab nationalism. For Iran, it was the Iranian nation and Islam.

From the beginning of the Iraqi invasion, Saddam Hussein played on the deep prejudices between Arabs and Iranians that date to the time the Arab army of Islam crossed the Shatt al-Arab into Persia. He described the war as a crusade to regain Iraqi territory usurped by the Persians. In one particular propaganda film unreeled over and over on Hussein's state-run television, Arab soldiers of Islam's first army shot arrows at helmeted Sassanians to the accompaniment of loud martial music. That image faded to an Iraqi missile blasting off to destroy Iranian positions dug in along the border that divides Arab Iraq from Persian Iran. Concurrently, Saddam Hussein's speeches characterized the Iranians as fire-worshipping Persians and invoked the legacy of Qadisiya, the seventh-century Arab defeat of the Persians, to boast that once more the Arabs would crush the tyranny of "the Magi."

In Iran, the Iraqi invasion tripped all the switches of Iranian nationalism. The *khak-e-pak*, the pure soil of Iran, had been invaded by Iraqi forces in a war that Iran had provoked but had not started. The millennia-old emotion of being invaded contributed to a powerful sense of solidarity and shared experience that blurred differences between classes, regions, and ethnic groups as the Iranians rushed to defend their territory and cultural distinctiveness. Vehicles used to evacuate women, children, and aged men from the violated border returned filled with clerics and theological students, secular intellectuals, young men in Western-style jeans, and tribesmen dressed in traditional costumes who carried the weapons they periodically used against the central government. Even some of Khuzestan's Arabs and the rebellious Kurds joined in the defense of Iran.

For a government torn by the dissensions of 1980, the outpouring of raw Iranian nationalism served the war and the revolution. To maximize the phenomenon, the national anthem, abandoned by a revolution that insisted that Islam tolerates no boundaries, sounded over the airwaves. So did martial music and snatches of Beethoven's Fifth Symphony, played to energize a people subjected to an "imposed war."

While drawing strength from Iranian nationalism, Khomeini and the political clerics damned the Iraqi invasion as a war against Islam. This too fed into the national psyche, arousing the sense of injustice and martyrdom so central to Shia culture. Psychologically, every Iranian Shia is conditioned from childhood to feel the great historic wrong committed against the Shia by the Sunnis and to accept as their task the recapture of Karbala. Thus, as the war marched on day after day, it became less a heroic defense of Iran with both its Persian and Islamic traditions and more a daily enactment of Shia themes of sacrifice, dispossession, and mourning.

It happened in part because Khomeini elevated the war to the realm of the spiritual by converting a territorial invasion motivated by political ambition into God's war against the infidel. In Tehran, four weeks after Iraq crossed the Iranian border, the ayatollah thundered, "[This war] is not a question of a fight between one government and another; it is a question of an invasion by an Iraqi non-Muslim Baathist against an Islamic country, and this is a rebellion of blasphemy against Islam."[10]*

Once Khomeini defined the war as a test for Islam rather than the defense of Iranian territory, he bound Iran to only one outcome—victory. That victory did not only mean the liberation of Iran's sovereign territory but the extension of the Islamic Revolution to Iraq. Consequently, peace would come only after Saddam Hussein, the secular son of Satan, surrendered to Islamic government. In this context,

*The Baathist party of Iraq through which Saddam Hussein rules combines socialism and Arab nationalism. Organized in the 1950s, it blames many of the woes of the Arabs on the burdens of traditionalism imposed by Islam.

the war soared above military strength and political compromise to become the supreme moral test, the ultimate challenge, the ennobling ritual of the Islamic Republic. But in defining both the war and the end result in terms of Islam, the regime became a prisoner of its own definition. The war would be fought in the universal interests of Islam, not the national interests of Iran. By the same measure, negotiation representing pragmatism for Iran became corruption for Islam.

Iran fought the long, incredibly costly war in four bloody stages: the heroic defense of 1980–81; the slaughterous attacks of 1982–84; the defensive entrenchment of 1985; and, in 1986–87, the grand offensives fought to end the conflict.

In the first weeks of the war, Iraq advanced deep into Iranian territory to pierce the heart of Iran's economy, Khuzestan. The valves of that heart were formed by the oil refinery at Abadan and the port city of Khorramshahr. The Iraqi war machine hit Khorramshahr first.

With no real army to defend them, the people of the town gathered at the central mosque. It is not much larger nor is it any more grandiose than a neighborhood mosque in a city. Its grandeur resides in the wounds of its recent history. That history is painted on the walls in two-dimensional figures in shades of brown, green, yellow, and blood red. A martyr carries the flag of the Prophet into enemy fire, a soldier lies wrapped in bloody bandages, a mother weeps over her slain son. My guide through the melancholy tableaus was Jamal Rahmani, one of the defenders of Khorramshahr. Crippled in one leg and limping on a cane, Jamal told me about October 1980. "The mosque turned into a military command center because this is where everyone came when we knew the Iraqis were advancing. The men who had weapons—any kind of weapon—went outside the town to try to delay the Iraqi advance." Sweeping his arm around the mosque's exterior courtyard, he said, "The women stayed here to tear cloth for bandages. When the fighting came closer, some of them left for the field to be nurses. None of it made any difference. The Iraqis kept coming. We pulled everything we could move into the road. They just kept coming and we kept retreating back toward the mosque. At the end, we were throwing Molotov cocktails at tanks. And then it was over." Khorramshahr fell on October 24, 1980.

In Tehran, then President Bani-Sadr and the political clerics squabbled over how to fight the war. In a dispute which pitted professionalism against piety, Bani-Sadr demanded that what was left of the American-trained army be mobilized and put in charge of the war effort. The mullahs insisted on turning the militarily unprepared but ideologically pure Revolutionary Guards into the vanguard of national defense.

The mullahs won in part because they controlled Iran's major assets in the war—men and commitment. Although Iraq fielded an army equipped with the best in Soviet technology, Iran, with three times Iraq's population, could afford higher casualties. It was the Revolutionary Guards who were willing to die in the confrontation with Saddam Hussein, the evil Yazid of Shia mythology. As a result, the Revolutionary Guards, now popularly called the Pasdaran, quadrupled in size. But with experience limited to putting down internal opposition to the Islamic Revolution, they were poorly organized and trained for war.

Nonetheless, Iran hung on through the first year of the war with an armed force patched together from the Pasdaran, the gendarmerie, the border police, the *komitehs*, and the army led by more than a thousand professional military officers freed from jail.* In June 1981, Iran pushed the Islamic Revolution toward Baghdad. From Tehran, Khomeini once more called the Shia of Iraq to overthrow Saddam Hussein, thereby laying the first brick in the new world order under Islam. But the Shia Iraqis ignored the call. Part of the reason resided in the financial stake they held in Iraq's socialist system. More important was the factor of identity. Iraqi Shia spoke Arabic rather than Farsi. Despite their minority status as Shia, they still saw themselves part of the Arab world, not the Iranian nation or the greater Islamic state envisioned by a man to whom they felt no particular allegiance. With tongue, blood, and identity denying Iran the Iraqi Shia, the Iranians were left to fight the war alone.

Iran opened the second phase of the war in the spring of 1982 with a series of military operations devised and conducted by the vilified professional army left from the reign of Muhammad Reza Shah. They retook Khorramshahr and drove the Iraqis out of Iranian territory. In conventional terms of liberating occupied territory from the enemy, Iran had won the war. It was time to respond to third-party offers to negotiate terms with the chastened enemy. But there was nothing conventional about this war or the domestic environment in which it was being fought. The mullahs still waged their death struggle with the Mujahedin and Ayatollah Khomeini still pursued an Islamic Re-

*At the beginning of the war, Reza Pahlavi, the heir to the Peacock throne, sent a message offering to serve as a pilot. The offer was declined.

public in Iraq as part of the ongoing Islamic Revolution. The *faqih* told his people, "If the war continues and if in the war Iran defeats Iraq, Iraq will be annexed to Iran; that is, the nation of Iraq, the oppressed people of Iraq, will free themselves from the talons of the tyrannical clique and will link themselves with the Iranian nation. They will set up their own government according to their wishes—an Islamic one. If Iran and Iraq can merge and be amalgamated, all the diminutive nations of the region will be joined."[11]

In the two years since it began, the Iran-Iraq War had largely stayed confined to the two participants. That changed in 1982. With Iran on the offensive and refusing to negotiate, the wealthy Arab states of the Persian Gulf contemplated with horror an Islamic juggernaut rolling through Iraq and on into their privileged domains. Despite consistent nervousness engendered by their size and temperament, the rulers of Kuwait, Saudi Arabia, and the principalities along the Gulf dropped their pseudoneutrality for a loose alignment with Iraq held together by money. That money bought Iraq sophisticated technology from the Soviet Union and the states of the West, none of whom wanted to see Iran win the war. Iran could have detached the Gulf states, the Soviet Union, and the Western powers from an Iraq that was only slightly more tolerable than the Islamic Republic by pulling the Islamic Revolution back into its own borders. But that was a price Khomeini and the militant clerics were unwilling to pay. With Iran demanding as the price of peace reparations and the trial of Saddam Hussein as a war criminal, the war went into Iraqi territory.

The clerics felt no imperative to make peace because the ongoing war continued to consolidate their power by providing justification for the reign of terror they pressed on the "traitorous" opponents of the regime. The Mujahedin, in an attempt to improve its position against the clerics, established close ties with Saddam Hussein, symbolically blessing the Iraqi invasion. To most Iranians, the Mujahedin became a pariah, deserving of whatever fate the regime chose to deal it. Yet the great force propelling the revolution and the war was still Islam. Losing much of the universal support for a war no longer seen as the defense of the Iranian nation, the revolutionary clerics continued to call the faithful to a cause. Leading them was Ayatollah Khomeini, the supreme religious guide, who sent men and boys to war for Islam and rallied women and girls to serve as "guardians of death."

In an environment where all the emotional symbolism belonged to the militants, leadership of the war passed once more from the professional military to the Pasdaran. Over the next eighteen months, war served as the canvas for revolutionary creativity. Combat, which painted on that canvas in blood, provided the opportunity for martyrdom to the recruits of the Vahid-e Basij-e Mustazafin (Unit of Mobilizations of the Deprived), the child of the Revolutionary Guards. The Basij operated from nine thousand mosques, enrolling boys below eighteen, men above forty-five, and women. Primarily the zealous products of poor, devout families from rural areas, they volunteered for temporary duty in God's war between school terms or in the interim dividing one season's harvest and the next season's planting. At the front, a Basij-i could be identified by his tattered leftover uniform and mismatched boots (often picked up on the battlefield), the bright red or yellow headband stretched across his brow declaring God's or Khomeini's greatness, and the large, imitation brass key, the key to paradise, that hung around his neck. The Basij-is gained fame as human minesweepers in the massive assaults that characterized the 1982–84 phase of the war. Boys as young as twelve, shaped by the fanaticism of the revolution, walked across minefields to clear the way for the advancing Pasdaran, followed by the army. Thousands joined the ranks of the dead. Many now lie in those seemingly endless graves in Behesht-e-Zahra.

Somehow many of the Basij-is survived the hell of war. One escorted me through the battlefields around Abadan. When I met him, I had to consider for an instant just where I was in time. With his large nose, flat head, and curly beard, he looked exactly like an ancient Persian who had just walked out of one of the reliefs at Persepolis. But he was a son of the Islamic Republic. He had gone to war in 1982 at the age of sixteen. By the age of twenty-two, he was a battle-scarred veteran. "Me," he announced, poking his finger at his chest, "I have wound here, here and here and one in my back. My hearing is bad too." Smiling broadly, he boasted, "I shoot RPGs at Iraqi helicopters." (The RPG is a rocket-propelled grenade launcher that is held on the shoulder.) He was full of war stories, firing them off in a nervous staccato. I asked him if he had ever seen Basij-is deliberately sacrifice themselves to the war. "Yes, yes! A group of us got trapped once on the other side of the river (the Shatt al-Arab). Iraqis were in front of us and land mines behind us. Seven boys—maybe fourteen, fifteen years old—they say, 'Let us go, let us go.' We—me and the others—said no. But they don't listen. They just run. Boom, boom, boom! The mines exploded. A little path opened up and we got out." He shrugged his shoulders. "Maybe if the young ones don't go I go. I believe in God and I would be rewarded with Paradise."

With the Basij leading the way, Iran's army crossed the Tigris River in February 1984, moving toward the Majnoon Islands, one of Iraq's richest oil fields. Iraq mounted a defense with mustard gas. As much a psychological tool as a military tactic, it stalled the Iranian advance. Still on the defensive, Iraq shifted the war to the Persian Gulf. Aiming to force the Islamic Republic to the bargaining table by economic means, Saddam Hussein declared a total exclusion zone around Kharg Island, Iran's main oil terminal in the Gulf. Throughout the spring of 1984, Iraq's new French-made Super Etendard warplanes, purchased with money from Saudi Arabia, Kuwait, and the UAE, attacked any ship bound into or out of Kharg Island. Benefiting from covert support from the United States, the Iraqi planes operated with intelligence data gathered by American AWACs based in Saudi Arabia. Iran had begun to pay the price of the militant clerics' acts of bravado, which failed to distinguish between the export of the revolution as a model for others to follow and revolutionary Islam as a vehicle for what many saw as an Islamic empire dominated by Iran. Plots against its Gulf neighbors, demonstrations during the *haj*, and support for radical Shia groups in Lebanon had led the West and the Arab states of the Gulf to judge Iraq as the less odious of the two combatants engaged in war. Still, Iran would not bend to peace without international condemnation of Iraqi aggression and the surrender of Saddam Hussein to Islamic government.

Despite the voluminous amounts of blood spilled on the battlefield, the general Iranian population had, so far, been spared the pain of total war. There was rationing, gasoline shortages, and electrical outages, but the war itself remained largely a volunteer effort fought on Iran's western frontier. Men who actually went to the front benefited from a government that took care of its own. The families of those who died collected a cash grant of 2 million rials, roughly thirty thousand dollars, from the Martyrs Foundation. Those crippled on the battlefield went on the priority lists for scarce goods, government jobs, and university positions. A war embraced first as a test of the values of the revolution and, second, as a vehicle to export that revolution had not even cost an inordinate amount. The shah's arsenal and ammunition depots had provided much of the matériel. But by the end of 1984 that was almost gone. In the future, a war on land and a war on the sea fought against a well-armed enemy would demand much more money and effort. The alternative, a negotiated peace, remained impossible for a regime captive of its own rhetoric and its own constituency. The masses who went into the streets for Khomeini in 1978–79 were the same people who were fighting the war. To justify their sacrifices, they required a victory for Islam. Without an Iraqi surrender that victory could not be claimed. So the war dragged on.

By the summer of 1985, the political clerics were finding it increasingly difficult to justify to everyone except their base constituency a war in which the enemy held very little Iranian territory. It was proving equally difficult to totally blame an unofficial inflation rate of about 35 percent a year, dwindling foreign reserves, and severe economic woes on the "imposed war" which the regime consistently refused to negotiate. Even the war's theological justification went under scrutiny by a number of clerics who argued two points. First, Islam sanctions self-defense, not aggressive war against other Muslims. And second, jihad, or holy war, intended to spread revolutionary Islam could not be declared in the absence of the Hidden Imam. On April 10, 1985, antigovernment demonstrations broke out in the Aban district of Tehran. They quickly spread through the city and jumped the miles to other cities. Ordinary people took to the streets to protest the war and, more ominously, the government. The political clerics responded to the unrest by shifting into their familiar defensive mode. Furious rhetoric condemned the protesters as agents of the radical left-wing opposition; jail doors slammed on demonstrators; and clubs wielded by religious vigilantes cleared the streets. By April 23, open opposition declined to silent resentment.

In its silence, much of Iran's population saw the spiritual rewards of Islamic rule dissolving in economic hardship. With shortages of everything, including food, haunting the land, those who had made money from revolution and war bought meat, butter, rice, and cooking oil on the black market at three to ten times the official ration price. The poor did without. Housing shortages caused by a population explosion encouraged by a government seeking numbers to promote the revolution and the migration of hundreds of thousands of war refugees to the cities shot rents up to astronomical levels which only the rich could afford. With no other option, the poor crowded into the shantytowns that sprouted on the edges of most major towns. Even the regime's most ardent supporters began to grumble that in wartime, revolutionary Islam's promised reign of justice had produced its own elite. Political necessity on the part of the clerics demanded that the war end before the divisions of society grew worse. But to preserve the sacrifices of the clerics' constituents, it had to end with some semblance of victory. That depended on wooing the Gulf states away from Iraq and gaining access to weapons and supplies. Consequently, the export of the revolution shifted to a lower gear in the summer of 1985. The verbiage the clerics fired at the Gulf states softened. And in Lebanon, Iran began to practice statecraft rather than revolution.

On June 14, radical Lebanese Shia hijacked TWA flight 847 en route from Athens to Rome. For three long days, the Boeing 727 shuttled back and forth between Beirut and Algiers while the hijackers terrorized the passengers. On one of the stops in Beirut, a young American navy diver named Robert Dean Stetham fell victim to Shia Lebanese anger against the United States. Brutally beaten, shot through the head, and dumped on the tarmac, Stetham became the battered symbol of Islamic extremism. The other thirty-nine Americans remaining on board disappeared into the slums of south Beirut. Over the next two weeks, power in Lebanon symbolically shifted from the United States to the Lebanese Hezbollah. While Amal, the mainstream Lebanese Shia organization, and Syria's Hafiz al-Assad lobbied for the hostages' release, Ali Akbar Hashemi Rafsanjani, the speaker of the Iranian Majlis, announced to the press that "Iran had no connection whatsoever with this incident."[12] Behind the scenes, he exercised his influence to win release of the hostages. In the end, Rafsanjani's action proved so helpful that American president Ronald Reagan publicly acknowledged the role played by Iran. In cooperation and acknowledgment, Iran saw the possibility of securing the desperately needed weapons for war with Iraq from the Great Satan. The Reagan administration, for its part, took hold of the prospect that the key to the release of the remaining American hostages held in Lebanon might be in the hands of the "fanatics and terrorists" in Tehran. Over the next fifteen months, an arms-for-hostages deal between the United States and the Islamic Republic of Iran unfolded in the deep recesses of international intrigue.

Two highly secret operations between August 30 and September 14, 1985, delivered badly needed arms supplies to Iran via Zionist Israel. In the quid pro quo, American hostage Benjamin Weir came out of captivity in Beirut. With each side achieving what it wanted, the arms-for-hostages arrangement represented a classic act of diplomacy. So as the winter of 1986 turned to spring, the United States and Iran danced around each other in a drape of secrecy. Then on May 25, 1986, a Boeing 707, painted a sinister black, parked on the apron of Tehran's Mehrabad Airport. Aboard were Ronald Reagan's former national security adviser, Robert McFarlane, and the National Security Council's Oliver North. They bore presents for the high-ranking Iranian officials they planned to meet—three sets of chrome-plated Magnum pistols in presentation boxes, a chocolate cake, and a pallet of spare parts for the HAWK missile. For three days, mutual suspicion and fear of the consequences of trafficking with the enemy barred negotiations. Privately Iran accused the United States of bringing only a quarter of the promised weapons. And the United States complained that Ali Akbar Hashemi Rafsanjani, the quarterback of the Iranian team, had reneged on his promise to meet with McFarlane and North.

It was not until November 3, 1986, that news of arms dealing between the United States and Iran got out by way of the Lebanese weekly *As Shiraa.** Rafsanjani scrambled to preempt domestic fallout from the revelation by arguing that Iran's war effort demanded weapons from any source. But for those fighting the war for Islam, the secret initiative with the Great Satan constituted nothing less than a betrayal of the revolution. To them, the needs of the state, even in time of a debilitating war, could never transcend the interests of Islam. Yet Ayatollah Khomeini, the *faqih*, both knew of and sanctioned contact with his great nemesis. And he never silenced Rafsanjani's repeated offers of Iranian assistance for the release of American hostages in exchange for American arms and access to Iranian funds frozen in the United States during the 1979 crisis over the seizure of the American embassy. Khomeini, like Rafsanjani, understood that victory in the war required weapons.

Even before the ill-fated American mission went to Tehran, bleeding Iran shifted back to the offensive on the battlefield in a grand attempt to end the war. On February 11, 1986, the seventh anniversary of Khomeini's return to Iran, one hundred thousand Iranian troops captured the Fao Peninsula, a swampy finger in the Shatt al-Arab that holds Iraq's strategic southern oil port. It put the Iranians only fifty miles from Basra, Iraq's second most populous city. Although the offensive claimed thousands of lives, it produced the biggest Iranian victory since the recapture of Khorramshahr in 1982. But unlike Khorramshahr, the Fao Peninsula lay inside of Iraq, not Iran. For the first time in five and a half years of war, Iran occupied a sizable amount of Iraqi territory. Once again conditions invited a negotiated settlement. And once again peace could not come because the Godless infidel, Saddam Hussein, refused to step aside for an Islamic government.

*In all probability, the story was fed to *As Shiraa* by Iranian hard-liners interested in torpedoing relations between Iran and the United States.

With the war raging on, Saddam Hussein put an ally in the field—the Mujahedin-e Khalq. Mujahedin headquarters had moved to Iraq under the aegis of Saddam Hussein when France expelled its leadership and hundreds of its members in June 1986 over concern about the organization's tie to terrorism. Sharing Hussein's goal of toppling the Islamic Republic, the National Liberation Army, the Mujahedin's military wing, took up positions alongside the Iraqi army. With the clerics' most hated internal enemy joining its most hated external enemy, the intertwined strands of domestic affairs and foreign policy wrapped ever tighter.

By now the government's slogan of "war, war until victory" was turning the conflict with Iraq into the revolution's most enduring legacy. Originally a convenient, perhaps essential, element in the clerics' maintenance of power, the war had merged into the consciousness and mythology of the revolution. Khomeini, the *faqih*, had defined the war in apocalyptic terms which brooked no compromise, envisaged no retreat, and allowed no discussion of the issue. Only he could change the course of the nation. But having declared the war to be holy, he would not compromise for peace. Consequently, the end of the war remained to be won on the battlefield.

On December 24, 1986, Iran launched what was heralded as the final offensive. Code-named Karbala 4, it rammed against the southern front around Basra.* Over fourteen weeks Iran threw wave after wave of the Basij, Pasdaran, and the army at some of Iraq's best-defended positions. The Iraqis met them with air power, heavy artillery, and mustard gas. While buses filled with men trying to cough up their seared lungs made their way to the rear, the soldiers of Ali, Hussein, and the Islamic Republic pressed the attack. Iraq's defensive positions ate the Iranians, particularly the Basij. While the dead were often borne northeast across Iran to be buried at Behesht-e-Zahra, the wounded went to field hospitals behind the lines as casualties of the never-ending war.

I noticed Batoul in a group of students and teachers at the women's theological school at Qom. She possessed a certain beauty but it was her quiet dignity that made her so distinctly different from the fifteen or so women around her. I asked the school's director who she was. Smiling, she said, "She is one of the brave ones—a nurse in the imposed war." Later I drew Batoul aside to talk to her about her

---

*Karbala 1 through Karbala 3 came in the first years of the war.

experiences. She told me she married at fourteen and went to the front with her husband at fifteen as part of the Pasdaran. For the next eight years, she rotated six months on the battlefield with two months in Tehran. I asked her how she coped with the carnage. A radiant smile lit her face as she answered, "The war was not too difficult to endure because you became immune to the suffering. I guess that is how you survive emotionally. I must say that occasionally something would really touch my heart. The third or maybe it was the fourth year of the war, a soldier was brought into the hospital unconscious. His arm had been blown off and he was bleeding badly. I was called to give him first aid. At the time, I was wearing a veil. When the patient regained consciousness, he looked at me and said 'Zahra' [Fatimah]." She ducked her head in pleasurable embarrassment. "He thought I was the daughter of the Prophet." I probed further to find out why she went to war. She quickly gave me an answer. "Because participating in the war was practicing Islam." Did she endure all the hardships and suffering for Islam or for Iran? Without hesitation, she answered, "Islam, of course."

Karbala 5 followed Karbala 4 by two weeks. For the next fifty days, the Islamic Republic once more slammed against the lines of secular Iraq. This time Iran broke through along a front six miles inside Iraq. Basra was again within striking distance. The city, founded as a base camp for the Arab invasion of Persia in the seventh century, took hit after hit from heavy artillery. But Iran could not deliver the knockout blow. There were not enough missiles, tanks, or artillery to consolidate the gains won by men. And even that seemingly inexhaustible asset was running low. Karbala 4 and Karbala 5 used up half the hundred thousand Basij-is deployed and a quarter of the Pasdaran's experienced officers.

Meanwhile in the Persian Gulf, what had become known as the tanker war escalated. Every time Iraq hit a vessel en route to Kharg Island, the Islamic Republic retaliated. Within the first five weeks of 1987, sixteen ships flying the flags of almost as many nations suffered damage. That Tehran had neither desired nor initiated the tanker war lost relevance in an environment in which Iraq reigned as the favored combatant. The Soviet Union made noises of intervention. But it was the mighty ships of the West, led by the United States, that went on patrol. In July, six Kuwaiti tankers raised the American flag. With Western aid to Iraq now overt, the balance in the Gulf tipped against the Islamic Republic. Undeterred, the hard-liners in Tehran pushed confrontation with the American Satan.* By September 1987, the narrow Gulf sea lanes resembled a shooting gallery in which Iran fired a .22 and everyone else unloaded shotguns. At last, the Islamic Republic was realizing the full political and military price of its arrogance and isolation associated with the export of the revolution.

Within Iran, the war had become the central, inescapable fact of life. Inflation roared through the economy, pushing the black market cost of low-grade beef to fourteen dollars a pound. Unemployment reached close to 40 percent. Meanwhile families continued to bury their dead. Day by day, the special wisdom and authority of the nation's spiritual guide, Ayatollah Ruhollah Khomeini, dripped away. The four-story-high portraits of the imam hung on public buildings in the glory days of the revolution faded and frayed. In April 1987, the month the land war again reached stalemate and the tanker war escalated, several hundred people boldly paraded down Tehran's Vali-ye-Asr Street calling for reconciliation with Iraq. In October, the Grand Ayatollah Qomi of Mashhad declared that there was no truth in the promise that those who died in the war against Iraq would go to heaven. His announcement came at a time when the working class and peasantry, taught for seven years that martyrdom is the ultimate achievement for the human being, were refusing to send their sons to suicide on the battlefield. Even the Revolutionary Guards had been forced to adopt conscription. In every class and every region, feelings of injustice and resentment grew. An Islamic government that had promised a better life now constantly extolled people to work hard, donate money to the nation's war chest, volunteer for the front, and rejoice over their martyred sons. Even though the Iranians were a people exhausted by revolution and war, there was no rest. On February 29, 1988, seventeen Soviet Scud-B missiles rained down on Tehran in the "war of the cities." Over the next seven weeks, the Iranian capital became an embattled city. At least a quarter of the population fled north, south, and east, anywhere they felt safe from a conflict that had moved from Iran's border to its heartland.

For the next four and a half months, one event after another tore at Iranian morale. Bombs hit the revered Friday Mosque in Isfahan and the city of Qom, the theological center of Shia Islam. On April 18, Iraq, with the help of chemical warfare, recaptured the Fao Peninsula. That same day, the United States Navy destroyed two Iranian oil

*The deteriorating situation in the Gulf influenced the Iranian decision to stage demonstrations at the 1987 *haj*.

platforms in the Persian Gulf in retaliation for an Iranian mine that damaged the frigate *Samuel B. Roberts*. In May, antiwar demonstrators once more marched in the cities. In June, Iraqi forces recaptured the Majnoon Islands, expelling the Iranians from the last important piece of territory the Islamic Republic held in Iraq. The battlefront now lay almost exactly where it was on September 22, 1980. Then on July 3, the *USS Vincennes* shot down Iran Air flight 655 over the Persian Gulf. Two hundred and twenty-four adults and sixty-six children died in the sixth worst disaster in aviation history. For days, Iranian television ran pictures of torn and charred bodies floating in the warm Gulf waters. Nonetheless public reaction, by Iranian standards, remained amazingly muted. In the place of outrage hovered a funereal sense of helplessness, isolation, and weariness. The war that had sustained the revolution seemed to be destroying the nation.

In mid-July, Ayatollah Khomeini appointed Ali Akbar Hashemi Rafsanjani to coordinate the flagging war effort. The speaker of the Majlis summoned Iran's military commanders to assess the situation. They quickly conceded that Iran could call on neither time nor resources to hold out indefinitely against Iraq, its Arab backers, and Western suppliers. Rafsanjani, joined by then-president Ali Khamenei, called together the ranking officials of the Islamic Republic. Through a long night, they argued the fate of the nation versus export of the revolution. In the end, a majority decided the revolution could be saved only by saving the nation. However, the final decision belonged to Khomeini.

Through the war, one third party and then another had made attempts of varying degrees to negotiate an end to the war. For a range of reasons including the obstinacy of the warring parties and the lack of serious commitment on the part of the potential negotiators, no viable peace plan emerged. Finally on July 20, 1987, the United Nations Security Council put Resolution 598 on the table. It called the parties to a cease-fire followed by negotiations aimed at relieving each party's most gnawing grievances.

On July 18, 1988, Khomeini grudgingly accepted the resolution. Two days later, he told the people of Iran, "I had promised to fight to the last drop of my blood and to my last breath. Taking this decision was more deadly than drinking hemlock. I submitted myself to God's will and drank this drink for His satisfaction. To me, it would have been more bearable to accept death and martyrdom. Today's decision is based only on the interest of the Islamic Republic."[13] In the end Ayatollah Khomeini proved to be more a nationalist than an Islamist.

The man who spent sixty-three days short of eight years driving Iran in a war for Islam had been forced to compromise the revolution's ideals for the sake of the state's survival. He could take comfort from Ali's instruction to the governor of Egypt: "Never reject a peace to which your enemy calls you and in which is God's pleasure, for in peace there is ease for your soldiers, relaxation from your cares and security for your land."[14]

When the guns finally fell silent, the costs of the war for Iran could be calculated in terms of the estimated $86.7 billion in military costs or the $28 billion in damage to the oil industry or the $23 billion in lost oil revenues. But it is the war's human debris, so visible in cemeteries, hospitals, and on the street, that gives the real measure of the war that Saddam Hussein imposed and Islamic ideology sustained. Iran's casualties numbered close to 750,000, more than the United States suffered in World War II. Almost any Iranian can testify to personal loss. In a mud-walled house in a small village, a woman wrapped in a chador drew deeply on a cigarette and told me about her son who stepped on a mine. An engineer in his early forties lost six cousins ranging in age from sixteen to forty-nine. A man selling fresh pomegranates in the bazaar in Tehran wept about his fourteen-year-old who never returned from the front. And a young, melancholy businessman described the day in 1988 when an Iraqi missile hit a Tehran apartment house, killing his wife, the mother of his five-year-old daughter. Those who survived the war's battlefields walk on crutches and canes. They live their lives without sight. They sell cigarettes on the street because a bullet in the head, too dangerous to remove, has closed the door on real employment. Thousands more escaped physical injury but not mental torture. Over and over, doctors and educators told me stories about a whole generation of men whose minds more than their bodies are damaged by the war.

It is in Khuzestan, on the border with Iraq, that the war and its legacy hang like a shroud. The flat, straight road running south from the provincial capital of Ahwaz passes between deserted fields where mounds of deadly gray soil mark deserted gun emplacements. Nothing grows where neither irrigation trenches nor plow can penetrate because of thousands of land mines hidden below the surface. Khorramshahr, the scene of the heroic but futile defense of 1980, is on that road. Like a skeleton trying to gather its own bones, the exhausted city struggles to put itself back together. The governor's office has been rebuilt at a traffic circle from which rises an artless steel monument to the Khorramshahr resistance. A government hostel hardly larger than a generous-sized two-story house provides food and rooms to the few guests who come this way. Khorramshahr lost to death and flight somewhere over 50 percent of its population during the war. Most of the refugees have not come back because there is so little to come back to. A row of new stores lines one side of the road on the edge of town. But they are little more than a facade for the absolute devastation which lies behind. The real measure of the destruction in Khorramshahr is an area in the center of town. Once the bazaar, it is leveled. Five years after the war ended, the only visible construction activity was one man sluggishly tossing yellow construction bricks off a flatbed truck. It carried a big sign on top of the cab that said For God.

The devastation of Abadan seems even worse. Perhaps it is because Abadan, a major site of the Iranian National Oil Company, was once so lovely. Palm trees stretching for miles behind the Shatt al-Arab created a tropical garden. They are all gone now, charred by the fire of war. Gone also are the houses, apartments, and shops which once made Abadan a jewel of Iranian towns. The refinery is back in production, sending its orange flame high into the black, moisture-laden night. And a section of the dock is functioning again. But because the river has yet to be dredged, only shallow-hulled boats can make their way this far upriver. On that dock, I met a man who lived in Abadan through the whole eight horrendous years of the war. He was past middle age, with thick glasses magnifying a face weathered by the sun. Why did he stay? "I stayed because I was resisting for my beliefs. I did nothing special to protect myself. As a Muslim, I was waiting for God's will." But he also spent eight years fighting for Iran. "I am proud. I have defended my land, not my city or my house but the soil of my country."

In less than a decade, the Islamic Republic of Iran had crushed the leftist rebellion led by the Mujahedin-e Khalq, pushed revolutionary Islam beyond the borders of Iran, fought a war in the name of Islam, and made peace in the name of Iran. In that same span of time and for half a decade beyond, the political clerics faced one another over issues of ideology and governance, with and without Ayatollah Khomeini.

12

Islamic Government: Religion, Culture, and Power

AYATOLLAH RUHOLLAH KHOMEINI, THE TOWERING FIGURE of the Islamic Republic of Iran, died on June 4, 1989, at the probable age of eighty-seven. The announcement of the death on Tehran Radio carried the tone of profound solemnity. "The lofty spirit of the leader of the Muslims and the leader of the noble ones, His Eminence Imam Khomeini, has reached the highest status, and a heart replete with love and God and his true people, who have endured numerous hardships, has stopped beating." The questions and unspoken doubts about the *faqih* that nibbled at Iranians in the last years of Khomeini's life gave way to enormous public grief. From across Iran, the disinherited who won Khomeini's revolution poured into Tehran. In one-hundred-degree heat, a black-clad throng numbering millions pushed toward a thirty-foot bier holding the glass, air-conditioned coffin containing the remains of the revolution's revered leader.

On the day of burial, the aged, gaunt body, wrapped in *kafan*, the traditional white burial shroud, was reverently laid in an open coffin and set on a litter. Summoning all the dignity the occasion demanded, the cortege began the journey to Behesht-e-Zahra. At every step, distraught mourners surged toward the coffin, grabbing for a piece of the precious shroud. Suddenly the litter rocked, tilted, and then turned, throwing the ayatollah's now half-naked corpse to the ground. Revolutionary Guards serving as escort quickly drew themselves into a ring to beat back the crowd while Khomeini's hysterical disciples bundled the body back into its burial box. Before the Guards could be swept aside by the stampeding crowd, a helicopter hovering overhead dropped low to snatch the corpse away from the frenzied mob. Six hours later, the Ayatollah Ruhollah Khomeini, safely encased in a sealed aluminum casket, was entombed. Nearby a Western-educated woman of the middle class watched quietly behind the concealment of *hejab*. She spoke for many in Iran. "I'll go to my grave hating him. But I cannot escape the reality that he was a giant."

The Khomeini era lasted a decade. In the years 1979 to 1989, Iran lived under the "neo-Shiism" conceived by Khomeini—an Islamic Republic in which the tenets of the faith constitute the rules of government and members of the *ulama* exercise authority as the political elite. In terms of Iranian culture, the theocracy endeavored to purge Iran's pre-Islamic past from society and nation. It was this commitment to the Islamic component of Iranian identity that provided the unifying force of the clerics who had donned the mantle of politics. But beyond the Islamization of Iranian society, the men in charge of Islamic government were divided over the fundamentals of governing. The issues fell into the categories of religion, the role of the state, and the export of the revolution. The political and religious style of Ayatollah Khomeini, fulfilling the role of *faqih*, kept each faction from dominating the other, often to the detriment of Iran. But Khomeini proved mortal. When he died, the Islamic Republic lost its all-important authority figure. In his absence, his heirs were left to struggle into the second decade of the revolution bleeding from their own divisions and bearing the burdens of the ayatollah's legacy.

In the euphoria of 1979, Islam constituted the great unifying theme of revolutionary Iran. Just as the Pahlavi shahs attempted to redefine Iran by elevating pre-Islamic Persian culture, Ayatollah Khomeini and the men around him sought to characterize Iran only by Islam. In what amounted to religious and cultural authoritarianism, the guardians of the Islamic Republic pruned Iran's Persian identity. With Islam constituting the raison d'être of the theocratic state, the enforcement of public morality became all-encompassing. Through law and intimidation, the mandate of *hejab* wrapped every woman, Muslim and non-Muslim, in layers of dark clothing, and strict sexual segregation descended on the whole society from schools to parks to the beaches of the Caspian Sea. The *komitehs* and the Sisters of Zeynab, operating as paramilitary enforcers of public morality, stalked males and females walking together, ensuring that they did not touch, and zealously watched for stray strands of hair escaping from women's scarves.

The authorities pounded art as well as mores into the Islamic mold. The themes of love and eroticism, present for centuries in Persian poetry, disappeared, replaced by verbal images of religion and revolution. The same applied to prose and to painting. In the filmmaking industry, controls clamped on by the Office of Islamic Guidance slashed production in 1981 to only seven movies, which were all made in one genre—the heroic Muslim male standing firm against corruption and injustice in the name of the revolution.

Essentially, the mullahs threw the Pahlavis' manipulation of Iran's cultural identity into reverse and traveled the same rails. Once more the calendar became a weapon in the identity wars as the names of the months on the pre-Islamic solar calendar underwent Islamic revision. And once more language experienced cultural purging as the clerical government officially abolished from Farsi Western words encouraged by the Pahlavis and reinstituted Arabic words discouraged by the shah. Non-Islamic first names such as Cyrus, Khosrow, and Shahram shrank from official favor to be replaced by Muhammad, Ali, and Hussein. Iranian national radio as well as television pumped out propaganda for Islamic government instead of Persian kingship. Under the threat of closure, newspapers devoted as much space to articles on Islamic history and on the faith's vital contemporary role in society as they had accorded to the glorification of the shah before the revolution.

In this cultural onslaught, the Pahlavis' secularization of education evaporated in the revolution's Islamization of all elementary and secondary schools. Revised textbooks erased the emphasis on Persia to write about Islam and the revolution. Religious instruction and the Arabic language returned to their central place in the curriculum. And roughly forty thousand teachers found themselves purged on grounds of insufficient piety in a system where devotion to Islam ranked as the supreme qualification for employment.

On the university level, the seven-member Council for the Cultural Revolution shut down all two hundred universities and colleges in June 1980. Behind closed doors, curricula and textbooks went through a bath of ideological purity that washed away Western concepts in education. Professors cleared of the ideological sins of Marxism, liberalism, capitalism, and nationalism underwent training in

Islam while those considered irreversibly tainted by the West lost their jobs. Once cleansed, the universities reopened in December 1982. In the new environment, students applying for admission gained acceptance through their knowledge of Islam and their attitudes toward the Islamic Revolution as much as by their academic skills.

The enforcement of this cultural conformity lay with the institutions of the Islamic state. The Revolutionary Guards from the beginning of the revolution served the critical function of providing stability and order for the new regime, including its cultural agenda. By the third year of the revolution, the Guards were no longer a collection of ad hoc vigilantes spontaneously spawned by neighborhoods and mosques. As the renamed Pasdaran, they possessed the structure and powers of a state-run military, a civilian police force, and an internal security organization combined. Other institutions of the revolution joined them in maintaining an obsessive atmosphere of ideological purity. The Ideological-Political Bureau, for one, assigned two thousand agents to the armed forces as political commissars. The Islamic Society, for another, established itself in workplaces, schools, universities, hospitals, neighborhoods, and large villages to promote the Islamic state and patrol its morals. But it was the Office of Propagation of Virtues and Prevention of Vice that held the forward position in the war on moral degeneracy. In one of its early acts, it leveled Tehran's teeming red-light district and sent over a thousand prostitutes to rehabilitation.

In the Shia state, where mullahs wore both the turbans of religion and the hats of government, a political cleric reigned in every village. Carrying the mandate of Tehran, he replaced the landlord as the most powerful person in the community. In the cities, the Friday prayer leaders, chosen by Ayatollah Khomeini from among his clerical collaborators, filled a political as well as a religious role, for it was they who delivered the political message that preceded the ritual of prayer.

The 1979 revolution, which raised high the Islamic dimension of Iranian culture and turned religion into politics, also brought to power a government promising the social transformation of Iranian society. As in all great political uprisings of the masses against the elite, Khomeini's "disinherited" released their full fury on Iran's upper class. In the wake of the shah's departure, mobs stormed the palatial homes of the rich to instantly redistribute wealth by way of furniture, silverware, refrigerators, and clothes. Even the Peacock throne that sat in

Gulistan Palace gave up some of its most important gems to looters. In the melee, rural migrants poured into urban centers in the expectation that Khomeini himself would distribute property to the deprived. Their expectations disappointed, they took squatter's rights in houses and apartments left vacant by those fleeing the rage of the revolution. But it was government seizure that so massively swept the property of the elite into the hands of an Islamic Republic vowing to level society. In the process, almost everyone in the upper strata of society lost something—or everything.

Just outside the town of Zanjan in western Iran, a summer moon rose over the courtyard of a once stately home. Tea, cookies, fruit, and a cake were passed around the table of one of the old thousand families that had once roosted near the top of the Iranian social hierarchy. Before the revolution, the aged patriarch who sat straight and proud in a wrought-iron chair owned thousands of acres of land and hundreds of villages. He and his two sons now survive on roughly three hundred of those acres. Deprived of income necessary for maintenance, their house is like a ghost of former times. It needs paint. One end is no longer habitable since the earthquake that struck two years after the revolution. The magnificent Persian carpets that covered the floors of the now deserted rooms are rolled and stacked in the stairwell to what remains of the second floor. Down a gravel path, a large swimming pool that once hosted holiday parties is dry and cracked. It seems that only the beds of roses around the courtyard have escaped the vendetta of the revolution.

The expropriation of properties began with that of the Pahlavis and their closest allies. Within a month of his return to Iran in February 1979, Ayatollah Khomeini ordered the possessions of the shah and "all persons who acquired wealth through relations with this family" seized for the benefit of the poor. They went under the control of the Bonyad-e Mostazafin, the Foundation for the Disinherited.* Backed by its own cadres of gun-toting Revolutionary Guards and Islamic judges ruling with an imprecisely worded law augmented with their own Islamic reasoning, the foundation went on the offensive. It confiscated businesses, industries, agricultural enterprises, office and

---

*This included the assets of the Pahlavi Foundation in Iran. Established in 1958 as a charity organization, it provided the cover for much of the royal family's corruption. In 1978, the foundation's total assets amounted to $3.2 billion. How much of that remained in Iran and how much was invested in the West is a question that neither the Pahlavi family nor the Islamic Republic has ever answered.

apartment blocks, carpets, paintings, antiques, jewelry, and, in at least one case, a family mausoleum at Behesht-e-Zahra. The foundation's assets multiplied over and over as the authorities sucked up the properties of those who died before the firing squads or fled the country. Some of these properties went into service to the revolution's social agenda. One Hollywood-style French chateau, complete with a bar in the middle of a huge swimming pool, became the reform school for the prostitutes burned out of Tehran's red-light district. What has happened to the rest of the seized property is one of the mysteries of the revolution. Rumors abound that many of the elite's European antiques went to the auction houses of Europe with the proceeds going into the pockets of the new elite of the revolution. Suspicions are fed by self-proclaimed eyewitnesses who report private auctions within Iran where selected clerics bought the treasures of Pahlavi Iran's upper class at white elephant prices. In any event, the foundation as a financial organization took command of assets that rank in worth second only to those of the state. At one time, administration of these extensive holdings employed eighty-five thousand people, a number that exceeded those required to run the National Iranian Oil Company.

In February 1980, Ayatollah Khomeini created a second foundation, the Martyrs Foundation, to provide for the welfare of the families of those who had died in the revolutionary movement of 1977–79. The following fall, it took responsibility for the martyrs of the Iran-Iraq War. With government funds and private contributions, the Martyrs Foundation became the most liberally endowed of the many foundations that spun out of the revolution. Then as now, these foundations as well as a cadre of others have both taken care of the needy and functioned as private fiefdoms of great wealth controlled by luminaries of the revolution.

The government's widespread expropriation of property, particularly business and industry, only exacerbated the staggering problems caused by the revolution and its prelude. The escaping elite drained $4 billion in capital from the country before the shah even left Iran. Compounding the loss, some of the industrialists and entrepreneurs created by the shah's development policies fled with hundreds of millions of dollars in borrowed money, leaving their staggering debts to the banks. Consequently, when the Bazargan government took over in February 1979, the treasury drained toward empty and the banking system rocked on the edge of collapse. In November 1979, the financial crisis worsened when U.S. president Jimmy Carter retaliated for the seizure of American hostages by freezing billions of dollars in Iranian assets on deposit in the United States. With a stroke of the presidential pen, Iran lost access to foreign exchange crucial to economic stability. This evaporation of capital poured one more ingredient into the boiling cauldron of the Iranian economy.

Afraid for their profits and their freedom, foreign contractors hired by the shah to build the infrastructure of his new Iran walked away from dozens of major government projects—roads, steel mills, petrochemical plants, and nuclear reactors. As a result, the shah's fast track to development ended and Iranian nationals working for these companies joined the unemployed. Committees of workers within functioning industries contributed to the chaos. In pursuit of higher wages, workers often expelled owners from their factories or held them hostage. Sometimes these instant labor unions arranged with sympathetic revolutionary committees to put members of Iran's historically thin entrepreneurial class in jail. This harassment, intimidation, and incarceration only fed the flight of entrepreneurial and managerial talent critical to the reconstruction of postrevolutionary Iran with its 2.5 million unemployed.

The new government desperately needed to jump-start production, reduce unemployment, and stem the flight of capital and expertise. Yet the corresponding imperatives created by the expectations of the revolution demanded that all vestiges of the old order be overturned in the interests of the underprivileged. Declaring its commitment to the masses who toppled the shah, the revolutionary government nationalized the banking system on June 8, 1979, and the privately owned insurance companies on June 25. On July 5, 1979, came the most sweeping nationalization measure of the revolution—the Law for the Protection and Expansion of Iranian Industry. Overnight the Islamic Republic acquired ownership of most of the country's privately owned industry and many of its businesses. Heavy industry including metals, automobile assembly, chemicals, shipbuilding, aircraft manufacture, and mining; light manufacturing spanning home furniture to soft-drink bottling facilities; and retail activities such as department stores and a supermarket chain all went under ownership of the government. In June 1980, government again reached out to officially seize dwellings left empty by fleeing owners. Many went to the rural migrants who continued to pour into the cities to collect their rewards from the revolution. Thus overnight deserted apartments joined first-class hotels as housing for the poor.

Despite the flurry of expropriation, common wisdom warned that the Islamic government faced serious political problems if economic

improvement did not come. But the revolution in the early years of
the Khomeini era chose to concentrate more on morality than economics. The core of the regime's ideology, so powerfully articulated by the
revered Ayatollah Khomeini, had lifted the revolution out of the material world of politics and placed it in the ethereal realm of the spiritual. Confirming that the revolutionary government gave priority to
moral needs over material well-being, Khomeini disparaged the revolutionaries who concerned themselves with such mundane and worldly
matters as the "price of watermelons." In a sense, Khomeini reflected
the Iranians' enduring conflict over the material and spiritual that
winds back into the Persia of the Achaemenians. He told the faithful,
"Some persons have come to me and said that now the revolution is
over, we must preserve our economic infrastructure. But our people
rose for Islam, not for economic infrastructure. What is this economic
infrastructure anyway? Donkeys and camels need hay. That's economic infrastructure. But human beings need Islam."[1]

Yet the revolutionary clerics cared enough about economics to
tend the interests of the mass of their constituency—the lower classes.
To hold their loyalty, revolutionary economics combined the idea of a
highly centralized economy on the lines of the Western welfare state
with the communal aspects of Islam. Together they created what
might be termed Islamic socialism. But not all the clerics' constituencies agreed. Between 1979 and the end of 1983, a widening dispute
over nationalization of business, expropriation of property, and state
control of the economy gathered in intensity and complexity. Rather
than adopting clear and consistent policies, the Islamic government
erected a tent under which the custodians of the revolution debated
economic philosophy and Islamic doctrine necessary to the revolution's
implementation. Among a variety of issues, it was land reform, the
great explosive issue between the clerics and the shah in 1963, that
first crystalized all the contradictions in the application of Islamic law
to matters of public policy, the search for social justice, the conflicting
authority of the Majlis and the Council of Guardians, and the nature
of the *faqih*, the ultimate arbiter in Islamic government.

In the first five years of the revolution, land reform emerged as the
most ambitious and concerted effort to transform the doctrine of the
Velayat-e Faqih into an instrument for social revolution and distributive justice. But Islamic injunctions on the economic life of Muslim
societies are ambiguous. As a result, it is possible to marshal up from
broad Islamic principles arguments for social justice that mirror the
egalitarianism practiced in Muhammad's first Muslim community and

arguments in defense of private property that mimic capitalism with a social conscience. This basic theological division surfaced in the debate on land reform.

Advocates of sweeping redistribution of land lined up behind the communal aspects of Islam. Drawing on the argument that land ultimately belongs to God alone, they insisted that the ownership of property is always "limited and conditional." Opponents, marshaling their own Islamic texts and traditions, claimed that Islam guarantees the right to private property and inherited wealth as well as the freedom to engage in the common contractual arrangements in Iranian agriculture such as rents, wage labor, and sharecropping. Within the Islamic reasoning of each group lay vested interests. On the side of private property stood many of the highest-ranking clerics who either belong to or are affiliated with rich landowning or merchant families. On the side of land distribution gathered clerics from the lower classes who held political and economic power only as a result of the revolution. In important ways, the continuing dichotomy between the schools of Islamic thinking on economics has less to do with Islam than with the clash of class interests. In the case of land reform, agitation for distribution of Iran's oldest asset came from the cabinet, the revolutionary zealots in the Majlis, the revolutionary organizations, and the villagers. Opposition flowed from the landowners, the bazaar, and the more conservative senior clerics.

In April 1980, the Revolutionary Council, functioning as the interim government, approved a sweeping land reform law intended to dismantle all but the smallest landholdings. Under the new law, the peasants and revolutionary organizations whirled into a frenzy of legal and illegal land seizures. In the ensuing chaos resulting from disputes over confiscated land, Khomeini, as the *faqih*, suspended land reform in November 1980. Hundreds of thousands of acres passed back to their original owners. But other hundreds of thousands remained in dispute in an atmosphere in which advocates for the peasants contrasted the moral corruption and exploitative nature of the rich with the nobility and goodness of the poor.

Under the terms of the 1979 constitution of the Islamic Republic, Khomeini passed the issue of land distribution to the Majlis. But parliament could not act alone. Legislation required religious certification by the Council of Guardians charged with ensuring that no law passed by the Majlis contravened Islamic law. In the Islamic Republic of the early 1980s, the council's twelve members all possessed strong connections with the landowning clergy and the *bazaaris*, who saw in government expropriation of land the shadow of a state-controlled economy that threatened their position as private entrepreneurs driving the Iranian economy. Beginning in mid-1982, the Council of Guardians wielded its veto against a cluster of legislation relating to private property on the grounds that it violated precepts of Islamic law. Articulating an economic position at variance with the goals of the radicals in control of the Majlis, the council functioned as the countervailing force to parliament.

If the Council of Guardians acted as the conservative force in the early years of the revolution, the Majlis performed as the most reform-orientated body in Islamic government. Established by the Constitutional Revolution that began in 1905, the Majlis, swamped by the tides of autocratic government and foreign intervention, never filled the role its creators envisioned. Yet the institution survived the collapse of the Constitutional Movement in 1911 and continued to serve as the empty shell of parliamentary democracy through the Pahlavi dynasty. When the Iranian revolution came, the Majlis rose like a genie to give Iranians more representative government than they had ever known. Elections have been neither entirely open nor free, since candidates for office must be certified by standards that ensure an individual's commitment to the goals and philosophy of the Islamic Republic.* Nonetheless, within the rigid rubric which guarantees that no one wins office who is not in some degree acceptable to the men in power, elections have been contested. And most Iranians have granted the Majlis a measure of legitimacy as a constrained voice of the people. Because of this expectation of at least a degree of popular will, the Majlis from the early years of the revolution held the potential for diversity. Conflicting political agendas did appear by 1984, when the political clerics and their allies who had used their majority in the Majlis to impose Islamic culture on Iranian society and dueled with the Council of Guardians over property rights began to exhibit profound differences among themselves over the nature and direction of the Islamic Republic. Those differences boiled down to a fundamental choice—the revolution or the state. It is this fundamental issue that continues to characterize Iranian politics by organizing the champions of clerical rule into two imprecise categories—radicals and moderates, or, perhaps more accurately, hard-liners and pragmatists.

*The exception is candidates running for the four seats reserved for Christians, Jews, and Zoroastrians.

* * *

The hard-liners hew to a revolutionary interpretation of Islam with its emphasis on an egalitarian society unmarked by sharp class divisions created by the undue accumulation of wealth. Although viscerally anti-Western, the hard-liners have consciously and unconsciously adopted Western socialist ideals and incorporated them into an Islamic model worthy of export. They see the Islamic Republic as the "redeemer state," rallying the power of Islam to create a new bloc of Islamic nations capable of defying both East and West. In their view, Iranian foreign policy centers on the export of the revolution, even by subversion and terrorism. In domestic policy, the hard-liners seek redistribution of wealth in the name of social justice. This means a centralized economy dominated by the state, massive land reform, and large-scale government control of foreign trade at the expense of the bazaar. In social policy, they demand a strict application of the Islamic moral code for reasons that are both cultural and political. In terms of culture, hard-liners live in fear that any relaxation of Islamic morality allows traditional Persian identity to resurrect, opening the way for decadent Western culture to creep back into Iran. In terms of politics, they hold the line against any moderation in the social atmosphere which might encourage Iranians exiled by the revolution to return, bringing with them their opposition to political Islam and the clerics position at the center of power. But the hard-liners' obsession with protecting the revolution is more than ideological and political. In contradiction to their own economic philosophy, many among the radicals are rich and important as a result of the private fortunes they have accumulated through the organs of the revolution, especially the Bonyad-e Mostazafin, the Revolutionary Guards, and a variety of other organizations. With a more flexible interpretation of the revolution and a more relaxed social atmosphere, the rationale for their fiefdoms would disappear and with it the fiefdoms themselves.

Portraying themselves as the champions of Islamic purity and the rights of the deprived, the hard-liners draw their following from the lower classes, the younger generation of clerical students, elements within the bureaucracy, and the all-important Revolutionary Guards. They enjoy the advantage of numbers, capitalizing on the inescapable truth that the revolution has responded to the needs of Iran's downtrodden. As evidence, they point to the revolution's history, in which a street peddler turned schoolteacher served as prime minister; a member of a revolutionary committee became governor-general of Khuzestan, then minister of oil; and an Islamic guerrilla went to Pakistan as ambassador. Perhaps all these men lacked the education and experience to serve their country well, but they reinforced the ideals of the revolution. By their very presence, hundreds of thousands of others from the lower classes saw their opportunity for upward mobility in Iran's social hierarchy reordered by revolution. Today it is most often those of the lower classes who hold the jobs in state-controlled enterprises of the Islamic Republic. And it is the lower classes who have both benefited from government services to the poor and responded to the ceremonies and rhetoric connected to the revolution.

The pragmatists are, in broad terms, radicals turned into moderates by the real-life experience of governing. Falling between the hard-liners and the conservatives ensconced in the Council of Guardians, they are less defined by ideology than by the recognition that Iran must live in the real world of economics and diplomacy. Forced to make a choice, they give priority to the nation rather than Islam.

Within the broad ideology of the revolution, the pragmatists support a free-enterprise economic system justified by Islam's sanction of private property. As a consequence, they oppose massive land reform, a highly centralized, state-controlled economy, and the Islamic socialism of the hard-liners. In the interest of economic growth, the pragmatists in 1983 began to offer nationalized enterprises to their former owners, to invite entrepreneurs and technologists living abroad to return in safety, to assure private businessmen their investments would be secure from nationalization, and to seek Western technology and trade.

Although the pragmatists share with the hard-liners a commitment to the export of the revolution, they reject subversion and violence in favor of projecting an image of Iran as a successful and prosperous Islamic community. Less fearful of the outside world than the hard-liners, they do not shrink from foreign powers, or alien ideologies, even those of the West. Interpreting Islamic moral codes more flexibly, they are more lenient in enforcing them. And because they tend to be nationalists more than Islamists, the pragmatists accept that Iranian traditions include those of Persia as well as Islam.

The pragmatists support, coming from the business community including the *bazaaris*, the middle class, and the bureaucracy, is fluid. Among its followers, some support the concept of Islamic government while others search the political horizon for the return of the secularists. A mixed lot of individuals and groups, they give support to the moderates among the political clerics as the best of the available choices on the political spectrum. Vastly different than the ideologues committed to the hard-liners, the pragmatists' one hope in politics is that tomorrow will not be worse than today.

In the Khomeini years, the proponents of private property versus distributive justice, free enterprise versus state control, lenient versus strict enforcement of the Islamic code of conduct confronted each other over virtually every major piece of legislation. As a result, government policy wallowed in the chaos of ideological confusion. Khomeini, as the *faqih*, commanded the power and the authority to give dominance to one faction or the other. But he refused, choosing instead to maintain a precarious balance between the conservatives, the pragmatists, and the radicals. It was a leadership style for which Iran continues to pay a heavy price.

Through its first critical years, the Islamic Republic stayed lashed together by the compelling bond of Ayatollah Ruhollah Khomeini's persona. To the pious Iranian masses, he was the man of religion, interested only in the good of the community. To the less pious, he was the intrepid defender of an independent Iran stalked by powerful nations of the East and West. Stern, demanding, and righteous, refusing to be seduced by materialism and power, Khomeini linked the Iranians to traditional faith and national identity. In response, his devoted followers conferred on him the title of imam. Although meaning leader rather than the sacred designation of the infallibles of Shiism, the title resonated with meaning, implying perfection and immortality. Defying all historical and theological prohibitions, Khomeini held a place in Iranian politics and culture that had never been occupied before nor is likely to be occupied by any other man again. Seemingly secured by divine mandate, his authority soared beyond limits. His will and his will alone bestowed legitimacy on parliament, on the constitution, on the Islamic state itself. Superseding the Persian tradition, where the mortal king rules hand in hand with Ahura Mazda, Khomeini, to his devotees, represented none other than the Hidden Imam.

Nonetheless, Khomeini in the infancy of revolutionary government floated above the ordinary affairs of politics. Every day, hundreds of common people thronged to his modest house in Qom to pour out their problems and partake of the wisdom of their imam. Then in January 1980, Khomeini entered a Tehran hospital after suffering a heart attack. On his release, he moved into a complex of small buildings clustered around the humble mosque of Jamaran off northern Tehran's Yasser Road, less than a mile down the mountain from Muhammad

Reza Shah's Niavaran Palace. Jamaran, meaning "Haven of Snakes," closed around the ayatollah. For the rest of his days, his life traced a precise pattern as he moved among the narrow, two-story house, a suite of nondescript offices, and the humble mosque hung with a crude balcony from which Khomeini addressed his followers. In the disturbances of 1981–83, the most powerful man in Iran backed one more step into isolation when fear of the Mujahedin constructed a tight wall of security around the compound. While Soviet-made SU-23 anti-aircraft guns scanned the sky, security guards along Yasser Road searched vehicles and their occupants. In contrast to the days in Qom, the number of people actually admitted to the compound declined to a carefully selected few. Khomeini stayed in public view only through the medium of state-run television, which every day filled blocks of time with pictures of the ayatollah receiving groups ranging from Majlis deputies to schoolchildren who had excelled in Islamic studies. In these meetings, the deference shown Khomeini exceeded the deference the sycophants of the shah showed their king. Within this isolation and the ceremony, the ayatollah fulfilled his powerful role as the *faqih*, the final source of authority.

When Khomeini made firm decisions such as holding the American diplomats hostage or continuing the devastating war with Iraq, he commanded absolute obedience. But the *faqih* seldom issued clear-cut decisions. Instead, he operated in the precise manner of the Shia religious leader. In a hierarchical tradition where it is difficult to determine the point at which the leader leads and the follower follows, Ayatollah Khomeini constantly tested the will of the people. Cognizant of the political clerics' basic differences on the application of Islamic law to the governance of a modern state, he listened to one faction and then to the other. When a major crisis demanded action, Khomeini retreated into seclusion and silence in order to focus his mind. More than dramatic effect, the ayatollah's isolation confirmed his total acceptance of the presence of God and of Satan, the light and dark of the universe. Caring nothing about the details of politics, Khomeini made his temporal decisions in the abstract realm of religious faith in which he sought to comprehend God's plan in unfolding events. When he spoke as the final arbitrator sensing the will of the people, he could rule on the side of a state-run economy or in defense of the private sector. He could grant extraordinary authority to the Islamic state, then retrieve it. He could, as he repeatedly did, endorse normalization of relations with the West and then remove himself as the words and deeds of the radicals kept Iran isolated. In this pattern of acceptance and rejection, Khomeini never took hold of the broad issues bedeviling the Islamic Republic. For he was the imam, balancing one faction against another in the interest of Islam or Iran or both. The ayatollah himself once said of his leadership style, "For the sake of maintaining balance among various factions, I have always issued bitter and sweet instructions because I consider all of them as my dear ones and children."[2]

In significant ways, Khomeini's style of circular leadership proved extremely effective in protecting the revolution. By wrapping the masses of deprived citizens in his clerical cloak, he provided political Islam a large, dedicated constituency. But by refusing to affirm on a consistent basis the interests of the *mostazafin* or any other constituency, Khomeini failed to give the Islamic Republic a uniform philosophy on anything other than control of the culture. Instead, the *faqih* exercised his enormous authority as a negative by preventing any one faction from gaining control of policy. Ignoring Iran's need for the order required to build the economy, Khomeini withheld his blessing from the moderation of the revolution that began in 1983. Instead, the *faqih*, the supreme authority of the Islamic state, only watched as the pragmatists and the hard-liners grappled for the steering wheel of the revolution.

In the fall of 1985, Khomeini again stayed silent while the political clerics hurled invectives against one another. The issue was the regime's failure to deliver the great socioeconomic goal of the revolution—equitable distribution of wealth. While rhetoric and social controls played ideologically to the pious poor, they and every other Iranian had become victims of an economy hobbled by war, heavy government intervention, and the unresolved dispute between the proponents of Islamic socialism and the champions of private property. In 1986, the speaker of the Majlis, Ali Akbar Hashemi Rafsanjani, admitted that there were "two relatively powerful factions in our country with differences of view on how the country should be run. . . . They may, in fact, be regarded as two parties without names."[3]

The ayatollah finally acted in June 1987 when Rafsanjani as speaker of the Majlis and Ali Khamenei as president persuaded him to dissolve the Islamic Republican Party. The purpose was to alleviate some of the unbearable pressure the party's core constituency put on the government to move even further in the direction of a state-controlled economy. Having achieved that, the pragmatists began the difficult task of convincing the imam that the interests of Iran superseded those of Islam. It was the only door out of both the Iran-Iraq War and the three-way impasse between the conservatives of the Council of Guardians, the hard-liners, and the pragmatists.

In January 1988, nine years after the revolution, Khomeini issued a sweeping *fatva* defining the powers of the Islamic state. He began by saying that the Islamic state derives its authority from the "absolute vice-regency entrusted by God to the Prophet," and like the Prophet's government exercises power by divine sanction over all matters— religious and secular. In the relationship between Islam and the state, the imam declared that in the wider interests of the community, an Islamic government has priority over all Islamic tenets, even over prayer, fasting, and the pilgrimage to Mecca. In what amounted to an addendum to the *Velayat-e Faqih*, Khomeini wiped away the last fragments of the historic Shia contempt for temporal authority. And for the second time in his life, he shook the theological foundations of the faith. The theory of the *Velayat-e Faqih* had pulled clerics out of the mosques and seminaries, where they extended legitimacy to or withheld it from the king on the basis of just rule, to make them government itself. Now, according to his critics, Khomeini had given government absolute, near divine power to rule over Islam. The ruling squashed the Council of Guardians and stabbed at the question troubling Iran's leaders since the revolution: When deciding the fundamental issues of public policy in the Islamic Republic, does ultimate authority lie in the mosque or in the state? By his ruling, Khomeini gave virtually unrestricted power to the state to regulate the affairs of the community. But he left the pragmatists and the hard-liners to fight out the details. For a little over a year, the pragmatists rode the wave of power.

The elections for the Third Majlis in April and May 1988 cut the number of mullahs in the membership almost in half, eliminating key hard-liners from government. With the cease-fire in the Iran-Iraq War, the ayatollah himself seemed less rigid in his demands on Islamic culture. Chessboards came out of the closet when Khomeini lifted the indictment of gambling. The black of mourning imposed on women by the revolution and war gave way to manteaus and scarves of subtle color. Despite protests by clerics in Qom, a *fatva* had already ruled as acceptable music "free of corrupt intentions." In this Tehran spring, Khomeini told the clerics and people alike that the old ways must pass. And so they did. The Tehran Philharmonic experienced a brief revival, bringing the music of Beethoven and Mozart back to the concert hall. On September 1, 1988, *The Merchant of Venice*, translated into Farsi, opened at a theater built during the shah's reign. When criticism again rose out of Qom, Khomeini told the nation not to "pay too much attention to what the stupid, backward or illiterate clergy might think."[4]

In the sunshine of moderation, the pragmatists rewrote foreign policy. Diplomatic relations with France, Britain, and Canada and strengthening relations with West Germany seemed to herald Iran's transformation from international pariah to member of the world community. But the rush to open up to the West coupled with the softening of the revolution shook the radicals and Ayatollah Khomeini. It was time for the *faqih* of the Islamic Republic to step in once more to redress the balance.

In September 1988, the month the Iran-Iraq War ended, a British publisher released a book titled *The Satanic Verses*. The author was Salman Rushdie, a forty-one-year-old former Muslim born in Bombay who lived and wrote in Britain. Combining the genres of traditional Arabic fable with modern magical realism, Rushdie weaves in his novel simultaneous stories that treat with skepticism sacred Islamic beliefs. He depicts the Prophet as Mahound, a term for the devil, and assigns prostitutes the names of the Prophet's wives. But more than anything, it is Rushdie's questioning of the authenticity of the Koran that inflamed Muslims within the House of Islam.* Muslim rage exploded in such diverse locations as India, South Africa, and Britain. At the time, Iran, caught up in the euphoria of the cease-fire with Iraq, expressed little interest in the Rushdie book. But in the winter of 1989, Ayatollah Khomeini picked up *The Satanic Verses* and flung it onto the fire of Iranian politics.

At 2:00 P.M. on February 14, 1989, the *faqih* of the Islamic Republic of Iran delivered a *fatva* on Tehran Radio. It read, "The author of *The Satanic Verses* book, which is against Islam, the Prophet, and the Koran, and all those involved in its publication who were aware of its content, are sentenced to death. I call on zealous Muslims to promptly execute them on the spot they find them so that no one else will dare to blaspheme Muslim sanctities." In the days that followed, lesser religious figures came forward with rewards estimated at anywhere from $1 million to $5 million for the person or persons who succeeded in killing Salman Rushdie.

---

*The original Satanic Verses are attributed to Muhammad by the tenth-century historian Abu Jafar al-Tabari. According to al-Tabari, Gabriel told Muhammad that a set of verses uttered by the Prophet were "Satanic" in origin. Consequently, they were excised from the Koran.

Like the aging Mao Tse-tung, who let loose the Cultural Revolution in China to purify his moderating revolution, Khomeini employed *The Satanic Verses* to obstruct the course being charted by Rafsanjani, President Ali Khamenei, and the other pragmatists. Coming down on the side of the hard-liners, he announced, "As long as I am around I shall not allow the government to fall into the hands of the liberals."[5] On the issue of what the *fatva* might do to improved relations with the West, he thundered:

> It is not necessary for us to go seeking to establish extensive ties because the enemy may think that we have become so dependent and attach so much importance to their existence that we quietly condone insults to beliefs and religious sanctities. Those who still continue to believe that and warn that we must embark on a revision of our policies, principles and diplomacy and that we have blundered and must not repeat previous mistakes; those who still believe that extremist slogans or war will cause the West and the East to be pessimistic about us, and that ultimately all this had led to the isolation of the country; those who believe that if we act in a pragmatic way they will reciprocate humanely and will mutually respect nations, Islam and Muslims—to them this [Rushdie's novel] is an example.[6]

Beyond internal politics, Khomeini's death sentence on Salman Rushdie represented his last attempt to export the revolution. For a decade, the aging ayatollah had strived to gain recognition as spokesman of the Islamic world. He failed, in part, because of the revolution's excesses at home and its support of extremist groups abroad that offended status quo regimes. More important, he was an Iranian Shia trying to capture Islam's largely Sunni audience. Before *The Satanic Verses*, Khomeini could speak only for the Iranians and some of the Shia of Lebanon. But in the growing fury over the novel among both Shia and Sunnis, Khomeini moved to the forefront of opposition to claim leadership of dar al-Islam. In the short run, it worked as the world shook to the power of the ayatollah's words. Salman Rushdie burrowed underground. His British publisher surrounded its offices with armed guards and his American publisher temporarily closed its New York office under the threat of bombs. As panic spread, booksellers pulled the volumes off their shelves to protect their employees against the firebombs already hurled into stores in Britain, the United States, and Italy. So pervasive was the fear that the government of the far-off Comoro Islands in the Indian Ocean threatened to expel any foreigner in possession of the blasphemous book. So it was that ten years after he toppled Muhammad Reza Shah, Ayatollah Ruhollah Khomeini again made the world quake. But in resurrecting the export of the revolution and redressing the balance between the hard-liners and the pragmatists, Khomeini wounded Iran.

With a few angry words, Ayatollah Khomeini blasted all the diplomatic gains eked out by the pragmatists over the previous year. Attempts to improve trade, unlock Iran's frozen assets, and woo capital-rich countries in Europe to join in the reconstruction of war-ravaged Iran disappeared in the death sentence imposed on Rushdie. In attempting to recoup some of the losses, President Khamenei suggested that the "wretched man" might be pardoned if he were to repent and apologize. Majlis speaker Rafsanjani suggested that the death sentence pronounced by Khomeini belonged in the realm of religion, not the affairs between states. Both failed. Member states of the European Economic Community that had warmed to Iranian overtures in defiance of the United States called their ambassadors home and slapped restrictions on economic and financial transactions with Iran. American determination forged in 1979 to keep Iran contained put on another suit of armor.

Ayatollah Ruhollah Khomeini, the charismatic figure with the flowing white beard and magnetic eyes, was now eighty-eight years old. The certitude of his mortality hung over the Islamic Republic, presenting it the challenge of choosing a successor for a man with no peer. As early as mid-1981, when the clerics took control of government, the question of Khomeini's heir stalked the custodians of the Islamic Republic. The revolution had succeeded because of the ayatollah's mystique, and Islamic government had survived because the *faqih* gave it legitimacy. By 1983, the war with Iraq, pockets of stubborn resistance to clerical government, and varying degrees of opposition to the *Velayat-e Faquih* from many of Shiism's ayatollahs made a smooth succession critical to the revolution's durability. Reacting to need, the regime, on July 14, 1983, submitted to the electorate the names from which eighty-three mullahs would be chosen for an Assembly of Experts to pick Khomeini's heir and to oversee the eventual transition. Over the next two years, the assembly etched in words and action the purely political nature of the *Velayat-e Faqih*. Ignoring traditional Shia theology, which bestows authority on the man recognized by his peers as the most learned Islamic jurist, the Assembly of Experts, in November 1985, picked Ayatollah Hussein Ali Montazeri as Khomeini's successor. Among the half dozen grand ayatollahs eligible for selection, Montazeri ranked as the youngest and, in many ways, the least eminent. Rather than religious, his credentials were political.

The product of a peasant family, Montazeri had studied with Khomeini at Qom. As a teacher at Faiziyeh Theological School, he went into the streets in 1963 to protest Muhammad Reza Shah's White Revolution. After Khomeini's expulsion from Iran, Montazeri sat at the center of the clerical network Khomeini left to oppose Pahlavi rule. He went to prison in 1974 and came out in 1978 in time for the revolution. In Khomeini's Iran, he served as Friday prayer leader of Qom and held membership in both the Revolutionary Council and the assembly that wrote the constitution for the Islamic Republic. Beginning in 1980, Khomeini had begun to transfer some of his power to Montazeri, and by 1983 all government offices hung a small picture of the chosen successor next to that of Khomeini. Yet the politically pristine Montazeri fell short of the theological requirements of the *faqih*. He could not claim descent from the Prophet nor did he possess the credentials of a revered scholar of Islamic law. His religious followers were few. And he lacked the all-important charisma. His selection had happened for one reason—he was the only one among the candidates for *faqih* who totally endorsed Khomeini's vision of Islamic government. But Montazeri, a relative moderate on domestic issues and a hard-liner in support of exporting the revolution, never took Khomeini's place.

On March 28, 1988, Khomeini snatched his mantle from the shoulders of Montazeri. Publicly, the imam told the nation that Montazeri had proved inadequate to the sweeping powers of the Supreme Jurisprudent. Privately, Khomeini would not forgive Montazeri's challenge to the *faqih*'s political reign. In defiance of Khomeini, Montazeri had urged an end to the war with Iraq a year before it came. In personal letters to the *faqih*, he criticized existing political conditions in the Islamic Republic. Citing the treatment of political prisoners, he charged, "Your prisons are far worse than those of the Shah and his SAVAK."[7] That was only the introduction to a litany of complaints. Montazeri complained that Khomeini lived in isolation from Iran's problems. He argued that political participation needed to be broadened and press censorship ended. Finally, he accused the regime over which Khomeini ruled of the ultimate sin of injustice. It all amounted to an intolerable affront to Khomeini's vision of Islamic government and his near divine role within it.*

Montazeri's removal left the Islamic Republic once more without an heir to Khomeini. And once again the regime faced its great theological problem—none of the grand ayatollahs from which Shia tradition dictated the choice be made agreed with the whole premise of Khomeini's *Velayat-e Faqih*. In the circumstances, the huge white banner that the Revolutionary Guards periodically stretched across the tall entrance gates of Jamaran took on urgent meaning: God, God, Keep Khomeini Alive Until the Mahdi's Revolution.

Constitutional reform in the summer of 1989 attempted to address the question of Khomeini's successor and other problems inherent in the 1979 document. But in correcting some of the faults, constitutional reform strengthened the existing system in which government can function only if the president and the supreme leader agree. Thus as the Council of Guardians had checked the Majlis, the spiritual leader checks the president. Yet as long as Khomeini lived, the constitutional changes meant little. The ayatollah delivered consensus in government, for he was the guide who showed "the way to submission to God, to the good society where the deprived will receive succor and self-realization, to the path by which the oppressed can gain the courage to stand up to oppressors, and to the unity of the community of believers."[8] Herein crouched the major weakness of the regime—dependence on the charismatic appeal of a mortal, aging, and ailing leader without an heir. Because the *faqih* existed as the keystone of Iran's Islamic government, the failure to find a successor for Khomeini threatened the clerics' position as the political elite.

By 1989, when none of the existing *marja-e taqlids* fit the regime's political criteria for *faqih*, the twenty-man council chosen to revise the constitution changed the qualifications. Under the new rules, any cleric "potentially" qualified to become a source of emulation could be chosen supreme leader. Consequently, the whole concept of the *faqih* altered. By separating the position of spiritual leader from its theological rationale, the men who amended the constitution stripped authentic religious legitimacy from the office of the supreme religious leader. Rather than rising to the position through the incremental, unstructured process defined by centuries of Shia tradition and practice, the

*Added to Khomeini's grievances against his successor was a scandal involving a friend of Montazeri's son-in-law who Montazeri refused to condemn even after he was executed on charges of murder.

spiritual leader now would be chosen through the same process of political consensus practiced by secular government. As a result, the *Velayat-e Faqih*, government by the just jurists of Islam, broke from its religious guidepost to follow the path of politics. It would do so without its great charismatic leader.

On his death in June 1989, Ayatollah Ruhollah Khomeini, a man of great intellect and legendary rigidity, left to Iran his complex legacy. In the most secular of ages, he had raised the power of religion to assert Iran's Islamic identity. To a whole generation empowered by his revolutionary government, Khomeini had affirmed Islam as a way of life and had established the faith as a means of governing a modern society. For a people haunted by alien invasions, he had delivered the conviction that only through religion can Muslims end the humiliation and exploitation of their societies by the West. It was as a theocracy reigned over by Khomeini fulfilling the role of the just jurist that the revolution triumphed over its own internal divisions, a war spanning as many years as World War I and World War II combined, economic devastation, and diplomatic isolation.

But Khomeini also left behind a government created specifically to provide a constitutional base for his leadership. Lacking a solid theological foundation in Shiism, Islamic government bestowed absolute power on the brooding ayatollah more for his political role as leader of the revolution than for his eminence as a religious figure. Nevertheless he became the imam to those in authority and to his devotees. This perception of Khomeini as more than human set impossible standards not only for his successor but for his government. In truth, the *Velayat-e Faqih* belonged only to Khomeini. Even before his death, Khomeini's Islamic government seemed incapable of coping with the challenges of a rapidly changing and increasingly interdependent world. More important to the Islamic Republic's future, Khomeini's model of government was proving ill-equipped to deal with the issues of economics, political consolidation, and cultural duality. To the elite created by the Iranian Revolution, this was secondary to their own survival. Burdened with the institutional and theological shortfalls of the *Velayat-e Faqih* as well as their own internal divisions, the men Khomeini left behind would refuse to allow the imam's death to deny the political clerics dominance over the politics and culture of Iran.

13

The Islamic Republic of Iran: The Failed Quest for Justice

HOT WIND PICKED UP DUST FROM A BARREN PLAIN AND blew it across a road that skirted south Tehran. Along that road, the poor and the pious from across Iran crept along in overloaded cars, trucks, and buses and strode on foot toward the gold-painted dome and soaring minarets of the massive tomb of Ayatollah Ruhollah Khomeini. They had come for the annual commemoration of the death of the aged, bearded man who so forcefully defines the Iranian Revolution.

The observance of Khomeini's death had spanned the preceding week. Mournful black banners hung from public buildings and stretched across the major streets of Tabriz and Gorgan and hundreds of other cities large and small. State-run Iranian television gave over its programming to artful video productions set to funereal music that remembered and glorified Khomeini the nationalist and Khomeini the *faqih*. In Tehran, the seat of the ayatollah's Islamic government, groups of Revolutionary Guards wearing black shirts, black pants, black headbands, and a variety of shoes marched down Vali-ye-Asr. With parade marshals setting the cadence, each man pounded his chest with his right fist as he followed a pickup broadcasting the imam's words over a loudspeaker. At the Kosar Hotel, chador-draped members of the Women's Organization of the Islamic Republic of Iran sat through the Conference on the Practical and Theoretical Conduct of the Late Imam Khomeini. But it was on Friday at the tomb of the revered ayatollah where the emotion and politics surrounding Khomeini's memory played themselves out.

Inside the massive structure the size of a stadium, a sea of women sat on carpets listening to the ceremonies. In the oppressive heat, a female Basij-i carrying a large aluminum drum circulated, offering cool water from a red plastic cup. Behind her, a man who lost three sons in the Iran-Iraq War wove through the densely packed crowd spraying fragrant rosewater from a canister strapped to his back.

Outside, men stood and sat between an enormous portrait of Khomeini bearing the ayatollah's words: God Almighty! Cut Off the Hand of Tyrants from the Muslim Lands! Cut Off the Root of Those Who Betray Islam. They faced a high podium from which Iran's current spiritual leader, Ali Khamenei, declared "the people should prove that they still adhere to the Imam's last will and advice."[1] In the elaborate ceremony which the government claimed drew two million people and which eyewitnesses, including myself, judged at only fifty thousand, the leadership of the Islamic Republic strained to claim legitimacy through its one charismatic leader.

The death of Ayatollah Khomeini, the spiritual guide of the Islamic Republic, left a void which no man could fill. The political clerics who inherited the Velayat-e Faqih have both allowed and, at the same time, hopelessly stood by as the ideals of the revolution have corroded in mismanagement, corruption, and severe economic hardship. Lacking a charismatic leader capable of bestowing legitimacy, the stewards of the Islamic Republic undergird their power through Islam and repression. Repeating the pattern of Muhammad Reza Shah in which the glorification of Persian culture and the imposition of a police state delivered raw power, the clerics impose Islamic culture and crush the voices of opposition. As in the prelude to the 1979 revolution, the Iranians are asking if Islamic government, like Pahlavi kingship, has moved from the light into the dark.

When Ayatollah Khomeini died on June 3, 1989, the choice of his successor as faqih remained bogged in a quagmire of theology and politics. Recognizing strength in unity, the political clerics solved the brooding question within twenty-four hours. They chose Ali Khamenei, the reigning president, as the spiritual leader of the Islamic Republic, the heir to the imam. The stooped, black-bearded Khamenei is another of the clerics in Qom who joined Khomeini's defiance of the shah in 1963 and operated his network during the years of exile. After the revolution, he helped found both the Islamic Republican Party and the Bonyad-e Mostazafin. He took command of the Revolutionary Guards Corps in December 1979 and in January 1980 became Friday prayer leader of Tehran, where he gained public renown for his fiery sermons. In June 1981, he shed blood for the Islamic Republic when a bomb planted by leftist opponents of the regime exploded, severely injuring Khamenei.

Khamenei's credentials to fill the position of *faqih* resided in politics rather than religion. A *hojjat ol-eslam* rather than an ayatollah, his selection as spiritual leader constituted a flagrant political act that confirmed an uneasily won consensus among the Islamic Republic's major political clerics. That still left the problem of what to do about the new leader's religious qualifications. Blatantly contravening the traditional hierarchical order of Shia Islam, the political clerics ignored the time-honored method of selecting religious leaders to confer on Ali Khamenei the title of ayatollah. In a system where mullahs increasingly acted more as politicians than as clerics, the Islamic Republic cut one more tie with its own theology.

But post-Khomeini Iran from 1989 to 1993 belonged less to the spiritual leader than to the new president of the Islamic Republic, Ali Akbar Hashemi Rafsanjani. With a touch of charisma, Rafsanjani fills a room with a quiet jollity that can charm and disarm. Rotund, with a moon face, the suggestion of an epicanthic fold, and an almost hairless face that grudgingly gives him only a mustache in a cultural climate demanding a full beard, Rafsanjani's appearance hints at Mongolian ancestry. Yet something else about Rafsanjani exceeds both his personality and physical features. It is an aura of infinite complexity that suggests a man who thrives at the game of intrigue.

Rafsanjani was born in 1934 into a well-to-do family of pistachio farmers in Kerman Province. He went to Qom to study theology in 1948. In 1963, he followed Ayatollah Khomeini into politics. Legend claims he provided the gun that assassinated the shah's 1965 prime minister, Hassan Ali Mansur. As a crucial link in Khomeini's postexile network, Rafsanjani went to jail in 1964, 1967, 1971, and 1972. Three years of prison began in 1975. On the eve of the revolution, Rafsanjani held a place within the galaxy of heroes in the Islamic opposition to Muhammad Reza Shah. After the revolution triumphed, he joined Ali Khamenei in founding the Islamic Republican Party. He escaped assassination in the bomb blast at IRP headquarters in June 1981 only because he left the rooms just before the bomb exploded.

In the machinery of the Islamic Republic, Rafsanjani's forte proved to be the Majlis. Elected as speaker in 1980, he shrewdly maneuvered through the twisting labyrinth of parliamentary procedure and oriental intrigue. He did so by building and consolidating his own network constructed from family and friends placed in pivotal positions as well as clans and cliques whose allegiance he won through mediating their disputes. Within the intrinsic limitations of an authoritarian state, the speaker built parliament into the revolution's most authentic institution, the voice of Iran's varied constituencies.

Rafsanjani is perhaps the prime example of Iran's revolutionary leaders who through a process of governing converted from zealous revolutionaries to pragmatic statesmen. Growing more concerned for the nation than the revolution, he began to hint at rapprochement with the United States as early as 1983. He masterminded the 1985 arms deal with the Reagan administration in order to secure the weapons Iran so desperately needed in the war with Iraq. In 1987, he prevented a showdown between the radicals and the pragmatists that would have damaged the state by convincing Khomeini to abolish the Islamic Republican Party. In 1988, he paved the way for Iran to end the war with Iraq. Caught in the web of Khomeini's perceived infallibility, Rafsanjani reluctantly stood behind the imam in the Rushdie affair and then attempted to separate a religious *fatva* from government policy. In the year before the ayatollah died, Khomeini still personified the revolution but Rafsanjani reflected the state. Still the speaker of the Majlis commanded the support of the Islamic radicals through his unwavering personal loyalty to Khomeini. Therefore when Khomeini died and Khamenei moved up to spiritual leader, the hard-liners who controlled the parliament backed Rafsanjani in an uncontested contest for president.

The new president faced an economy wrecked by revolution, war, and conflicting ideologies. Through the Khomeini decade, Iran had zigzagged from one economic policy to another, all conceived and implemented largely by men trained in religion. Now with the end of the Iran-Iraq War feeding the delayed expectations of a population promised a better life by the revolution, Rafsanjani and the pragmatists realized that domestic production had to increase in order to ease some of the shortages, particularly consumer goods. But intention ran into a wall of reality and ideology. Oil prices slid downward, worsening the shortage of foreign exchange. The United States still refused to release Iranian assets frozen in 1979, which denied the government desperately needed cash. Borrowing proved difficult because the Khomeini legacy, sacrosanct to most in government, demanded Iran stay free of foreign debt that often invited foreign control. In this economic environment, in which the standard of living refused to rise, Rafsanjani set Iran on the course of reform. He heavily weighted his cabinet with technocrats, many of whom were graduates of either American or European universities. And he once more called Iranian professionals, entrepreneurs, and industrialists living abroad to come home under his personal protection.

Foreign policy also acquired a new face crafted from the pragmatists' assessment that Iran could not rally the economy in the closet of isolation. The test of that new foreign policy came when Iraq's Saddam Hussein invaded Kuwait in August 1990. While a half million American troops poured into the Persian Gulf, Iran remained meticulously neutral in a determined effort to allow pragmatism and national interest to triumph over religious ideology. In the most critical event for Iran in the post-Khomeini era, Khamenei as the *faqih* backed the pragmatists. Shortly after Saddam Hussein crushed the Shia uprising in southern Iraq that occurred in the aftermath of the Iraqi defeat in the Gulf War, a diplomat assigned to Tehran observed, "The revolution is finally over. It died a month ago when Iraq bombed holy shrines in Najaf and Karbala, cities sacred to Iranian Shiites, without an Iranian response. It died when Iraq began massacring Iraqi Shiites without a single protest march in this overwhelming Shiite society, and only a belated peep from its leader. It died when the country decided to stop exporting its Islamic revolution and concentrate on the mess inside."[2]

A large part of that internal mess involved exchange rates between the Iranian rial and foreign currency. Rafsanjani vowed to bring order to a system in which the government exchanged rials for dollars at 70 to 1 while the black market dealt somewhere around 1,350 to 1. He would do it by freeing Iranian currency from the heavy hand of government control, a policy that signaled a move away from the rigid state-run economy toward some degree of capitalism. The issue of how many rials converted to one U.S. dollar struck the core of the clerics' great political-ideological divide. On one side massed the advocates of distributive justice, holding to their ideology regardless of the cost to the overall economy; on the other side were the proponents of economic recovery through free-market forces. Hiding in the pronouncements of each faction were the vested interests of individuals. Rafsanjani wanted to gain control over the institutions of the revolution while these same revolutionary organizations wanted to preserve their profits delivered by the privilege of drawing dollars from the

Central Bank at 50 percent of their market value against the Iranian rial.

Still the battle to transform Iran's highly centralized, heavily subsidized, stagnating economy into a vibrant, decentralized free-market system inched forward. In less than a year, the elimination of subsidies shot up the cost of chicken 30 percent, caused the price of postage stamps to triple, and increased international airfares purchased in local currency eightfold. In the interest of protecting the average citizen against total free fall, the government continued to sell gasoline at one-fourth its actual production cost. Nevertheless most of the population, particularly the poor, took a hard hit from economic reform. But Rafsanjani and the reformers moved on. In April 1992, the president maneuvered many of the hard-liners out of the Majlis by the devilish requirement that incumbents pass a difficult written test on Islam before they could stand for reelection. That shifted parliament to the right, toward Rafsanjani and his reform program. But within a month, the regime faced violence from the poorest of the poor when government attempted by decree to reclaim land occupied by squatters' shanties ringing most of Iran's cities.

In August 1991, the Tehran district of Bagher Abad rioted against municipal agents who attempted to demolish illegally constructed shacks. A March 1992 protest by disabled war veterans against the mismanagement of the Foundation of the Disinherited spread. Two to three thousand protesters set buildings ablaze in Arak, 150 miles southwest of Tehran. Shiraz rumbled. On May 30, 1992, Mashhad exploded when demolition squads and security forces moved into a squatter area. Torch-carrying rioters set fire to government buildings. In the conflagration, the city's main library with its extensive collection of Korans burned and tax records disappeared. Computers and other equipment that refused to ignite flew out of the top floor of the Ministry of Culture and Islamic Guidance. Quickly the clerics from the right and left of the political spectrum buried their differences and went on the attack. While officials blamed the violence on "foreigners" and the Mujahedin, the Basij and the Revolutionary Guards, the shields of Islamic government, came from near and far to put down the disturbances. Executions of four perpetrators followed. Finally, the clerics set about repairing the political damage among the lower class through the defense of Islamic culture. After a nine-week run that sold thirty thousand tickets, *Victory in Chicago*, a stage comedy about a failed search for justice in crime-ridden Chicago of the 1930s, closed under orders of the Ministry of Culture and Islamic Guidance.

Despite some high-profile enforcement of the revolution's cultural agenda in the wake of the spring riots, the general easing of the social strictures of the revolution continued. After years of banning popular music, stores now sold a tightly regulated selection of music tapes. And Walt Disney films along with some other American films judged morally fit populated a handful of video stores operated by proprietors who had passed the government's stringent virtues test. In every city and town, merchants in narrow storefronts sold cosmetics, curling irons, and flashy costume jewelry to women in *hejab*.

I arrived in Iran in the early fall of 1992, three months after the riots in Mashhad. For the next month, I wandered through the Bakhtiari pasturelands in the Zagros Mountains, the cities of Tehran, Isfahan, and Shiraz and the villages along the Caspian Sea. Regardless of the thirteen-year campaign to wipe the vestiges of the West from Iran, I saw fast-food restaurants selling fried chicken under red-and-white striped awnings that mimicked those of Kentucky Fried Chicken. The Caspian seafront town of Babal sported a hamburger stand called McAli's. In a hotel in Isfahan an old Muzak system scratched out the Beatles hit "Yesterday." The kiosks that stand at every busy intersection in every city carried the newspapers *Kayhan* and *Salaam*, the voices of the hard-liners. But beside them was the satirical magazine *Golagha*, lampooning figures in the government with full-color cartoons. *Time*, *Newsweek*, and the *Economist* were there also, sometimes weeks out of date and deprived of their seminude photos and alcohol ads by the scissors and ink brushes of the censors.

I found among the middle class that attitudes about government run by clerics were cautiously upbeat. The unfolding economic reforms promised to allow Iran to begin the process of recovery from revolution and war. Hope dwelled in economics, for few believed that the clerics were willing to open up the political system, where the all-powerful *faqih* guaranteed the political clerics' privileged position in Iranian politics, society, and culture. Under the *faqih*'s jurisdiction, the guardians of Islamic government continued to certify who could run for public office. As a result, the Majlis elections in the spring of 1992 had represented a contest in which voters chose between candidates qualified for election by their Islamic credentials. Still, it was a start toward the democracy Iran had never really known.

I returned to the Islamic Republic for another long stay in May 1993. I knew a rise in subsidized milk prices in January had sparked mob attacks on grocery stores. I also knew there had been violence in Abadan earlier in the spring. Yet Iran as a whole seemed more relaxed than the year before. I set up headquarters in a small, privately owned hotel in Tehran and began to explore the country once again. Even more than the year before, I saw evidence of economic reform and cultural flexibility. The big, new orange-and-purple buses in Tehran were subsidizing the two-cent bus fare by slapping ads for Samsung and Braun on their sides. Cinemas plastered with movie posters packed in customers for two American films, both starring Kevin Costner. But it was content rather than the star that put them on the screens of the Islamic Republic. *Dances with Wolves* dramatized the American exploitation of the Indians and *JFK* paraded the conspiratorial nature of the United States government.

In the summer of 1993, everyone complained about the economy. Inflation had driven the price of meat so high that some families were able to break a diet of rice and vegetables only one time a week. In the cities, particularly Tehran, soaring rents hit the middle class and the poor alike. Still, there existed a certain confidence in a future free of the Iran-Iraq War and street fighting between political opponents. Like the previous year, this confidence was encouraged by what seemed like a definite shift by government to a rational, consistent economic policy.

It was in June 1993 that Ali Akbar Hashemi Rafsanjani stood for reelection. The competing factions among the clerics joined forces and the system produced three other candidates for an election that guaranteed the regime stayed in power. Still Rafsanjani went on television to assure the voters that subsidies would continue on bread, sugar, water, electricity, tea, and milk. And a televised debate brought together proponents and opponents to discuss economic reform. In the run-up to the election, campaign posters papered walls of towns and cities reminding voters that it was Rafsanjani who represented the revolution in the first presidential election since the death of Khomeini.

Over and over I saw the link forged between Rafsanjani and the revolution. A little over a week before the vote, men lined up shoulder to shoulder around Ferdowsi Square to lift their hands in prayer in order to remind people to vote for Rafsanjani and Islam. Zahra Mustafavi, president of the Women's Organization of the Islamic Republic and daughter of Ayatollah Khomeini, issued a public statement reading, "The Women's Society . . . has endorsed Hashemi Rafsanjani in the upcoming election for president. . . . Because Mr. Rafsanjani was a student of the Late Imam Khomeini, all Iranians are urged to vote for him."[3] At Khomeini's tomb seven days before the electorate cast its ballots, Ali Khamenei, the spiritual leader, told the crowd that the failure to vote meant a vote against Islam. It carried weight. As one supporter of the clerics told me, "Rafsanjani has the experience of the revolution. That's important. The country must have its leadership in the hands of people who suffered its history."

Although everyone recognized the election of Rafsanjani as a foregone conclusion, the government hustled to turn out a big vote to give internal and external validity to the Islamic Republic. Many of the regime's opponents who had talked of boycotting the election marched to the polls to have their identity cards stamped in order to protect themselves against political recrimination delivered in a dozen ways by a highly centralized government.

The day of the election I went to the polls with a family from west-central Tehran. In the two blocks we walked, we saw posters for all the candidates. But it was Rafsanjani's name on a huge balloon striped red, yellow, and blue floating from the top of an apartment house that grabbed attention. Inside the mosque-turned-polling place, the men went straight ahead and the women turned left, for like everything else in the Islamic Republic, voting is sexually segregated. Except for the all-female election staff swathed in chadors, the polling place differed little from those in the West. My friends presented their identity cards and waited for the voter registration list to be checked and their ballots to be issued. There were no voting booths with curtains providing privacy. But neither was an election official hanging over the big rectangular table where voters marked their ballots. No one seemed to mind that I looked over her shoulder to see whom she was voting for. Not everyone I observed voted for Rafsanjani, although a majority did.

The election results gave Rafsanjani 63.2 percent of the nearly seventeen million ballots cast. The following day, the reelected president commented, "I hope that the government with its efforts in the Second Five-Year Development Plan will respond to this confidence of the people to succeed in removing their needs and difficulties. . . ."[4] The language of Ali Khamenei, the spiritual leader, proved more graphic. "The Iranian people, through their massive turnout in the elections, slapped in the mouth of their enemies and infuriated them."[5] That massive turnout was 57.6 percent of eligible voters.

Besides bestowing at least a degree of legitimacy on Rafsanjani's presidency, the election of 1993 reflected the Islamic Republic's ongoing attempt to define itself after Khomeini's death. It seemed at the time that the regime would continue to evolve in a moderate direction, moving away from heavy-handed Islamic socialism and broadening its popular support. In that process, the regime would have to decide the ultimate cultural issue of whether Iran interprets itself only by Islam or if it is willing to also accept its Persian identity.

During Rafsanjani's first term, the government had seemed to be willing to allow the two poles of Iranian culture to move toward reconciliation. A government in which the pragmatists held the upper hand sought the broad-based consensus needed to attack Iran's massive problems. That depended on a successful appeal to Iranian nationalism with both its Persian and Islamic components. Consequently, the revolution's Islamic rhetoric modified. Spokesmen of Islamic government conceded that although all pre-Islamic societies, including Persia, had lived in ignorance and darkness, Persian society had proved superior to all others.

In more contemporary terms, the Central Bank discreetly reopened its doors on the Iranian crown jewels. On Wednesday afternoon, anyone with the admission price of roughly four dollars could go down steep carpeted steps into the dazzling exhibit of prerevolutionary Iran ruled by kings. The globe of gold and jewels that once sparkled in Nasir ed-Din Shah's throne room is there next to a tiered, gilt throne embellished with the lion of Persia. So are the crowns of emeralds, rubies, diamonds, and pearls that sat on the heads of the Qajars. Alone in a glass case near the entrance is the plumed Pahlavi crown. According to the museum's curator, the same man who served the shah, the collection remains intact for the people of Iran.

This reconnection with pre-Islamic and prerevolutionary Iran found an advocate in Rafsanjani. In April 1992, he had become the first revolutionary leader to make an official visit to Persepolis. Among the same ruins that the zealots of 1980 wanted to raze to dust, the president of the Islamic Republic declared, "Standing in the middle of these centuries old ruins, I felt the nation's dignity was all-important and must be strengthened. Our people must know that they are not without a history."[6] It appeared that at last the Islamic Republic was beginning to understand the Iranians' dual identity.

But before Rafsanjani could either restore some balance to the Iranians' cultural identity or accomplish economic reform, he and the pragmatists found themselves in full retreat. The reason was the bitter medicine required to revive the economy. Reduction or elimination of subsidies to state-run services that began in March 1994 had increased the price for telecommunications 60 percent, gas 100 percent, and electricity at plants and factories 300 percent. Domestic airline fares had jumped 100 percent. Other products and services provided by the government experienced similar rises. When I returned to Iran that summer, the optimism I had observed in 1993 was gone in an atmosphere in which concern about individual and family survival dominated. Fear and anger gripped taxi drivers and university professors as they watched the rial slide to three thousand to the dollar. In addition, the anticipation that social restrictions would be eased had evaporated, leaving those who had put hope in Rafsanjani to improve their lives as immobilized as the president himself. Over and over I heard the same refrain: "This government is like every other government of Iran. The only thing it is interested in is maintaining the privileges of those in power."

By the summer of 1995, forces related and unrelated to economic reform inflicted their pain on a country already hurting. In a market where prices drifted lower, oil revenues refused to provide the desperately needed cash the economic reformers anticipated; foreign debt registered at forty billion dollars; and rice that had sold for seventy rials a kilo in the shah's time now cost seven thousand in an economy in which average per capita income clung to a quarter of what it was in 1979. In one measure of severe economic times, marriage had become so expensive that Rafsanjani called for wider use of the Shia practice of temporary marriage to provide men and women "physical comfort."

Economic stress coupled with the government's continuing efforts to impose administrative order on an unruly country sparked riots and demonstrations that began in June 1994. On Ashura, the day the martyred Hussein is mourned, a bomb planted in the women's section of the Imam Reza Mosque in Mashhad detonated, killing at least twenty-five people.* On August 9, 1994, Qavin, ninety miles northwest of Tehran, rose against central authority. Ten days later, thousands of people in Tabriz, Iran's third largest city, rioted. Demonstrations at the University of Tehran in November called for the execution of "capitalists" and denounced lawmakers for favoring wealthy merchants over the poor. In April 1995, Akbarabad, a shantytown on the edge of Tehran, exploded when bus fares increased. By the time the riots were quelled perhaps as many as thirty people had died. The next day hundreds of police officers lined the streets as local authorities bused in thousands of Basij-is to march in pro-government demonstrations. It was evidence not only of how far short the pragmatists had fallen in

---

*Among the groups suspected in the bombing are the Sunnis whose mosque in Mashhad was razed by local authorities earlier in the summer.

attempting to revive the Iranian economy but also how divided the political clerics remained on issues of ideology and economics.

At the beginning of Rafsanjani's second term in 1993, the parliament which the president had so boldly pruned of hard-liners the preceding year had proved no more willing to rally behind the president's reform program than the previous one. In the rising tide of public protest over the punishment associated with economic reform, a new coalition had gathered to torpedo the pragmatists' foreign exchange policy and the modernization of the economy. They also aimed at Rafsanjani himself, who many of the political clerics saw as employing economic reform as a means of weakening the clergy's grip on domestic affairs. In the service of revolutionary ideology and self-interest, the new alliance in the Majlis brought together old adversaries—the hard-liners and the right-wing conservatives who had done battle against each other in the early years of the Islamic Republic. They were joined on major issues by Ali Khamenei, the *faqih*. Formerly allied with the president, Khamenei began to employ his constitutional power as the final authority in the Islamic Republic to both sabotage the pragmatists and block Rafsanjani from emerging as Iran's uncontested political leader. Deviating from Ayatollah Khomeini's practice of moving back and forth between opposing groups in order to maintain balance, Khamenei most often took the side of the hard-liners. Consequently, on the three great ideological issues that have divided the political clerics since the early 1980s—state intervention in the economy, the enforcement of strict Islamic codes of conduct, and relations with the West—the hard-liners gathered their allies to block the threatened dominance of the pragmatists over public policy in the Islamic Republic. As Rafsanjani tries to hang on into the twilight of his presidency, the impasse remains. But the label of hard-liner or pragmatist fails to recognize the multitude of factions within each camp as the political clerics vie for purely personal power. Repeating the traditional pattern operating under kingship, the personal interests and family interests of individual clerics too often rank as greater priorities than the national good. Consequently, narrow interests combine with revolutionary ideology to hold Iran at the mercy of a state-run economy, clerical mismanagement, and personal greed. That leaves the Iranians to ponder the results of the revolution they greeted with such widespread joy and expectation.

As in most revolutions, the Iranian Revolution has produced gains and inflicted losses. Among the gains is the social nature of the revolution that overthrew kingship. The masses who crushed the Pahlavi throne also pulled the struts out of the old hierarchical order, toppling the traditional elite that had dominated Iran since the Achaemenians. Although a new elite rose with Islamic government, it sat at the top of a society shaped more like a plateau than a pyramid. For the Islamic Republic represents the culture of the masses rather than the culture of the privileged. In this new social order, *hejab* not only enforces public morality, it renders the material distinctions between the haves and the have-nots less discernible.

Although the government which rules it is greatly flawed, Iran now exhibits genuine elements of a republic. Power no longer concentrates in the person of a king but operates from multiple centers. The Majlis, that representative voice of the people created by the Constitutional Revolution, has gathered strength as an institution in the years since 1979. Public debate, although constrained, echoes through the land. And a press representing different viewpoints is active in a climate of caution.

Education has opened up to the masses, dramatically improving literacy rates for both males and females. Access to health care has grown and social services have expanded under the guidance of a government seeking to weave a social fabric in which the individual is no longer totally dependent on hierarchical relationships. Even women have gained certain advantages in the Islamic state, including education, greater job opportunities, and the right in divorce to recover the value of a wife's labor over the duration of the marriage. But through the revolutionary leaders' own vested interests, their mistakes, and factors beyond government control, the negative results of the Iranian Revolution loom large.

In the revolution's two phases, the Iranian people ruptured. Perhaps as many as three million fled either the rage against the privileged or the repression imposed by the clerics. In economic terms, they took with them the capital and skills necessary to build a new Iran. In terms of Iranian society, the exodus physically broke the great extended families, the foundation blocks of society. They are now divided between those living abroad and those remaining in Iran. For the exiles, feelings of alienation in an adopted land and the powerful emotional pull of historic Iran bring some back to the Islamic Republic. But few stay because they cannot survive in the present economy or they refuse to live within the social strictures imposed by clerical government. So they return West with their dreams of the Iran that was rather than the Iran that is.

The pain for those who never left Iran is often no less than for those who did. A female intellectual tearfully talked about her daughter, a nine-year-old student in Tehran's International School when the revolution began. Forced into *hejab*, she begged to leave the Islamic Republic. Her mother finally agreed in 1984 to send her to her uncle in Canada. Since that time mother and daughter have been together a total of three weeks. But when I asked this same mother about how she felt about welcoming the émigrés back, her fiery reply was, "Those of us who have suffered the revolution don't feel good about them. Some are coming back and acting like nothing has changed. They did not go through the intellectual process that people who stayed did. We have grown and matured. They have not. We have gone through the process of self-education and evaluation. They have not." And so the Iranian people look at each other over the chasm of distance and identity, pondering whether they are forever divided.

Despite the massive exodus abroad following the revolution, the Islamic Republic has experienced a population explosion. In 1978, the population stood at roughly thirty-six million. Today it is over sixty million, the result of government policy in the early years of the Islamic Republic that encouraged one of the highest birthrates in the world. The assumption of the revolutionaries in charge of government was that large numbers of Iranians would help the Islamic Republic propagate its ideology. Instead increased population has added yet another burden to the Islamic Republic. Facing housing shortages, too few jobs, overburdened educational and health systems, persistent demands for infrastructure, and threatened water supplies, the leadership is now aggressively pushing population control. Although achieving falling birthrates, a population in which 40 percent is under the age of fourteen means that the Islamic Republic will live for decades with the consequences of its earlier population policy.

Sadly, this greatly expanded population has never experienced either the equality or the community of ordinary men and women that the rhetoric of the revolution promised. In early 1979, the Iranians who united to topple the Pahlavi dynasty considered themselves bound together by mutual ideals. For a brief moment, common courtesy spawned by revolutionary fervor dictated that everyone in an old, hierarchical society address each other as brother and sister. Then the scramble for power began, separating Iranians into groups competing for control of the economy and the culture. The clerics and their followers became the dominant group in control of import licenses and access to favorable exchange rates, scarce resources, and land.

Today the Islamic Republic is rife with corruption. Perhaps nothing symbolizes ill-gotten gains more potently to the man on the street than the mullah gripping a briefcase under his cloak as he steps into a new, air-conditioned, chauffeur-driven Peugeot. Less visible but no less resented are the clerics and high-ranking government officials who have moved into the confiscated homes of the *taghoot*, as the wealthy Westernized supporters of the shah were called. Although Ali Khamenei as the spiritual guide has declared, "Officials of the Islamic government must live a simple life and stay away from tendencies to comfortable or luxurious lifestyles," many political clerics and their allies continue to build personal kingdoms of wealth and privilege.[7]

Some of the largess falling to the clerical alliance comes from the foundations. After the government-owned oil industry, they are the largest manufacturers, traders, and real estate developers in the country. At the same time, they reap huge subsidies from government. The bloated giant of the *bonyads* is the Mostazafin Foundation, the Foundation of the Oppressed, that swept up the confiscated property of the Pahlavis and other wealthy families in the early days of the revolution. The roughly seven hundred companies now under its control make cars and pharmaceuticals, import steel and chicken, and operate most of Iran's hotels. It even owns property on Fifth Avenue in New York. In 1995, the foundation's assets were estimated at twelve billion dollars, with yearly earnings of perhaps one hundred million.* The Mostazafin Foundation, the Martyrs Foundation, and most of the other so-called charity organizations are accountable neither to shareholders nor to the government, but only to the man who sits at its head, or to the *faqih*, Ali Khamenei. Rather than real businesses concerned with profits and losses, they are cornucopias of wealth for the Islamic Republic's elite. As an example of how profits take precedence over public welfare, a large part of the output of the pharmaceutical industry goes to the black market rather than the pharmacies, creating a chronic shortage of reasonably priced drugs. One Iranian complained to me, "Because of the mullahs, sometimes there is not an aspirin in Tehran."

In an attempt to prevent more civil disturbances over the rising cost of living, the Majlis is beginning to shine the light of inquiry on

---

*The president of Bonyad Mostazafin is Mohsen Rafighdoost. He moved out of his father's fruit shop in the bazaar to become Ayatollah Khomeini's chauffeur and bodyguard. On the imam's orders, he founded the Revolutionary Guard. That put him in position to build the assets of the Foundation of the Oppressed.

the foundations. In 1995, preparation began on a report on the Mostazafin Foundation intended to determine if its primary purpose is charity or profit. But reining in the foundations will be difficult. First, people in high places are the *bonyads'* chief beneficiaries and, secondly, a portion of the foundations' profits are channeled to the "martyrs and the oppressed" who keep the clerical regime in power.

Unfortunately for the people of the Islamic Republic, corruption is not isolated to the *bonyads*. In the bureaucracy charged with everything from stamping a form to clearing a shipment through customs to scheduling a court case, nothing gets done without a bribe. Even the Revolutionary Guards, the guardians of public morality, have become corrupt. Hefty fees paid in advance keep the Pasdaran away from parties of the rich where alcohol is served. Lesser bribes in lesser social classes smooth the departure of religious vigilantes who have burst through the door to shut off Western music and collect a payoff for keeping the offenders out of jail.

Although the stain of corruption is on all layers of the Islamic Republic, its damage has penetrated to the core of the clergy in charge of the Islamic Republic. The perception of most Iranians outside the revolutionary diehards is that every high-ranking cleric in government is corrupt. President Rafsanjani is rumored to control the pistachio market, own the Mitsubishi plant, and take a cut on all import taxes collected at Iran's major port on Qeshem Island. Ali Akbar Nateq-Noori, speaker of the Majlis, has had little success in denying that he owns four houses gifted by the government. Even the family of Imam Khomeini is suspect. The fact that Zahra Mustafavi, the ayatollah's daughter who heads the Women's Organization, travels the streets in a new Mercedes adds resonance to the whispers that before his death, her brother, Ahmed, was the richest man in Iran. It is in this environment of fact and rumor that the majority of the Iranian population believes that government runs on the precepts of power and privilege, not on the principles of the revolution.

Society in the Islamic Republic resembles that of Pahlavi Iran in that it is seemingly irrevocably split between a small, very rich minority, a larger middle class struggling to survive, and the overwhelming majority of the poor. This gaping chasm between rich and poor stands as testament to the brutal reality that the Islamic Republic has not been able to deliver on the one great social goal of the revolution—the equitable distribution of economic resources. It is as if the hourglass of power that turned over in 1979 changed everything and changed nothing. In the Islamic Republic as in Pahlavi Iran, north and south Tehran continue to symbolize the great socioeconomic divisions in Iran. As the new elite look down on the sprawling city below the mountains, what was written about the Iran of Muhammad Reza Shah in 1960 now describes the Iran of the clerics. "Throughout the city new wealth can be seen but not touched by vast numbers of the population; and increased education itself creates expectations which the government does little to fulfill."[8]

As a result, the schism between a diminishing core of loyalists to the revolution and the rest of Iranian society is growing. The opposition gathers in groups inside and outside Iran. In their political and cultural viewpoint, they span the whole history of Iran's turbulent twentieth century. The monarchists cling to the Persian component of Iranian identity, condemning the Islamic Republic as alien to the historical requirements of Iran and bemoaning the reordering of the traditional hierarchy. The ideological descendants of the Constitutionalists of 1906 and the Nationalist Movement of Muhammad Mossadeq dream of justice and equality postulated both in the Persian cultural tradition and the Islamic religion, and of democracy and liberty conceived in Iran's engagement with the West.* There are also those among the masses whose marching feet did so much to create the Islamic Republic and whose bleeding bodies contributed so much to saving it in the war with Iraq who remember Ayatollah Khomeini's words uttered from exile in 1972: "Once the clergy is corrupted, the world is corrupted."[9]

The opposition to rule by the clerics remains fragmented and quiescent in part because the proponents of politicized Islam have proven as intolerant of dissent as their royal predecessor. Evin Prison, stormed in February 1979 to free political prisoners of Muhammad Reza Shah, now holds the political prisoners of clerical government. Even so, the Islamic Republic has never built and operated an internal security system approaching in size, efficiency, and ruthlessness that of the shah. Rather, surveillance is erratic, repression fitful, and terror decentralized. In essence, the clerics stay strong enough to govern but supple enough to survive. Consequently, there is freedom of the press

---

*The Mujahedin-e Khalq no longer constitutes a political option in Iran. Living on the largess of Saddam Hussein, the group claims an army, a parliament in exile, and a future president of Iran. All operate within a cult of personality built around the Mujahedin's long-time leader, Masoud Rajavi. While the Mujahedin remains the most widely feared opposition group because of periodic raids across the Shatt al-Arab, it is also the most discredited among the Iranian people who have not forgotten the Mujahedin's support of Iraq in the war against Iran.

and there is censorship. There is the absence of a police state and the presence of repression in which an Iranian constantly wonders if he is being spied on, if his telephone is tapped, or if the Pasdaran will strike. Although the Bahais and evangelical Christians are the primary victims of outright persecution, everyone is sensitive to the growing parallels with the oppression of the shah.

The clerical regime, like that of Muhammad Reza Shah, has long reached out beyond the borders of Iran to eliminate foes. In recent years, the most high-profile assassination was that of Shahpur Bakhtiar, the shah's last prime minister. He was strangled and then repeatedly stabbed in his Paris home on August 6, 1991. France convicted the killers, claiming they acted on orders from Tehran. Although the Iranian government has never publicly accepted responsibility for his death, Bakhtiar joined at least sixty-three other Iranians abroad who have been killed or wounded since the shah was overthrown.

Of more concern to the Iranians of the Islamic Republic was the arrest of a well-known intellectual in 1994. Ali Akbar Saidi Sirjani authored fifteen books on Iranian history and legend that explore the differences between Iranian culture with its Persian component and Islamic culture promoted by the ruling mullahs. His contention that Iranians possess a pre-Islamic tradition of respect for individual rights and opposition to tyranny led the government to ban his books in 1991. Following his arrest three years later, Sirjani, according to the hard-line newspaper *Kayhan*, confessed to charges of espionage and drug abuse. For eight months, Iranian intellectuals and international human rights advocates protested the writer's detention. Then on November 28, 1994, Ali Akbar Saidi Sirjani died in prison of a sudden and unexpected heart attack, the same fate that befell Jalal Al-e Ahmad and Ali Shariati during the reign of Muhammad Reza Shah.

In an environment in which the oppressed of Pahlavi Iran have become the oppressors of the Islamic Republic, a disillusioned member of the middle class told me, "This government is making the same mistake as the shah by keeping all power within their own group. The shah tried to shut out the Shiites. Now the Shiites shut out everyone else."

Denied an officially sanctioned outlet for political protest, resistance to the clerical regime is following indirect, even passive forms. As a result, the threat posed to the existing order is not so much what people do against the government but what they refuse to do for it. The organs of the Islamic state issue orders and people ignore or circumvent them. Apathy and cynicism permeating all layers of society serve to keep the numbers the regime needs for legitimacy away from Friday prayers, anniversary celebrations that mark the events of the revolution, and elections. In what amounts to an act of rebellion, the unhappy generation that has grown up under the cultural restrictions of the revolutions reaches out to anything Western. It all proves that Iran is today what it has always been—a land of heresy and heterodoxy in which the individual continually rejects accepted wisdom to search for his own divine truth.

Having failed to deliver on the economic promises of the revolution, refusing to open up the political process, and increasingly forced to rule with the iron hand of repression, the clerics continue to anchor their legitimacy in Islam, just as the Pahlavi dynasty attempted to ground its authority in resurrected Persia.

During the emotionally frenzied days of the revolution, surging crowds numbering in the hundreds of thousands descended on the University of Tehran every Friday to pray to Allah and shout the slogans of politicized Islam. It is quieter now, but the dwindling faithful of Islamic government continue to come to partake of the politics of prayer. On a November day when the skies were clear and the air touched with a chill, a steady stream of worshipers tranquilly filed through the gates of the university. At the mosque, they crowded into a vast, sloping rectangle paved with poorly finished cement and covered with a corrugated Fiberglas roof. Divided by a forbidding wall, the women sat on one side in irregularly strewn clusters while the men, kneeling on everything from finely woven prayer rugs to rough burlap sacks, lined up in precise rows to wait for the prayers to begin. Much from the tumultuous days of the revolution resides in this place. And much of the regime's modus operandi exhibits itself here. At the head of the prayer area, roughly ten feet off the ground, a platform holds an open, framed box from which the prayer leader delivers his sermon. Thirty yards back, scaffolding set within the crowd provides a perch for a television camera that focuses eye to eye with the speaker. Every word spoken, every gesture given, goes out to the nation twice—once live and once on tape broadcast on Friday evening.

On this day, the presiding cleric began the ceremonies by preaching on the new world order and Iran's place within it. The message fell far short of passionate oratory, yet on cue, clenched fists darted out of the crowd to wave back and forth in the air to the cadence set by the speaker. The vitriolic revolutionary slogans sounded again just as they had Friday after Friday in late 1978 and early 1979. Then as suddenly as it rose, the crowd quieted for the ritual of prayer. With the political message still ringing in their ears and television cameras panning their ranks, men and women bowed toward Mecca.

Seeking political control through cultural control, the clerics of Islamic government have drilled a whole generation of Iranian children with Islam. They control the nation's cultural life and try to direct its intellectual life. They send the Revolutionary Guards to the mountain trails where young people hike to race up and down the paths keeping boys and girls properly separated. They lock women in *hejab* as a political statement of the power of the revolution. And they ban satellite dishes because the spiritual leader warns, "Our enemies are encouraging young people to turn away from Islamic belief" and, by implication, the Islamic state.[10] In government offices, airports and schools, on buses and billboards, mosques and grain silos, the pictures of Khomeini and Khamenei hang like sacred symbols of Islam. Yet for too many people the question remains: Is the Islamic Republic a government drawing its authority from the basic tenets of Shia Islam or is it another in a long line of authoritarian governments in the twisted, tortuous pattern of Iranian history? With religion as the only legitimating force of clerical government, it is somehow appropriate that the most serious challenge facing the political mullahs comes from within Shiism itself.

In the Iranian revolution, the *ulama* assumed a political role unprecedented since 1501, when the clerics of Shiism became the authenticators of the legitimacy of the monarch. That division and that link between temporal and religious authority ended with the Islamic Republic. Particularly after 1981, members of the *ulama* rather than secular authorities took responsibility for the day-to-day business of running a government. Today they remain the wheels and cogs of the Islamic Republic. It all stands in stark contradiction to Shia tradition in which believers present quiescent but unyielding opposition to governmental authority in the absence of the Twelfth Imam.

Even before the revolution began, Ayatollah Shariatmadari and others warned against the corrupting effect of political power in a system of governance in which there is no division between the realm of God and the realm of the state. By extension, these critics of the concept of the *Velayat-e Faqih* feared religion's involvement in secular politics would open the clergy to public scrutiny and wrath, eroding its special position in Iranian society. But with the support of Ayatollah Khomeini, mullahs-turned-politicians imposed their views upon the dissenting clerics through public rebuke, ridicule, intimidation, censorship, and house arrest. Yet within a decade, the experience of the Islamic Republic proved the prediction of the clerical opponents of the *Velayat-e Faqih*. The mullahs' direct involvement in the affairs of state has laid the blame for the ills of society and the failings of government at the feet of the clerics of Shia Islam, undermining the clergy's once considerable moral authority. As a result, the learned jurists in the Shia theological schools of Qom and Mashhad are again debating what the Iranian Revolution really means in terms of governance and religion. And they are asking the mullahs of the *Velayat-e Faqih* if it is Islam that is the revolution's one great martyr.

Leading the public rhetoric is Abdul Karim Soroush, a Muslim philosopher who began the revolution as part of the regime. He is now held in contempt by the major powers of the Islamic Republic. Although banned from the airwaves, his popular university lectures and evening discussions at a Tehran mosque continue. The thrust of Soroush's thinking is that the sacred texts of Islam are, by definition, unalterable. But man's understanding of them is not because of any number of variables including historic era, geographical location, the social and cultural environment of the time, as well as the existing level of scientific knowledge. Dismissing the possibility of absolute truth, Soroush challenges anyone's claim to the right to impose his own interpretation of the sacred texts or to lead the Muslim community on terms of divine right. In essence, "Soroush opposes the clergy's traditional privilege of interpreting and carrying out the will of the Prophet. Beyond that, his thinking includes an implicit attack on the institution of the *valayet-e faqih.* . . . one of the two pillars of the Islamic republic, the other being the popular sovereignty embodied in the parliament and president of the republic, elected by universal suffrage."[11] In other words, the Islamic state claims legitimacy only if it is democratic and humanistic.

Soroush's audience includes the 98 percent or more of the 80,000 clerics in Iran who are not part of Islamic government. Fulfilling their traditional role of religious guide and source of succor for oppressed people, they see the prestige and influence of the clergy ebb in the failures of the Islamic Republic. While some still recognize the divine legitimacy of the *faqih*, others hold that the spiritual guide's authority derives solely from the popular will, and that, like other elected officials, popular will can remove him from power.

Another source of clerical opposition to the concept of the *Velayat-e Faqih* resides in the Shia theological center at Najaf. Like Ayatollah Khomeini in his days of exile in Iraq, Shiism's most esteemed clerics cannot be silenced by censorship imposed by the government of Iran. When the Islamic Republic's political clerics made an audacious attempt to elect Ali Khamenei as spiritual leader of all Shia in December 1994 following the death of Ayatollah Ali Araqi—the reigning *marja-e taqlid*—it was the clerical leadership in Najaf who forced a reversal. Khamenei's rejection by the legitimate hierarchy of Shiism confirmed the great dilemma of Iran's clerical government. The *Velayat-e Faqih* which bases its legitimacy on an interpretation of the Shia authority figure is led by a spiritual leader who is a politician rather than a revered jurist of Islamic law. Even the diehards of politicized Islam realize the contradiction. In the absence of a powerful figure of Islam filling the Iranian need for a charismatic leader, the supporters of the Islamic Republic grieve for Ayatollah Khomeini. A poem read on the fourth anniversary of Khomeini's death cried

> *Oh, Alas*
> *The separation*
> *The sky is full of clouds*
> *The sun does not shine anymore*
> *The earth looks like a desert*
> *He has been gone for four years and he has not come back.*
> *We were small plants he made into big trees.*
> *We were butterflies that flew around his flame.*[12]

In the Islamic Republic, as it was in Muhammad Reza Shah's state, it is questionable whether the regime in power will retain possession of the spiritual charisma that bestows authority in Iranian political culture. As the *Velayat-e Faqih* struggles through its second decade the parliament, the courts, the *ulama*, and the people all harbor deep uncertainty not only about who determines what, or who rules whom, but also what the future principal of rule, the future charisma, will be.

While grappling with this central question of authority and legitimacy, the leaders of the Islamic Republic also face, as part of that same question, the definition of Iranian identity. Just as the Pahlavi dynasty attempted to do, the clerics are once again trying to undergird their political power by removing one of the two poles of Iranian identity. But stalking the Islamic Republic's rigid enforcement of the rules and mores of Shiism is the reality that the Iranians' cultural duality always poses the Iran of the ancient Persians against the Iran of Islam, the Zoroastrian god Ahura Mazda against the Muslim god Allah,

Persepolis against Mecca. The end of the Pahlavi dynasty demonstrated that efforts to separate these two components of Iranian culture
or to give one precedence over the other are short-lived and futile. For
while the beard on the face of a Basij-i is part of the identity battle
now raging in Iran, so is the look of awe registered by a group of little
schoolgirls dressed in *hejab* peering up at the massive platform of
Persepolis. In the expression of those children is seen the question the
West has asked for almost two decades: Who are the Iranians?

They are heirs to the civilizations of Persia and Islam just as Westerners are heirs to the cultures of Greece and Rome and the religions
of Judaism and Christianity. But unlike Westerners who divide the
secular from the religious, the Iranians have never separated their legacy from man and their legacy from God. Although Persian tradition
claims the Zoroastrian god Ahura Mazda and Shia Islam prays to the
Islamic Allah, the Persian and Islamic components of Iranian culture
share, at the deepest level, a perpetual tension between the transcendental and the mundane, the spiritual and the secular. It is within this
tension that much of Iranian history and behavior occurs and it is in
the resolution of this tension that the salvation of Iranian society lies.
For as long as religion and politics remain at odds over culture and
governance, the Iranians as a people suffer. And as long as human suffering prevails, the quest for justice will drive all aspects of Iranian
society.

Although the fusion of the transcendentalism of religion and the
realism of politics has been implied throughout the life of the Iranian
nation, it was never achieved in ancient Persia and perhaps in Islam
only fleetingly under the first four caliphs and in the early Abbasid
dynasty. In the Iran of Persian culture and Shia Islam, the Safavids, in
the sixteenth century, did attempt to join that which is spiritual and
that which is secular by combining the institution of ancient Persian
kingship and the concept of the Shia immamate. It did not last long
after the demise of the dynasty's founder, Ismail. Instead, the king sat
on the throne commanding all the power of the state, while religion
tended the nation's soul and kept alive the promise of justice at the
end of time.

Iran's meeting with the West that began in the late nineteenth
century only intensified the ancient tension between mundane politics
and transcendental religion. In the technology and ideas of the West,
the orthodoxy of Islam found much to fear and the absorptive nature
of the Persians much to like. As a result, the agitation between traditionalism and modernity joined the strain between spirituality and re-

alism. Yet out of these two tensions came the Constitutional Revolution that gave Iran a parliament, introducing in theory the legitimization of the ruler through the will of the people. In devising a new basis of authority, the Iranians contradicted the tradition of divine kingship certified by the *ulama* of Islam. But while the king, the *ulama*, and the people shared both a secular and spiritual bond in the Constitution of 1906, Pahlavi power over five decades held Iran in the old mold of ruler-based politics in which the secular dominated the religious. In the Iranian Revolution of 1979, kingship was subordinated to religion, but then the spiritual abdicated to the mundane as all politics passed into the hands of a new elite committed to the preservation of its interests.

Contrary to Shia tradition, Ayatollah Khomeini's *Velayat-e Faqih* represented the boldest attempt in Iranian history to subject all the cultural, social, economic, and political aspects of the society to the transcendental ideal of the "government of God." Yet in function, it is government by a cadre of clerics manipulating the ancient order of hierarchy and authority in a system dominated by the ruler. This reality about the nature of Iran's Islamic government lies at the heart of the current debate about the nature of the *Velayat-e Faqih*. Voicing the perpetual tension between the transcendental and the mundane, Iranians are asking if the authority of the *faqih* comes from the will of Allah or the will of the people.

This is the core question for Iranians who as an ancient, fiercely independent people are painfully groping for a new identity defined in terms of their unique Persian-Shia heritage. In the process, the stress between the religious and political realms of Iranian society can only intensify. Despite a regime that has sought isolation to protect its own version of Iranian culture, Iran cannot escape from the influences of the twentieth century's increasingly global civilization. Nor can the clerics pretend that the elevation of a false spirituality over secular government has benefited Iranian society as a whole. In spite of all the gains that clerical government claims have accrued to the lower classes as a result of the revolution, Islamic government has not satisfied the Iranians' ancient quest for justice. Instead the ideal and implementation of justice which joins the transcendent and the mundane is no more a reality than it was under kingship. This is the great challenge to the stability of the Islamic Republic. As R. K. Ramazani has pointed out, "Without justice, there can be no durable order and without liberty there can be no justice."

The central question is whether the Islamic Republic is in danger of losing the *farr*. In the service of its own power, an elite is trying to impose on an essentially cosmopolitan culture its own particular interpretation of Shia Islam. The iron hand can hold power for the clerics for a while, forcing the Iranians to continue to struggle through the communal pain associated with the search for themselves. But in the end, the regime will either have to open up to major reforms that could make it a true government of the people or retain the rule of the *faqih* in a way that will lose the support of the masses.

In what might be the gathering twilight of the current phase of the Iranian revolution, I stood one night on the balcony of an apartment house set on a hill in northwest Tehran. Through an ethereal glow created by dust and lights, I looked out over the city. Attracted by space and illumination, my eye rested on Azadi Square and the monument built by Muhammad Reza Shah in 1971 to celebrate his own version of Iran. Farther south, I saw the soaring minarets of Ayatollah Ruhollah Khomeini's tomb. They rise out of the massive structures of a constantly expanding complex built to Islam and politics. But neither the king nor the ayatollah nor the systems of rule that they devised and administered met the needs, demands, and yearnings of the Iranian people in the twentieth century. As a result, the Pahlavi construction of an Iran defined by Persia and kingship is gone. Khomeini's Iran of Islam and political clerics survives in the grip of menacing cultural, social, economic, and political tensions. Perhaps one day another monument will stand below the mountains, one built by the Iranian people who allow both their Persian and Islamic identities to lie at peace in the soul of the nation.

Epilogue

In the closing years of the twentieth century, the Iranians are draped in a cloak of tragedy woven from the threads of their own history. In that history that spans twenty-five hundred years, a people in possession of enormous gifts, holding a distinct and highly refined culture, have struggled against the harshness of their natural environment, the repeated invasion of alien forces across their borders, and the oppression of their own governments. In this century, they have waged two revolutions aimed at establishment of a just society. Now they debate their future in the shambles of their present. Deliverance from the travails of society and nation will come neither easily nor quickly. Fissured by ethnicity, language, tribe, and family, historically ladened by illiteracy, hierarchy, and poverty, and void of a tradition that seeks the common good, the Iranians are painfully groping their way through the unfinished revolution. Although the process must be internal, the United States holds an enormous stake in the outcome. The reason is embedded in the core elements of strategic interests—geography and resources. Because of Iran's location and natural resources, American self interest demands that the United States care, and care deeply, about how the Iranians complete the Iranian revolution. Anything less invites uncertainty at best, disaster at worst, for American strength and prosperity.

U.S. strategic concerns have already thrust American power onto Iran's doorstep. Every day at sunrise, a needle-nosed FA-18 roars down the runway of an American aircraft carrier and screams into the sky to begin yet another patrol of the Persian Gulf. The shallow, turquoise waters below its wings lack the energy of the Atlantic, the expanse of the Pacific, or the beauty of the Mediterranean. But this body of water that is more a lake than an ocean, holds within its floor and shores the viscous, black petroleum on which the very survival of the industrialized West depends. Access to the West's lifeblood was threatened in 1990 when Saddam Hussein invaded Kuwait. The great powers who would later stand by to watch the Serb's bestial plunder of Bosnia swiftly gathered behind the United States to liberate the sheikdom of Kuwait. In the 1991 Gulf War, an American-led armada took command of the seas, high-tech aircraft rained down death and destruction on Iraq, and a land army numbering over a half million rolled across the desert to crush the army of the upstart Saddam Hussein. The most technically advanced war machine in history bludgeoned a lesser foe for one reason—to protect oil. Yet in the aftermath of the Gulf War, the United States, the decisive leader of the coalition that humiliated Saddam Hussein, disregarded the imperative to develop a realistic policy capable of securing the Persian Gulf, the alpha and omega of its strategic interests. Rather than viewing the Gulf as a region, the United States concentrates on caging Iraq in a punishing embargo and maintaining politically uncertain Saudi Arabia as the anchor of the Gulf's defense. Meanwhile, two hundred miles across the Persian Gulf from Dhahran, the major U.S. weapons depot in Saudi Arabia, the Islamic Republic of Iran lives as the pariah of American policy, isolated by anger, fear, and perception.

Current American policy on Iran began in that calamitous year of 1979 when the fall of Muhammad Reza Shah left the United States stunned and adrift in the crucial Persian Gulf. When disciples of Ayatollah Khomeini captured the American embassy, anger took over from confusion. And anger and suspicion have led four administrations to flounder in what is in essence a rudderless boat carrying the vital interests of the United States.

The shock of the unexpected Iranian revolution and the trauma of the unsolved hostage crisis consumed the Carter administration. In 1981, Ronald Reagan took office sporting the image of a sheriff armed against an outlaw. Eight years later, he left the presidency riding high in the saddle, dragging behind him the carcasses of the American adventure in Lebanon, the Iran Contra Affair, the attack on the *U.S.S. Stark*, and the downing of Iran Air flight 655.

In 1989, George Bush entered the Oval Office. Generally proclaimed the best prepared president on foreign policy since Richard Nixon, he coaxed China further along the path away from Mao Tse-tung's brand of Marxism. He presided over the collapse of the Soviet Union with sensitivity coupled with an understanding of just how much the end of the Cold War changed the world. But Bush and his advisors clung to American attitudes about revolutionary Iran shaped by the images of 1979 and the death sentence Ayatollah Khomeini imposed on Salman Rushdie. In spite of the moderating revolution that came in the wake of Khomeini's death, the United States refused to inch toward conciliation. Pointing to the end of superpower rivalry as well as the Iranians' historic distrust of Russia, the Bush administration insisted that the Islamic Republic held no options. If the West stood firm, the clerics in Tehran eventually would be forced to normalize relations with the United States and Europe on terms and conditions laid down by the West. Then came the Gulf War.

In the eight months between the invasion of Kuwait and the cease-fire that ended the Gulf War, the Bush administration watched Iran walk the fine line of neutrality between the hated Saddam Hussein and the Great Satan of revolutionary rhetoric. But the Islamic Republic was not neutral. By staying clear of the conflict and supporting all United Nations sanctions on Iraq, the leadership of the Islamic Republic lined up with the United States. Nonetheless, when George Bush laid out before Congress his grand plan to protect the Persian Gulf, Iran was denied a voice in the security of its own region. Thus when the Bush presidency gave way to that of Bill Clinton, the wall the United States had built around Iran after 1979 remained unbreached. It was left to the new administration to strengthen the fortifications.

A novice at foreign policy, President Clinton chose as his secretary of state the seasoned diplomat Warren Christopher. Christopher had headed Jimmy Carter's team of negotiators that spent fifteen months attempting to free the American hostages captured with the U.S. embassy in Tehran in November 1979. When he took over American foreign policy in 1993, Christopher still carried the scars of that battle. But the Clinton administration's tough policy on Iran that began the day it took office has gained sustenance from factors beyond the personal attitudes of the secretary of state.

The first of those factors is the American people. The collapse of communism in 1989 that took with it the Soviet Union eliminated the evil empire against which the United States had directed its energy and its treasure for forty years. Almost overnight Americans who knew no other way to look at the world except in terms of certain right and absolute wrong were cut adrift in a sea of ambiguities. Psychologically needing a new villainous enemy to engage their nation's moral energies, the attention of Americans focused on Iran, and then in 1990, on Iraq. Following the neutering of Saddam Hussein, it returned to Iran and the ideology of revolutionary Islam.

American anxiety produced by what is imprecisely but viscerally termed "Islamic fundamentalism" is nothing new. The West has always been disquieted by the passion of Islam. But not since the Crusades has the Christian West been so frightened by a challenge that circumvents political and military might to strike at Western civilization itself. For resurgent Islam not only denounces what it sees as economic and cultural imperialism promoted by the West but condemns the West's whole way of life.

The very term "Islamic fundamentalism" was given common coinage at the zenith of the Iranian revolution. Since then it has grabbed and held an American public emotionally scarred by military casualties and civilian hostages in Lebanon; violence inflicted against Westerners by Islamic militants in Algeria and Egypt; fear engendered by the shadowy group that detonated a bomb in New York's World Trade Center; and anger roused by the endless slogans of Islamic zealots that damn the West. Regardless of the range of grievances and geography of militant Islamic groups, the American mind sees the Islamic Republic of Iran as the font of Islamic extremism.

Into American fears of resurgent Islam led by a militant Iran, American allies pour their vested interests. Confronting internal political opposition voicing the call of Islam and needing to justify in an era of shrinking U.S. budgets the $5 billion in American aid that they share each year, Israel and Egypt have taken the forward position in vilifying the Islamic Republic. Dependent on American support to shore up their shaky regimes, Saudi Arabia's House of Saud and the governments of several other states in the churning Muslim world have joined the chorus of alarm. Together they have conjured the fear-inspiring image of revolutionary Iran marching at the head of an army of a hundred million Muslims screaming for the destruction of the West.

Together the American need for a clearly defined enemy, the warnings of Israel and other self-interested nations about imminent peril posed by the Islamic Republic, and the actions and rhetoric of revolutionary Islam itself, bolstered an administration that came to office determined to increase American pressure on the Islamic Republic of Iran. While the director of the CIA, James Woolsey, warned that Iran sought to do no less than dominate its neighbors and project its influence across the Middle East, the administration shaped its Middle East policy around something called "dual containment." Naming the mullahs of the Islamic Republic along with Saddam Hussein as dire threats to world peace and Western interests, the United States announced it would vigorously pursue the political and economic isolation of both Iran and Iraq. This quarantine of each country would continue until behavior judged unacceptable to the United States changed. Unable to surrender to American conditions for dialogue without rousing their own hard-liners, Rafsanjani and the pragmatists of the Islamic Republic watched the door through which they planned to escape Iran's economic crisis close.

The Clinton administration has marched on. In pursuit of the Iranian component of dual containment, the administration continues to refuse to release Iran's remaining assets frozen in 1979. It has increased funding to the Central Intelligence Agency's efforts in the Gulf, igniting Iranian memories of 1953. It attempts and frequently succeeds in applying the same pressures imposed by preceding administrations to bottle up loans to Iran from multinational institutions like the World Bank and the International Monetary Fund. Yet in the first three years of Bill Clinton's presidency, Iranian behavior refused to bend to American perceptions and demands.

Despite urging from Europe that the diplomatic climate between Iran and the West can open up only when the death edict on Salman Rushdie is lifted, the Islamic Republic continues to insist that it cannot, and will not, contravene what is a religious ruling issued by Ayatollah Khomeini. Nor is Iran willing to end its role as the leader of the opposition to the Middle East peace process between Israel and its Arab neighbors that the United States so painstakingly tends.

At the same time, the Islamic Republic stands charged of fomenting Islamic revolution from North Africa, through the Middle East, and on into Southwest Asia. In the absence of any proof of either official sponsorship or sanction, Iran's accusers link the Islamic Republic to militant Islamic groups in Algeria, Egypt, Jordan, Lebanon, Tunisia, Gaza, and the West Bank. Several carry the despised tag of terrorist. Consistently denying any government policy that supports export of the revolution by any means other than ideological dissemination, President Rafsanjani has failed to preclude the very real possibility that Iranian aid does flow to these same groups by way of zealous clerics who command their own networks and sources of funding.

What has proved measurable for an aroused West is Iran's continuing military buildup. In a campaign for arms that has grabbed the attention of not only the United States but Iran's neighbors in the Gulf, the Islamic Republic is gathering missles and submarines from China, North Korea, and Russia. It culls the black markets of Central Asia and international arms dealers for spare parts and secondhand weapons to fill the Islamic Republic's arsenal depleted by the war with Iraq. Some of these arms along with contingents of troops have taken up places on the islands of Abu Musa and the two Tunbs at the entrance of the Strait of Hormuz through which 20 percent of the world's oil requirement must pass. Western angst refuses to be calmed by the fact that neither the Iranian deployment on these islands nor Iran's antiquated submarines can actually maintain a blockade of the Strait. Western anxiety also resists the solid argument that Iran, dependent on free navigation to export oil and import food and capital, would commit economic suicide by shutting the waterway. Yet while lacking the ability and the intention to close the Strait of Hormuz, the men in charge of revolutionary Iran nonetheless realize that in escalating their country's military presence at the mouth of the strait Iran is positioned to inflict temporary but severe pain on an American, Iraqi, or Israeli adversary that might attack the Islamic Republic.

Threats of a preemptive military strike came from Israel in early 1995 when alarm bells rang over Iran's apparent drive for membership in the elite nuclear club. From Russia, Pakistan, China, the former Soviet republics of Ukraine, Kazakhstan, Turkmenistan, and Azerbaijan as well as from scattered private companies of Europe, Iran appeared to be assembling the pieces of technology required by nuclear weapons. Further evidence, rumor, and innuendo put Iranian and foreign scientists recruited from the former Soviet Union and Pakistan in Iranian laboratories. At Bushehr on the hot, humid southern coast of Iran, the nuclear power plant begun by Muhammad Reza Shah stirred to life as Iran declared its intention to produce nuclear power. As a consequence, all of the fears and dire predictions raised by the Clinton administration and the accompanying voices of self-interest sounding from Israel and the Arab Middle East seemed to be materializing. Consequently in April, 1995 following the conclusion of a contract between Conoco Oil Company and the Islamic Republic to develop a new oil field in the Persian Gulf, the administration slapped an embargo on trade between the United States and Iran. Briefing reporters after the announcement, Warren Christopher called America's allies to join the embargo. Branding the Islamic Republic an "outlaw state" that cannot be permitted to function in the international community of trade and diplomacy, the secretary declared, "No other regime employs terror more systematically as an instrument of national policy—to destroy the [Middle East] peace process, to intimidate its neighbors and to eliminate its political opponents."[1]

To the detriment of both parties, the United States demonization of Iran is mirrored in the Islamic Republic's demonization of America. For the most political of reasons, hostility to the United States is woven into the very mythology of the revolution. It was the American link with Muhammad Reza Shah that fed the nationalism attending the destruction of the Pahlavi dynasty. The humiliation of the American giant in the hostage crisis of 1979 won popular support for the Islamic Republic. U.S. complicity with Iraq helped provide the emotion and the masses necessary to sustain the Iran-Iraq war. And now the United States serves a regime mired in economic chaos as the foreign conspirator plotting the destruction of Iran. Over the years, the Islamic Republic has invested so much time and energy sustaining a revolutionary mythology centered on confrontation with the United States that the regime can neither psychologically nor politically give up the Great Satan.

In this environment of mutual recrimination, the United States and the Islamic Republic face each other over a cauldron filled with experience and perception. Iran sees containment, cultural repression, and threats against the very survival of the revolution. The Clinton administration sees a living menace, a terrorist state that if left to its own devices will someday use nuclear weapons to bully its neighbors, subvert Israel, and dominate oil transport routes essential to global commerce.

Beyond imagery and rhetoric, what are the realities of Iranian behavior? Particularly since the Gulf War, the pragmatists within the Islamic Republic have endeavored to end the isolation imposed on the nation by revolutionary fervor. With both successes and failures, the Islamic Republic toils to improve relations with its Arab neighbors on the other side of the Persian Gulf. Emissaries of the Islamic Republic fan out across Central Asia carrying the message of cooperation and mutual interest. The Karun River project on the border with Saddam Hussein's Iraq remains a highly prized goal despite the bitter legacy of the Iran-Iraq war. The permanent mission of the Islamic Republic of Iran to the United Nations actively participates in the affairs of the U.N. And Iran continues to be a signatory to the Nuclear Nonproliferation Treaty, allowing international inspectors access to Iranian nuclear facilities. In essence, the pragmatists of the Islamic Republic show every evidence of trading confrontation for cooperation for one reason—economic survival. But they do so in an atmosphere charged with emotion and in a pattern of national behavior etched with destruction. For the history of Iranian foreign policy demonstrates time and again that when Iran feels truly threatened it pursues power unrealistic to conditions through means inappropriate to its goals.

Currently, Iran feels gravely threatened. The Islamic Republic sees itself surrounded by dire threats to its security. Saddam Hussein's Iraq, beaten but not vanquished, crouches on Iran's western border. Saudi Arabia, still hostile to the Iranian revolution and armed to the teeth with American weapons, lies just across the Persian Gulf. To the north, the Central Asian republics barely contain the turmoil that has swirled out of the collapse of the Soviet Union. To the east, the shambles of Afghanistan appear forever violent while Pakistan and India possess nuclear capability. Back in the Persian Gulf, the United States, the avowed enemy of the Islamic Republic, maintains nineteen warships, two hundred aircraft carrying sophisticated technology of destruction, and twenty thousand seamen and airmen.

But it is not only security Iran feels it is denied. In its relations with other countries, the Islamic Republic wants what every Iranian government has wanted—respect. To Westerners, the Iranian's desire for protection and stability is more easily understood than their demand for honor. Yet with a passionate pride that resides in the uniqueness of their culture, the Iranians of the Islamic Republic, like the Iranians of Pahlavi Iran, desperately want recognition as an old, cultured civilization deserving of respect and position among the nations of the world. On one level, this demand for a role in international affairs in line with its perception of itself explains why the Islamic Republic propagates its revolution abroad, tries to muscle into the diplomatic arena of the Middle East through rhetorical opposition to the Arab-Israeli peace process, and rearms and explores the nuclear option in an atmosphere of poisonous rhetoric that masks the insecurities of an immensely proud nation. There are those who forcefully argue that once Iran achieves a place at the table of nations, the need to prove its worth diminishes. But the Clinton administration refuses to listen.

Once a young, brash America seemed to understand old, complex Iran. When it established diplomatic relations with Persia in 1882, the United States listed as one justification for its decision to engage in diplomatic intercourse the fact that Iran represented "the oldest government in the world."[2] But since 1979, the United States has chosen to isolate Iran in a chamber of containment. The irony is that containment is isolating the United States rather than Iran. After calling its allies to the embargo imposed by the Clinton administration in early 1995, the United States finds itself alone. America's European allies refuse to cooperate. Japan continues to purchase four hundred thousand barrels of oil a day from the Islamic Republic. Economically strapped Russia bobbed and weaved before announcing in the spring of 1995 that it would go ahead with the sale of nuclear reactors to Iran. Even South Africa has defied American displeasure to trade with the Islamic Republic of Iran. Meanwhile it seems every country except the United States and Israel is tilling the Iranian market, allowing Iran to escape the full brunt of the embargo. Although it has paid a price in massive foreign debt, the Islamic Republic has been able to rebuild war-damaged areas and launch economic development projects with loans and investments by friend and allies of the United States who see their interests served through engagement with the Islamic Republic.

The deep cleavage lying between the United States on one side and most of the rest of the world on the other results from differing opinions about the political possibilities present in revolutionary Iran. The Europeans, the Japanese, and others judge that, for the foreseeable future, there are only two viable options on the Iranian political spectrum—the pragmatists led by Hashemi Rafsanjani and the hard-line disciples of Ayatollah Khomeini's rigid ideology of militant Islam. The West's interests obviously lie with the pragmatists and the promise of a moderating revolution. But the pragmatists can win only by improving the economy. That requires that Rafsanjani and company break Iran out of the diplomatic and economic isolation surrounding it. Without that breakthrough, Iran falls to the hard-liners. Under their control, the Islamic Republic either shifts back to the wrath and the zeal of the early 1980s or sinks toward anarchy produced by a government that can claim little authority. Neither of these dark scenarios provides either stability or a measure of security for American interests in the vulnerable Persian Gulf. That leaves the United States and other nations with high stakes in the Gulf the delicate and demanding task of leading the Islamic Republic along the path of moderation that can come only with improvements in the economy and incorporation into the world community.

For forty plus years, the United States contained the Soviet Union as it now attempts to contain Iran. But when Mikhail Gorbachev's policy of openness birthed the term *perestroika*, the United States began to engage the Soviet Union and then the Russian federation. But the Clinton administration as the Bush administration before it has refused to do the same with Iran. In a repeating pattern established when Iran accepted the cease-fire with Iraq in 1988, the United States has closed its eyes to the changed circumstances created by the death of Ayatollah Khomeini and the ascendancy of President Hashemi Rafsanjani. Since his election in 1989, Rafsanjani has clearly pursued policies geared to the creation of an open-market economy, the alleviation of deep-rooted social and political problems blocking development, and the integration of Iran into the world community. But while fear that the ultra-nationalists will rise to power in Russia drives, in part, the American partnership with its former adversary, a similar threat that Islamic radicals will gain control of Iran in the parliamentary and presidential elections of 1996 and 1997 has yet to push the U.S. toward a policy of reconciliation with the pragmatists of the Islamic Republic. Nor is there any apparent recognition that simply and quietly backing away from the containment policy is more likely to serve the United States' enlightened self interest far more than the ever-escalating confrontation that has so far proved counterproductive. Instead the Clinton foreign policy team holds tight to containment that threatens to accomplish exactly what the administration wants the least—an even more bellicose Iran.

It has been almost two decades since Muhammad Reza Shah departed Iran, taking the American position on the eastern side of the Persian Gulf with him. Yet in all those years, the United States has never seriously grappled with the issues of Iranian culture that might explain Iranian behavior. Nor has it considered any policy toward the Islamic Republic beyond confrontation. As a result, the United States's rejection of Iran's claim to security, respect, and a place at the table of nations fires the Iranians' potent nationalism and stokes their obsession with conspiracy.

Precipitated by centuries of intrigue in which the weak have sought protection from the strong, nothing happens in Iran that Iranians do not somehow perceive as a conspiracy against themselves and their nation. Precisely because they are a people who carry the burdens of political, economic, and cultural domination the Iranians bitterly feel they were betrayed by the British and Russian conspiracy to dismantle the Constitutional Revolution of 1905–11, the U.S.-sponsored countercoup that restored Muhammad Reza Shah to his throne after he fled a nationalist coup in 1953, and the CIA and Israel's Mossad who trained much of SAVAK, the Shah's discredited security force that kept the political opposition in line. Now in Iranian eyes, Iran is being betrayed again by an American government conspiring to destroy the Islamic Republic. Reality gives substance to the imagery. The Islamic Republic carries bitter memories of United States actions in the Iran-Iraq War that crippled Iran's navy, destroyed Iranian offshore oil installations, and downed an Iranian civilian aircraft. And today Iran suffers not only the American quarantine but the indignity of the label "terrorist" applied most forcefully by the United States. This feeling of victimization that burrows in the mind of every Iranian trips the powerful images in the Iranians' collective psyche—courage against injustice, martyrdom in service of the will to survive. As a result, the United States policy of containment contravenes its whole reason for being by serving the revolutionary government. For it functions as the foil for the old Iranian habit of exploiting the foreigner to escape the problems of domestic society. In this century, Muhammad Reza Shah used his American partnership to escape the ideological divisions and deep structural flaws in Iranian society. Now the mullahs of the Islamic Republic are feeding and exploiting anti-American sentiments toward the same end. It works because the Islamic Republic that has failed at so much claims the emotional call to Iranian nationalism as its one great achievement. The revolutionary government has given Iran a sense of independence by refusing to bow to external pressures. Thus in spite of the Iranians' displeasure, even despair, with the ideology, administration, and repression of the Islamic Republic, Iranian nationalism holds the people to the regime. Thus regardless of what the Clinton administration's foreign policymakers regard as legitimate concerns addressed by legitimate means, the Iranians see in the United States's much touted containment policy invasion by quarantine, assault on national independence, and conspiracy to destroy Iran. It all adds up in the Iranian mind to a dire threat to national survival.

Before dragging the United States further down the path of failed policy, the Clinton administration needs to heed Robert McNamara's advice about understanding the adversary. On the twentieth anniversary of the fall of Saigon, McNamara wrote a book on the Vietnam War that is more than history. The former secretary of defense to John F. Kennedy and Lyndon B. Johnson verbalized the awful truth that American policymakers over the decade of the Vietnam tragedy overestimated the ultimate goals of the enemy and misunderstood the nature of its adversaries. The same charge can be laid on the current Clinton administration. But this time the subject of American misconceptions is Iran. While the mistakes of the Vietnam era damaged the social contract between the United States government and the American people, the wounds inflicted by the conflict pierced the spirit more than the body. But the miscalculations on Iran threaten the Persian Gulf, the wellspring of Western industrial might. And this time the enemy exaggerated by American perception is not a peasant army. It is a nation occupying the western side of the Persian Gulf reaching for nuclear weapons.

As happened in Vietnam, the United States is in danger of creating a monster from an adversary. Isolation to force Iran to alter its behavior in the murky realm of politicized Islam and to renounce nuclear armament fails both to evaluate realistically the threat of the Islamic Republic or to understand the Iranian people. Because Iran is a separate culture, religiously heretical to many Muslims among Islam's overwhelmingly dominant Sunni sect, the Islamic Republic might channel aid to political groups, but it cannot lead a unified movement of militant Islam against the West even if it wanted to. And while the United States sees Iran's occupation of the islands at the entrance to the Strait of Hormuz and its nuclear program as offensive, the Iranians see it as a defensive response to profound fears of invasion from forces stronger than themselves. The diplomatic and economic isolation of Iran that the United States continues to so doggedly pursue even against the collective will of its European allies only exacerbates these emotions and perceptions. Thus as the mistakes of the Kennedy and Johnson administrations led America into a wrenching war, the mistakes of the Clinton administration are shaping another disaster for American foreign policy. This time the theater of that calamity is not the jungles of Southeast Asia but the strategically vital Persian Gulf.

Endnotes

1. An anthropological mystery beyond speaking a dialect of Persian, the Kurds regard themselves as an ancient Aryan people whose bloodlines remain unsullied by the generous mixing of foreign blood that has taken place among some of Iran's other ethnic groups. Although more Kurds are Sunni rather than Shia Muslims, they dismiss religion as inconsequential to the central issue of their existence—Kurdish nationalism. Like the Kurds, the Azerbaijanis possess their own distinct identity. Although they push frequently and fervently for the right to speak their own language, run their own schools, and command a level of autonomy in their own affairs, they are more integrated into Iranian culture, economics, and political life than the Kurds.

2. According to the Iranian government, there are currently 1.2 million people in Iran who live a nomadic life. But the number of settled people who still identify themselves by tribal affiliation is several times higher.

3. Most Iranian Jews speak Farsi, adhere to Persian culture more than Jewish culture, and live scattered within the general population. Generally, they do not share the passionate attachment to Israel which characterizes many Jewish groups.

CHAPTER 1 THE GLORY OF PERSIA

1. Maneckji Nusservanji Dhalla, *Zoroastrian Civilization: From the Earliest Times to the Downfall of the Last Zoroastrian Empire 651 A.D.* (New York: Oxford University Press, 1922), 33.
2. Clive Irving, *Crossroads of Civilization: 3,000 Years of Persian History* (New York: Barnes and Noble Books, 1979), 19.
3. *Encyclopaedia of Religion and Ethics* quoted in Adda B. Bozeman, *Politics and Culture in International History* (Princeton, N.J.: Princeton University Press, 1960), 46.
4. Words from a Zoroastrian ceremony.
5. Clive Irving, *Crossroads of Civilization*, 76.
6. Esther 1:4.

CHAPTER 2 THE INVASION OF ISLAM

1. Koran, Sura 49:10.
2. Richard N. Frye, *The Heritage of Iran* (London: Cambridge University Press, 1975), 214.
3. Jalal Al-e Ahmad quoted in Eli Kedourie and Sylvia G. Haim, eds., *Towards a Modern Iran: Studies in Thought, Politics, and Society* (London: Frank Cass, 1980), 142.
4. Quoted in Manocher Dorraj, *From Zarathustra to Khomeini: Populism and Dissent in Iran* (Boulder, Colo.: Lynne Rienner Publishers, 1990), 50.
5. Abdulaziz Abdulhussein Sachedina, *Islamic Messianism: The Idea of Mahdi in Twelver Shiism* (Albany: State University of New York Press, 1981), 6–7.
6. Quoted in Manocher Dorraj, *From Zarathustra to Khomeini: Populism and Dissent in Iran*, 66.
7. Quoted in Donald N. Wilber, *Iran: Past and Present* (Princeton, N.J.: Princeton University Press, 1958), 87.
8. Iranian poet quoted in Clive Irving, *Crossroads of Civilization*, 104.
9. Michael C. Hillman, *Iranian Culture: A Persianist View* (New York: University Press of America, 1990), 42.

CHAPTER 3 GOD AND STATE

1. Jalal Al-e Ahmad, *Plagued by the West (Gharbzadegi)* (Delmar, N.Y.: Caravan Books, 1982), 13.
2. Quoted in Clive Irving, *Crossroads of Civilization*, 123.
3. Quoted in A. Bausani, "Religion in the Saljuq Period." J. A. Boyle, ed., *Cambridge History of Iran*, vol. 5 (London: Cambridge University Press, 1968), 538.
4. David Morgan, *Medieval Persia 1040–1797* (London: Longman Publishers, 1988), 79.
5. Ibid.
6. Jalaladdin Rumi, *Selected Poems from the Divani Shamsi Tabriz*, ed. and trans. Reynold A. Nicholson (Cambridge: Cambridge University Press, 1977), 128.
7. *Collected Poems of Muhammad Hafez Shirazi*, ed. Muhammad Qazvine and Qasem Ghani (Washington, D.C.: Foundation for Iranian Studies, 1986), 43.
8. Jalaladdin Rumi, *Selected Poems from the Divani Shamsi Tabriz*, 124.
9. Marshal G. S. Hodgson, *The Venture of Islam: Conscience and History in World Civilization,* vol. 1 (Chicago: University of Chicago Press, 1977) 377–8.
10. Michael M. Mazzaoui, *The Origins of the Safavids: Shiism, Sufism, and the Gulat* (Wiesbaden: Fraz Steiner Verlag GMBH, 1972), 72–73.
11. Quoted in Roger Savory, *Iran Under the Safavids* (Cambridge: Cambridge University Press, 1980), 18.
12. Ibid., 23.
13. Quoted in Roy Mottahedeh, *The Mantle of the Prophet: Religion and Politics in Iran* (New York: Pantheon Books, 1985), 173.
14. Quoted in Roger Savory, *Iran Under the Safavids*, 21.
15. Hasan Rumlu quoted in I. P. Petrushevsky, *Islam in Iran* (Albany: State University of New York Press, 1985), 321.
16. Quoted in Roy Mattahedeh, *The Mantle of the Prophet*, 171.
17. Quoted in Clive Irving, *Crossroads of Civilization*, 141.
18. Ibid., 157.
19. Pietro Della Valle, *The Pilgrim: The Travels of Pietro Della Valle*, trans. George Bull (London: Hutchinson and Company, 1989), 118–19.
20. Ibid., 119.
21. Vita Sackville-West, *Passenger to Tehran* (New York: Moyer Bell, 1990).

CHAPTER 4 THE FACES OF AUTHORITY: FATHER, KING, AND CLERIC

1. Quoted by William H. Forbis, *Fall of the Peacock Throne: The Story of Iran* (New York: Harper and Row, 1980), 23.
2. Pietro Della Valle, *The Pilgrim: The Travels of Pietro Della Valle,* 170–1.
3. Ann K. S. Lambton, *Qajar Persia* (Austin: University of Texas Press, 1987), 93.
4. Koran, Sura 53: 39.
5. Koran, Sura 9: 35.
6. James A. Bill and Carl Leiden, *Politics in the Middle East* (Boston: Little, Brown, and Co., 1979), 156.
7. Quoted in Charles J. Adams, ed., *Iranian Civilization and Culture: Essays in Honor of the 2500th Anniversary of the Founding of the Persian Empire* (Montreal: McGill University Institute of Islamic Studies, 1972), 85.
8. Ann K. S. Lambton, *Qajar Persia,* 195.
9. Abdulaziz Abdulhussein Sachedina, "Activist Shi'ism in Iran, Iraq, and Lebanon," in *Fundamentalisms Observed,* ed. Martin E. Marty and R. Scott Appleby (Chicago: University of Chicago Press, 1991), 425.
10. Koran, Sura 2:115.
11. Roy Mottahedeh, *The Mantle of the Prophet: Religion and Politics in Iran,* 144.
12. Abdulaziz Abdulhussein Sachedina, *The Just Ruler in Shiite Islam: The Comprehensive Authority of the Jurist in Imamite Jurisprudence* (New York: Oxford University Press, 1988), 29.
13. Quoted in Robin Wright, "Teheran Summer," *New Yorker,* September 5, 1988, 72.

CHAPTER 5 KING AND NATION: IRAN'S FIRST REVOLUTION

1. Quoted in Richard N. Frye, *Persia* (New York: Schocken Books, 1960), 67.
2. Quoted in Ervand Abrahamin, "Oriental Despotism: The Case of Qajar Iran," *International Journal of Middle East Studies* (January 1974): 11.
3. Hamid Algar, *Islam and Revolution: Religion and State in Iran 1785–1906* (Berkeley, Calif.: University of California Press, 1969), 148.
4. Quoted in Abbas Amanat, "The Downfall of Mirza Taqi Khan Amir

Kabir and the Problem of Ministerial Authority in Qajar Iran," *International Journal of Middle East Studies* (vol. 23, no. 4 November 1991): 588.

5. Quoted in Mangol Bayat, *Iran's First Revolution: Shi'ism and the Constitutional Revolution of 1905–6* (New York: Oxford University Press, 1991), 67.

6. Ann K. S. Lambton, *Qajar Persia*, 248.

7. Quoted in Mohsen M. Milani, "Shiism and the State in the Constitution of the Islamic Republic of Iran," in *Iran: Political Culture in the Islamic Republic*, ed. Samih K. Farsoun and Mehrdad Mashayekhi (London: Routledge and Company, 1992), 135.

8. Mangol Bayat, *Iran's First Revolution*, 127.

9. Edward G. Browne, *The Persian Revolution of 1905–1909* (Cambridge: Cambridge University Press, 1910), 118.

10. Quoted in Edward G. Browne, *The Persian Revolution of 1905–1909*, 120.

11. W. Morgan Shuster, *The Strangling of Persia: Story of the European Diplomacy and Oriental Intrigue that Resulted in the Denationalization of Twelve Million Mohammedans* (New York: The Century Co., 1912), xxi.

12. Article II of the supplement to the 1906 Iranian constitution.

13. Edward G. Browne, *The Persian Revolution of 1905–1909*, 444.

CHAPTER 6 REZA SHAH: TO THE GLORY OF IRAN

1. Kenneth Rose, *Superior Person: A Portrait of Curzon and His Circle in Later Victorian England* (New York: Weybright and Talley, 1969), 229.

2. Quoted in Mangol Bayat, *Iran's First Revolution: Shi'ism and the Constitutional Revolution of 1905–6*, 244.

3. *Spectator*, December 9, 1911, 999.

4. W. Morgan Shuster, *The Strangling of Persia*, 182.

5. Ibid., 331.

6. Quoted in L. P. Elwell-Sutton, "Reza Shah the Great: Founder of the Pahlavi Dynasty," in *Iran Under the Pahlavis*, ed. George Lenczowski (Stanford: Hoover Institute Press, 1978), 18.

7. Ibid., 24.

8. Quoted in *Atlantic Monthly* (October 1926): 553.

9. Ibid.

10. Quoted in L. P. Elwell-Sutton, "Reza Shah the Great," 34.

11. Quoted in Roy Mottahedeh, *The Mantle of the Prophet*, 64.

12. Quoted in William Shawcross, *The Shah's Last Ride: The Fate of an Ally* (New York: Simon and Schuster, 1988), 59.
13. Harold Nicholson, "Marginal Comment," *Spectator*, September 5, 1941, 234.

CHAPTER 7 THE SHAH AND THE PRIME MINISTER:
IRAN'S SECOND REVOLUTION

1. *Time*, September 29, 1941, 24.
2. Soraya, *The Autobiography of Her Imperial Highness* (Garden City, N.Y.: Doubleday and Co., 1964), 64.
3. Quoted in James A. Bill, *The Eagle and the Lion: The Tragedy of American-Iranian Relations* (New Haven: Yale University Press, 1988), 59.
4. Quoted in Richard Cottam, *Nationalism in Iran* (Pittsburgh: University of Pittsburgh Press, 1979), 152.
5. William Shawcross, *The Shah's Last Ride: The Fate of an Ally*, 64.
6. Quoted in William H. Forbis, *Fall of the Peacock Throne: The Story of Iran* (New York: Harper and Row, 1980), 57.
7. Roy Mottahedeh, *The Mantle of the Prophet*, 133.

CHAPTER 8 THE SHAH AND THE AYATOLLAH: PERSIA AND ISLAM

1. Roy Mottahedeh, *The Mantle of the Prophet*, 294.
2. Jalal Al-e Ahmad, *Gharbzadegi*, 33.
3. Ibid., 67.
4. Quoted in R. K. Ramazani, "Intellectual Trends in the Politics and History of the Musaddiq Era," in *Musaddiq, Iranian Nationalism and Oil*, ed. James A. Bill and William Roger Louis (London: J. B. Tauris, 1988), 318.
5. *Newsweek*, March 28, 1960, 39.
6. Harold H. Martin, "Iran's Good King," *Saturday Evening Post*, April 14, 1962, 18.
7. Quoted in James A. Bill, *The Eagle and the Lion*, 146–7.
8. Quoted in R. K. Ramazani, "Who Lost America? The Case of Iran," *Middle East Journal*, vol. 36, no. 1 (Winter 1982): 16.
9. Quoted in Robin Wright, *In the Name of God: The Khomeini Decade* (New York: Simon and Schuster, 1989), 50.
10. Ibid.

11. Ibid., 51.

12. Reza M. Behnam, *Cultural Foundations of Iranian Politics* (Salt Lake City: University of Utah Press, 1986), 76.

13. Quoted in William Shawcross, *The Shah's Last Ride: The Fate of an Ally*, 115.

14. *Time*, June 14, 1963, 35.

15. Interview with Sandra Mackey, June 15, 1992, McLean, Virginia.

16. Quoted in L. P. Elwell-Sutton, "Reza Shah the Great," 28.

17. Jalal Al-e Ahmad, *Gharbzadegi*, 108.

18. Quoted in Hamid Dabashi, *Theology of Discontent: The Ideological Foundation of the Islamic Revolution in Iran* (New York: New York University Press, 1993), 453.

19. Roger Savory writing in *Iranian Civilization and Culture: Essays in Honour of the 2500th Anniversary of the Founding of the Persian Empire*, ed. Charles J. Adams (Montreal: McGill University Institute of Islamic Studies, 1972), 78.

20. Quoted in James A. Bill, *The Eagle and the Lion*, 184.

21. Quoted in William Shawcross, *The Shah's Last Ride: The Fate of an Ally*, 116.

22. Ibid.

CHAPTER 9 THE PERSIAN EMPIRE OF MUHAMMAD REZA SHAH

1. *Time*, March 26, 1951, 31.

2. "Joint Chiefs of Staff Intelligence Committee Memorandum for the Joint Strategic Plans Committee and the Joint Logistic Plans Committee," Washington, D.C. April 13, 1955, 273.

3. Quoted in William Shawcross, *The Shah's Last Ride: The Fate of an Ally*, 83.

4. Harold H. Martin, "Iran's Good King," *Saturday Evening Post*, April 14, 1962, 18.

5. *Life*, May 31, 1963, 54.

6. Quoted in Roy Mottahedeh, *The Mantle of the Prophet: Religion and Politics in Iran*, 245–6.

7. *Newsweek*, January 24, 1977, 48.

8. Quoted in L. P. Elwell-Sutton, "Nationalism and Neutralism in Iran," *Middle East Journal* (Winter 1958): 29.

9. Betty Friedan, "Coming Out of the Veil," *Ladies Home Journal*, June 1975, 98.

10. Sattareh Farman Farmaian, *Daughter of Persia: A Woman's Journey*

from Her Father's Harem Through the Islamic Revolution (New York: Crown Publishers, 1992), 274.

11. Reza Baraheni, "America in Cahoots with the Shah," *Nation*, March 12, 1977, 308.

12. R. K. Ramazani, "Who Lost America? The Case of Iran," 7.

13. Muhammad Reza Shah quoted in Oriana Fallaci, *Interview with History* (Boston: Houghton Mifflin Company, 1976), 267.

14. Ibid., 268.

15. Reinhard M. Sorge, "Iran Ancient and Ageless," *Saturday Evening Post* (Fall 1971), 47.

16. *Time*, September 18, 1978, p. 32.

17. Ahmad Shamlu, "Anthem for the Bright Man Who Went into Shadows," translated by Esmail Khoi, *Major Voices in Contemporary Persian Literature* (Austin, Texas: Literature East and West, 1976), 187–188.

18. Muhammad Reza Shah quoted in Betty Friedan, "Coming Out of the Veil," 102.

19. Quoted in Hamid Dabashi, *The Theology of Discontent*, 112.

20. Ibid., 179.

21. *Newsweek*, November 28, 1977, 65.

22. Quoted in James A. Bill, *The Eagle and the Lion*, 233.

CHAPTER 10 THE DOUBLE REVOLUTION

1. Quoted in Hamid Dabashi, *Theology of Discontent*, 431.

2. Ibid.

3. Quoted in Fouad Ajami, *The Vanished Imam: Musa al Sadr and the Shia of Lebanon* (Ithaca: Cornell University Press, 1986), 25.

4. Cheryl Benard, "Islam and Women: Some Reflections on the Experience of Iran," *Journal of South Asian and Middle Eastern Studies*, vol. IV, no. 2 (Winter 1980): 25.

5. Sijavash Kasrai quoted in Ahmad Karmim-Hakkak, "Revolutionary Posturing: Iranian Writers and the Iranian Revolution of 1979," *International Journal of Middle East Studies*, vol. 23, no. 4 (November 1991): 515.

6. William H. Sullivan, *Mission to Iran* (New York: W. W. Norton, 1981), 57.

7. *Newsweek*, January 29, 1979, 38.

8. *Newsweek*, February 12, 1979, 44.

9. Quoted in Shaul Bakhash, *The Reign of the Ayatollahs: Iran and the Islamic Revolution*, rev. ed. (New York: Basic Books, 1990), 39.

10. Hamid Dabashi, *Theology of Discontent*, 476–7.

11. 1980 Amnesty International Report, p. 52.

12. *Newsweek*, April 30, 1979, 47.

13. Ibid.

15. Quoted in Shaul Bakhash, *The Reign of the Ayatollahs: Iran and the Islamic Revolution*, 78.

16. R. K. Ramazani, "Who Lost America? The Case of Iran," 21.

17. Shahram Chubin and Charles Tripp, *Iran and Iraq at War* (Boulder, Colo.: Westview Press, 1988), 37.

18. Quoted in Shaul Bakhash, *The Reign of the Ayatollahs*, 156.

CHAPTER 11 THE INTERNAL AND EXTERNAL:
WARS FOR THE IRANIAN NATION

1. *Time*, July 13, 1981, 30.

2. *Newsweek*, September 7, 1981, 33.

3. Quoted in R. K. Ramazani, "Iran's Export of the Revolution: Its Politics, Ends and Means," *Journal of South Asian and Middle Eastern Studies*, vol. 13, nos. 1 and 2 (Fall/Winter 1989): 79.

4. The Constitution of the Islamic Republic of Iran, Chapter I, Article 11.

5. Foreign Broadcast Information Service, October 10, 1982.

6. *Kayhan*, August 24, 1983.

7. *New York Times*, August 4, 1987.

8. Ibid.

9. Quoted in Shahram Chubin and Charles Tripp, *Iran and Iraq at War*, flyleaf.

10. Ibid.

11. Ibid., 164.

12. Quoted in Robin Wright, *In the Name of God: The Khomeini Decade*, 131.

13. Foreign Broadcast Information Service, Near East and South Asia, July 21, 1988.

14. *A Shiite Anthology* (London: Muhammadi Trust of Great Britain and Northern Ireland, 1981), 80.

CHAPTER 12 ISLAMIC GOVERNMENT:
RELIGION, CULTURE, AND POWER

1. John W. Limbert, *Iran: At War with History* (Boulder, Colo.: Westview Press, 1987), 15.
2. BBC Summary of World Broadcasts, February 24, 1989.
3. *Financial Times*, February 9, 1988.
4. Robin Wright, *In the Name of God*, 192.
5. Reuters News Service, February 23, 1989.
6. Quoted in R. K. Ramazani, "Iran's Export of the Revolution: Its Politics, Ends and Means," 91.
7. Ahmad Khomeini's letter, Resalat, cited in Shaul Bakhash, *The Reign of the Ayatollahs: Iran and the Islamic Revolution*, rev. ed. 282.
8. Richard W. Cottam, "Inside Revolutionary Iran," *Middle East Journal*, vol. 43, no. 2 (Spring 1989): 177.

CHAPTER 13 THE ISLAMIC REPUBLIC: THE FAILURE OF JUSTICE

1. *Tehran Times*, June 6, 1993.
2. *New York Times*, April 8, 1991.
3. *Kayhan*, June 3, 1993.
4. *Tehran Times*, June 14, 1993.
5. *Tehran Times*, June 17, 1993.
6. *New York Times*, May 8, 1992.
7. *New York Times*, April 12, 1992.
8. Stanley Cooperman, "Iran's False Front," *Nation* (September 24, 1960): 177.
9. Quoted in Hamid Dabashi, *The Theology of Discontent: The Ideological Foundations of the Islamic Republic*, 459.
10. *New York Times*, December 21, 1994.
11. Eric Rouleau, "The Islamic Republic of Iran: Paradoxes and Contradictions in a Changing Society," *Middle East Insight*, vol. X, no. 5 (1995): 56–57.
12. Recorded by Sandra Mackey at the Conference on the Practical and Theoretical Conduct of the Late Imam Khomeini sponsored by the Women's Organization of the Islamic Republic of Iran, Tehran, Iran, June 2, 1993.

Epilogue

1. *Washington Post*, May 8, 1995.
2. R. K. Ramazani, *The United States and Iran: The Patterns of Influence* (New York: Praeger, 1982), 6.

Selected Bibliography

ABRAHAMIN, ERVAND. "Oriental Despotism: The Case of Qajar Iran." *International Journal of Middle East Studies* 5, no. 1 (January 1974): 3–31.

ADAMS, CHARLES J., ED. *Iranian Civilization and Culture: Essays in Honour of the 2500th Anniversary of the Founding of the Persian Empire*. Montreal: McGill University Institute of Islamic Studies, 1972.

AJAMI, FOUAD. *The Vanished Imam: Musa al Sadr and the Shia of Lebanon*. Ithaca, N.Y.: Cornell University Press, 1986.

AL-E AHMAD, JALAL. *Plaughed by the West (Gharbzadegi)*. Translated by Paul Sprachman. Delmar, N.Y.: Caravan Books, 1982.

ALGAR, HAMID. *Religion and State in Iran, 1785–1906*. Berkeley: University of California Press, 1989.

AMANAT, ABBAS. "The Downfall of Mirza Taqi Khan Amir Kabir and the Problem of Ministerial Authority in Qujar Iran." *International Journal of Middle East Studies* 23, no. 4 (November 1991): 577–99.

ARJOMAND, SAID AMIR. "Introduction: Shi'ism, Authority, and Political Culture." In *Authority and Political Culture in Shi'ism*, edited by S. A. Arjomand. Albany: State University of New York Press, 1988.

BAKHASH, SHAUL. *The Reign of the Ayatollahs: Iran and the Islamic Revolution*. Revised edition. New York: Basic Books, 1990.

———. "The Politics of Land, Law, and Social Justice in Iran." *Middle East Journal* 43, no. 2 (spring 1989): 186–201.

BANUAZIZI, ALI. "Iran's Revolutionary Impasse: Political Factionalism and Societal Resistance." *Middle East Report* 24, no. 6 (November-December 1994): 2–8.

BARAHENI, REZA. "America in Cahoots with the Shah." *The Nation* (March 12, 1977): 307–8.

BAUSANI, A. "Religion in the Saljuq Period." In *Cambridge History of Iran.* Vol. 5. Edited by J. A. Boyle. London: Cambridge University Press, 1968.

BAYAT, MANGOL. *Iran's First Revolution: Shi'ism and the Constitutional Revolution of 1905–6.* New York: Oxford University Press, 1991.

BEEMAN, WILLIAM O. *Language, Status, and Power in Iran.* Bloomington: Indiana University Press, 1986.

BEHNAM, M. REZA. *Cultural Foundations of Iranian Politics.* Salt Lake City: University of Utah Press, 1986.

BENARD, CHERYL. "Islam and Women: Some Reflections on the Experience of Iran." *Journal of South Asian and Middle Eastern Studies* 4, no. 2 (winter 1980): 10–26.

BILL, JAMES A. *The Eagle and the Lion: The Tragedy of American-Iranian Relations.* New Haven, Conn.: Yale University Press, 1988.

———. "Power and Religion in Revolutionary Iran." *Middle East Journal* 36, no. 1 (winter 1982): 22–47.

———. "The Politics of Extremism in Iran." *Current History* 81, no. 1 (January 1982): 9–13.

BILL, JAMES A., AND CARL LEIDEN. *Politics in the Middle East.* Boston: Little, Brown, and Company, 1979.

BONINE, MICHAEL E., AND NIKKI R. KEDDIE, EDS. *Modern Iran: The Dialectics of Continuity and Change.* Albany: State University of New York Press, 1981.

BOZEMAN, ADDA B. *Politics and Culture in International History.* Princeton, N.J.: Princeton University Press, 1960.

BROWNE, EDWARD G. *The Persian Revolution of 1905–1909.* Cambridge: Cambridge University Press, 1910.

BURRELL, R. M. "Ruler and Subject in Iran." *Middle East Studies* 25, no. 2 (April 1989): 253–61.

CHUBIN, SHAHRAM, AND CHARLES TRIPP. *Iran and Iraq at War.* Boulder, Colo.: Westview Press, 1988.

COOPERMAN, STANLEY. "Iran's False Front." *The Nation* (September 24, 1960): 176.

COTTAM, RICHARD W. "Inside Revolutionary Iran." *Middle East Journal* 43, no. 2 (spring 1989): 168–85.

———. *Nationalism in Iran.* Pittsburgh: University of Pittsburgh Press, 1979.

DABASHI, HAMID. *Theology of Discontent: The Ideological Foundations of the Islamic Revolution in Iran.* New York: New York University Press, 1993.

DAVIS, DICK. *Epic and Sedition: The Case of Ferdowsi's Shahnameh.* Fayetteville: University of Arkansas Press, 1992.

DELLA VALLE, PIETRO. *The Pilgrim: The Travels of Pietro Della Valle.* Translated by George Bull. London: Hutchison and Company, 1989.

DHALLA, MANECKJI NUSSERVANJI. *Zoroastrian Civilization: From the Earliest Times to the Downfall of the Last Zoroastrian Empire 651 A.D.* New York: Oxford University Press, 1922.

DURRAJ, MANOCHER. *From Zarathustra to Khomeini: Populism and Dissent in Iran.* Boulder, Colo.: Lynne Rienner Publishers, 1990.

ELWELL-SUTTON, L. P. "Reza Shah the Great: Founder of the Pahlavi Dynasty." In *Iran Under the Pahlavis*, edited by George Lenczowski. 85–127. Stanford: Hoover Institute Press, 1978.

———. "Nationalism and Neutralism in Iran." *Middle East Journal* 12, no. 1 (winter 1958): 20–32.

FALLACI, ORIANA. *Interview with History.* Boston: Houghton Mifflin Company, 1976.

FARMAN FARMAIAN, SATTAREH. *Daughter of Persia: A Woman's Journey from Her Father's Harem through the Islamic Revolution.* New York: Crown Publishers, 1992.

FORBIS, WILLIAM H. *Fall of the Peacock Throne: The Story of Iran.* New York: Harper and Row, 1980.

FRIEDAN, BETTY. "Coming out of the Veil." *Ladies Home Journal* (June 1975): 71+.

FRIEDL, ERIKA. *Women of Deh Koh: Lives in an Iranian Village.* Washington, D.C.: Smithsonian Institution Press, 1989.

FRYE, RICHARD N. *The Heritage of Iran.* London: Cambridge University Press, 1975.

———. *Persia.* New York: Schocken Books, 1960.

HAAS, WILLIAM S. *Iran.* New York: Columbia University Press, 1946.

HASAN, HADI. *A Golden Treasury of Persian Poetry.* Delhi: Ministry of Information, 1966.

HILLMAN, MICHAEL C. *Iranian Culture: A Persianist View.* New York: University Press of America, 1990.

———. *Iranian Society: An Anthology of Writings by Jalal Al-e Ahmad.* Lexington, Ky.: Mazda Publishers, 1982.

HIRO, DILIP. *Iran under the Ayatollahs.* London: Routledge and Kegan Paul, 1985.

HODGSON, MARSHALL G. S. *The Classical Age of Islam.* Volume 1 of *The*

Venture of Islam: Conscience and History in a World Civilization. Chicago: University of Chicago Press, 1977.

————. *The Expansion of Islam in the Middle Periods*. Volume 2 of *The Venture of Islam: Conscience and History in a World Civilization*. Chicago: University of Chicago Press, 1977.

HUNTER, SHIREEN T. *Iran after Khomeini*. New York: Praeger, 1992.

————. "Islam in Power: The Case of Iran." In *The Politics of Islamic Revivalism: Diversity and Unity*, edited by Shireen T. Hunter. Bloomington, Ind.: University of Indiana Press, 1988.

IRVING, CLIVE. *Crossroads of Civilization: 3000 Years of Persian History*. New York: Barnes and Noble Books, 1979.

KARMIN-HAKKAK, AHMAD. "Revolutionary Posturing: Iranian Writers and the Iranian Revolution of 1979." *International Journal of Middle East Studies* 23, no. 4 (November 1991): 507–31.

KEDDIE, NIKKI R. *Roots of Revolution: An Interpretive History of Modern Iran*. New Haven: Yale University Press, 1981.

KEDDIE, NIKKI R., ED. *Saints and Sufis. Muslin Religious Institutions in the Middle East since 1500*. Berkeley: University of California Press, 1972.

KEDDIE, NIKKI R., AND ERIC HOOGLUND, EDS. *The Iranian Revolution and the Islamic Republic*. Syracuse, N.Y.: Syracuse University Press, 1986.

KEDOURIE, ELIE, AND SYLVIA G. HAIM, EDS. *Towards a Modern Iran: Studies in Thought, Politics, and Society*. London: Frank Cass, 1980.

LAMBTON, ANN K. S. *Qajar Persia*. Austin: University of Texas Press, 1987.

LIMBERT, JOHN W. *Iran: At War with History*. Boulder, Colo.: Westview Press, 1987.

MARTIN, HAROLD H. "Iran's Good King." *Saturday Evening Post* (April 14, 1962): 17–25.

MAZZAOUI, MICHEL M. *The Origins of the Safawids: Shiism, Sufism, and the Gulat*. Wiesbaden: Fraz Steiner Verlag GMBH, 1972.

MILANI, MOHSEN M. *The Making of Iran's Islamic Revolution: From Monarchy to Islamic Republic*. Boulder, Colo.: Westview Press, 1988.

————. "Shiism and the State in the Constitution of the Islamic Republic of Iran." In *Iran: Political Culture in the Islamic Republic*, edited by Samih K. Farsoun and Mehrdad Mashayekhi. London: Routledge and Company, 1992.

MILLSPAUGH, ARTHUR C. *Americans in Persia*. Washington, D.C.: The Brookings Institute, 1946.

MORGAN, DAVID. *Medieval Persia 1040–1797.* London: Longman Publishers, 1988.

MOTTAHEDEH, ROY. *The Mantle of the Prophet: Religion and Politics in Iran.* New York: Pantheon Books, 1985.

NICHOLSON, HAROLD. "Marginal Comment." *Spectator* (September 5, 1941): 233–34.

O'DONNELL, TERENCE. *Garden of the Brave in War: Recollections of Iran.* Chicago: University of Chicago Press, 1980.

PETRUSHEVSKY, I. P. *Islam in Iran.* Albany: State University of New York, 1985.

PISCATORI, JAMES. "The Rushdie Affair and the Politics of Ambiguity." *International Affairs* 66, no. 4 (October 1990): 767–89.

RAMAZANI, NESTA. "Women in Iran: The Revolutionary Ebb and Flow." *Middle East Journal* 47, no. 3 (summer 1993): 409–28.

RAMAZANI, R. K. "Iran's Expert of the Revolution: Its Politics, Ends and Means." *Journal of South Asian and Middle Eastern Studies* 13, no. 1 (fall-winter 1989): 69–93.

———. "Intellectual Trends in the Politics and History of the Musaddiq Era." In *Musaddiq, Iranian Nationalism and Oil,* edited by James A. Bill and William Roger Louis. London: J. B. Tauris, 1988.

———. *Revolutionary Iran: Challenge and Response in the Middle East.* Baltimore: The John Hopkins University Press, 1986.

———. "Burying the Hatchet." *Foreign Policy* 50, no.4 (fall 1985): 52–74.

———. "Who Lost America? The Case of Iran." *Middle East Journal.* 36, no. 1 (winter 1982): 5–21.

———. *The United States and Iran: The Patterns of Influence.* New York: Praeger, 1982.

———. *Iran's Foreign Policy 1941–1973: A Study of Foreign Policy in Modernizing Nations.* Charlottesville: University of Virginia Press, 1975.

RAMAZANI, R. K., ED. *Iran's Revolution: The Search for Consensus.* Bloomington, Ind.: Indiana University Press, 1990.

ROEMER, H. R. "The Safavid Period." In *Cambridge History of Iran.* Vol. 6, London: Cambridge University Press, 1986.

ROSE, KENNETH. *Superior Person: A Portrait of Curzon and His Circle in Late Victorian England.* New York: Weybright and Talley, 1969.

ROULEAU, ERIC. "The Islamic Republic of Iran: Paradoxes and Contradictions in a Changing Society." *Middle East Insight* 11, no. 5 (July-August 1995): 54–58.

RUMI, JALALADDIN. *Selected Poems from the Divani Shamsi Tabriz.* Edited and translated by Reynold A. Nicholson. Cambridge: Cambridge University Press, 1977.

SACHEDINA, ABDULAZIZ ABDULHUSSEIN. "Activist Shi'ism in Iran, Iraq, and Lebanon." In *Fundamentalism Observed*, edited by Martin E. Marty and R. Scott Appleby. Chicago: University of Chicago Press, 1991.

―――. *The Just Ruler in Shiite Islam: The Comprehensive Authority of the Jurist in Imamite Jurisprudence*. New York: Oxford University Press, 1988.

―――. *Islamic Messianism: The Idea of Mahdi in Twelver Shiism*. Albany: State University of New York Press, 1981.

SACKVILLE-WEST, VITA. *Passenger of Teheran*. New York: Moyer Bell, 1990.

SALEHI, M. M. *Insurgency through Culture and Religion*. New York: Praeger, 1988.

SAVORY, ROGER. *Iran under the Safavids*. Cambridge: Cambridge University Press, 1980.

SHAMIU, AHMAD. "Anthem for the Bright Man Who Went into Shadows." Translated by Esmail Khoi. In *Major Voices in Contemporary Persian Literature*. Austin, Texas: Literature East and West, 1976.

SHAWCROSS, WILLIAM. *The Shah's Last Ride: The Fate of an Ally*. New York: Simon and Schuster, 1988.

SHIRAZI, MUHAMMAD HAFEZ. *Collected Poems of Muhammad Hafez Shirazi*. Edited by Muhammad Qazvini and Qasem Ghani. Washington, D.C.: Foundation for Iranian Studies, 1986.

SHUSTER, W. MORGAN. *The Strangling of Persia*. New York: The Century Company, 1912.

SIMPSON, JOHN. *Inside Iran: Life under Khomeini's Regime*. New York: St. Martin's Press, 1988.

SORAYA. *The Autobiography of Her Imperial Highness*. Garden City, N.Y.: Doubleday and Company, 1964.

SORGE, REINHARD M. "Iran Ancient and Ageless." *Saturday Evening Post* (fall 1971): 46–47.

SULLIVAN, WILLIAM H. *Mission to Iran*. New York: W. W. Norton, 1981.

STODDARD, PHILIP H., DAVID C. CUTHELL, AND MARGARET W. SULLIVAN, EDS. *Change and the Muslim World*. Syracuse, N.Y.: Syracuse University Press, 1982.

WILBER, DONALD N. *Iran: Past and Present*. Princeton, N.J.: Princeton University Press, 1958.

WRIGHT, ROBIN. "Islam, Democracy, and the West." *Foreign Affairs*. 71, no. 3 (summer 1992): 131–45.

————. *In the Name of God: The Khomeini Decade*. New York: Simon and Schuster, 1989.

ZARRINKUB, ABD AL-HUSAIN. "The Arab Conquest of Iran and Its Aftermath." In *The Cambridge History of Iran*. Vol. 4. London: Cambridge University Press, 1975.

Index

and religious authority combined, 102; and Shariati's opposition to Shah, 264–65; Sufism sect developed, 74–79; Sunni-Shia split, 41, 44–53; and Zoroastrianism, 17*n.. See also* specific concepts and sects

Islamic culture: and Islamic Republic, 335–37, 361–62; need to combine with Persian culture, 377–80; and political control, 374–75; tension with ancient Persian traditions, 5–10; and Western culture, xxii, 135–36

Islamic Empire: Abbasid dynasty, 57–58, 67–68, 107; and Buyid dynasty, 60–61; founded, 41–52; and Ghaznavids dynasty, 61–62; Golden age of, 67; as Ilkhanate, 70–71; and kingship ideal, 68–72; Mongol invasion of, 75–76; Persian break with, 6; and Saffarid dynasty, 61; and Samanid dynasty, 61; Seljuk Turk invasion of, 67–68, 75; and Shia, 6, 107; and Shia-Sunni split, 49–55; Umayyad dynasty, 50–57. See also Persia; Persian culture; Persian Empire

Islamic fundamentalism, fear of, 384

Islamic government or state: and Constitution of 1979, 292–93; *fatva* defining, 349; ideal of, and Islamic Empire, 97–98; Khomeini argues for, 233–34, 237, 286–88; Motahhari argues for, 266; secular revolutionaries vs., 288–300; vote for, 288–89, 296. *See also* Iran, Islamic Republic of

Islamic Jihad, xviii, 315, 315*n.*

Islamic law: and Constitution of 1906, 150–51; and justice, 103; and Mossadeq, 203; Reza Shah reforms, 178–79; Shia vs. Sunni concept of, 115–16. *See also* Sharia

Islamic Left, 303–9

Islamic militants: and export of Iranian revolution, 310–11, 386, 392; West's fear of, xix–xx, 384, 392

Islamic Nations party (Hezb-e-Millat-e-Islami), 230

Islamic Republican party (IRP), 297, 300, 303*n.*, 307, 358; dissolved, 348–49, 359; meeting bombed, 304, 358

Islamic Revolution: export of, 302, 309–16, 325–27, 386; Khomeini argues for, 275; theological debate over, 116. *See also* Revolution of 1979; Iran, Islamic Republic of

Islamic Society, 337

Ismail (successor to imam Jafar al-Sadiq), 77–78

Ismail, Shah of Iran, 81–85, 82*n.*, 124; and kingship ideal, 98–99, 276

Ismail (Turkoman conquerer), 6

Ismailis, or Seveners (Shia sect), 77–78

Israel, 243, 313, 315*n.*, 326, 384, 385, 387

Istakhr (city), 33; siege of, 47

Jafar al-Sadiq (sixth imam), 77–78

Jalula, Battle of, 46

Jami (poet), 73

Japan, 161, 389

Jews, 4, 14, 16, 17*n.*, 22, 89

JFK (film), 363

Johnson, Lyndon B., 247, 391–92

Jordan, 385

Julfa Railway, 168

Juma, Ayatollah Imam, 172

Junayd, Sheikh, 79–81

Justice ideal (just rule): Ali as model of, 54, 104, 266, 274; and authority figures, 93–94; and charismatic leadership, 97–99, 101–2; and early Islam, 48–49, 50, 103–4; and Hussein, 104–5; and Islamic Republic, 341–46, 348–49, 356, 360–61, 366–72, 372–74, 379–80; and Islamic Revolution, 309, 353; Mazdakism and Manichaeism, 36; and Muhammad Reza Shah, 213, 228–29, 240, 266; and Qajar, 127–28; and Reza Shah, 158; and Revolution of 1979, 274–75; and Sassanians, 35–36; and Shia, 53, 54, 93–94, 102–6, 118–19, 136; and Zoroastrianism, 17, 24, 26, 36

Justice Ministry, 179

Karbala 4 offensive, 328–29

Karbala 5 offensive, 329

Karbala, Battle of, 55, 76, 104, 222, 233; holiday in mourning for, 105–6; and Revolution of 1979, 279–80; and Reza Shah, 180, 189; site bombed, 360

Karim Khan (ruler of Zands), 125

Kar Kiya Mirza Ali (ruler of Gilan), 81

Karun River project, 387

Kashani, Ayatollah Sayyed Abol-Qasem, 197–98, 203–4, 205, 209–10, 223

Kayhan International (newspaper), 251–52

Kazakhstan, 386

Keermani, *Hojjat ol-eslam*, 290

Kennedy, John F., 219–20, 247, 391–92

Khalkhali, *Hojjat ol-eslam* Sadeq, 290–91